SLOG OR SWAN

British Army Effectiveness in Operation Veritable, February and March 1945

Dermot Rooney

Helion & Company

Helion & Company Limited
Unit 8 Amherst Business Centre
Budbrooke Road
Warwick
CV34 5WE
England
Tel. 01926 499 619
Email: info@helion.co.uk
Website: www.helion.co.uk
X, Formerly Twitter: @helionbooks
Visit our blog https://helionbooks.wordpress.com/

Published by Helion & Company 2025
Designed and typeset by Mach 3 Solutions (www.mach3solutions.co.uk)
Cover designed by Paul Hewitt, Battlefield Design (www.battlefield-design.co.uk)

Text © Dermot Rooney 2024
Images and maps © as individually credited

Every reasonable effort has been made to trace copyright holders and to obtain their permission for the use of copyright material. The author and publisher apologise for any errors or omissions in this work and would be grateful if notified of any corrections that should be incorporated in future reprints or editions of this book.

ISBN 978-1-804516-69-0

British Library Cataloguing-in-Publication Data.
A catalogue record for this book is available from the British Library.

All rights reserved. No part of this publication may be reproduced, stored in a retrieval system, or transmitted, in any form, or by any means, electronic, mechanical, photocopying, recording or otherwise, without the express written consent of Helion & Company Limited.

For details of other military history titles published by Helion & Company Limited contact the above address or visit our website: http://www.helion.co.uk.

We always welcome receiving book proposals from prospective authors.

Contents

List of Illustrations	iv
List of Maps	v
Abbreviations	vii
Acknowledgements	x
Introduction	xii
1 Context and Planning	29
2 Artillery and Effectiveness	48
3 Tactics and Logistics	82
4 Command or Control	101
5 Infantry and Armour	122
6 Urban Attrition	143
7 Manoeuvre Warfare	170
8 Battle Morale	196
Conclusion: Memory and Imagination	216
Bibliography	224
Index	238

List of Illustrations

Figure 1: Abridged organisational chart for 21st Army Group on 8 February with focus formations in bold.   30

Figure 2: Abridged organisational chart for 1 Fallschirm-Armee with focus formations in bold.   43

Figure 3: Swann's data on number of shells fired and attacker casualties per defending company, excluding losses to mines.   58

Figure 4: Abridged organisational chart for 30 Corps with focus organisations in bold.   59

Figure 5: Part of the Groesbecker Bach 'flooded anti-tank ditch' (on a much drier day) where "A" Company attempted to cross. Buildings on the left are part of the old town, those in the distance are post-war.   67

Figure 6: Swann Report data for shells fired per square kilometre and attacker casualties per defending company. Trend line excludes the three delayed attacks.   79

Figure 7: Swann Report data for shells per square kilometre and unit-derived data for attacker casualties per defending company.   79

Figure 8: An AVRE carrying a fascine (left) following another with a Small Box Girder bridge. In the distance between them is a turretless "Jumbo" bridge-layer.   86

Figure 9: Abridged organisational chart for 44 Brigade.   89

Figure 10: An idealised armoured breach based on the method attempted by 44 Brigade.   91

Figure 11: Abridged organisational chart for 15 and 43 Division.   103

Figure 12: 5 Duke of Cornwall's Light Infantry in quick lift to Materborn on 4/7 Dragoon Guards' Shermans.   109

Figure 13: A Jagdpanther from Pzjgr 655 north of Materborn village.   118

Figure 14: Abridged organisational chart for 52 Division.   125

Figure 15: Forest-clearing drill trialled in the Broederbosch.   132

Figure 16: Post-war image of Goch's market square and its main churches.   144

Figure 17: Abridged organisational chart for Goch battles.   145

Figure 18: 'Small Box Girder Bridge in position over the anti-tank ditch north of Goch'. This picture was probably taken on the coup de main crossing on 19th.   152

Figure 19: Aerial view of central Goch on 23 February, with overlay showing British front at 07:30 on 19th.   159

Figure 20: Abridged organisational chart for 53 Division.   173

Figure 21: Abridged organisation chart. Note The Coldstream infantry separated from their armour.   188

Figure 22: Infantry deaths per day for 15 and 53 Divisions during Veritable.   209

Figure 23: 53 Division battle casualties and battle exhaustion cases 1944–45.   210

Figure 24: 4 Welch deaths during Veritable.   212

Figure 25: 4 Royal Welch Fusiliers casualties and prisoners during Veritable.   213

List of Maps

Map 1: A post-war outline of Operations Veritable and Grenade.	xiii
Map 2: Chapters, themes, and geographic setting.	xxiii
Map 3: Original concept for what became Operation Veritable, labelled 'Right Corps of Second Army'.	33
Map 4: Ground and fixed defences.	38
Map 5: Veritable's Army and Corps plans.	40
Map 6: Barrage phases and battalion attacks on Veritable's D-Day.	55
Map 7: 4 Royal Welch Fusiliers attack on De Horst.	61
Map 8: 10 Highland Light Infantry schematic showing a mix of what was planned and what transpired.	65
Map 9: 10 HLI attack showing the depth of the barrage pause area, mattress impact and company manoeuvre.	68
Map 10: 2 A&SH attack south of Kranenburg.	71
Map 11: 9 Cameronians Aatack on Frasselt.	73
Map 12: 154 Brigade attack into the Reichswald.	76
Map 13: The 15 Division plan to break through and break out of the Westwall main defence.	90
Map 14: Breakthrough and partial breakout by 44 Brigade, D+1 04:00 To 17:00.	95
Map 15: Situation at 23:59 on 9 February (D+1).	104
Map 16: The Materborn salient before the 43 recce probe (front 9th 23:59) and just before the 5 DCLI final attack (front 11th 14:00). Note the cloister building, church and 'Tiger Corner'.	111
Map 17: Final attack on Materborn 11 February (D+3) 14:00 to 17:00.	115
Map 18: 52 Division outline plan.	126
Map 19: 157 Brigade plan and notable enemy, with insert from 4 KOSB history.	128
Map 20: Positions and intentions on the morning of 17 February.	135
Map 21: Outline of operations to capture Goch.	146
Map 22: Battalion axes, company group objectives and artillery concentrations for the initial assault of Operation Spider.	149
Map 23: Main events around the coup de main.	151
Map 24: Outline of 51 Division's plans for attacking Goch.	156
Map 25: 5 Black Watch positions around 06:00 19 February.	157
Map 26: British forward line at 06:00, 19 February.	161
Map 27: 51 Division's planned attacks for the night of 20/21 February.	163
Map 28: 5 Black Watch attack and Kampfgruppe counter 20/21 February.	164
Map 29: Operation Leek, 53 Division's earlier plan to capture Weeze.	174
Map 30: 6 RWF's two-bite plan.	176
Map 31: 6 RWF attack on Höst.	178

Map 32: 71 Brigade's second plan (left) and execution.	180
Map 33: The five steps of Operation Daffodil, 53 Division's later plan to capture Weeze.	182
Map 34: 71 Brigade plan and barrage.	183
Map 35: 1 East Lancs and Robinforce, 1 March.	184
Map 36: Breakout and pursuit from Weeze to the Bönninghardt Plateau.	186
Map 37: Irish Group actions 4 and 5 March. 1. Unopposed Battalion Group attack. 2. Unsuccessful Company Group attack. 3. Successful Platoon Group attack. 4. the original planned attack.	190
Map 38: Grenadier Group actions 5 March.	192
Map 39: The Spandicker Ley plan.	198
Map 40: Spandicker Ley 23:00 to 04:30.	200
Map 41: Spandicker Ley counterattacks.	201
Map 42: 53 Division crossing the plateau.	203
Map 43: 4 Welch and 6 RWF attacks south of Alpen.	205

Abbreviations

A&SH	Argyll and Sutherland Highlanders.
AFV	Armoured Fighting Vehicle.
AGRA	Army Group Royal Artillery.
APC	Armoured Personnel Carrier.
Arty	Artillery.
AT	Anti-Tank.
AVRE	Armoured Vehicle Royal Engineers.
BAOR	British Army of the Rhine.
Bde	Brigade.
Bn	Battalion.
C-in-C	Commander-in-Chief.
Cam H	Cameron Highlanders.
Cams	Cameronians.
CMHQ	Canadian Military Headquarters.
CO	Commanding Officer.
Comms	Communications.
COS	Chief of Staff.
Coy	Company.
CRA	Commander Royal Artillery.
CWGC	Commonwealth War Graves Commission.
DCDC	Defence Concepts and Doctrine Centre.
DCLI	Duke of Cornwall's Light Infantry.
DCM	Distinguished Conduct Medal.
DG	Dragoon Guards.
Dgns	Dragoons.
Dir	Director.
Div	Division.
DOW	Died of Wounds.
DSO	Distinguished Service Order.
DTI	Directorate of Tactical Investigation.
East Yorks	East Yorkshire Regiment.
East Lancs	East Lancashire Regiment.
Engrs	Engineers.
FAA	Forward Assembly Area.
Fd	Field.
FIBUA	Fighting in Built Up Areas.
FJ	Fallschirmjäger (paratrooper).
FJD	Fallschirmjäger-Division.
FJR	Fallschirmjäger-Regiment.
FM	Field Manual.
FMS	Foreign Military Studies.
FOO	Forward Observation Officer.

Fwd	Forward.
Gen	General.
GHQ	General Headquarters.
Glas H	Glasgow Highlanders.
GR	Grenadier-Regiment.
GSO	General Staff Officer.
HLI	Highland Light Infantry.
Inf	Infantry.
Instr	Instruction.
ISUM	Intelligence Summary.
KIA	Killed in Action.
KOSB	King's Own Scottish Borderers.
KRRC	King's Royal Rifle Corps.
LWDC	Land Warfare Development Centre.
MC	Military Cross.
MOD	Ministry of Defence.
Mons	Monmouths / Monmouthshire Regiment.
MORU	Military Operational Research Unit.
MM	Military Medal.
NA	National Archives, UK.
NARA	National Archives and Records Administration, USA.
NATO	North Atlantic Treaty Organisation.
NORTHAG	Northern Army Group.
OO	Operation Order.
Op	Operation.
OP	Observation Post – static, mobile, or airborne.
ORS	Operational Research Section.
Oxf Bucks	Oxfordshire and Buckinghamshire Light Infantry.
Pdr	Pounder
PGD	Panzergrenadier Division.
PGR	Panzergrenadier Regiment.
PIAT	Projector Infantry Anti-Tank.
Pl	Platoon.
Poss	Possible.
PW	Prisoner of War.
PzJgr	Panzerjäger (tank hunter).
RA	Royal Artillery.
RAC	Royal Armoured Corps.
RASC	Royal Army Service Corps.
RAF	Royal Air Force.
Rd	Road or round.
RE	Royal Engineers.
Recce	Reconnaissance.
Regt	Regiment.
Rly	Railway.
RSM	Regimental Sergeant Major.
RTR	Royal Tank Regiment.
RWF	Royal Welch Fusiliers.
SHAEF	Supreme Headquarters Allied Expeditionary Force.

Sigs	Signals.
SITREP	Situation Report.
SL	Start Line.
SLI	Somerset Light Infantry.
Sp	Support.
SP	Self-Propelled.
Sqn	Squadron.
SRY	Sherwood Rangers Yeomanry.
SSVC	Services Sound and Vision Corporation.
Stug / StuG	Sturmgeschütz (assault gun).
StuH	Sturmhaubitze (assault howitzer).
TA	Territorial Army.
Tac	Tactical.
TD	Territorial Decoration or Tank Destroyer.
Tk	Tank.
Tp	Troop.
Tpt	Transport.
USMC	United States Marine Corps.
Veh	Vehicle.
Wilts	Wiltshires, Wiltshire Regiment.
WO	War Office.
Worcs	Worcesters, Worcestershire Regiment.

Acknowledgements

The wonderful collection of people who helped with the book could be classed as academics, soldiers, "amateur" historians, publishers, friends, and family, but most occupy three categories, and some fit five, so apologies if I put you in the wrong slot. Some of the people mentioned provided fantastic material that was sadly whittled away to achieve the final word count but will surely resurface in another guise one day.

Of the academic historians and professional analysts, three lovely men took special interest in the project: Jonathan Boff who got me started, Jonathan Fennell who took me on, and Greg Kennedy got me over the finish line. Although Greg was paid for his time, he deserves special thanks and surely some kind of bonus for taking on an oddball project at an awkward time, and then steering it and me with cheer, insight, and rigour. Top Bloke. Able assistance was provided by Chris Tripodi (stylish), Ignacio Morales (finding Monty), Kunika Kakuta (virtual group hugs), Charles Kirke (guns, cultures, and command), John D. Salt (guns, giggles, and graphs), Rowland Goodman (arty suppression insider), David Rowland (bravery, Balchin, and all things effectiveness), Pete Dudley (cybernetics), Stuart Burdett (calm), Rob Jones (more guns), Roger Lloyd-Williams (battle exhaustion), Dave Robson (urban), Dave Richardson (stoicism), and Paul Syms (towel locating).

The good people at the National Archives at Kew, the British Library at Boston Spa and at King's made research a joy, made Byzantium less daunting and tolerated my excitement at finding scribbled marginalia in spice-scented war diaries. The resolute staff of regimental museums provided permission to use proprietary images, and out of print or unpublished documents that have been of especial value. Honourable mentions are deserved by Gerry O'Neill from the KOSB Museum, Deborah Vosper at Bodmin Keep, Keith Jones and Nick Lock of the RWF Museum, Siân Mogridge of the Royal Artillery Museum, and Robert Cazenove of the Coldstream Guards Association.

When the project moved to being a proper book, the team at Helion were patient with my many maps and figures, endured many geeky tweaks and changes, and put up with me sobbing about having to change all the "ized" words back to "ised". Especial thanks go out to Duncan Rogers, Stephen Ede-Borrett, and the inimitable Kim McSweeney. Thanks also to Neil Powell at battlefieldhistorian.com who sourced many images for the book.

Serving and retired soldiers who answered numpty questions include Peter Knox of the seminal SSVC video, Jason Boswell of US armour fun, Shaun Chandler and Steven Smith of the Infantry Battle School, Malcolm Abbey of the Royal School of Artillery, Matt Baker, Paul Knight and Don Oldcorn of the Land Warfare Centre, and Peter Cook of something-on-artillery-but-I-lost-my-notes-sorry. Paul Johnson gave bridging tips despite me ballsing up an Inf Wing do back in the 1990s. Paul Aldridge regularly cycled over the Pennines with books in his teeth. Paul Stevens patiently explained radio wave propagation at least twice. John Cotterill found me an updated version of Balchin's 'Battle Morale' and sold me on the interaction of patrolling and morale. Glyn Taylor taught me about the pillbox problem, Sappers, and social Zooming. Sergio Miller, Jim Storr, Wilf Owen, Cole Petersen, and Roger Antolik gave me advice on load, urban and command. Officers (commissioned, warrant, and otherwise) from the RTR, 1 RGR, and 1 & 2 Mercian helped with the sadly deleted tactical psychology ratings and sometimes fed me curry.

I am especially indebted to the many amateur historians who have developed a deep understanding of units, operations, or arms for the love of history, family, or regiment, and then given their time and wisdom to an unknown geek who asked vague questions via social media. These include John Hendry, who kindly allowed the use of his father's memoirs, Lee Richards for access to psyops diaries, Paul Woodadge for letting me gas, Nikolas Lloyd for providing prompt Churchill facts, and Adam Bruce-Watt for putting the 15 Division diaries online then giving hints and tips on archival research. The fine people on WW2Talk are a singular tribe of mainly-amateurs who were totally helpful throughout the project. These include Chris Camfield for generously sharing the diaries of 54 AT Regt, "AB64" for providing access to the near-unobtainable history of HQRA 52 Division, John "Tolbooth" Bagley for filling gaps in the 1 Lothian story, "Dbf" for all the Irish Guards depth, and Rob "Buteman" McAllister for the missing Mattress facts. Dominating this band is the noble "Stolpi" who kept the Veritable story alive through mines and mud, took me for my first tour of the battlefields, and knows more about the ground and lore of the operation than anyone has a right to.

Finally, I must thank those friends and family who do not fit into any of the above categories. These include Our Jim for listening and linking, Alice Munro for German tips, Bob King, Dan Griffiths, Duncan Kerry, Jeremy and Jono Butt, Gandey Munro, Chrispy Tebb, Anne Whittaker and, let's face it, pretty much anybody in the Wapentake who made the mistake of asking "are you doing summat about World War Two?" and then endured a good half hour of the Feynman technique. But of course, the greatest thanks go to the loves of my life, Joey, Evan, and Bill. They shared a house with a bear who wasn't always cuddly, and they propped him up whenever he got a thorn in his paw. Thank you. NNX.

Introduction

WELCOME TO VERITABLE – MINES AND MUD – A MURKY PAST – HASTINGS VERSUS BUCKLEY – MORE THAN THE REICHSWALD – A NEARLY BOTTOM-UP APPROACH – NECESSARY ADMINISTRATION

Forgotten Victory?

On 8 February 1945, First Canadian Army, with 30 British Corps as its main fighting component, launched the supposed 'Forgotten Victory' of Operation Veritable.[1] With overwhelming firepower from armour and airpower but chiefly artillery, the aim was to break through the most northerly part of the *Westwall* (known to the Allies as the Siegfried Line) and then burst out into the open country beyond to fight a battle of manoeuvre. The breakout was to be achieved within two days and, with luck, would lead to the capture of the Rhine bridges at Wesel on the third or fourth day. Meanwhile, on 10 February and 120km to the south, the Ninth US Army was to launch Operation Grenade, striking northeast across the Rur (Roer) just as the Germans were deploying their reserves to meet the Anglo-Canadian force (Map 1).[2] These two jaws of the Allied pincers would apply pressure so rapidly that the defenders would be unable to concentrate force and would be defeated in detail west of the Rhine.

Veritable was a meticulously choreographed concentration of force that allowed seven British and Canadian divisions to launch a surprise attack against a section of the Westwall defended by a weak German division full of half-trained medical cases. The Germans were relying on boggy ground and dense woods to delay any advance, but the Allies would negate this advantage by striking mid-winter when frozen ground would allow rapid armoured movement. Unfortunately for the Allies, two unforeseeable events undermined their plan: an early and unexpected thaw on the eve of the operation turned the ground into a morass, and German engineers flooded the Rur, which caused the American attack to be postponed for two weeks. Then the combination of thaw, persistent rain, and German breaching of dykes along the Rhine severely hampered Allied movement, slowing Veritable to a crawl as 30 Corps spent over a week fighting through the *Klever Reichswald* (Kleve Imperial Forest). By that time *1. Fallschirm-Armee* had moved up powerful reserves including *47. Panzerkorps* to forestall the Anglo-Canadian attack.

Expecting to face one or two second rate infantry divisions, First Canadian Army fought at least nine, including three *Fallschirmjäger*, two *Panzer*, and one *Panzergrenadier* division. Yet mines and mud hampered the Allied attack far more than enemy action. Lieutenant General Brian Horrocks,

---

1 M. Zuehlke, *Forgotten Victory. First Canadian Army and the Cruel Winter of 1944–45* (Madeira Park: Douglas & McIntyre, 2014).
2 P. B. Randel, *A Short History of 30 Corps in the European Campaign 1944–1945* (Hanover: 30 Corps, 1945), p.59.

INTRODUCTION xiii

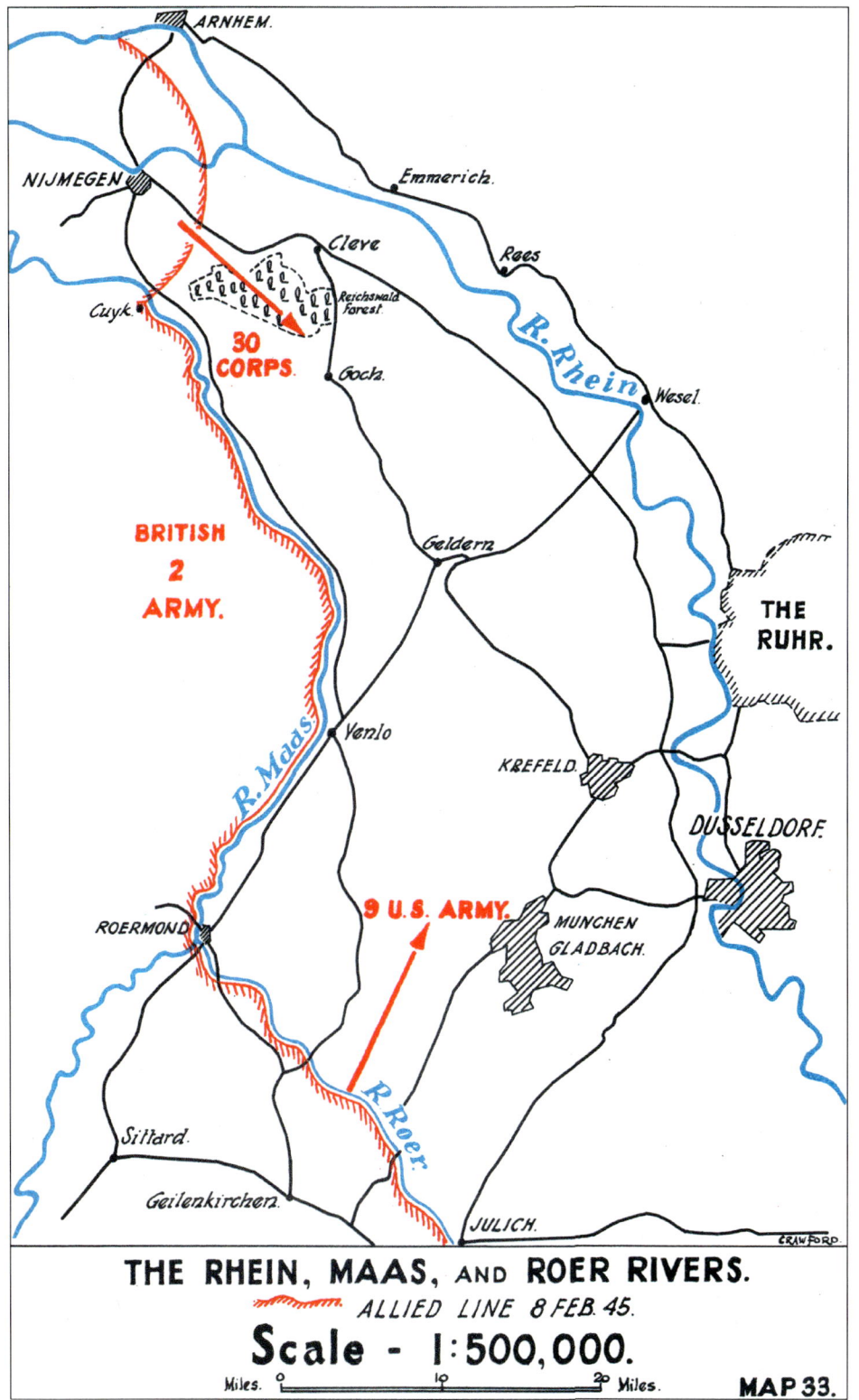

Map 1: A post-war outline of Operations Veritable and Grenade. (Randel, *Short History*)

the commander of 30 Corps, summed up the operation as having 'no room for manoeuvre and no scope for cleverness' and, 'a slog in which only two things mattered, training and guts.'[3] Instead of breaking out into a favourable manoeuvre space, 30 Corps spent a month grinding through successive layers of prepared defences. Joined by Guy Simonds's 2 Canadian Corps in the second week, the Allied force bludgeoned its way through the rain-soaked forests while tanks 'bogged to their turrets in the heavy going.'[4]

The Allies were therefore forced to switch to their contingency plan. In a repeat of the scheme used in Normandy, the British and Canadians drew in German reserves to ensure American success when the Rur floods subsided. This approach allowed Operation Grenade to achieve a breakthrough, so the combination of Anglo-Canadian mass and American velocity secured victory. Veritable's unavoidable attrition favoured the Allies, who suffered 16,000 casualties while the Germans lost 50,000 in killed, wounded and prisoners, a loss the *Wehrmacht* could not bear; *1. Fallschirm-Armee* was bled white by the time it withdrew across the Rhine on 10 March. When the Allies crossed the great river two weeks later, the opposition was a husk, capable only of mounting desperate and futile rearguard actions.

The above narrative is a distillation of official sources and the few histories that devote more than a handful of pages to Veritable. The work for this book uncovered many problems with the Veritable narrative, but they were uncovered almost by chance. *Slog or Swan* began as a PhD study of tactical psychology (the techniques soldiers use to make the enemy run, hide, and surrender) and aimed to enhance the quantitative historical analysis used by the UK Ministry of Defence; an approach that combines primary and secondary source material to create a sample of detailed battle descriptions that are then subject to statistical tests. It is a rigorous, almost pedantic, way for the armed services to answer fundamental questions like "what force ratio worked best in urban combat?", "what was the best mixture of armour and anti-armour weapons?" or "how much artillery was needed to suppress an enemy defence?"[5]

The focus of the PhD changed for administrative reasons, but by that time the sample of battle descriptions had uncovered a story that conflicted with the Veritable narrative.[6] The dates, times and places were usually the same, but examining the operation almost from the bottom up produced a much richer picture – a picture that often reversed the accepted lines of causation. For example, a story of a failing attack saved by the timely intervention of armour often became an attack that failed because the armour arrived too late. An attack that needed a mass of artillery support because British troops lacked fighting spirit became an attack where fighting spirit was destroyed by artillery fratricide. Then the reasons for late armour and artillery fratricide were found to be no fault of the tankies and gunners involved, but were due to problems with doctrine, command, and the structure of divisions. Examining the detail of battalion group battles, how brigades and divisions sequenced those battles, then working up to corps interactions revealed an operation that was not simply a slog. And even when it was a slog, mines and mud were rarely the main problem.

Analysis of the mass of primary source data uncovered an operation that was less a forgotten victory, more a subtly obscured failure. First Canadian Army did beat *1. Fallschirm-Armee* but

---

3 J. Ellis, *Brute Force: Allied Strategy and Tactics in The Second World War* (London: Deutsch, 1990), p.424; W. D. and S. Whitaker, *Rhineland. The Battle to End the War* (London: Leo Cooper, 1989), p.85.

4 R. Woollcombe, *Lion Rampant, The Memoirs of an Infantry Officer from D-Day to the Rhineland* (London: Black & White, 2014 [1955]), Kindle 2961.

5 The best summary of defence historical analysis can be found in D. Rowland, *The Stress of Battle: Quantifying Human Performance in Combat* (London: HMSO, 2006), passim.

6 The administrative reasons included covid lockdown blocking access to Land Warfare Centre experts who were due to test the tactical psychology rating method.

did so very slowly and with overwhelming physical advantages, falling far short of being the 'final round' or the 'knockout blow' that Montgomery saw as opening the road to Berlin.[7] Many veterans shared the view that, 'It was the culminating point in the campaign, for it was the main entry into Germany and, for those who are lucky enough to be alive to look back on it, it was the beginning of the end of the war.'[8] Contemporary sources and memoirs reflect a 'controlled yet infectious enthusiasm' marked in many diaries with the words 'This might be the end.'[9] But when Veritable failed to achieve rapid victory, it was repackaged as a tough but uninteresting enabling action, an action that served to make a tidy battlefield before crossing the Rhine. The repackaging of the operation and its lack of cinematic glamour have since served to hide Veritable from objective analysis.

With close to half a million men fighting a month-long series of battles, Veritable dwarfed the Arnhem disaster that preceded it, the Rhine crossing that followed it, and any of the named operations that formed the Anglo-Canadian Northwest Europe Campaign. By the end of Veritable, 11 British and Canadian divisions, three independent armoured brigades, one commando brigade and 14 battalions of 79 Armoured Division had been deployed. The only British divisions in theatre that were not deployed were 7 Armoured and 49 Infantry.[10] Veritable was second only to Normandy for combat intensity, and a close second at that. The 52 Division history described Veritable as 'one of the most bitter series of battles ever fought by men. Leaving aside the effects of intensive bombing in the Ruhr, it is doubtful if any area of God's earth outside Stalingrad was ever so smashed up by the conventional military weapons.'[11] The scars of Veritable are plainly visible today, in the misshapen development of market towns and in a chain of artificial lakes where Allied fire missions smashed through the water table along the Dutch-German border.

Yet with hundreds of titles examining Normandy and Arnhem, there are only four works that give serious attention to Veritable, and each was undermined by the limitations of its source material.[12] Veritable's historiography has been extremely sensitive to the initial conditions set by the earliest reports from within 21st Army Group. Some units produced slim summaries of their experience, but most were beaten to publication by 'Montgomery's Scientists' in No. 2 Operational Research Section, who produced influential reports while the operation was still being fought.[13] Those studies were wrapped into 21st Army Group's post-operation report, which (being written by planners) spent more time describing the original plan than the month of fighting that followed, and in so doing set a trend for representing Veritable as a successful, centrally driven activity.[14]

---

7 Montgomery 'Personal message from the C-in-C (To be read out to all Troops)' February 1945.
8 53 Recce Regt, 'Operation "Veritable"', UK National Archives file WO 223/94. Hereafter, all files prefixed WO and CAB are from the National Archives.
9 R.W. Thompson, *The Battle for the Rhineland* (London: Westholme, 1958), p.157.
10 Anon, *An Account of the Operations of Second Army in Europe 1944–1945* (Germany: 21 Army Group, 1945), p.323. Veritable might have been the largest named British operation of the war, Operation Overlord being the name given to the whole Northwest Europe Campaign.
11 G. Blake, *Mountain and Flood. The History of the 52nd (Lowland) Division, 1939–1946* (Glasgow: Jackson, 1950), p.147.
12 Thompson, *Rhineland*; J. Dennis (dir.), *Battle for the Rhineland* (Services Sound and Video Corporation, 1984); Whitakers, *Rhineland*; Zuehlke, *Forgotten Victory*.
13 For example, M. Swann, 'Fire Support in Operation Veritable – Effect on Forward Defensive Positions', reproduced in 21 Army Group, *Operational Research in North West Europe* (Hanover: 21 Army Group, 1945), pp.177–183. Reproduced again in Copp, T. (Ed.), *Montgomery's Scientists. Operational Research in Northwest Europe. The Work of No.2 Operational Research Section with 21st Army Group June 1944 to July 1945* (Waterloo ON: Laurier Centre, 2000), pp.359–371. For reader convenience, footnotes use page numbers from the Copp reproduction.
14 21 Army Group, *Operation Veritable. Clearing the Area Between the R Maas and the R Rhine, 8 Feb – 10 Mar*

Two Canadian post-operation reports followed: one covered the first half of Veritable; the other described Blockbuster, a subordinate operation led by 2 Canadian Corps in the last fortnight of Veritable.[15] These reports politely corrected a few omissions in the 21st Army Group document (particularly regarding the contribution of General Harry Crerar, the commander of First Canadian Army) but did not address the many 30 Corps actions in the second half of Veritable. As a result, professional historians have overlooked a quarter of the operation. Meanwhile, in contrast to the tendency of British and American authors to fixate on Normandy and Market Garden, Canadian historians have been rightly proud of their national contribution to Veritable. So, despite providing only 20 percent of Veritable's manpower, there has been a far greater word count devoted to the activity of Canadian forces.[16]

Despite the dominance of Canadian historiography, the most influential source has been the 1947 British Army of the Rhine (BAOR) *Battlefield Tour*, a lavishly illustrated document used to train generations of British officers in Montgomery's post-war masterplan doctrine.[17] The *Battlefield Tour* expands the tendency to underplay problems in execution, with two-thirds of its content focused on planning and barely a mention of fighting beyond the second day. The relevant chapters in the two nations' official histories are abridged versions of their respective post-operation reports. Each adds a little depth from selected formation and unit histories, but both include substantial factual errors and omissions.[18]

These shortcomings echo through the three most complete written operational level histories. Thompson's *Battle for the Rhineland* is a colourful account by an embedded journalist that spends only a quarter of its pages on Veritable, has some factual errors, but includes many wonderful insights missed from later works.[19] The Whitakers' *Rhineland: The Battle to End the War* is an impressive labour of love, and one of its authors commanded a Canadian unit in Veritable; it builds on a wealth of veteran interviews but covers several other operations and sometimes overlooks British actions.[20] Zuehlke's *Forgotten Victory* refines the Whitakers' work and builds on Terry Copp's broader Canadian-focused histories but, being part of a national commemoration series, gives each Canadian battalion three times the attention of any British division.[21] Less substantial works on Veritable include considerable factual errors.[22]

1945 (Hanover: 21 Army Group, 1945), passim.

15 J. B. Conacher and W.E.C. Harrison, 'Operation "Veritable": The winter offensive between the Maas and the Rhine, 8–25 Feb 45 (preliminary report)' (Canadian Military Headquarters, report no.155, 1946); P. A. Mayer, 'Operation "Blockbuster": the Canadian offensive west of the Rhine, 26 Feb – 23 Mar 45 (preliminary report)' (Canadian Military Headquarters, report no. 171, 1947).

16 J. Williams, *Long Left Flank: The Hard-Fought Way to the Reich 1944–1945* (London, Leo Cooper 1988), passim; T. Copp and R. Vogel, *Maple Leaf Route: Victory* (Alma OT: Maple Leaf Route, 1988), passim; T. Copp, *Cinderella Army: The Canadians in Northwest Europe, 1944–1945* (Toronto: University Press, 2006), passim; T. Copp, *The Brigade. The Fifth Canadian Infantry Brigade in World War II* (Mechanicsburg: Stackpole, 2007), passim.

17 British Army of the Rhine, *Battlefield Tour, Operation Veritable. 30 Corps Operations Between the Rivers Maas and Rhine, 8–10 February 1945* (Germany: BAOR, 1947), WO 106/5846.

18 C. P. Stacey, *Official History of the Canadian Army in the Second World War. Volume III, The Victory Campaign* (Ottawa: Queen's Printer, 1960), pp.460–526; L.F. Ellis, *Victory in the West. Vol. II* (London: HMSO, 1968), pp.253–277.

19 Thompson, *Rhineland*.

20 Whitakers, *Rhineland*.

21 Zuehlke, *Forgotten Victory*.

22 P. Elstob, *Battle of the Reichswald* (London: Macdonald, 1971); K. Ford, *The Rhineland 1945: The Last Killing Ground in the West* (Botley: Osprey, 2000); L Clark, *Arnhem. Jumping the Rhine 1944 and 1945* (London: Headline, 2009), pp.258–266.

A strong indication of Veritable's historiographic shortcomings is that, second to the Whitakers, the most thorough analysis is the three-part documentary *Battle for the Rhineland* by the Services Sound and Vision Corporation (SSVC). Aside from its accessibility (it is free to view online) the main strength of the SSVC documentary is that it was informed by a 1980s effort to update the *Battlefield Tour* and has serving NATO officers apply a robust soldier-scholars' critique of the operation. However, like the written histories, the SSVC documentary's basic structure and most of its conclusions are dependent on those early and incomplete official narratives.[23]

The historiographic weakness of the Veritable narrative can be illustrated by one of the division-sized subordinate operations. In the second week of Veritable, when 30 Corps stalled northeast of the Reichswald, 52 Lowland Division was tasked with breaking out to the south of the forest and then hooking east to capture Weeze (between Goch and Geldern on Map 1).[24] This expedient adaptation to the masterplan would have encircled Goch, a Westwall keystone, nullifying its defensive value and inevitably causing its evacuation. But 52 Division was stopped halfway to Weeze and stayed there for another 10 days. Meanwhile, two other divisions spent four days and thousands of tonnes of artillery ammunition fighting through Goch in a desperate urban battle. The bold attempt to bypass Goch appears only in war diaries, a few soldier memoirs, and circumspectly in the 52 Division history.[25] All other sources cover this potentially pivotal event with no more than a paragraph, typically describing it as 'flank protection' or 'mopping up'; or omitting it entirely.[26] It is almost impossible to imagine a history of Normandy or Arnhem omitting a week of activity by a whole division, but this seems acceptable in Veritable's fragmented historiography.

British Army Effectiveness

The tendency to overlook Veritable has skewed the debate on British Army effectiveness, mostly towards Normandy, where 21st Army Group was finding its feet, and to a lesser extent to Market Garden with its now-obvious conceptual flaws. Yet 21st Army Group was arguably at the height of its powers when Veritable was launched, with more artillery, armour, and air support available than in France, Belgium, or Holland. There were fewer infantry divisions in theatre (losing 50 and 59 while gaining 52) but most battalions were overmanned on Veritable's D-Day. Granted, many good men had been lost and their replacements were often retrained anti-aircraft gunners, but the ratio of novices to veterans was close to that in Normandy and, judging by censorship reports, the men were less 'browned off' and more 'bloody-minded' than they had been in August 1944.[27] Since landing in Normandy, commanders and staff had learned their trades or been replaced, and the higher-level coordination that had been so difficult to exercise in England had been tested and refined. By the time Veritable launched there had been time to refit, reorganise, retrain, and even take some well-earned leave. Above all, Antwerp's port was open and was delivering enough supplies to feed the industrial consumption that came with 21st Army Group's conception of manoeuvre warfare.[28]

---

23 SSVC/Dennis, *Rhineland*; author interview with Peter Knox, 2018. Another useful online source is British Army, *Fighting In Built Up Areas (FIBUA), Part 3: Goch* (c1984).
24 157 Brigade Operation Order No. 9 (OO 9), 16 Feb. 1945, Brigade diary (WO 171/4420).
25 Examples for 52 Division include: 5th Battalion (Bn), King's Own Scottish Borderers (5 KOSB) war diary, Feb 1945, WO 171/5216; P. White, *With the Jocks. A Soldier's Struggle for Europe 1944–45* (Stroud: Sutton, 2000), pp.182–195; Blake, *Mountain*, pp.146–158.
26 Elstob, *Reichswald*, p.146; Stacey, *Victory Campaign*, p.490.
27 A. Allport, *Browned off and Bloody-minded: The British Soldier goes to War* (London: Yale, 2015).
28 J. Fennell, *Fighting the People's War: The British and Commonwealth Armies and the Second World War*

Assessments that overlook Veritable are therefore very likely to reach invalid or incomplete conclusions about British Army effectiveness, but many prominent studies stop at the end of 1944.[29] Meanwhile, authors who include 1945 often leap over Veritable and race to the finish on Lüneburg Heath.[30] Liddell Hart, the most influential early critic of British soldiers and commanders, has Veritable only as an unnamed cause for Allied bickering.[31] Despite a firepower focus and the claim that Veritable opened with 'the heaviest barrage of the whole war', Ellis's *Brute Force* spends only two paragraphs on the operation, while Bidwell and Graham's *Fire-Power* gives Veritable two vague pages.[32] In sources that assesses both Market Garden and Veritable, the former averages four times the word count. The most balanced is Fraser's *And We Shall Shock Them*, with seven pages on Market Garden to four on Veritable.[33] At the other extreme (excluding the many sources that fail to mention Veritable at all) is McKee's *Race for the Rhine Bridges*, with 123 pages on Market Garden but only three on Veritable and Grenade, even though these operations raced for 10 Rhine bridges.[34] The repeated focus on the first half of the Northwest Europe campaign inevitably leads to misperceptions about the campaign and British Army effectiveness.

One of the greatest misperceptions springs from Veritable being labelled the "Battle of the Reichswald" even though only two of the 11 Allied divisions fought in that forest, and only for about a week. This may seem pedantic (the Battle of Hastings was not fought in Hastings after all) but with Veritable, the ambiguity in official accounts and the powerful imagery of forest fighting has created a perception that the operation was all about the Reichswald. For example, Ford's *Rhineland 1945* claims:

> The commander of the Canadian 1st Army planned for two divisions to attack into the Reichswald (British 51st and 53rd Divisions) while two other divisions (Canadian 2nd and British 15th Divisions) provided flank protection outside of the forest to the north … with the intention of securing the line Gennep–Asperden–Cleve. This was the final objective of "Veritable"…[35]

This is an extreme example, but it reflects the generally weak conception of why and how Veritable was fought: it reverses the main effort, puts the final objective 20 kilometres too far north, and gives the false impression the forest had some strategic value. It is unlikely that any history would claim the Norman objective at Hastings was to secure Hastings, but for Veritable the equivalent perception is widespread.

The confused and casual treatment of the operation began to change with Stephen Hart's *Colossal Cracks*, which repeatedly refers to Veritable when exploring the interaction between 21st

---

(Cambridge: University Press, 2019), pp.589–591.

29 The best of the deliberately curtailed assessments include: T.H. Place, *Military Training in the British Army, 1940–1944* (London: Cass, 2000); D. French, '"Tommy is No Soldier": The Morale of the Second British Army in Normandy, June–August 1944', *Journal of Strategic Studies*, 19 (1996), pp.154–178; C.J. Dick, *From Victory to Stalemate: The Western Front, Summer 1944* (Lawrence KS: University Press, 2016).

30 D. French, *Raising Churchill's Army. The British Army and the War Against Germany 1919–1945* (Oxford: University Press, 2000), p.268.

31 B. H. Liddell Hart, *History of the Second World War* (London: Cassel, 1970) devotes 13 pages to Normandy (pp.543–547), four to Arnhem (dispersed across pp.558–567), but only three sentences to Veritable and Grenade (pp.677–678).

32 Ellis, *Brute Force*, p243–244; S. Bidwell and D. Graham, *Fire-Power. The British Army Weapons and Theories of War 1904–1945* (Barnsley: Pen & Sword, 2004 [1982]), pp.289–291.

33 D. Fraser, *And We Shall Shock Them: The British Army in the Second World War* (London: Hodder & Stoughton, 1983), pp.341–348, 386–390.

34 A. McKee, *The Race for the Rhine Bridges* (London: Pan, 1956), pp.57–179, 191–194.

35 K. Ford, *Rhineland 1945*, p.25.

Army Group's concepts of firepower, mass, and morale.[36] This more Veritable-friendly approach has continued in works by John Buckley, Charles Forrester, and Jonathan Fennell.[37] All these authors happen to align on the more charitable side of the British Army effectiveness debate, each pushing against the judgemental view presented by Liddell Hart then expanded by D'Este, Hastings, Beevor, and the mainstream media.[38] For brevity, these two camps are aligned here behind two protagonists, with Max Hastings as exemplar of the cynical "anti-British" school and John Buckley the charitable "pro-British" faction. Hastings depicts the British soldier as unwilling, his commanders incompetent, and his weapons ineffective but plentiful.[39] For Hastings, the British conducted 'workmanlike campaigns' against the *Wehrmacht*'s 'extraordinary fighting performance' but failed on almost every dimension except the massing of physical strength that was itself a product of American industry.[40]

Buckley only half disagrees with this conclusion, acknowledging that, being the product of a democratic state, the British soldier lacked the will, aggression, and tactical competence of the indoctrinated German. But Buckley suggests British commanders countered these shortcomings by playing to their strengths in mass, firepower, planning, intelligence, engineering, medicine, and logistics; a deliberate effort to avoid the collapse in morale that would follow excessive casualties or operational failure.[41] The British approach, Buckley argues, was 'a holistic and modern attitude to the conduct of "war", as opposed to the fighting of "battles"'.[42] Buckley has Montgomery and his subordinates balancing the components of fighting power, developing a conceptual component (how to fight) that used the physical component (material strength) to protect the moral component (will to fight). In the summer of 1944, this caused 21st Army Group to adopt 'operational and tactical methods that emphasised risk aversion' but then a more flexible, problem-solving attitude developed in the winter of 1944–45.[43] The result was a fighting system involving 'greater use of night attacks, armoured personnel carriers, flame-throwers and the support of engineering and close support equipment, all covered by lethally responsive and heavy artillery and air support.'[44] The new operational concept united these physical capabilities to better overcome those ingrained moral shortcomings. Buckley, therefore, claimed that in 1945 the British Army applied operational art

---

36 S. A. Hart, *Montgomery and "Colossal Cracks": The 21st Army Group in Northwest Europe, 1944–45* (Westport CT: Stackpole, 2000) was based on S. A. Hart, 'Field Marshal Montgomery, 21st Army Group and North-West Europe, 1944–45' (KCL PhD thesis, 1995). Hereon, Hart, *Colossal Cracks* and Hart, 'Montgomery'.

37 J. D. Buckley, *Monty's Men: The British Army and the Liberation or Europe, 1944–45* (New Haven CT: Yale, 2014), passim; C. Forrester, *Monty's Functional Doctrine: Combined Arms Doctrine in British 21st Army Group in Northwest Europe, 1944–45* (Solihull: Helion, 2015), passim; J. Fennell, *People's War*, passim.

38 Liddell Hart, *Second World War*, passim; C. D'Este, *Decision in Normandy* (London: Harper Collins, 1983), passim; M. Hastings, *Overlord: D-Day and the Battle for Normandy 1944* (London: Pan, 1985), passim and *Armageddon: The Battle for Germany 1944–45* (Basingstoke: Macmillan, 2011), passim; A, Beevor, *Arnhem: The Battle for the Bridges, 1944* (London: Viking, 2019), passim.

39 Hastings, *Armageddon*, Kindle 516, 935, 2064, 2173, 3363.

40 Hastings, *Armageddon*, Kindle 823, 725, 1495, 1504, 1778–2063.

41 Buckley, *Monty's*, pp.296–303.

42 Buckley, p.297.

43 Buckley, p.298. For convenience, divisions are considered the lowest operational level, where most named operations were planned (Ops Spider, Sprat, Leek, and Daffodil will be seen later) making everything below a division distinctly tactical. To understand some of the difficulties of defining the operational level and operational art try reading S. Naveh, *In Pursuit of Military Excellence: The Evolution of Operational Theory* (London: Cass, 1997), passim, or the more concise summary in J. Storr, *Something Rotten: Land Command in the 21st Century* (Havant, 2022) pp.20–21.

44 Buckley, p.302.

to overcome German tactical excellence; a level of artfulness that is usually attributed only to Russian or American armies.[45]

A salient difference between Hastings and Buckley is their treatment of Veritable. Hastings uses 4,000 words to sketch the operation as a set-piece battle that descended into a chaos of mud, overcaution, incompetence, and exhaustion.[46] His presentation relies on snapshots of memoir to illustrate these themes, but with its visceral seasoning removed Hastings presents a narrative that is thinner than the generic summary related at the start of this chapter. Hastings presents Veritable with little preamble, relates how it was fought with pluck, determination, and exhaustion but then moves on having offered little in the way of analysis. By contrast, despite claiming there was little new to say about Market Garden, Hastings gives it a 14,000-word description detailing tactical events and weaving the operation's planning, outcome, and implications into his wider assessment.[47]

Buckley also tips his word count towards Normandy and Arnhem, but the scales are more evenly balanced, giving Veritable 6,000 words to Market Garden's 10,000.[48] The real difference in approach is most evident in the breadth of sources; where Hastings relies on memoirs, Buckley includes higher commanders' papers, the post-operation reports, operational research studies, and key items from Copp's work.[49] Buckley examines the main events in greater detail and depth than Hastings, then extends the assessment to his wider conclusions. Both authors present Horrocks's moral and physical slog, but Buckley also includes the conceptual element of 'no room for manoeuvre'. From Buckley's perspective, the exceptional conditions of Veritable countered British strengths in planning, logistics, and intelligence, sorely tested their medical and engineering expertise, and thereby forced some reversion to mass and firepower. Yet, as if accepting this partial exception proves the rule, Buckley suggests his characterisation of British Army effectiveness differs from that of Hastings partly because it gives more weight to Veritable.[50]

Does either author correctly appreciate Veritable's operational and tactical implications? Both works make little reference to sources that describe tactical events in Veritable, and consequently both authors share a shallow analysis of those events. Shallowness is inevitable when spanning a whole campaign, but for Normandy and Arnhem, Hastings, and Buckley (and others) build on a foundation of tactical research by earlier authors.[51] That foundation is lacking for Veritable. So, for example, when Hastings or Buckley express their views on 30 Corps' failure to capture Arnhem on 20 or 21 September, they draw on earlier assessments that accessed the diaries and histories of the units involved. The absence of previous primary research means they could not do this when relating the repeated failure of 30 Corps to capture Weeze between 10 February and 1 March. Indeed, neither author mentions these events because they have not been the subject of a tactical assessment. There are glimpses of the Weeze failures in memoirs and unit histories, but the glimpses form a collection of narrow and unrelated views spread across five divisions.

It is therefore likely that Hastings sees only a slog in a bog because that is the main theme of memoirs. Likewise, Buckley sees planning, logistics and intelligence as saving graces because

---

45   Naveh, *Military Excellence*, passim; S. D. Biddle *Military Power: Explaining Victory and Defeat in Modern Battle* (Princeton: University Press, 2004), passim; M. Vego, 'On Operational Art', *Strategos*, 1/2 (2017), pp.15–39.
46   Hastings, *Armageddon*, Kindle 7633–7770.
47   *Armageddon* names Veritable twice, Market Garden 28 times.
48   Buckley, *Monty's* pp.208–231, 265–281.
49   Notably: BAOR, *Tour*; 21 Army Group, *Veritable*; Copp, *Cinderella*.
50   Buckley, p.302.
51   For Normandy, Buckley draws on: L. Clark, *Orne Bridgehead* (Stroud: Sutton, 2004); P. Warner, *D-Day Landings* (London: Random House, 1990) and eight similar titles.

commanders and staff wrote the early official narratives. There is a chance that Hastings and Buckley have unwittingly built their views of Veritable on sand. Given Veritable's scale, and its expected outcome, the weakness of this foundation has undermined the whole debate on British Army effectiveness.

In one respect this book tests the Hastings and Buckley theories to inform the debate on British Army effectiveness, but it is also an attempt to assess the existing narratives of Veritable by examining the operation at the tactical level. The book evaluates the strands of Veritable's historiography in official narratives, memoirs, and formation histories against a wide range of primary sources, then binds those strands together to describe the components of effectiveness in British Army units during the operation. However, the book cannot claim to be a complete tactical history of Veritable because of the need to trade depth for breadth. To access, assess and synthesise all of the British (let alone Canadian and German) sources at the tactical level would be beyond the scope of one author. The tactical detail and the enormity of Veritable demanded a focus on British units in 30 Corps when they were on its line of main effort – that being the point of main effort or *schwerpunkt* as it changed over time.[52] This approach reduced the number of battles examined from over 200 to a more manageable 60.

Other deliberate trade-offs concerned the processing of Canadian, German and airpower sources. Efforts to mine each of these seams greatly increased the author's data processing burden but (with a few exceptions) added little value to the assessment. For Allied airpower, the lack of detailed secondary studies and this author's unfamiliarity with the primary material were problematic, but the main constraint was the limited discernible impact on battalion group battles.[53] Canadian secondary sources were of immense value in shaping the work, but primary source access was often difficult and the material of limited relevance to British unit performance on the 30 Corps main effort. For German sources, these obstacles were magnified by the language barrier and by the fragmented nature of the material, but sources have been exploited wherever possible.[54]

As a result of these constraints, the source material in *Slog or Swan* is overwhelmingly drawn from British Army units and formations. But of course, they are the subject of the main research question: How did British units and formations fight in Operation Veritable? There are many strands to this question. Was Veritable, as Horrocks claimed, just a slog in a bog? Was there really no room for manoeuvre and no scope for cleverness? How did planning, intelligence and logistics shape tactical battles? How did command systems function to manage the operation? How did units use artillery firepower? How did they coordinate infantry and armour? How did 30 Corps fight set-piece battles, urban battles, and battles of manoeuvre? How did the Corps transition between the set-piece break-in battle to more fluid breakthrough, breakout, and exploitation/

52　Montgomery used schwerpunkt and *aufrollen* in his *The Armoured Division in Battle*, (Holland: 21 Army Group, 1944), p.15.

53　A similar lack of data and effect were noted in T. Copp, *Fields of Fire: The Canadians in Normandy* (Toronto: University Press, 2003), xiii. Veritable had many days where air was unavailable but even on clear days, command system problems usually precluded the use of air support within 2km of friendly troops.

54　The four pages covering Veritable in the German official history were translated by a friend but offer few insights. R. D. Müller (Ed.), *Das Deutsche Reich und der Zweite Weltkrieg – Band 10/1: Der Zusammenbruch des Deutsches Reiches 1945* (München: Deutsche Verlags-Anstalt, 2008), pp.282–285. Promising titles like H. Bosch, *Der Zweite Weltkrieg zwischen Rhein und Maas* (Geldern: District Historical Association, 1977) were found to be based primarily on Allied sources with little additional information of relevance. The most useful German sources were online fora (see Acknowledgements), the 'arguably self-serving' and certainly vague post-war interviews with German generals and H. G. Guderian, *From Normandy to the Ruhr: With the 116th Panzer Division in World War II* (Bedford PA: AUSA, 2001), passim. The 'self-serving' quote is from J. Wood, 'Captive Historians, Captivated Audience: The German Military History Program, 1945–1961', *Journal of Military History*, 69 [2005], pp.123–147.

pursuit phases of operation? Instead of repeating what generals or previous historians have said, *Slog or Swan* will attempt to answer these questions by looking at what units did, then, as the book's subtitle suggests, examine what made units effective and ineffective.

The book also aims to inform current force development by providing a detailed example of how fundamental factors interact to make a fighting organisation effective or ineffective. Many studies have used historical operations to inform force development, but they tend to build on secondary sources, compare multiple operations, and draw broad strategic, or operational level, conclusions.[55] This book aims to illustrate themes more narrowly by describing their impact at the lower tactical levels that are familiar to a wider military audience.

Disproving Wellington

Many academic studies adopt a purely thematic approach, but this did not suit Veritable because there is no reliable tactical or operational history to provide context.[56] Siting the thematic elements at the start and end of the book, with a large descriptive block in between, or addressing every theme at the end of each descriptive chapter, increased the word count or lost so much tactical detail that the reader would have been unable to assess bias in the author's selection of evidence.[57] Then, because the themes are so intertwined (for example, with manoeuvre dependent on firepower and command systems) their relationships and impact only become fully apparent when examining the operation from start to finish. Indeed, the reader can only judge the conduct of later battles in the light of previous planning and fighting.

Despite the limitation of a thematic structure, certain themes were more evident during particular phases of the operation, so it has been possible to use each chapter to examine a theme. For example, operational planning is a natural fit to Chapter 1, which also puts Veritable in its strategic context. Then firepower naturally fits Chapter 2, which describes Veritable's D-Day and its massive opening fire plan. However, it is not until Chapter 8, near the end of the operation and the book, that it is possible to examine the role of morale. This is convenient because morale was dependent on planning, artillery, tactical logistics (introduced in Chapter 3), command systems (Chapter 4), infantry-armour cooperation (Chapter 5), and on the conduct of urban battles (Chapter 6) and manoeuvre operations (Chapter 7). These chapters and themes follow the 30 Corps line of main effort and are shown in context on Map 2.[58]

As the book grew from tactical psychology research, only the firepower theme was chosen prior to data collection – artillery being used to suppress more than kill defenders. All other themes grew from the data and from the progress of battles rather than a doctrinal template or previous research findings. Although the author's reading and experience as a military psychologist and operational researcher shaped this process, the themes appeared from tracing the causes and effects in a large sample of battles. The assessment often includes concepts that would have been alien to

---

55 T. N. Dupuy, *Future Wars: The World's Most Dangerous Flashpoints* (London: Sidgwick & Jackson, 1992); Naveh, *Military Excellence*; Biddle, *Military Power*.
56 The absence of a reliable narrative meant some historians and soldiers who could converse freely about the many subordinate Normandy battles, or knew which division landed where in Market Garden, confused Veritable with earlier and much smaller operations, or had difficulty seeing past the mines and mud cliché.
57 These approaches work well with narrower samples of combat, as in C. Stockings, *Bardia: Myth, Reality and the Heirs of Anzac* (Sydney: UNSW, 2009), and J. D. Clayton, 'The Battle of the Sambre, 4 November 1918' (Birmingham PhD thesis, 2015).
58 Base map from R. Gill and J. Graves, *Club Route in Europe: The Story of 30 Corps in the European Campaign* (Hanover: 30 Corps, 1946), p.128.

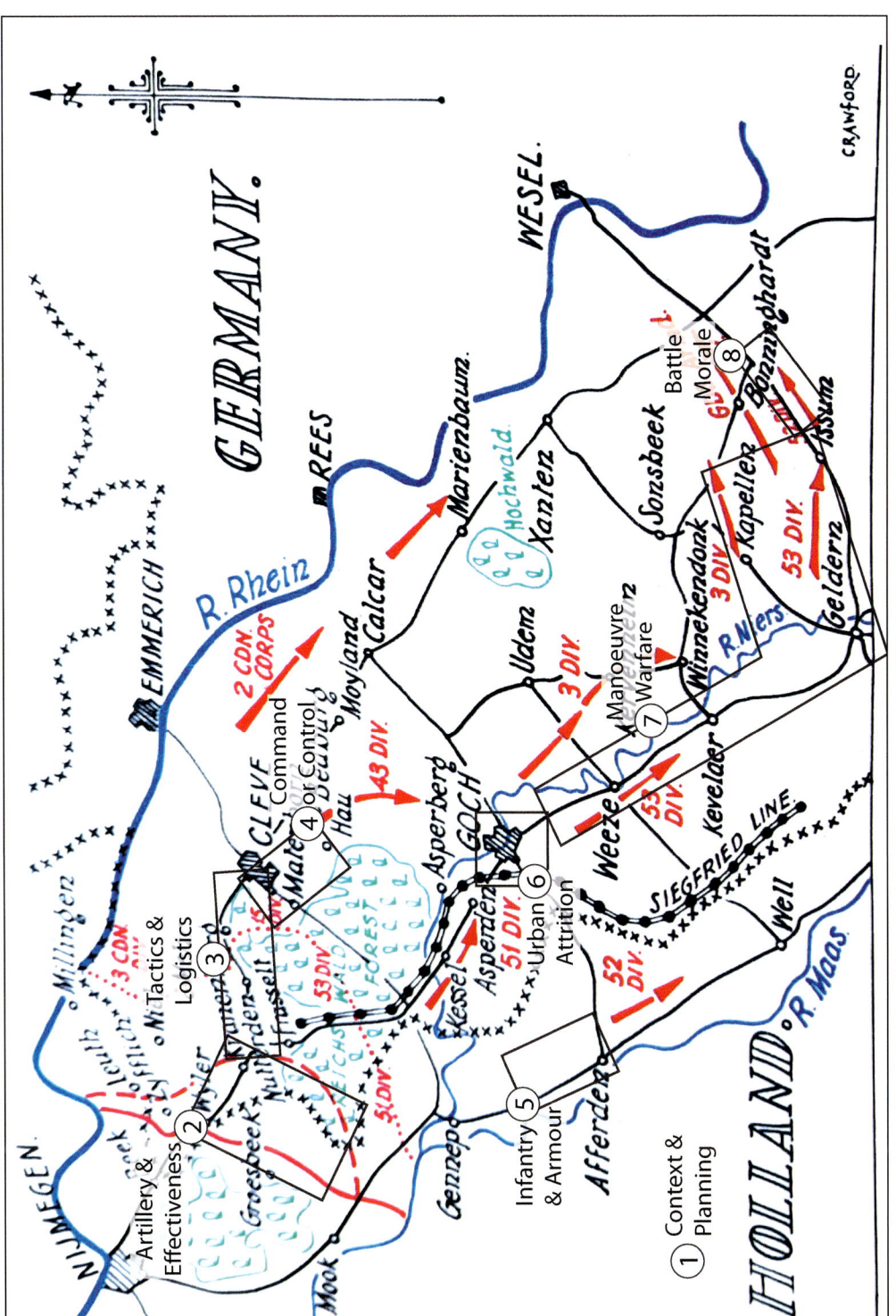

Map 2: Chapters, themes, and geographic setting. (Gill and Graves, *Club Route*)

the soldiers who fought Veritable; "suppression" is a 1970s term, "command system" is from the 2000s, and the author was unaware of "tactical logistics" before searching for words to explain the observed phenomenon. These terms would sit awkwardly in a purely historical study but offer the best root to transfer lessons from 30 Corps to current force development activities.

Each chapter opens with a brief introduction to the operational and thematic context and ends with a thematic conclusion. However, the main body of most chapters is a description that allows the reader to understand the causal chain and assess the impact of each theme. Later chapters begin to combine themes, allowing readers to see the interaction of factors throughout the operation. The descriptive component of chapters is far from exhaustive: with the 60 battle descriptions averaging 4,000 words each, the whole would be outside the scope of a readable book. So, while a chapter can involve a dozen battalion group battles, only those that best illustrate the theme are related in any detail, with the remainder summarised to provide context and indicate the extent to which a theme was common to all battles.

The main body of the project was primary historical analysis, with each battle description drawn from as many as 20 sources and some chapters drawing on nearly 100 sources for their descriptive component. Mapping was essential for understanding the flow of battle, and most of the maps included in *Slog or Swan* are the result of a ponderous projection of original overlays, aerial photographs, orders, action summaries, gird references and timings onto contemporary and modern mapping. Most maps in the book are based on the 1:25000 sheets the infantry was issued, but then zoomed in or out to fit the page. In these cases, north is always up, and each grid square is a kilometre across. (British, Canadian, and American forces went metric in 1944 but told most soldiers that a grid square was 1,000-yard box.) Like the originals, maps are sometimes blurry, inaccurate, and poorly aligned, so a road on one sheet can become a field boundary on the sheet that joins it. Some woodland ends dramatically where map sheets meet. On maps near the national border, lines of latitude do not travel east–west but lean slightly to allow the German grid to join up with the Dutch grid. Despite their flaws, these maps give a much better feel for what commanders used to inform their decisions. It is merely a coincidence that this approach was much cheaper than creating new maps from scratch.

Data collection was guided by published campaign summaries, then the analysis of each battle began in the central battalion's diary or history before drawing other sources into an iterative cycle of refinement and correction. Late in the project a chance find changed this process. A footnote in Hart's 'Montgomery' led to Harris's 'Liberation Campaign', a detailed history of the Northwest Europe Campaign produced for the Cabinet Office, which seems to have been lost to subsequent historiography.[59] Harris produced two volumes on Veritable that cross-reference war diaries, making them an ideal start point for the last quarter of the analysis. Harris also referred to otherwise inaccessible corps, army and army group documents that were especially useful for providing the context for each chapter.

Using such a wide range of sources was not naïve empiricism but an essential step in understanding the course of each battle. Even the most complete and balanced secondary sources, including Harris, abridge actions for the sake of readability, while primary sources were biased by their physical and organisational perspectives. For example, some units' diaries were found to ascribe the capture of a position to a dogged frontal assault by their own men, either not knowing or neglecting to mention that another unit had outflanked the position causing the defenders to surrender or withdraw. So, while units' strengths and casualties can often be estimated from one

---

59 G. W. Harris, 'Liberation Campaign North-West Europe: The Battle of the Rhineland' Part I (CAB 44/257) and Part II (CAB 44/258), hereon Harris 'Rhineland I' and 'Rhineland II'. The series is described in D. Rooney 'Opening the Second Draft of History: Liberation Campaign 1944–45', *Mars & Clio*, Autumn 2024, pp.12–25, in press.

or two sources, the tactical events become clear only after compiling a battle description from multiple perspectives. Only by reconciling different descriptions of events in time and space was it possible to reliably assess how and why a battle was won or lost. As one reviewer put it: 'You're trying to disprove Wellington by speaking to as many guests as possible.'[60]

The "guests" in this case were the junior officers and signallers compiling war diaries and communication logs. These are imperfect sources: the logs depend on access to working radios and therefore have many gaps, while diaries were often back-filled hours after the events they describe, and on rare occasions possibly weeks later. Yet together the diaries and communication logs represent a body of material that is consistently closest to the events that inform historical discourse. The diaries vary in completeness and readability: some appear to have been written as the first draft of a glowing unit history, others are critical, self-critical, and glaringly at odds with later publications. Most are straightforward descriptions of the main events with timings and grid references that allow the sequence of events to be plotted on a map. Although some diaries provide pages of description for a single action, others use only a couple of sentences, and this inevitably skewed the assessment. There is similar variation in histories and memoirs, with 10 books on the Sherwood Rangers Yeomanry, while other units have no accessible history.[61] The diaries and communication logs also help to correct published unit histories, which tend to hide uncomfortable incidents, and nearly always omit dull but critical facts to enhance readability.

The "nearly-bottom-up" approach owes much to the truly bottom-up studies presented at the pivotal Edinburgh University Soldier Experience conference and most notably extended in Copp's work on the Canadian Army's Northwest Europe Campaign.[62] However, the analysis in *Slog or Swan* required a level of completeness in source material that does not exist below battalion level. For example, the memoirs accessed for the project include Woollcombe's *Lion Rampant*, which provides an accessible company level view in 15 Division, but the next nearest memoir is Sydney Jary's platoon-level view in 43 Division.[63] These wonderful lower-level sources are exploited wherever possible but the wide gaps between them mean they can only occasionally add useful detail and there is no potential to unite them into a coherent picture of how companies or platoons combined to fight a battle or operation. The most relevant study to apply a bottom-up approach is Louis Devine's comparison of 43 and 53 Divisions. Both these formations fought in Veritable and Devine's thesis contains a wealth of useful material, but the longitudinal approach, stretching from before Normandy until the end of the war leaves little space for tactical detail. As a result, Devine's analysis of battles relies heavily on published histories that often conflict with the evidence from primary sources.[64]

---

60 'The history of a battle is not unlike the history of a ball. Some individuals may recollect all the little events of which the great result is the battle won or lost, but no individual can recollect the order in which, or the exact moment at which, they occurred, which makes all the difference as to their value or importance.' Wellington in T. Babington Macaulay, *The History of England from the Accession of James II* (Philadelphia: Porter & Coates, 1855), p.481. Unlike Wellington's time, British Second World War communication logs and war diaries recorded times, places, and events almost as they happened.

61 There are eight titles between T. M. Lindsay, *Sherwood Rangers* (London: Burrup, Mathieson & Co, 1952) and J. Holland *Brothers in Arms: One Legendary Tank Regiment's Bloody War from D-Day to VE-Day* (London: Bantam, 2021).

62 P. Addison and D. Calder (eds), *Time to Kill: The Soldier's Experience of War in the West 1939–1945* (London: Pimlico, 1997); Copp, *Fields of Fire*.

63 S. Jary, *18 Platoon* (Winchester: Light Infantry, 2003).

64 L. P. Devine, 'The British Way of War in North West Europe 1944–45: A Study of Two Infantry Divisions' (Plymouth University PhD thesis, 2013), passim. A. Holborn, *The 56th Infantry Brigade and D-Day* (London: Continuum, 2010) applies a similar 'worm's-eye view' of a single brigade using extensive veteran interviews but includes no maps and has few battle descriptions making tactical assessment problematic.

Cross-referencing sources involved the correction of basic errors (particularly place names and the identity of flanking units) and perennial mundane problems such as written orders that inconsistently relate changes to a plan, or communication logs that note the time an event was reported rather than the time it occurred. Some of the jargon in diaries was unfamiliar to this author, and technical terms were used inconsistently by units.[65] For example, "start line", "H-Hour", "barrage" and "Tiger" meant different things to different diarists. Cross-referencing and compression to reach a marketable word count meant many descriptive sentences were distilled from six or more sources, which made footnotes unworkably dense. To retain readability while demonstrating rigour and guiding future research, footnotes only display those source disagreements that are relevant to later conclusions. Readers wishing to reassess any battle in more depth can find all the relevant sources in nearby footnotes and the bibliography.

Data collection focused on material from eight divisions (3, 15, 43, 51, 52 and 53 Infantry; 79 Armoured and Guards Armoured) and three independent armoured brigades (8, 34 and 6 Guards). With their reconnaissance, artillery and engineer components included, this amounted to 18 diaries for the average division. Corps, army, and army group records brought the total to 192 primary sources. Thirty-one unit and formation histories proved useful in constructing battle descriptions and providing context, as did memoirs, biographies, and operational level histories, despite these often being at odds with primary records. The unavoidable reliance on British sources meant German force size and composition was usually only an approximation derived from intelligence summaries, corroborated against the few usable German sources.

The battle descriptions include crude measures of mission success: for British units this was usually a matter of comparing objectives stated in orders against those achieved in execution. Objectives for German units had to be implied but were usually obvious: typically to defend a town, village, or a piece of forest-covered high ground, or to delay the British advance. In most cases it was clear which side prevailed. Where possible, the cost of success and failure was also measured in terms of soldiers killed, wounded, missing, and captured, and armoured vehicle losses. The figures given in diaries were corroborated at different command levels and against the records of the Commonwealth War Graves Commission (CWGC). To better convey the human cost, especially in terms of its subsequent morale implications, British casualties are expressed in terms of the cost to "fighting strength", the approximate number of soldiers engaged in close combat, rather than the considerably higher war establishment or strength return for a battalion.[66] In common with previous defence assessments of historical battles, any conflict between sources regarding force composition or casualties was averaged unless there was reason to distrust a source.[67]

To identify chains of causation and their effect on battle outcome, each battle description was then subject to a crude form of root cause analysis, a technique adapted from studies of accidents

---

[65] For example, the author lost an hour of analysis time working out that a 'Crusader Tower' was not a medieval siege engine but a tracked vehicle for towing artillery.

[66] One reason for using fighting strength is that casual comparison to the extremes in some First World War battles exaggerates the supposed morale deficit in the Second World War British Army. A typical 1918 battalion comprised 1,000 men, with 916 in rifle companies, so 500 casualties would have been 50 percent of the battalion or 54 percent of its fighting strength. In Veritable, a battalion of 819 men suffering 500 casualties would lose 61 percent of the total but that could be 100 percent of its fighting strength. Fighting strength varied considerably and had to be interpolated from periodic returns and statements in diaries. Sometimes battalions deployed only three of their four companies and most had a proportion of each company left out of battle, but the dismounted carrier platoon might be used in a close combat role.

[67] R. C. Thornton and D. Watson, 'Historical Analysis of Infantry Defence in Woods' (Defence Operational Analysis Centre report, 1993).

and complex system failures.[68] Previous historical studies do not appear to have used this approach, but it is simply historical method writ large, as it involves asking 'why?' repeatedly to create linked segments of description and causation. The main benefits of this approach were the structure it forced on the data preparation and the alternative explanations it raised for success or failure. The much-delayed attack on Weeze illustrates the value of this approach. A top-down anti-British assessment might attribute the delay to over-cautious commanders, where a pro-British author might blame the weather. Innate overcaution and weather may have been contributory factors, but they were factors that units and formations could not change. The more detailed analysis presented here has instead identified problems with 30 Corps' equipment, planning, communications, organisation, logistics and operational concept: problems that units and formations could have corrected, had they been aware of them.

This nearly-bottom-up approach therefore represents an almost forensic history of how units fought in Operation Veritable. The book challenges the cynical and charitable views of British Army effectiveness and corrects the omissions and biases of existing narratives of Veritable. It shows how the 'forgotten victory' was a failure at the operational level, but it also shows how units usually overcame the British Army's conceptual and organisational problems to tactically defeat the last best hope of the *Wehrmacht* in the west.

---

68   R. J. Latino, *Patient Safety: The PROACT® Root Cause Analysis Approach* (London: CRC Press, 2009), passim; G. Wangen, et al, 'An Empirical Study of Root-Cause Analysis in Information Security Management', paper delivered to Emerging Security Information Systems and Technologies conference, 2017.

1

Context and Planning

SEPTEMBER 1944 TO FEBRUARY 1945 – AFTER ARNHEM – ANOTHER RACE TO THE RHINE – RAPIER BECOMES BLUDGEON – FANATICAL *FALLSCHIRMJÄGER* AND SICK OLD MEN – INTELLIGENCE AND DECEPTION – CONFLICTING AIMS MAKE HOLLOW PLANS

Planning is Everything

John Keegan warns historians against assuming a unit's actions result from higher orders (rather than the improvisations and accidents that so often shape behaviour) but there is a lesser-known tendency to imagine that operational plans result from the methodical processes espoused in doctrine pamphlets.[1] In fact, plans are often born of almost arbitrary decisions made in a particular context then executed in very different circumstances when subordinates lack the time and information to assess the validity of the original decisions.[2] The planning for Veritable was dominated by arbitrary decisions and its execution was filled with improvisation and accident, but very little of this is reflected in the existing historiography, which portrays a rigorously planned activity that neatly fit into Eisenhower's broad front strategy to achieve both concentration of force and surprise.[3] Sources routinely praise the 'masterful piece of planning', the 'thorough and accurate staff work' by planners who 'by all accounts performed magnificently', and the 'three long months of meticulous planning [for] the greatest single military operation ever undertaken by Canadian troops.'[4]

---

1   J.D.P. Keegan, *Face of Battle: A Study of Agincourt, Waterloo and the Somme* (London: Barrie & Jenkins, 1976), pp.27–34; Development, Concepts and Doctrine Centre, *Understanding and Intelligence Support to Joint Operations* (Shrivenham: DCDC, 2011), p.6–5.
2   C.A. McCann, R. Pigeau and A. English, 'Analysing Command Challenges using the C2 framework', (Defence Research and Development Canada report, 2003). Market Garden is an excellent example of iterative planning problems, perhaps best described in P. Harclerode's *Arnhem: A Tragedy of Errors* (London: Arms & Armour, 1994), passim.
3   P. Warner, *Horrocks: The General Who Led from the Front* (London: Sphere, 1984), p.123.
4   Whitakers, *Rhineland*, p.32; Dennis/SSVC *Rhineland*; P.D. Dickson, *A Thoroughly Canadian General: a biography of General H.D.G. Crerar* (Toronto: University Press, 2008), pp.384–390; J.A. Macdonald, 'In search of Veritable: Training the Canadian Army staff officer, 1899 to 1945' (Royal Military College of Canada master's thesis, 1992), p.2. Macdonald based his thesis on the assumption that examining 'a military operation as successful as VERITABLE promised to offer all the criteria necessary to determine how well

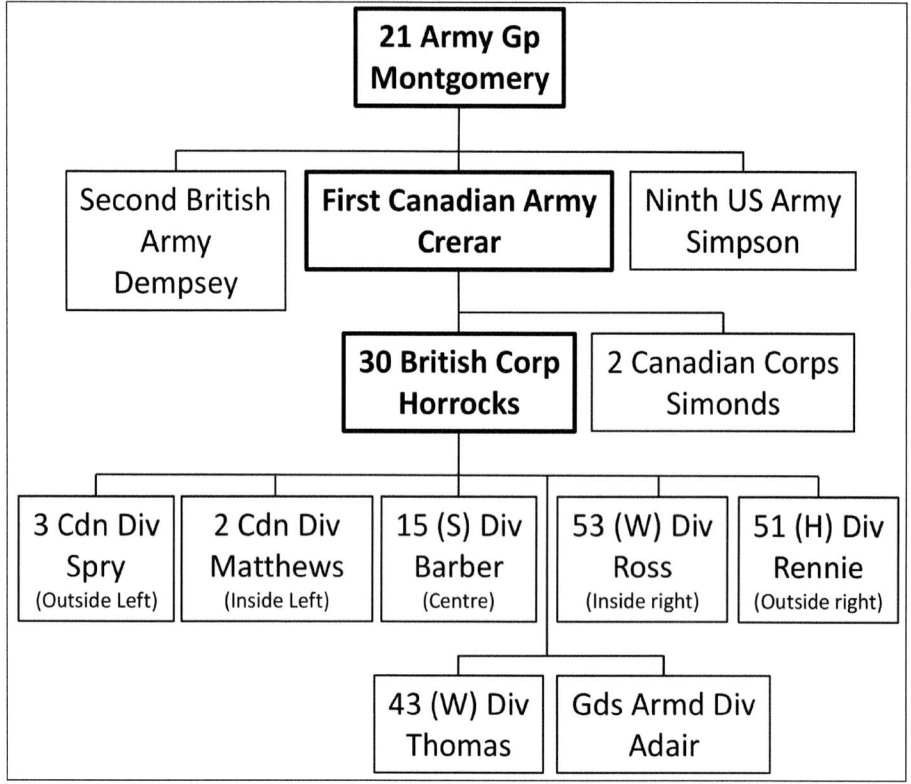

Figure 1: Abridged organisational chart for 21st Army Group on 8 February with focus formations in bold.

Guided by official narratives, units and formations produced histories that emphasised the high quality of Allied planning but had difficulty reconciling this with their own experience of intense friction and unexpectedly hard fighting. Mines, mud, and the delayed American attack were used to explain the gap between such great planning and difficult execution, as were concrete bunkers, Tiger tanks, fanatical *Fallschirmjäger* and the forbidding Reichswald, all of which were conveniently outside the control of 21st Army Group planners. This narrative was then recycled in the biographies of Montgomery, Crerar, and Horrocks, the key commanders shown at Figure 1.[5] Many components of this semi-official core narrative are factually correct, but they are framed by a description of planning written by the planners, and the whole is inevitably skewed as a result.[6]

That uncritical narrative spilled over into later assessments that presented only minor variations to the story of a Montgomery masterplan colliding with mines and mud.[7] The planning paragon in

---

Canadian staff officers performed their duties', p.3.

5   N. Hamilton, *Monty: The Field Marshal, 1944–1976* (London: Hamish Hamilton, 1986), pp.369–376; Dickson, *Thoroughly Canadian*, pp.384–390; Warner, *Horrocks*, pp.123–125. Warner (p.118) makes the astounding claim that Horrocks 'could scarcely be expected to have a detailed knowledge of all the ground he was approaching, but others should have done and should have briefed him.'

6   The plan-centred narrative was aided by administrators' ability to publish early. For example, BAOR, *Administrative History of 21 Army Group* (Hanover: Publisher unknown, 1945) was a plush publication quickly distributed through the Allied commands then copied into British and Canadian post-operation reports.

7   Ellis, *Victory*, pp.254–260; Hart, 'Montgomery', p.119; Hastings, *Armageddon*, Kindle, 7633.

the *Battlefield Tour* seems to have shaped Stephen Hart's view that Montgomery insisted formations follow his masterplan: 'This attitude was evident in "Veritable", which was continued inexorably day after day in accordance with the phases outlined in the original plan.'[8] A few later sources succeed in identifying flaws in the plan, with the Whitakers and the SSVC documentary correctly noting that the thaw was predictable, and that the operation was delayed by Anglo-American bickering.[9] Yet thaw and bickering also make a partial view that appears alongside strangely ambivalent presentations of the gulf between Veritable's planning and execution.

With its focus on battalion battles, *Slog or Swan* is not overly concerned with higher command, but planning, intelligence and deception have been presented as Allied strengths that countered the fragile morale of British soldiers and the *Wehrmacht*'s tactical superiority. Planning also helped set the conditions in which units fought, and so some assessment is essential for understanding unit performance. This chapter shows how the initial conception of Veritable split in two, with one plan based on rapid manoeuvre, the other on steady attrition, but neither plan taking sufficient account of weather, ground, or enemy. The chapter introduces the idea that these competing operational conceptions exacerbated a dissonance between First Canadian Army and 30 Corps, then shows how Allied intelligence and deception were not the paragons described in official sources. Subsequent chapters will examine the extent to which these problems undermined operational effectiveness.

Arnhem's Ashes

Veritable was born from the death of Operation Market Garden. On 21 September 1944, four days after the Arnhem drop, the fate of 1 British Airborne Division was already sealed. Colonel Frost's force on the road bridge had surrendered and the rest of the Division was trapped in a tiny pocket, kilometres from a viable crossing. With the bridge in their hands, *SS Panzer* troops headed south to block 30 Corps and 82 US Airborne Division just north of Nijmegen. From that point on, Market Garden would mutate into an effort to rescue 1 Airborne Division and defend Nijmegen.[10] Yet on that same day, Montgomery issued the following directive to his Chief of Staff:

1. If we are to take quick advantage of the good situation we have achieved in the general area GRAVE – NIJMEGEN – ARNHEM, it will be necessary for the right Corps of Second Army to develop a strong thrust on the axis GENNEP – CLEVE – EMMERICH.
2. Having established itself in the CLEVE [Kleve] area, this Corps would operate in a S.E. direction between the RHINE and the MEUSE [Maas], directed on the N.W. corner of the RUHR.
3. The remainder of the Second Army would then move on HAMM.
4. But the right Corps of Second Army is at present holding a front facing east through DEURNE and WEERT, so as to protect the right flank of the Army. It cannot take on the task outlined in para 1 unless it is relieved from this protective role.
5. The task is to isolate and capture the RUHR. The best way to do this is to take quick advantage of our favourable situation and deliver a strong left hook with Second Army.

---

8   Hart, 'Montgomery', p.119. Following Hart, Hastings has Veritable as 'a characteristic Montgomery setpiece', *Armageddon*, Kindle, 7633. Later chapters will show considerable adaptations to the plan that were hidden from Hart's sources.
9   Whitakers, *Rhineland* pp.14–24, 29–43; SSVC/Dennis, *Rhineland*, part 3.
10 N. Hamilton, *Monty: The Battles of Field Marshal Bernard Montgomery* (London: Hodder & Stoughton, 1994), p.460.

First US Army should use its left wing in a holding role, so that Second Army can develop its full potential.
6. I consider that the inter-Army Group boundary should be adjusted <u>at once</u> as follows:
<u>All incl 12 Army Group:</u>
HASSELT – WEERT – ASTEN – DEURNE – VENRAY – MAASHEES.
Exact and detailed boundary to be settled between Second British and First US Armies.
7. If I were in full command and control of the operations to capture the RUHR, I would at once order the above adjustment of boundary.
8. As things stand at present, the command set-up is such that I can only recommend it. But I have been directed to co-ordinate the action of the Armies on the Northern route. Therefore I definitely recommend this new boundary.
9. I have cabled my recommendation to the Supreme Commander. Bring the matter up at the conference tomorrow.

[Signed] B. L. Montgomery
Field Marshal,
C-in-C 21 Army Group.
21-9-44

The directive was accompanied by the schematic at Map 3.[11]

In hindsight, Montgomery's proposal for a right turn near Nijmegen seems delusional or duplicitous, especially as it coincided with a failed attempt to regain control of First US Army. Yet even at the time, the logic must have been questionable: if the Arnhem crossing were as secure as Montgomery implied, why would the next step be to divert one-third of Second Army's strength to threaten the Ruhr from the wrong side of the Rhine? Eisenhower approved the scheme, but Montgomery's aspirations dwindled as German counterattacks increased. Two days later, Hamm was off the menu and 1 Airborne Division had been relegated to a feint force, serving only to distract the Germans from the new main effort, that right turn near Nijmegen.[12]

The next day, 24 September, preparations began for withdrawing 1 Airborne Division and revealed the true logic behind Montgomery's scheme. Accepting that Arnhem was lost transforms the right turn from an irrational diffusion of effort into the quickest way to reach the next set of Rhine bridges, 60 kilometres upstream (southeast) at Wesel. Getting to Wesel would involve breaching the Westwall at its weakest point, then outflanking the rest of the defensive line, potentially trapping German forces on the wrong side of the Rhine. However, by the 24th the right turn had been overtaken by events; Second Army was struggling to hold the Nijmegen supply corridor open, and it was accepted that the drive on Wesel would have to wait until the immediate fallout of Market Garden had been cleaned up.[13]

Despite the changed circumstances, the true logic of the right turn endured and Second Army formally adopted responsibility for preparing the operation, which was then codenamed "Gatwick", and would use 30 Corps and 8 Corps in a two-pronged drive north and south of the Reichswald (just like Montgomery's suggestion at Map 3).[14] Gatwick was postponed on 7 October because 'more immediate commitments' came to prominence, most obviously

---

11 Directive to COS in 21 Army Group Future Operations Planning (WO 205/247).
12 Hamilton, *Field Marshal*, pp.80–84, 210.
13 Hamilton, *Field Marshal*, pp.83–84; 15 Division diaries, Sep 44 (detailed later but transcriptions are free online at 15thscottishdivisionwardiaries.co.uk).
14 Harris, 'Rhineland I', p.78.

CONTEXT AND PLANNING 33

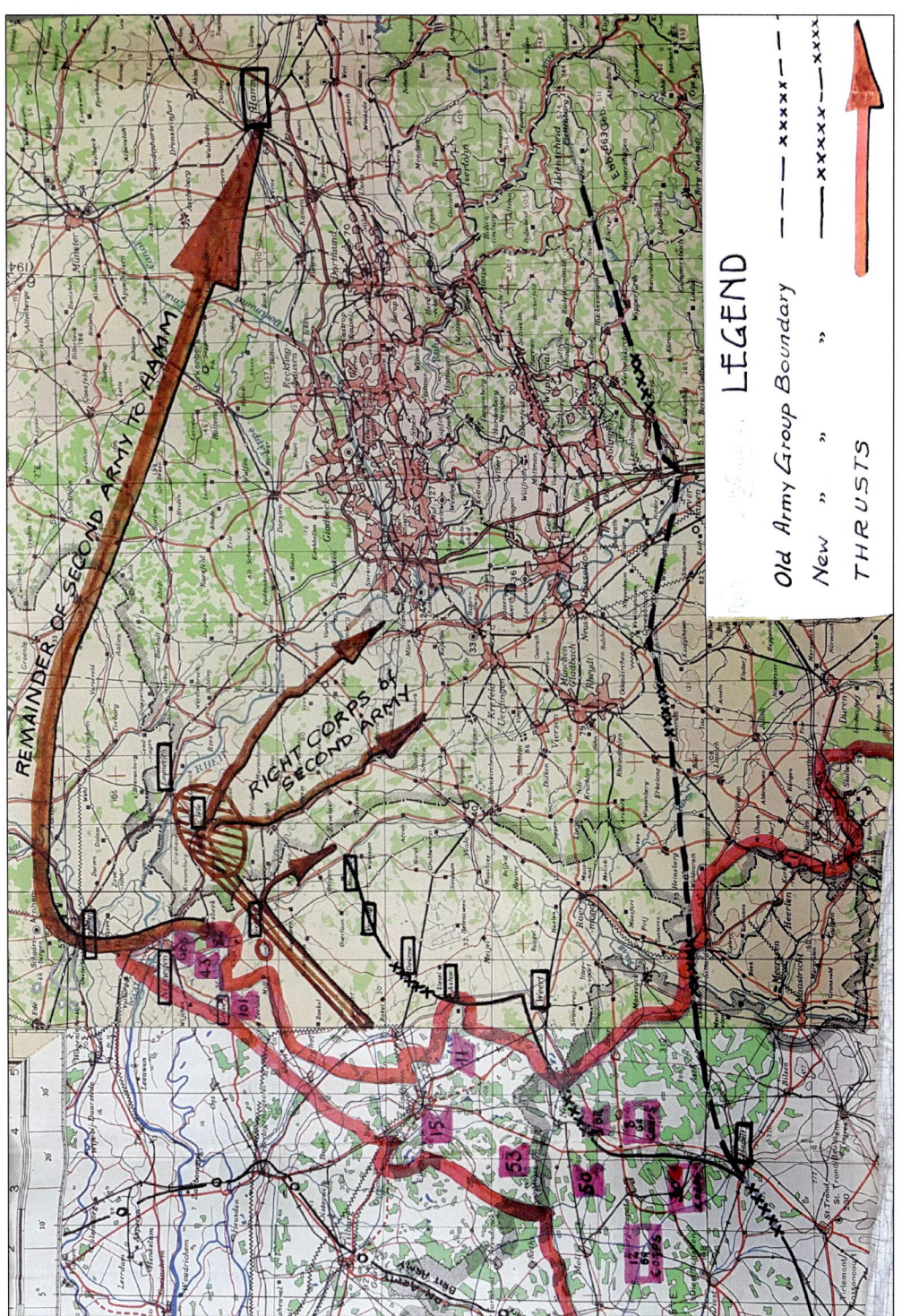

Map 3: Original concept for what became Operation Veritable, labelled 'Right Corps of Second Army'. (National Archives, author's photograph)

securing the Scheldt to resolve Allied supply problems.[15] There were other pressing operations under consideration, notably clearing the huge German pocket west of the Maas centred on Venlo (50km south of Nijmegen), and Horrocks's preferred move, another Rhine assault just east of Arnhem.[16]

Tactical misgivings also played a part in Gatwick being abandoned, with the ground and defences considered too difficult for a hasty attack. One of the brigades assigned to Gatwick noted that the operation was 'happily abandoned after one day's reconnaissance.'[17] Unfortunately, this decision did not come soon enough for the 1,000 people killed in the towns of Kleve and Emmerich, which were bombed on 7/8 October in preparation for the aborted Operation Gatwick.[18] The right turn stayed on Montgomery's to-do list but the responsibility passed to 30 Corps, which renamed the operation "Wyvern", after 43 Division's emblem.[19] By 28 October, Wyvern was to involve four infantry divisions, one armoured division and three independent armoured brigades in a scheme remarkably close to that finally employed on 8 February.[20]

Wyvern was itself abandoned a few weeks later because 30 Corps was sent to clear the Geilenkirchen salient south of Roermond in Operation Clipper (10 to 22 November). Responsibility for the right turn then passed to Crerar's First Canadian Army, which renamed it Valediction. In addition to replacing 30 Corps with 2 Canadian Corps, Valediction was paired with a northwards thrust by the American 12 Army Group, which was expected to meet the Canadians 20 kilometres south of Wesel. The main problem with this scheme was that 2 Canadian Corps was considerably weaker than the reinforced 30 Corps assigned to Wyvern, so on 28 November Crerar informed Montgomery that Valediction was impracticable.

Montgomery gave a dismissive reply, claiming Crerar had misunderstood the intention as there was never any prospect of launching Valediction until the spring. A week later Montgomery performed a U-turn and ordered Crerar to launch Valediction as soon as possible.[21] This change of heart was partly because the Scheldt and left flank were secure, the German presence west of the Maas was much-reduced, and flooding had ruled out a crossing near Arnhem.[22] However, it seems the main inspiration for the renewed urgency was that Eisenhower and Montgomery had patched up their differences again and were seemingly united in their conviction of the need for decisive operations that 'pointed very definitely to the Ruhr'.[23] This reconciliation was perhaps encouraged because Valediction could fit both Monty's and Ike's divergent ambitions and operational concepts. To Eisenhower, Valediction would be part of the broad front clearing up to the Rhine,

---

15　B. L. Montgomery, *21 Army Group: Normandy to the Baltic*, (London: Hutchinson & Co, 1946), Kindle 3382.
16　For example: Montgomery, *21 Army Group*, Kindle 3382-3400; BAOR, *Tour*, 1; WO 205/247; Conacher and Harrison, 'Veritable', p.2; 12 Army situation maps, library of congress loc.gov/item/2004629029.
17　Advocate, *From Normandy to the Baltic: The Story of the 44th Lowland Infantry Brigade of the 15th Scottish Division from D Day to the End of the War in Europe* (Germany: Wasers, 2017 [1945]), Kindle 1018; 44 Brigade diary, 7 Oct 44; N. Scarfe, *Assault Division* (London: Collins, 1947), pp.154–155.
18　M. Middlebrook and C. Everitt, *Bomber Command War Diaries* (Barnsley: Pen & Sword, 2014), Kindle 866, claims 641 civilians and 96 soldiers killed in Emmerich but offers no figure for Kleve; liberationroute.com claims 500 civilians killed in Kleve.
19　Macdonald, 'In search of Veritable', p.172; Stacey, *Victory Campaign*, pp.437–438; 'Notes on the Operations of 21 Army Group', WO 205/972A, p.41; 15 Division diary, October.
20　Harris, 'Rhineland I', p.78. The tank brigades equipped with Churchill infantry support tanks were renamed 'armoured type 2' in January 1945.
21　H. Darby, and M. Cunliffe, *A Short History of 21 Army Group* (Aldershot: Gale & Polden, 1949), pp.98–99; 21 Army Group *Veritable*, pp.1–2; B. Horrocks, E. Belfield. and H. Essame, *Corps Commander* (Toronto: Griffin House, 1979), pp.149–156; Stacey, *Victory Campaign*, p.436.
22　'Operations of 21 Army Group, 6 June 1944 – 5 May 1945', WO 205/952a, p.42.
23　Conacher and Harrison, 'Veritable', p.3.

but it was also set to be the first and the strongest of the broad front blows, giving Montgomery scope to attempt another knifelike thrust towards the Ruhr.[24]

In early December Valediction was renamed Veritable and given a provisional launch date of 1 January. Having returned from the Geilenkirchen salient, 30 Corps was placed under command of First Canadian Army and would lead the attack, at least until Kleve and Goch were captured and there was enough space for a two-corps front, at which point 2 Canadian Corps would join the fight. For Veritable's first phase 30 Corps was to be further expanded, to comprise five infantry divisions, an armoured division and the three independent armoured brigades.[25]

Preparations had barely begun when, on 16 December, the German *Wacht am Rhein* offensive struck through the Ardennes and 30 Corps was rushed south to form the backstop guarding Brussels. Even when the Ardennes fight was at its most desperate, most of 30 Corps was kept out of contact so Veritable could launch as soon as the German attack culminated. For this fifth iteration of the planning cycle, Veritable kept its name but Montgomery's operational concept shifted to become a rapid counter-offensive, striking towards Wesel while the bulk of Germany's western strength was still embroiled in the Ardennes.[26] Planners examined three options for launching Veritable quickly: the first involved only 2 Canadian Corps; the second bolstered the Canadians with divisions from 30 Corps as they returned from the Ardennes (rather than waiting for all of 30 Corps to assemble and echelon through); the third switched roles, with 2 Canadian Corps leading, then 30 Corps following up.[27]

None of these options were enacted, seemingly because Montgomery favoured Horrocks to lead the attack, and Canadian planners were wary of anything short of a laboriously prepared assault. The Canadian chief planner, Lieutenant Colonel Pangman, had already reported a worrying lack of detail in 30 Corps documents when he took over Veritable in mid-December, particularly for the operation's first phase, which was 'never precisely defined'.[28] Pangman's team believed there would only be slight advantages of speed and surprise from launching Veritable quickly, and although they considered 2 Canadian Corps sufficient to break through the Westwall, they worried the Corps might not be strong enough to break out:

> An unfortunate time lag might develop before the necessary regrouping could take place, by the insertion of another corps headquarters and additional formations, to maintain the momentum of the attack. Time would thus be given to the enemy to strengthen his several layback lines of defence and the later stages of Operation 'VERITABLE' might well prove to be as difficult, or even more so than the first phase.[29]

This proved to be an ironic and prophetic assessment, but its immediate effect was that it made Veritable too slow to be a riposte to *Wacht am Rhein*. First Canadian Army chose to wait for all of

---

24   This strategic schism is this author's speculation. Either Montgomery gave up his earlier narrow ambitions for Veritable then regained them after the Ardennes or, as suggested here, held onto them without telling Eisenhower. The latter view would also help explain the divergence of plans in First Canadian Army and 30 Corps.
25   Conacher and Harrison, 'Veritable', (pp.3–4) suggests the name change on the 13th but WO 205/9 uses 'Veritable' on 9 Dec. The overlap of operation names might reflect Valediction never gaining traction outside First Canadian Army.
26   Conacher and Harrison, 'Veritable' pp.4–5; Hamilton, *Battles*, pp.496–497, 529, 531.
27   There is no record of the second option being considered but it was common practice in the Canadian and British formations throughout the campaign – planners would have been remiss for not considering it.
28   Macdonald, 'In search of Veritable', p.196. Pangman was GSO 1 Plans.
29   Macdonald, 'In search of Veritable', p.197.

30 Corps to return and the combination of difficult logistics and Allied bickering meant the move took far longer than expected.[30] Veritable therefore changed back from a rapid counter-offensive to being part of the broad front, at least as far as SHAEF and First Canadian Army were concerned.[31]

Come the new year, 21st Army Group had three armies, and three operations aimed at Wesel. In addition to Veritable, Ninth US Army had come under British command to launch Operation Grenade northwards from the River Roer (as shown at Map 1), but between these was a third prong, Operation Ventilate, which had Second British Army crossing the Maas near Venlo and taking the shortest route to the Wesel.[32] Ventilate is a fascinating example of compromises in coalition planning, as it started life as an alternative to Veritable, become a contingency should Veritable stall, then turned into a backup in case Grenade was cancelled. It eventually dwindled to an administrative move prior to crossing the Rhine but despite this confusion, Ventilate was a worked-up plan that may well have solved many of Veritable's later problems.[33]

Plan Early, Plan Twice

At the end of January, Ninth Army was given authorisation to launch Grenade, 'possibly with a target date 15 February – though this is not certain', and on 1 February Veritable's D-Day was fixed as 8 February.[34] At this point aggressive American efficiency and a powerful desire to not play second fiddle were activated, bringing Grenade's launch date forward to the 10th.[35] Finally, after five and a half months of disjointed planning, four different names and five or six operational concepts, 21st Army Group was ready to send 30 Corps to Wesel. And after all that preparation, the blow was set to be a real haymaker. The initial assault had grown from two or three divisions in September to seven in February, with even more force to be added once 2 Canadian Corps joined in.

---

30 The bickering is ably covered in Ellis, *Victory* (Ch 9), the move less so (pp.259, 336). It is generally accepted that *Wacht am Rhein* culminated in late Dec, but Eisenhower retained 30 Corps until 16 Jan. Conacher and Harrison, 'Veritable', p.7; C.B. MacDonald, *A Time for Trumpets: The Untold Story of the Battle of the Bulge* (London: Harper Collins, 2018) Kindle 13826-13849.
31 Conacher and Harrison, 'Veritable', pp.5, 8; Stacey, *Victory Campaign*, p.442.
32 T. W. Parker and W. J. Thompson, *Conquer: The Story of Ninth Army, 1944–1945* (Washington: Infantry Journal, 1947), Chapter 4.
33 Crerar recalled Ventilate being cancelled on Feb 4 (D-4) because too few US divs had been transferred to Second Army. Ninth Army put the decision later, attributing cancellation to Second Army divs being transferred to Crerar. Troops assigned to Ventilate were told their role was to cut off Germans retreating from Veritable and only learned on 12th (D+4) that the operation was 'Likely NOT to happen' unless Veritable stalled. Later chapters will show that Veritable had already stalled by that date. The confusion surrounding Ventilate's viability can be seen in conference notes from 16 Jan, where Montgomery suggested the operation was cancelled, and a directive of 21 Jan, suggesting it was not. Second Army and 21 Army Group documents (WO 205/708-716, 205/972A, 205/9); Conacher and Harrison, 'Veritable', pp.12–13; Parker and Thompson, *Conquer*, p.158; T.R. Stone, 'He had the guts to say no: A Military Biography of General William Hood Simpson' (Rice University PhD thesis, 1974), pp.134–162; Blake, *Mountain*, pp.159–160; Notes on 156 Brigade conference, 1 Glasgow Highlanders (1 Glas H) diary (WO 171/5191) 12 Feb 1945.
34 21 Army Group, 'Considerations concerning Operations 'VERITABLE' and 'GRENADE'', WO 205/9.
35 The Veritable core narrative presents the timings for the two operations as part of Montgomery's careful sequencing to catch German defenders wrongfooted as they sent reserves north (e.g. Hamilton, *Field Marshal*, p.372); B. Horrocks, *A Full Life* (London: Collins, 1960), p.243). However, it is clear from chapter 4 of Parker and Thompson, *Conquer*, that the launch of Grenade was brought forward by Ninth Army's efforts.

To assess the operational plans that grew from this process, it is necessary to take a closer look at the ground over which Veritable would be fought and (in the official narratives) was to become so surprisingly unsuitable for manoeuvre warfare. As Map 4 shows, the area of operations was bounded in the northeast by the Rhine and in the southwest by the Maas.[36] The attack would launch from Groesbeek Heights, just to the east of Nijmegen (A on Map 4). This is where 82 US Airborne Division had landed in September, and the Heights had marked the front line since then. The 30 Corps objective was the two bridges at Wesel (B) 50 kilometres southeast of Groesbeek and just across the Rhine.

The whole area was low-lying, much of it less than 20 metres above sea level, with the highest points rarely exceeding 100 metres. The higher ground was generally comprised of forest-covered ridges and plateaus that dominated the flat cultivated areas around them. The northern strip of floodplain (C) was waterlogged following the thaw and in danger of being inundated if German engineers opened dykes along the Rhine. A narrower strip 100–200 metres either side of the Maas was also prone to flooding.

The flood plains would force the opening moves of Veritable into a bottleneck just eight kilometres wide (D) that was mostly filled by the plug of the Reichswald (E), 80 square kilometres of managed woodland divided into a rough grid by unpaved rides. Between the British start lines near Groesbeek and 'the sinister blackness of the Reichswald' lay an open area of flat farmland, dotted with hamlets and copses, and criss-crossed by streams, drainage channels, cart tracks, and a few paved roads.[37] This terrain pattern was repeated right across the operational area, with a patchwork of higher woodland and flatter open farmland, much of which was polder-like floodplain. The many farms were served by a collection of market towns.

The main road from Nijmegen to Wesel ran through a strip of open but higher ground on the northern edge of the Reichswald and was the best chance to reach the Wesel bridges quickly. Both sides recognised this corridor as key terrain for the initial attack and made their plans accordingly. The area south of the Reichswald was to be the secondary axis for 30 Corps, as the roads here were less developed and more difficult to reach, requiring either a fight through the edge of the forest or across the Maas.

The main and secondary axes passed through a series of defensive belts. The forward defence line was a two-kilometre-deep system of earthworks, minefields, and wire, running north to south along the flat open ground between Groesbeek and the Reichswald (marked as two bands near D), which then continued southeast along the Maas. A few kilometres behind this lay the Westwall's main defence line, which the Allies expected to include well-constructed concrete fighting positions that ran right through the Reichswald. Despite the main effort bypassing the forest, these defences were a concern for 30 Corps because of the severe casualties suffered by US troops fighting in the combination of woods, wire, mines, and interlocking fire from concrete pillboxes in the *Hürtgenwald*.[38]

Spurs of defensive works reached back from the Westwall to incorporate the towns of Kleve (F) and Goch (G) into the main defence. These two communication hubs were expected to be heavily fortified but most of their civilian populations had been evacuated following the October bombing of Kleve and Emmerich for the abandoned Operation Gatwick. Further east were other towns and villages that had less developed defensive works, but both sides expected every urban area to serve as a fortress. The final defensive belt was the Schlieffen Line (H), which the Allies called the

---

36 These paragraphs are compiled from multiple intelligence summaries listed later, the secondary sources cited previously and two weeks walking the ground. Maps 4 and 5 are based on an insert from 21 Army Group, *Veritable*.
37 Horrocks, *Full Life*, p.243.
38 C. B. MacDonald, *Siegfried Line Campaign* (Washington: Centre for Military History, 1993), pp.474 & 492.

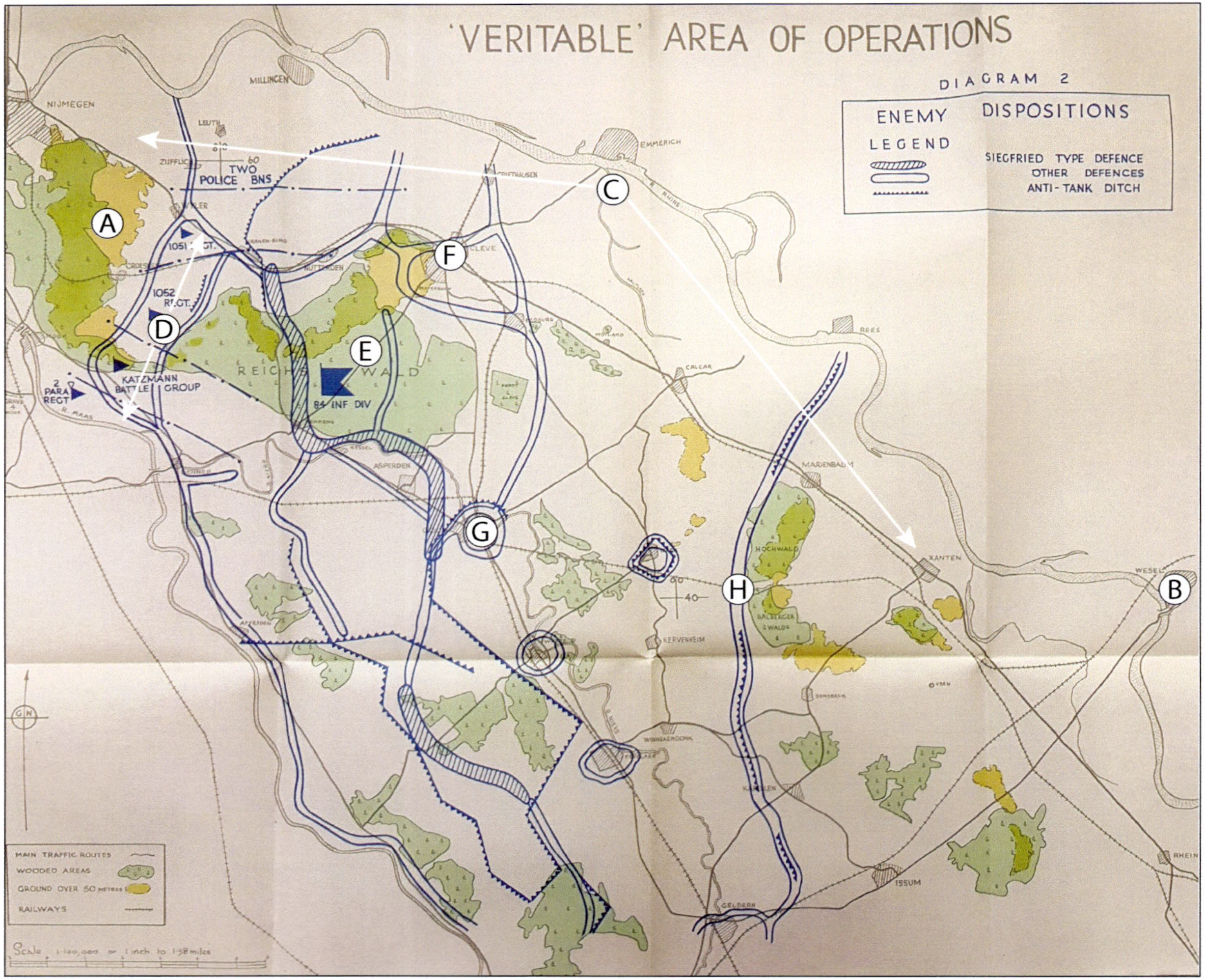

38 SLOG OR SWAN

Map 4: Ground and fixed defences. (21 Army Group, Veritable)

Hochwald layback. In mid-January this was little more than a single anti-tank ditch covered by a few trenches, but in the weeks preceding Veritable, work had begun to extend the earthworks back into the *Hochwald* (above the H) and *Balberger Wald* (below). Beyond these forests lay another block of the more open patchwork country, leading up to Wesel.

As with many previous 21st Army Group operations, the small number of metalled roads and the difficulty in moving armour off-road in wet weather would prove critical. The chance of poor going helped undermine Allied schemes back in September, when Veritable was still called Gatwick, but there had been a near continuous hard frost since November and plans were built on the hope that this would continue and allow armour to move and fight cross country. Although official narratives tend to give the impression that the thaw came on the eve of battle, the long-range forecast on 21 January had predicted it, and prompted Montgomery to demand a wet weather contingency plan.[39] So, when the thaw came a full week before Veritable's D-Day, it was sudden but far from unexpected.

Two markedly different operational concepts evolved from Veritable's disjointed planning process, but instead of one plan for hard ground and one for soft, one was Canadian, the other British. First Canadian Army envisaged a steady, three-phase operation:

> Phase 1. Clear the Reichswald and secure the line Gennep–Asperden–Kleve.
> Phase 2. Breach the 'second defensive system east and south-east of the Reichswald' and secure the line Weeze–Uedem–Kalkar–Emmerich.
> Phase 3. Break through the Hochwald layback and secure the line Geldern–Xanten.[40]

This plan was built around the assumptions that 'the enemy will strongly man and fight his several lines of organised defences' and that each line would need to be battered in a massive set-piece battle. Once each phase was complete, 'it will be necessary to move up the artillery and supporting weapons and commence the next phase with co-ordinated and heavy fire support, and with controlled movement.'[41] These phase lines are shown in yellow at Map 5.

The more energetic 30 Corps plan (shown as red arrows with division numbers) was explained with a soccer analogy:

> Outside left (north), 3 Canadian Division would attack late on D-Day to provide flank protection by securing the northern plain.
> Inside left, 2 Canadian Division would capture the village of Wyler and the first section of the main road, then be "pinched out" by the divisions either side of it.
> Centre-forward, 15 Scottish Division would fight through the Westwall and along the corridor between floodplain and forest, secure the key terrain of the "Materborn Feature" south of Kleve, then break out and exploit eastwards.
> Inside right, 53 Welsh Division would shadow 15 Division, protecting its southern flank by securing the northern half of the Reichswald.
> Outside right, 51 Highland Division would attack through the southwest corner of the Reichswald then secure Veritable's secondary axis towards Goch.[42]

Two more formations poised behind 15 Division were ready to burst out into open country once the Materborn Feature had been secured:

---

39 Conacher and Harrison, 'Veritable', p.10; SSVC/Dennis, *Rhineland*, part 1.
40 Ellis, *Victory*, p.256.
41 Conacher and Harrison, 'Veritable', p.13.
42 15 Division Operation Order no. 8 (OO 8), 4 Feb, Division diary (WO 171/4194).

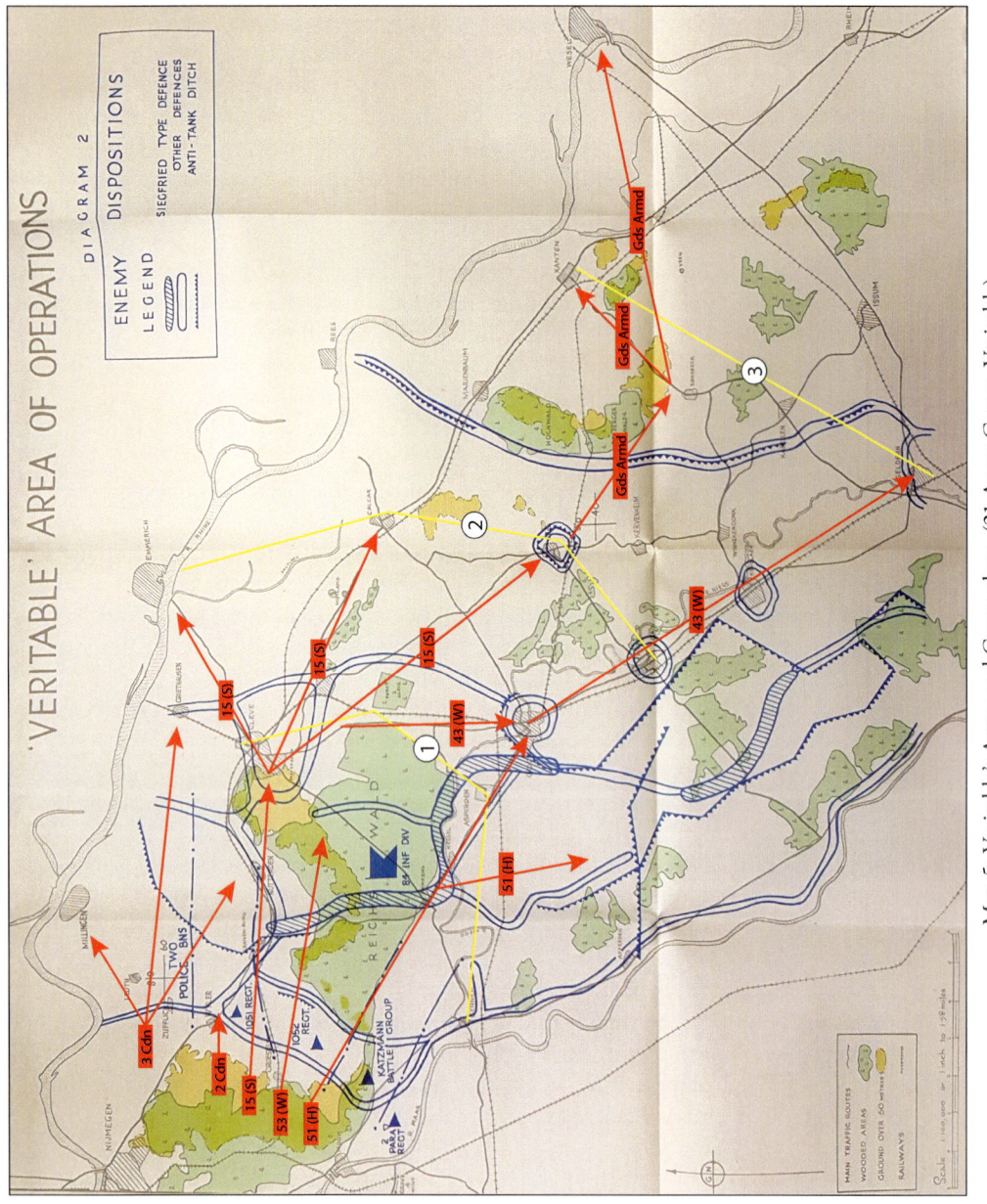

Map 5: Veritable's Army and Corps plans. (21 Army Group, Veritable)

First reserve, 43 Wessex Division would strike south from Kleve, through Goch, Weeze, Kevelaer and Geldern, cutting the Venlo–Wesel road.

Second reserve, Guards Armoured Division was more like a quarterback. It would overtake 15 Division near Uedem, then hook around the southern edge of the Hochwald to strike Wesel.[43] Guards' orders stated that, 'the Corps Comd will accept great risk to push a division across the river.'[44]

A quick scan of Map 5 might suggest the British plan nested quite neatly within the Canadian framework, but this is an artefact of mapping, with Corps arrows pointing to Army phase lines because they shared the obvious landmarks. The Canadian and British versions of Veritable inevitably shared logistic, assembly, deception, and engineer sub-plans, all of which were dictated at Army level, but these were mere servants of radically different operational concepts.[45]

Where the Canadian plan was to bash through the Reichswald and the Hochwald, the British plan was to dash around them, paying only lip service to a second phase and any actions by 2 Canadian Corps. Fifteen Division was to break out from the Materborn Feature within 24 hours and push mobile forces south and east before German reserves could deploy, then 43 Division was to 'elbow' its way past other formations and race through Goch outflanking the German divisions along the Maas, allowing Guards Armoured an unhindered dash to the Wesel bridges while the Canadians were still back near Kleve and Nijmegen.[46] In his memoirs, Horrocks gives the impression he saw bouncing a bridge as an outside chance, and perhaps he did, but a rapid dash to Wesel was explicit in the 30 Corps plan, and capturing a bridge was central to Guards Armoured Division's orders.[47]

By contrast, the Canadian Army plan paid its lip service to breakout, exploitation, and manoeuvre, with Phase One clearing the whole of the Reichswald before moving to Phase Two. Clearing the Reichswald was expected to be laborious in any weather and would require 53 and 51 Divisions to push their units beyond the boundaries set by 30 Corps and into the heart of the forest. Then, although Crerar suggested 30 Corps had a chance of reaching his third phase line within a few days, he saw this as an outside chance, and this line did not even go to Wesel.[48] A useful indication of the caution in the Army level planning is the contingency developed in case of a spontaneous German withdrawal behind the Rhine before 8 February; an event that required five days' notice before any advance, an astoundingly lengthy period for anyone versed in the manoeuvre warfare conception dictated by Montgomery's newer pamphlets.[49]

Army and Corps were at odds in other ways too, and the most harmful may have been inclusion of both the Canadian infantry divisions in 30 Corps' D-Day order of battle. This was not the

---

43   15 Division OO 8.
44   Guards Armoured Division Planning Notes No. 2, 22 February (diary, WO 171/4103).
45   Macdonald, 'In search of Veritable' (pp.198–199) outlines these subordinate plans.
46   BAOR, *Tour*, p.86.
47   Horrocks, *Full Life* (p.246) 'hoped secretly to bounce one of the bridges over the Rhine.' See also, P. Forbes, *The Grenadier Guards in the War of 1939–1945* (Aldershot: Gale & Polden, 1949), p.202, and D.J.L. Fitzgerald, *History of the Irish Guards in the Second World War* (Aldershot: Gale & Polden, 1949), p.559. As late as 4 March, Guards units were being 'warned to be prepared to jump the WESSEL bridge if opportunity occurred', 2 Welsh Guards diary, 'Operation "Veritable": brief summary of events' (WO 171/5152).
48   Conacher and Harrison ('Veritable', p.16) has Crerar stating on 4 February: 'If everything breaks in our favour – weather ground, air support, enemy dispositions and reactions – I would not be surprised if the armour of 30 Corps reached the Geldern–Xanten line in a few days.' This does not ring true as it was stated four days after the thaw and was followed by a reiteration of the three-week, three-phase plan. Curiously, the Whitakers (*Rhineland*, p.31) use this quote but extend Crerar's line along the Rhine to Wesel.
49   Notably *Armoured Division in Battle*, passim.

result of any measured assessment to match ends and means but an operational distraction caused by horse trading outside the chain of command:

> Gen Simonds [2 Canadian Corps] sent Gen Crerar a note pointing out the repercussions and bad taste which would come out of this from our Canadian soldiers – to be left out of THE battle – probably the one that ends the war. Gen Crerar saw Monty the following day and apparently as a result 3 Cdn Div was included in the attacking divs.[50]

This attempt to muscle-in on the British scheme did nothing for Canadian prestige as 30 Corps staff simply split a one-division flank protection task into two, so both Canadian divisions would still be left out of 'THE' battle, unless of course something went horribly wrong.

The German Defenders

The enemy is the greatest source of uncertainty in any plan, but this is not apparent in the Veritable narrative: to demonstrate the superiority of Allied intelligence, official sources emphasise the accuracy of the predicted rate at which German reinforcements would arrive; to show the effectiveness of the Allied deception, sources recount *Oberkommando der Wehrmacht* (*OKW*) listing the location of 30 Corps as 'unknown' until a few days after Veritable launched.[51] These observations are supported by primary sources, but they are isolated facts presented without the wider context that shows Allied intelligence and deception were less than the perfection implied.

On Veritable's D-Day, 30 Corps was to strike the right wing of *General der Fallschirmtruppe* Schlemm's *1. Fallschirm-Armee* (Figure 2), which was responsible for 80 kilometres of the front, running from the Rhine just east of Nijmegen, to Roermond on the Maas. The immediate opposition to 30 Corps was *84. Infanterie Division* under *Generalmajor* Heinz Fiebig. Sometimes mislabelled a *Volksgrenadier* formation by Allied sources, *84. Division* was formed from fragments of others in early 1944, then 'smashed almost completely' in the Falaise Pocket, where its previous commander was captured.[52] In September 1944, Fiebig was tasked with rebuilding *84. Division* and in October the Division was sent to the Kleve sector to block any eastward Allied thrust from Nijmegen. At the extreme right of *1. Fallschirm-Armee*, *84. Division* was the most northerly formation on the Westwall, the most northerly formation west of the Rhine and was responsible for defending the gap between the Maas and the Rhine.[53]

When 30 Corps attacked, *84. Division*'s main force comprised three regiments (each of two battalions) plus artillery, engineers, labour units, and a fusilier battalion. Contrary to the laydown shown in Map 4, in the days before Veritable launched, the northern flood plain was defended by *Grenadier-Regiment 1052* (*GR 1052*), the area around the main road to Wesel by parts of *GR 1051*

---

50 Diary of Brigadier N. E. Rodger, 2 Canadian Corps BGS, 10–13 Dec, quoted in Macdonald, 'In search of Veritable', p.218; Copp, *Cinderella*, p.201. Rodger may have transposed division numbers; Veritable Planning Notes 4, 30 Corps diary (WO 171/346), has 3 Canadian Division in the order of battle, not 2.
51 Horrocks et al *Corps Commander*, p.182.
52 Fiebig interview, 'The 84th Infantry Division during the battles from the Reichswald to Wesel' (National Archives of the USA Foreign Military Studies [NARA FMS] B-843,1948), p.3. BAOR, *Tour* (p.8) gives the Volksgrenadier label because *84. Division* had three regiments, then seems to have assumed the rest of the Division's structure from that.
53 53 Division Diary, Appendix B to ISUM 190, 22 Feb; Stacey, *Victory Campaign*, p.463; Fiebig, '84th Infantry', pp.3, 7; K. Ford, *A Luftwaffe General: General der Fallschirmtruppe Alfred Schlemm* (Southampton: Self-published, 2018) Kindle 338–462; BAOR, *Tour*, p.8.

CONTEXT AND PLANNING 43

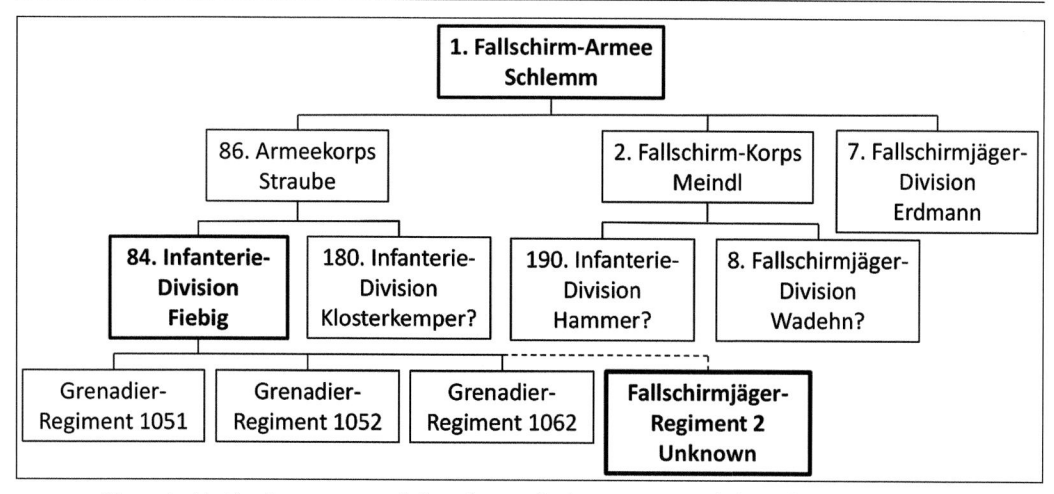

```
                        ┌─────────────────────┐
                        │ 1. Fallschirm-Armee │
                        │       Schlemm       │
                        └──────────┬──────────┘
        ┌──────────────────────────┼──────────────────────────┐
┌───────┴────────┐         ┌───────┴─────────┐        ┌───────┴────────┐
│ 86. Armeekorps │         │ 2. Fallschirm-  │        │ 7. Fallschirm- │
│    Straube     │         │   Korps Meindl  │        │ jäger-Division │
└───────┬────────┘         └────────┬────────┘        │    Erdmann     │
        │                           │                 └────────────────┘
┌───────┴───┬───────────┐    ┌──────┴──────┐
│ 84.       │ 180.      │    │ 190.        │ 8. Fallschirm-
│ Infanterie│ Infanterie│    │ Infanterie- │ jäger-Division
│ Division  │ Division  │    │ Division    │ Wadehn?
│ Fiebig    │ Kloster-  │    │ Hammer?     │
│           │ kemper?   │    │             │
```

Figure 2: Abridged organisational chart for 1 Fallschirm-Armee with focus formations in bold.

and *Füsilier-Bataillon 84*, while the open ground in front of the Reichswald was defended by *GR 1062*, though this changed slightly on the eve of the attack. Five or six battalions were deployed in the forward defensive line on D-Day, with the Westwall's main defensive belt containing most of the Division's artillery, part of *GR 1051*, *Pionier Bataillon 184*, and *Magen Bataillon 276*, the latter being comprised of men with chronic stomach ailments.[54]

There is considerable disagreement concerning the strength of *84. Division*'s left flank but intelligence from 51 Division combined with fragments from German sources suggest *Fallschirmjäger-Regiment 2* (*FJR 2*, once part of *2. Fallschirmjäger-Division*) came under command of *84. Division* in January and took over its left flank, as indicated at Map 4.[55] Part of the historiographic disagreement arose because, in the few days before Veritable launched, *FJR 2* was itself reinforced by parts of *FJR 20* from Schlemm's reserve formation, *7. Fallschirmjäger-Division*. This reinforcement coincided with a battalion of *GR 1222* (from *180. Division*) arriving to relieve part of *GR 1062*, just on the boundary with *FJR 2*.[56] The result of all this activity was that *84. Division* gained around 2,000 men in January and perhaps another 1,000 just before Veritable's D-Day. The operational and tactical impact was that 51 Division, the 'outside right' of 30 Corps, was set to attack an enemy much stronger than that indicated by intelligence, and perhaps twice as strong as that faced by any other division.

The competence and commitment of soldiers in *84. Division* has also been subject to debate. Some secondary sources have given undue prominence to the stomach battalion (a common inclusion in line infantry divisions since 1943) and perhaps confused the mistaken *Volksgrenadier* honorific with *Volkssturm* (an ill-equipped, untrained paramilitary levy) to suggest the whole formation

---

54 Stacey, *Victory Campaign*, p.463; Fiebig, '84th Infantry', p.3; 51 Division ISUM (intelligence summary) No.49 (WO 171/4245).
55 Fiebig '84th Infantry' claimed a 500-man parachute battalion was attached 'in the very last moment' but Stacey, *Victory Campaign*, p.463, has a 'well-equipped formation of 2000 men'. Later sources have tended to choose one of these alternatives then move towards surer ground.
56 30 Corps 'Enemy situation – 7 Feb 45'; 51 Division ISUMs 49 and 324; Fiebig, '84th Infantry', p.3; Ford, *Luftwaffe General*, Kindle 449; H. Stimpel, *Die deutsche Fallschirmtruppe 1942–1945: Einsätze auf Kriegsschauplätzen im Osten und Westen* (Hamburg: Mittler & Sohn, 2001), p.354; formation summaries at lexikon-der-wehrmacht.de.

was filled with sick old men and ill-trained boys.[57] The more balanced contemporary assessments suggest the Division was an 'average second rate' formation.[58] This would put the *Grenadiere* from *84. Division* at a lower standard than *Fallschirmjäger* and *Panzergrenadiere*, or even line infantry from 1940, but certainly not the dregs implied by some sources.

There are similar contradictions concerning the armour support for *84. Division*, with secondary sources having the powerful tank destroyer battalion *schwere Panzerjäger-Abteilung 655 (PzJgr 655)* or a company of *Sturmgeschütz* assault guns under command on 8 February, but no reliable primary source relates any contact with armour until the evening of the 10th and these arriving in small packets from somewhere far to the southeast.[59] When aggregated, these points of contention present *84. Division* as anything from 8,000 sick old men to a competent 13,000-man force plus an armoured battalion and a fanatical paratrooper regiment. The Division's likely composition when 30 Corps attacked was 10,000 slightly sub-par soldiers plus 2,000 somewhat more effective *Fallschirmjäger* troops, but no armour.

The Division's guns were provided by *Artillerie Regiment 184*, with a mixed bag of 70–80 field pieces ranging from 75mm infantry guns up to 152mm howitzers, with many being old Soviet arms. There were also four batteries of towed anti-tank guns from *Panzerjäger-Abteilung 184*, each equipped with a dual purpose 88mm gun and three captured Russian 76.2mm guns. Two or three *Nebelwerfer* multi-barrelled rocket launchers were also attached to the Division. All sources have artillery ammunition in short supply, with many suggesting a limit of 20 rounds per gun, though first-hand operational research found some guns with more than 60 rounds at the ready on D-Day.[60]

The ground was as great a concern for Fiebig as it was for Allied commanders. The Westwall extension was started in 1939, so it followed the Dutch-German border more than the lay of the land. Although the earthworks had been hurriedly improved in autumn 1944, Fiebig complained it was tactically unsound, being overlooked by Allied positions on the Groesbeek Heights and so close to the water table that some trenches could be only 1.2 metres deep. Fiebig's requests to pull back to more defensible ground were denied, however, presumably to avoid the political implications of giving up part of the Reich without a fight. Fiebig admitted that the Reichswald was an obstacle for the Allies but claimed it gave him little advantage because of the diktat to defend forward. Also, unlike the Allies, Fiebig knew there were no hardened fighting positions in his area, merely a scattering of concrete troop shelters.[61]

---

57 Allen *One More River* (p.32) bases its low opinion on basic errors, with *84. Division* including '719th Regiment made up of old men, and the 176th Regiment who were nearly all semi-invalids.' Neither regiment was part of *84. Div.* For an example of Volksgrenadier-Volkssturm confusion see MacDonald, *Time for Trumpets*, Kindle pp.623, 799.

58 Swann/Copp, 'Fire Support', p.360.

59 BAOR, *Tour*, p.8; 21 AG, *Veritable*, p.8. Ellis, *Victory*, p.254. The formal abbreviation for this unit appears to be *sPz.Jg.Abt. 655* but *PzJgr 655* is smoother. The first reliable report of German armour was on the morning of the 10th (15 Division comms log, 101100) but BAOR, *Tour* and sources following it, claim an 88mm *Jagdpanther* platoon captured on the 9th and assault guns in *84 Division* on the 8th. 43 Division intelligence for 10 and 11 Feb (Division diary, WO 171/4207) suggests one or two SP guns supporting *84. Division* on D-Day but was based on radio intercepts of mistaken sightings of Allied vehicles or German vehicles destroyed the previous September. The 51 Division comms log includes a report of 'SPs' firing on 7 A&SH on 9 Feb, but this is not mentioned in any Bn or Brigade diaries, where the first reliable report of armour is on the 13th (153 Brigade diary, WO 171/4409). Stimpel (*Fallschirmtruppe*, pp.348, 358) makes no mention of *PzJgr 655* and has the only armour in *1. Fallschirm-Armee* provided by *Fallschirmjäger-Sturmgeschützbrigade 12 (FJ-Stug-Brigade 12)* 50km south, near Venlo.

60 Fiebig, '84th Infantry', p.6; BAOR, *Tour*, p.8. 21 AG, *Veritable*, p.8; Copp, *Montgomery's Scientists*, pp.337–348.

61 Fiebig, '84th Infantry', pp.3–7. For an overview of concrete fortifications in the Veritable area see *After the*

According to the Veritable core narrative, the German defenders were completely surprised by a deception plan that used fake road moves, fake radio traffic and fake news leaked to civilians to indicate an attack on Utrecht in the northern Netherlands, but there is no record of this information reaching German commanders.[62] Then, despite the elaborate concealment efforts lauded in Allied reports, there were many clues to Veritable's true purpose, with poor light discipline among troops, many recorded instances of disguises being unavailable, and daylight movement bans ignored.[63] From the German side, Fiebig cited 'lively reconnaissance' in the air and on the ground, live artillery registration, and the building of bridges over uncontested sections of the Maas, which all pointed to Kleve and *84. Division* rather than Utrecht. Fiebig also mentioned the use of movement light ("Monty's Moonlight", created by reflecting searchlights off the cloud base, see Chapter 3), which, being a centrally controlled asset, suggests an army or corps decision to compromise security. To cap all this, interrogation of Allied prisoners on 4 February provided a strong indication that a major operation was due on the Veritable axis.[64]

For German battalions, the long-expected attack was seen as imminent from 5 February (D-3) and preparations were made accordingly.[65] Allied troops strongly suspected that they had been rumbled, with one diary noting on 5 February: 'It is appreciated that the enemy realises the weakness of this sector, and there are indications that he has noticed mov[ements] or suspects additional mov[ements] in assembly areas.'[66] By 7 February there was 'little doubt that the enemy is expecting an offensive by the British or Canadian Armies to develop shortly.'[67] This was made most evident when Canadian troops woke that morning to find 'The tide's in!'[68] German engineers were so sure the attack was coming they opened dykes on the Rhine to flood the area north of Kleve (C on Map 4).

It therefore seems the Allied deception and concealment plans did little more than make the picture slightly murkier for German commanders. While *OKW* did not expect the Veritable axis to be the main thrust, it was an organisation controlling a 700-kilometre front with plausible threats along its entire length. Below that, *Heeresgruppe H* interpreted reports of activity in the Veritable assembly area as a threat to the north, but this seems to be more due to old fears of having forces cut off in the Netherlands than the new deception. Meanwhile Straube, commander of *86. Armeekorps*, saw his main threat on the Operation Ventilate axis through Venlo to Wesel, but he was ignored by his junior, Fiebig, and his superior, Schlemm.[69] Fiebig recalled his personal appreciation as: 'Where could the conditions be more favourable for the enemy than in the Kleve sector; here the Westwall was in the main just an imaginary line [and] it was not necessary to cross the river as everywhere else further south.'[70]

Battle, 159 (2013), p.17.
62 BAOR, *Tour*, pp.11–12. German units in Utrecht may have seen things differently but no record of their assessments could be accessed.
63 30 Corps outgoing messages 051100 (to keep footnotes a little tighter they use a six-figure date time format) 'Orders re lighting are not being observed in all cases' and 062045 'Incidental traffic NIJMEGEN area still excessive and endangering security' and was to be addressed by the 'drastic action' of allowing no daylight movement without a pass signed by a brigadier or higher (WO 171/4076).
64 Fiebig, '84th Infantry', Stimpel, *Fallschirmtruppe*, p.354; Bosch, *Zweite Weltkreig* pp.190–194.
65 Interrogation Report on Major Potratz, *Füsilier-Bataillon 84*, ISUM 75, 34 Armoured Brigade diary (WO 171/4363).
66 '53 Welsh Division Artillery Op Instr No 24, 5 Feb 45', 53 HQRA diary (WO 171/4282).
67 'Enemy situation – 7 Feb 45' 51 Division diary (WO 171/4245).
68 Whitakers, *Rhineland*, p.43.
69 'German Wehrmacht in the last days of the war' (NARA FMS C-020, undated) pp.181–182; Fiebig, '84th Infantry', pp.4–5; Whitakers, *Rhineland*, pp.4–8; Ford, *Luftwaffe General*, Kindle 338–462.
70 Fiebig, '84th Infantry', pp.4–5.

Schlemm's logic, at least as far as he recalled it after the war, was that the southern threat (Grenade) was impractical if German forces still held the Rur dams and could flood that river at will, while Utrecht was simply too far from the Ruhr. This left Venlo (Ventilate) or Kleve (Veritable). The latter seemed the better option because it did not require an opposed river crossing.[71] Commanders' recollections are notoriously self-serving, but Fiebig and Schlemm reflect the logic behind Montgomery's original left turn. They are also corroborated by the chief of staff of *116. Panzer-Division* (part of *47. Panzerkorps*, which would counterattack 30 Corps on D+4) who had nothing to gain from painting Fiebig or Schlemm as insightful.[72] On balance, the *Wehrmacht*'s real problem was not in deciding where the next blow would fall but in the lack of forces to counter it. Yet despite their severe resource and movement constraints, German actions speak louder than post-war words: the Rhine dykes were blown, *GR 1222* and *FJR 20* elements were transferred to *84. Division*, and *116. Panzer-Division* was moved towards the Veritable area. These actions show that the deception plan, while laudable, could not hide the movement of the massive Allied force.

Even with the advantages of air supremacy and ground superiority, the Allied intelligence picture was just as murky as that in *Heeresgruppe H*. In terms of collection assets there was a huge gap between infantry patrols at the lowest tactical level, and Ultra intercepts at the strategic level. Both extremes were becoming less useful as the campaign wore on, often producing disconnected fragments of information, but it was inconsistent collation, analysis and dissemination of intelligence that made the picture confusing.[73] All 30 Corps divisions had access to the same source information prior to the operation, but their intelligence cells reached radically different conclusions. Fifty-One Division had *84. Division* backed up by an infantry division in Goch and a fictional *Panzer* division on Crerar's third phase line between Xanten and Geldern.[74] Contrarily, reports from 15 and 43 Divisions did not mention any reserves in the Veritable area, while 53 Division gave two separate pictures, each containing one of the reserves suggested by 51 Division.[75]

No sighting or intercept reports were presented to support the existence of the supposed infantry reserve (*180. Division*, centred further south on the Maas had some troops in Goch) and the only evidence reported for the *Panzer* reserve was an air reconnaissance report of anti-aircraft guns covering trench-digging near the Hochwald.[76] The most plausible explanation for the diversity of assessments is that confirmation bias or 'decision-based evidence-making' had intelligence cells making assessments that fit their version of the plan.[77] The divisions set for breakout roles (15 and 43) interpreted information to conform to the breakout of the 30 Corps plan. Divisions with less glamorous roles saw opposition more suited to First Canadian Army's caution.

---

71 Ford, *Luftwaffe General*, Kindle 338–462.
72 Guderian, *Normandy to the Ruhr*, pp.370–373. Meindl, the commander of *2. Fallschirm-Korps* during Veritable, also claims to have independently spotted the Allies' true intentions: 'II Parachute Corps: Part 3, Rhineland (15 Sep 1944 to 21 Mar 1945)' (NARA FMS B-093, 1947).
73 Later chapters will examine the limitations of infantry patrols and armoured reconnaissance, though sadly only briefly. L. G. M. Buckholt, 'Signal Security in the Ardennes Offensive' (Command and General Staff College Masters thesis, 1997), pp.57–60, shows the reduced value of Ultra by this stage of the campaign, with German command systems making more use of the civilian telephone system. Intelligence cycle as outlined in DCDC, *Understanding and Intelligence*, pp.3–4.
74 'Enemy situation – 7 Feb 45', 51 Division diary.
75 'Special int summary No. 2', 15 Division diary (WO 171/4194), 6 Feb. When 15 Division mentions a reserve late on 9 Feb (ISUM 198) it is *7. FJD*. 43 Div, ISUMs, Division diary (WO 171/4207), 3–9 Feb; 53 Div, ISUM 176, 8 Feb 45, and 'O.O. No. 27' 4 Feb, Division diary (WO 171/4276); 71 Brigade OO 1, 1 HLI diary, (WO 171/5202), 7 Feb.
76 30 Corps ISUMs 591 and 592 (WO 205/954), 7 and 8 Feb.
77 Quote from Lieutenant Colonel (Retd) Bruce Pennell. Cognitive biases are briefly examined in Ch 4.

Conclusion

The original aim of this chapter was simply to put the assessment in the context of the wider campaign and describe the ground and enemy facing 30 Corps, but by summarising the planning process and products, it has identified some of the shortcomings with Veritable's historiography and with Allied planning. The chapter has supported the observations of those operational histories that showed Allied bickering delaying Veritable and noted the predictability of the thaw, but it has also identified contributions from within 21st Army Group that have previously been overlooked. Rather than the planning paragon presented in official narratives, Veritable started life more like an expedient reaction to a field marshal's embarrassment than a realistic concept of operations. That initial conception lost its relevance as the strategic and operational contexts changed along with the weather, but the only variation in the plan was to add more mass and further delay the launch of the operation.

Within First Canadian Army, the evolving conceptions of the operation, and the repeated switching of responsibility, spawned a split between the plans developed at army and corps levels. The two plans diverged when Operation Wyvern became Valediction, leaving 30 Corps still set on salvaging September's race to the Rhine, while First Canadian Army fixated on November's sluggish contribution to the broad front strategy. The historiography of Veritable has overlooked this bifurcation and the confusion that it created, encouraging some erroneous conclusions about the efficacy of Allied planning.

It is tempting to see more to this split, with the divergence between army and corps being rooted in the personalities and expectations of commanders and national chains of command. On one side, the Canadian "Cinderella Army" prided itself on professional, procedural aggression. It was led by Crerar, the civilian engineer turned gunner then staff officer; a 'cold and remote figure' but a public servant in nearly the purest sense.[78] On the other hand, was the 'flamboyant panache of 30 Corps'; renowned from the desert and the great swan up Club Route Europe, it projected an image of rapid manoeuvre.[79] Thirty Corps was led 'from the front' by Horrocks 'the Actor', a charismatic career soldier and armour advocate.[80] There is insufficient evidence to lift this comparison above cliché, but the divergence between army and corps may reflect a cultural or habit-ingrained influence on operational art. It is clear, however, that the conflicting operational concepts, combined with the logistic, assembly, concealment, deception, and engineer plans made for a complicated scheme that was resistant to the change needed to account even for the inevitable and predicated thaw. Despite fighting through autumn and winter in the Netherlands, there was little practical consideration of the implications the thaw would have on Veritable once troops crossed the start line.

Other lauded aspects of Veritable's planning and preparation do not bear scrutiny either. Judged against the failings of the Ardennes and Arnhem, Veritable's intelligence shortfall was a workaday problem but an intelligence assessment that trebled the enemy's strength was a profound error. Yet in the years since, the 'mines and mud' narrative has been used as an excuse for the operation's failures (themselves obscured) and hidden its planning flaws. This is most evident in the BAOR *Battlefield Tour*, which altered the presentation of planning and execution to such an extent that they almost overlap, thereby preventing generations of soldiers from learning the lessons of history and instead teaching them that planning, and the masterplan, were everything.

---

78 P. D. Dickson, *Thoroughly Canadian*.
79 M. Henniker, *An Image of War* (London: Leo Cooper, 1987), p.225, original emphasis. Panache is emphasised throughout Gill and Graves, *Club Route in Europe*.
80 D. E. Delaney, *Corps Commanders: Five British and Canadian Generals at War, 1939–45* (Vancouver: UBCPress, 2011) pp.10–58.

2

Artillery and Effectiveness

8 FEBRUARY 1945 – A NEW D-DAY – NEUTRALISATION AND SUPPRESSION – FIREPOWER FIGURES – A HIDDEN WELSH VICTORY – KEYS TO KRANENBURG – SWANN REPORT REVISED – FORGETTING FIRE AND MANOEUVRE – THE PERILS OF OVERKILL

On Artillery

If there is one thing all sides of the effectiveness debate agree on, it is that the British Army was good at using artillery.[1] While most of the debate tails off before Veritable, Hastings and Buckley both portray Veritable's D-Day fire plan as a prime example of British artillery effectiveness. Beyond that their positions diverge, with Hastings presenting artillery as a crutch and a bludgeon, while Buckley considers gunnery to be part of a balanced and proficient fighting system. Yet Veritable's weak historiography encouraged Hastings's artillery assessment to lean on a few Normandy-centred studies, then skim through Veritable to confirm that view.[2] The same historiographic weakness meant Buckley's more rigorous assessment met official sources that (as with planning) exaggerate the effectiveness of Veritable's artillery.[3]

Official sources make grand claims like, 'well over half a million rounds were fired without a single case being reported of a round falling short', and 'the Germans were completely stunned by the terrific artillery support and it was largely thanks to this that 15 (S) Div, in spite of the bad going, succeeded in getting its crossings over the SIEGFRIED LINE.'[4] This chapter will show how the first of these statements is false, and how the second misses the real lessons of the artillery fire plan. In doing this, the chapter will also expose the inconsistency in British use of artillery and its roots in a failure to retain concepts and skills developed in the First World War.

Veritable's historiography has the D-Day fire plan as massive, but vaguely so, with the number of guns ranging from 1,000 to 2,000 and around half a million rounds fired. Sources agree that the main effect of the fire plan was psychological, but this is also vague: the Whitakers describe defenders as 'overawed', 'temporarily stunned', 'shell-shocked' and 'bomb happy'; Thompson has

---

1 Bidwell and Graham, *Fire-Power*, passim; Place, *Military Training*; Ellis, *Brute Force*, passim; Dennis / SSVC *Rhineland*.
2 In this respect Hastings relies on classic academic studies, notably: Place, *Military Training*, p.170; French, *Churchill's Army*, pp.255–256, 268, 285.
3 Buckley, *Monty's Men*, pp.271–272.
4 Conacher and Harrison, 'Veritable', p.25; BAOR, *Tour*, p.65.

them dazed in places but resolute in others.[5] Although these authors may not have known it, their presentation of fire and effect was based on an operational research study that analysed 12 battalion attacks from Veritable's D-Day to define the psychological effect of artillery fire. The study became known as the Swann Report and was subject to an iterative homogenising of its findings.[6] Despite being almost forgotten and having a few awkward flaws, the Swann Report still sits at the heart of NATO warfighting doctrine and is still the most complete description of suppressive fire produced by any army in any war.

To examine the psychological effect of Veritable's D-Day fire plan, and therefore the employment and effectiveness of artillery firepower throughout the operation, this chapter will begin with a brief history of indirect suppressive fire in the British Army, then describe the Veritable fire plan and its assessment in the Swann Report. The chapter will then reassess those 12 battalion attacks to highlight problems with Swann's source data, the British conception of firepower, and with using operational level sources to draw conclusions about tactical effectiveness.

Suppressive Fire

"Suppression" is a catch-all term adopted in the 1970s to describe the psychological effects of fire.[7] Despite a vague and classified definition in NATO doctrine, it is simpler to apply this term retrospectively rather than detail the inconsistent use of other terms such as blinding, pinning, neutralising, fixing, or the moral(e) effect.[8] Suppression is a temporary degradation in combat effectiveness caused by incoming fire, a human reaction that is fundamental to modern warfare from the battle drills taught to riflemen right up to corps manoeuvre. The history of suppression reaches back to *Anabasis*: 'A rush of the heavy infantry at full speed under cover of a storm of missiles, lances, arrows, bullets, but most of all stones hurled from the hand with ceaseless pelt …. Overwhelmed by this crowd of missiles, the enemy left their stockades and their bastion towers.'[9] The crowd of missiles may have incapacitated some defenders, but the main effect was that the immediate threat of being hit by an arrow or stone outweighed longer-term concerns about the Greeks getting over the wall. There are glimpses of suppression right through military history, and though it seems to have been taught by word of mouth, enough of a record remains to show that armies understood the effect very well.[10]

That understanding was lost in the early twentieth century when artillery became primarily an indirect fire system, so gunners lost sight of suppression and became fixated on destruction. The bureaucracy of trench warfare eventually generated enough information to allow armies to reacquire a conception of suppression, but it was far from a smooth progression. The British Army

---

5 Whitakers, *Rhineland*, pp.47, 53, 62; Thompson, *Rhineland*, pp.145, 162.
6 Major Michael Swann, later Lord Swann, is best known for the influential 1980s study *Education for All*, which was dubbed the Swann Report, but that label was already used by military operational researchers to refer to his Veritable study. When the current author joined a team of military psychologists in the 1990s, he was given a copy of the 1945 Swann Report as one of five "must read" sources. A good example of homogenising is in Hastings, *Armageddon* (Kindle 1936) which uses a summary from French, *Churchill's Army* (p.268) alongside a general comment by Alanbrooke, both of which were rooted in the Swann Report.
7 Directorate of Combat Developments, 'The Fort Sill Fire Suppression Symposium' (Fort Sill: DCD, 1980).
8 The definition is part of NATO Standardisation Agreement 4513, and a version of it can be accessed via standards.globalspec.com.
9 Xenophon, *Anabasis*, (Gutenberg eBook, 2013 [c380BCE]), book 5-2.
10 War Office, *Field Service Regulations 1909* (London: War Office, 1912), pp.135–139; Bidwell and Graham, *Fire-Power*, pp.13–14.

generated a profusion of ideas on the physical and psychological effects of fire, and the relative benefits of a long preparatory bombardment versus a fiercer onslaught immediately before an assault. The psychological effect gradually came to prominence, but by 1916 was seen only as something akin to draining Moran's bank of courage through the casualties, disorganisation and distress caused by a long bombardment.[11] In 1917 a conception of shock came to the fore, with a long bombardment 'calculated to reduce the enemy's moral by its insistence, a short one by its intensity.'[12]

At the same time, suppression by barrage became the primary function of close support fire. Historians sometimes follow non-gunner sources who describe a whole fire plan as a barrage, but the term was originally used to describe a static line of fire to act as a barrier. By 1945, artillerymen used the term to refer only to a rolling or creeping block of fire preceding an assault, and that definition is used throughout this book. Like the fire and movement described in *Anabasis*, a barrage forced defenders into cover while attackers followed the fire as closely as possible, "crowding", "leaning into" or "hugging" the barrage. The barrage did not aim to wear down or shock the enemy but to prevent them from returning fire while the assaulting infantry crossed the killing area of no man's land and got into or through a position before the defenders could react.[13]

The First World War suppression debate can therefore be seen a competition between three theories:

a) *Eroding* enemy will to fight through a long bombardment.
b) *Shocking* the enemy with an intense bombardment.
c) *Preventing* the enemy returning fire long enough for friendly infantry to assault.

Each was a genuine effect, but by 1918 it was evident that "preventing" (for want of a better word) required fewer shells and accounted for most of the difference in defence resistance. Eroding required an extended and expensive fire plan that advertised the coming assault; shocking required a lot of guns, denuding other fronts or demanding a very narrow front; both options smashed ground, towns, and roads, slowing the friendly advance and making reinforcement and resupply difficult. In contrast, preventing with a barrage-hugging attack needed just enough fire to encourage the enemy to take cover, and therefore used fewer guns, did less physical damage and was more likely to achieve surprise.

The preventing effect soon wore off, so the assault force had to strike quickly to reap the full reward. The most effective units advanced to within 30 metres of the barrage, preferring to lose of a few men to friendly artillery over losing many to enemy machine-guns. The gap between fire and assault came to be so important that pamphlets encouraged units to anticipate six percent casualties to friendly artillery.[14] It seems that the adage "artillery conquers, infantry occupies"

---

11 War Office, *SS98/4 Artillery in Offensive Operations* (London: War Office, 1916); C.M. Wilson (Lord Moran), *The Anatomy of Courage* (London: Constable, 1945). The Stationery Service pamphlets used here can be found in appendices to W. S. Marble, 'The infantry cannot do with a gun less: the place of artillery in the BEF, 1914–1918' (King's College London PhD thesis, 1998), which is available as a free Gutenberg eBook.
12 War Office, *SS139/4 Artillery in Offensive Operations* (London: War Office, 1917). At that time 'shock' was delivered by the assault of infantry, cavalry or tanks and the debate struggled with terms to describe the difference between insistent and intense fire.
13 These terms are all used in the diaries that form the core of this book but see also J. R. A. Bailey, *Field Artillery and Firepower* (Oxford: Military Press, 1989), pp.132–134.
14 A. F. Becke, 'The Coming of the Creeping Barrage', *Journal of the Royal Artillery* 58:1 (1938), passim; M. Middlebrook, *The First Day on the Somme* (London: Penguin, 2001), p.279.

needed the caveat "as long as the infantry arrive quickly". The main difficulty with adopting and retaining the preventing concept was that soldiers who had been under fire could easily recognise erosion and shock, and could understand that increasing the volume of fire would have a greater effect. Preventing was a more complicated interaction of fire and manoeuvre that required rigorous collective training to get results.

Efforts to calculate the number of rounds needed to suppress while avoiding overkill have prompted historians to suggest the success of a barrage was 'determined by long division' with 3,840 shells per square kilometre per hour (km²/hr) needed to suppress.[15] However, this figure was derived from multiple sources, with one stating a rate of fire, another the number of guns, and another the rate at which the barrage crept forward. To add further confusion, different formulae were tested right up until the end of the war, leaving no clear statement for future generations.[16] As a result, on the eve of the Second World War, the only echoes of a suppression formula appear to reside in US doctrine, which mixed eroding, shocking and a little preventing but increased the rate of fire up to an astounding 96,000 shells per km²/hr. That doctrine offered no figures for the duration of the suppression after effect (the critical time period before suppression wore off), but it was implied that an assault must follow within minutes of fire being lifted.[17]

For most of the Second World War, 'Any small morale effects, if they existed, were regarded as a useful bonus' to the destructive effect, and it was a month into the Northwest Europe campaign before 21st Army Group began to search for insights into the phenomenon.[18] According to operational researchers, it was 'not till 1945 that it could be stated that the morale effect, measured in terms of reduction of enemy opposition, was generally several times [i.e., five or six times] as great as the effect due to casualties to enemy men and material.'[19] Meanwhile attacks were failing because commanders expected artillery to destroy, erode, or shock the enemy much more than it did, and units were inconsistently hugging barrages, or not using barrages at all.

A study of four battalion battles from Operation Clipper (November 1944) produced valuable indications of a suppressive effect, with the 'most outstanding' being the attack where 5 Dorsets followed a will-eroding four-hour bombardment of 6,500 shells per km²/hr onto the village of Bauchem.[20] With defender casualties estimated at 10 to 15 percent, and attacker casualties around one percent of fighting strength, the defending company 'offered not the slightest resistance' and

---

15 R. Prior and T. Wilson, *Command on the Western Front: The Military Career of Sir Henry Rawlinson 1914–1918* (Barnsley: Pen & Sword, 2004), pp.312–313. The rate referred to shells per 25-yard square and has been scaled up and roughly metricised to make an easier comparison with the Swann data. There were also efforts to relate success to weight of fire (the volume of explosive dropped onto a position) but, as Swann found, the number of shells was a more reliable measure. For simplicity, this chapter focuses on the number of shells.

16 J. Hughes, 'The Monstrous Anger of the Guns: The Development of British Artillery Tactics 1914–1918' (University of Adelaide PhD thesis, 1992), passim; W.S. Marble, 'The infantry cannot do', passim.

17 For example, US War Department, *Field Artillery Field Manual: Firing, FM 6-40* (Washington: War Department, 1939), passim. British doctrine at the time was focused on mathematics and cartography with effects on soldiers hidden in appendices: Royal Artillery, *Programme Shoots (Barrages and Concentrations)* (Larkhill: Publisher unknown, 1942).

18 J. C. Dorward, and R. E. Strong, 'The effects of bombardment, the current state of knowledge.' Military Operational Research Unit (MORU) Report No. 3, 1946, passim. T. Copp, 'Operational Research and 21st Army Group' *Canadian Military History*, 3(1) pp.71–84, 1994. Anon, 'Fire Support of Seaborne Landings Against a Heavily Defended Coast. Summary of a Report by an Inter-Service Committee.' (CAB 80/77/19, 1943), passim.

19 Dorward and Strong, 'Effects of bombardment', para 4(a). Square bracket insertion from para 11(d).

20 All quotes in this and next paragraph from Anon (likely M. Swann), 'The effect of artillery fire on enemy forward defensive positions in the attack on Geilenkirchen (Operation Clipper)' (ORS 2 report No. 22, 1944) / Copp, *Montgomery's Scientists*, pp.353–358.

those who were in fighting positions (rather than troop shelters or cellars) were said to be 'absolutely yellow coloured'. To try shocking defenders, the other three Clipper attacks involved higher rates of fire that lasted only 20 to 40 minutes before the assault. In these actions, attack and defence casualties were believed to be around five percent and there were no yellow-coloured reactions, but defenders still surrendered with little opposition. Even in the attacks following shorter fire plans, the after effect was deemed to be 'much more than a mere "keeping down of heads"' because one of these attacks met little resistance a full 30 minutes after fire had lifted.

Although the report's authors suggested the results from this small sample be treated with caution, they recommended two types of fire: 4,300 shells per km²/hr for four hours to achieve 'an overwhelming effect and paralyse all resistance', and 5,800 shells per km²/hr for 30 minutes to have a 'strong demoralising and disruptive effect', but lacking the 'mental and physical breakdown' of the longer fire plan. The Clipper report therefore brought the conception of suppression back towards that of 1917, with defenders shocked, their morale eroded, or a mix of the two. The preventing concept was explicitly discounted by the report emphasising that one instance of an assault delayed by 30 minutes and by making no mention of barrage hugging.

The Fire Plan

The Veritable fire plan should be considered to have started with the bombing of Goch and Kleve, which Horrocks requested be 'taken out' by the RAF on the night of 7 February to slow German reinforcement and demonstrate the futility of resistance.[21] In terms of aircraft per resident, both raids far outstripped the bombing of Dresden and the effect was profound. Lotte Seiler wrote of her experience four kilometres from the epicentre of the Kleve bombing:

> My Dear,
> The first night of horrors has come to an end. At 2200 hrs I was awakened by the shooting. The entire grounds of the building were covered with hundreds of flares and it was light as day … For fully 20 minutes bombs were coming down all around us the air blast effect was so intense it prevented me from reaching Edith's room. All the windows had already been blown open, but no glass was broken … Outside the refugees are trekking down the road and all the Westwall labourers are leaving the district with bag and baggage … The Air Force are still here, but have everything packed, a breakthrough by the Americans has been expected for days. This night will probably be followed by many similar ones and one will have to get accustomed to all these crashes …[22]

High above Lotte, Richard Dimbleby recorded a report for the BBC from one of the Lancasters bombing Kleve: 'And what an astounding sight it is that lies immediately ahead of us as we go into Kleve. There is the town, the junction we are attacking, lit like London on its brightest day. But not lit only by the light of flares, the lights of bombs that are bursting and incendiaries that are bursting too …'[23] The morale effect of the two raids, like the whole heavy bomber campaign, is still debatable and there must have been some physical effect on *84. Division* but no record could be found. The main recorded effect of the Kleve bombing was that it made the main road

---

21 Horrocks, *Full Life*, p.247.
22 53 Division ISUM 193 (diary, WO 171/4276).
23 'Richard Dimbleby reports from a bomber raid over Germany' bbc.co.uk/sounds. For the pilot's version see J.W. Gee, *Wingspan: The Recollections of a Bomber Pilot* (Unknown: Self-published, 1988), pp.158–164.

to Wesel impassable to 30 Corps. It also seems likely that it gave Schlemm a final confirmation of the Veritable axis and therefore, contrary to intentions, drew German reserves to the Kleve area.[24]

The subsequent artillery fire plan was built on the lessons in the Clipper report and aimed to extend the Bauchem effect to the whole of *84. Division*. Combining Swann's data, 30 Corps records, and a 1946 recount provides gives a clearer picture of how massive the fire plan was.[25] All told, 1,852 weapons lobbed explosive shells onto *84. Division*. Guns ranged from a handful of 240mm super-heavies, down to 264 40mm Bofors guns, with the largest proportion of fire from 576 25pdr (88mm) field guns. The 1946 recount gave a figure of 500,891 shells fired but missed 30 Corps records of an additional 156,450 shells from the combination 17pdr (76mm) anti-tank guns, Sherman tank guns (75mm), 4.2-inch (110mm) heavy mortars and the Bofors guns. Both sources overlooked indirect fire from battalions' 3-inch (81mm) mortars, plus a few armoured squadrons whose commanders felt the need to add to the cacophony. Some on-call and repeat fire missions may have gone unrecorded too. The Veritable preparation therefore exceeded 650,000 shells, with the total weight of shell between 6,000 and 8,500 tonnes.[26] In addition, three million .303-inch (7.7mm) rounds were fired indirectly from 188 Vickers medium machine-guns.[27]

To put this in context, the famous artillery-heavy attacks of the Somme and Alamein fired more shells than Veritable, but the Somme's 2,029 guns fired their 1.7 million shells over eight days across a 22-kilometre front, and Alamein's 1,000 guns fired their million shells over 12 days and 32 kilometres.[28] Veritable focused on a 10-kilometre front and probably fired most of its shells in 14 hours, making it at least three times the intensity of the Somme and Alamein. A wider, though unavoidably shallow, survey of secondary sources reveals many fire plans that were larger but far less intense, and a few that were more intense but much smaller. No battles were found that were unequivocally larger and more intense than Veritable. The battles of Valenciennes and Hamel (both 1918), Tunisia Plain (1943) and Bauchem (1944) were more intense but on narrower fronts.[29] It is notable that Crerar was an artillery planner for Hamel and Valenciennes, while Horrocks was corps commander for Tunisia Plain and Bauchem, so they both had experience of battles where firing more shells correlated with success.[30]

The comparison with earlier battles could give the impression of the Veritable fire plan as an incessant and intense rain of shells as seen in movies or firepower demonstrations, but on average only one shell fell in each 100-metre square every three and a half minutes. Although far less threatening than a movie fire plan, such a volume of fire would give any exposed upright person

---

24   Despite many other sources noting the intensity of the Kleve bombing, Schlemm only recalls the Veritable artillery fire plan as a warning to launch reserves (Ford, *Luftwaffe General*, Kindle 427).
25   Swann, 'Veritable'; HQ 30 Corps to 2 Canadian Division, 23:25, 2 Feb, 30 Corps GS diary (WO 171/4076); MORU, 'Memorandum: Operation Veritable' (CAB 106/991). The 30 Corps figures are additional rounds brought forward to support the D-Day fireplan. Given the subsequent shortage of rounds (Ch 5) it seems safe to assume these rounds were all fired.
26   The lower tonnage is extrapolated from Swann (p.367) by multiplying the average per square kilometre by the area attacked, then conservatively estimating the extra weight from the later ammunition total. The higher figure is from Hart 'Montgomery' (p.130) which has 'over 8,377 tons' in a MORU report (mistakenly cited as CAB 106/1120).
27   Corps diary, HQ 30 Corps to 2 Canadian Division, 23:25, 2 Feb.
28   Bailey, *Field Artillery*, Annex A, pp.338–342; Hughes puts the number of Somme shells at around 1.5 million: 'Monstrous Anger', p.91.
29   Bailey, *Field Artillery*, Annex A; Stacey, *Victory Campaign*; Hughes, 'Monstrous Anger' pp.144, 145, 268; RA history, 1914–18. As only secondary sources were examined there is a chance that the reported figures for guns and rounds are inaccurate, as was the case with Veritable.
30   P.D. Dickson, *Thoroughly Canadian*, pp.64–67; Horrocks, *Full Life*, pp.166–172.

little chance of surviving more than 20 minutes.[31] Averages also hide the intricacy of the fire plan, which had four main components: preparatory fire, counter-battery fire, pepper pot and barrage. Preparatory fire began at 05:00 with most of the traditional artillery plus 3.7-inch (94mm) anti-aircraft guns firing indirectly, with all these focused on the destruction of headquarters, communication hubs and gun positions.[32] Half an hour later preparatory fire was augmented by the pepper pot, which aimed to suppress forward defensive positions. The pepper pot was named for its liberal scattering of small projectiles but the 4.2-inch mortar was powerful ordnance and weapons were focused on specific targets, often cycling between targets, and leaving gaps to encourage defenders back into the open.[33] At 07:30 a smoke screen was fired onto the forward positions as a ruse to prompt German defensive fire, then there was a complete cessation of fire for 10 minutes to allow radar, flash detection, and sound-ranging teams to locate German batteries. The few German batteries that did engage, received a prompt and heavy response.[34] While general preparatory fire continued, most of the field and medium guns began the barrage at 09:50.

Before describing the barrage, preparatory fire from the Land Mattress rocket batteries needs to be introduced. Slow to reload and sight-in but rapidly fired, a single 32-tube Mattress launcher (known to some German defenders as the 'Churchill-Organ') could project almost as much explosive power as two medium gun regiments.[35] In 20 seconds, a battery's 12 launchers could saturate an area roughly 400 metres square with a weight of explosives equivalent to all Veritable's 262 medium guns firing for a full minute. This storm of steel was expected to have an overwhelming morale effect, but safety concerns and the dominant perception that suppression worked through erosion and shock meant that all Mattress missions were complete at least an hour before their targets were assaulted.[36]

The barrage consumed perhaps half the shells fired on D-Day, with over 400 guns firing at a steady rate to produce a band of fire running over 4,500 metres north to south ahead of the three central divisions. The depth of the barrage comprised five lines, 100 metres apart, with the two lines farthest from assault troops engaged by medium guns (5.5-in, 140mm) but the three closest engaged by the lighter 25pdr field guns. The 25pdr's predictable fire and small blast radius allowed infantry to hug the barrage more closely. The rate of fire increased during the barrage but still averaged only a little over one shell per minute for every 100-metre square. The main boundaries of the barrage are marked by the white lines overlaid on Map 6, which is taken from the original Swann Report.

Fire fell on the opening barrage line for 40 minutes while units formed up behind it then at H-Hour (10:30) all the guns lifted to fire to engage a line 300 metres further east. The attacking battalions followed. Fire on the second line continued for 12 minutes before lifting again and

---

31 Figures extrapolated from Swann, 'Veritable'. Artillery vulnerability calculations from Anon, 'Field Artillery, Volume 6, Ballistics and Ammunition', (Department of National Defence, Canada, 1992) 4:3.
32 CRA 15 Division, OO 2. 'Op 'VERITABLE' Phase I (GILBERT)', 15 Division HQRA diary (WO 171/4197).
33 21 Army Group, 'Operation Veritable', p.16. Rotation of fire is stated in sources but the effect only implied, e.g., CRA 53 Division, 'Op Veritable – Arty Fire Plan', 53 Division HQRA diary (WO 171/4282).
34 Operational research found this was not as overwhelming as later sources implied, but it was still formidable. P. Johnson, 'Effect of counter-battery fire in Operation Veritable' ORS 2 Report No. 29, April 1945 (WO 291/1331), reproduced in Copp, *Montgomery's Scientists*, pp.337–348.
35 Stimpel, *Fallschirmtruppe*, p.350.
36 D. Knight, *The Land Mattress in Canadian Service* (Ottawa: Service Publications, 2003), p.12. BAOR, *Tour* (p.71) lays out the figures a little differently and gives the impression that Mattress missions were fired close to the assault (p.21), but the Rocket Regt task list in 'Operation Veritable – Fire Plan' (53 Division HQRA diary) contradicts this.

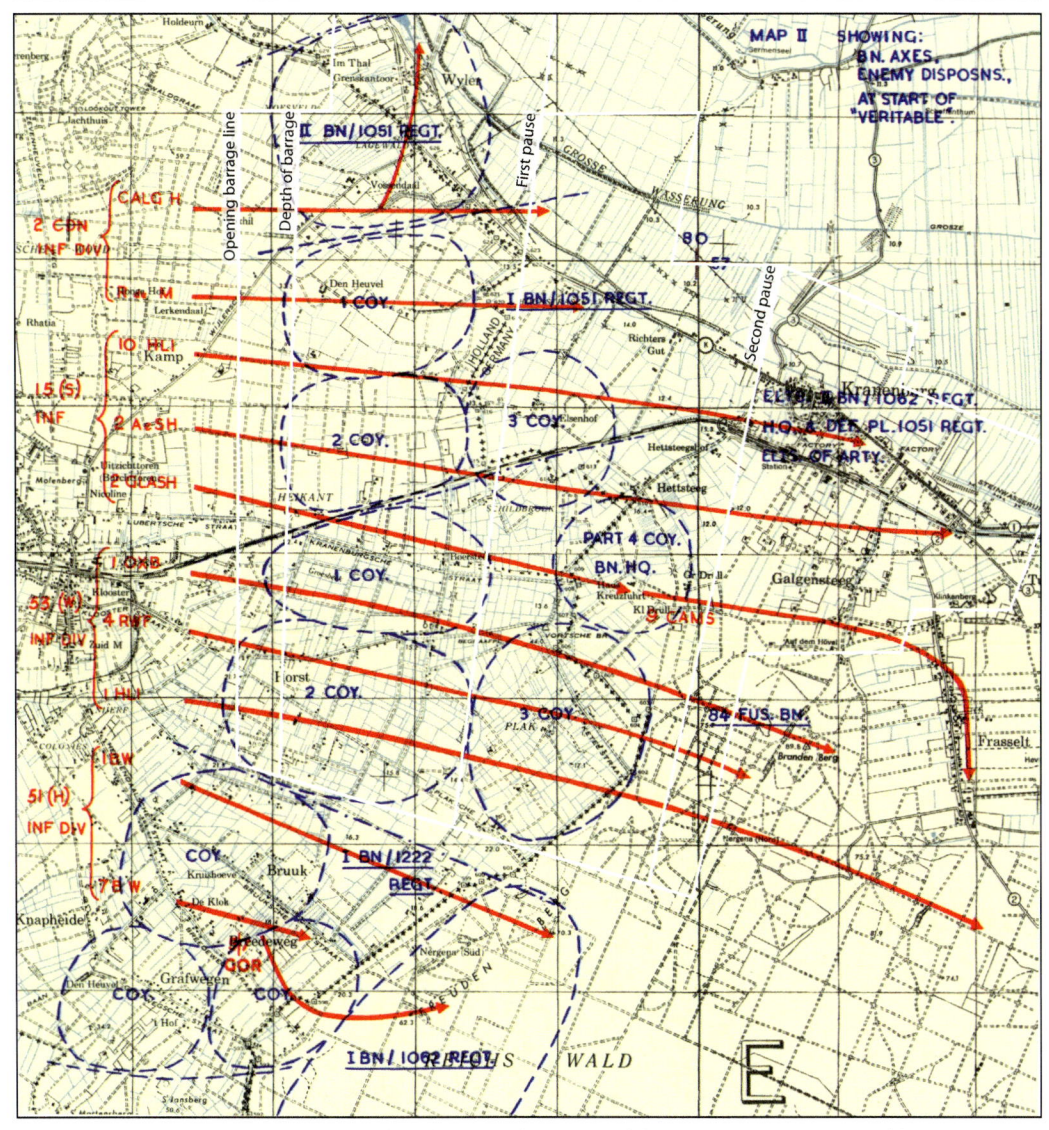

Map 6: Barrage phases and battalion attacks on Veritable's D-Day. (Swann, 'Veritable')

repeating this process every 12 minutes. The barrage therefore moved at an average of 25 metres per minute, a common rate for First World War attacks, though these typically used 100-metre lifts. To help troops hug the barrage, yellow smoke shells were included in the western edge one minute before each lift. To allow battalions time to catch up and reorganise, or to let other units echelon through, there were five periods where fire would loiter for up to 70 minutes: at the start and end of the barrage, and during three pauses in between. The final loitering phase began at 16:00 and lasted until 16:40 by which time units were expected to have secured all their objectives.[37]

---

37   CRA 15 Division, OO 2; smoke details in CRA 53 Division, 'Op Veritable – Arty Fire Plan'.

In the south, 51 Division's attack was not supported by a barrage, through the reasons for this are unclear.[38] Instead, 51 used a series of timed linear concentrations onto likely enemy positions that were intended to achieve the suppressive effect but did not hit the open ground between positions. Flanking moves by the Calgary Highlanders (2 Canadian Division) and 9 Cameronians (15 Division) also used timed concentrations for the period when they were attacking at an angle to the barrage.[39]

The immediate operational effect of Veritable's D-Day fire plan was in little doubt. Between 10:30 and 18:00, 30 Corps advanced nearly seven kilometres behind its barrage, soundly defeating *84. Division*.[40]

> The Corps artillery preparation for Operation "VERITABLE" so numbed the enemy's will and ability to resist that little opposition was encountered when our divisions attacked at 1030 hours this morning. It was thought at first that 84 Inf Div had anticipated our attack by false fronting back to the position along the Western edge of the REICHSWALD, but identifications and the number of enemy killed and PW show that we hit four battalions fair and square in their proper localities.[41]

By early evening there were 1,100 prisoners in the 30 Corps cage, with many more still heading back through Allied lines. Although Crerar and Horrocks did not know it, at that point there was no formed defence between 30 Corps and the Wesel bridges, 40 kilometres further east. The effect of the fire plan was more varied at the tactical level, with some battalions suffering below two percent casualties (very like Bauchem) and easily achieving their objectives on time, while others lost 15 percent of their fighting strength and had to repeatedly restart their attacks. This variation in victory was linked to differences in the fire plan, terrain, and tactics, and was the cornerstone of the Swann Report.

The Swann Report found the destructive effect of the fire plan to be almost negligible, reporting only 60 defender casualties to indirect fire, with a similar number of casualties inflicted by assault troops. As in the Operation Clipper study, increasing weight of shell was seen to reduce attacker casualties, but the number of shells had the greater effect: as a later report put it, 'the thing that counts most of all is the number of bangs.'[42] However, where the Clipper report implied the after effect could last up to 30 minutes, Swann suggested that assaults launched even 15 minutes after fire lifted had a much tougher time. Prisoner interviews and the comments of an artillery observer convinced Swann that Mattress fire was indistinguishable from the 'general unpleasantness' and that the carefully crafted phases of fire were perceived as incessant.[43]

Swann used firing data, casualty reports, and interviews to propose three levels of suppression:

---

38   Swann, 'Veritable', BAOR, *Tour*, 21 Army Group 'Veritable' and J.B. Salmond, *The History of the 51st Highland Division* (Edinburgh: Blackwood & Son, 1953) give no reason. It is possible 51 Division was confident in reports of German positions or out of practice with the complicated procedure for barrage laying.
39   9 Cameronians diary (WO 171/5168). Given limited access to Canadian records, the use of timed concentrations by the Calgary Highlanders is speculation but seems highly likely.
40   Defeated but not destroyed. *84. Division* survived the whole operation by being trickle fed reserves but lost its original total strength several times over. Guderian, *Normandy to the Ruhr*, Ch 10; Fiebig, '84th Infantry'.
41   30 Corps ISUM 592 (WO 205/954).
42   Anon, 'The Morale Effects of Artillery' MORU Memorandum No. 7, 1946 (WO 205/1164); Copp, *Montgomery's Scientists*, pp.373–375.
43   Swann, 'Veritable', p.362.

1. *Stopping movement* occurred during preparatory fire, when just 650 shells per km²/hr was 'quite enough to keep officers and everyone else firmly in their dugouts'.
2. *Stopping firing* was evident during the barrage when the rate of fire reached 6,500 shells per km²/hr. At this rate, after-effects were 'certainly present and, when the fire support was followed up closely, the enemy surrendered at once.' However, Swann suggested that this rate was overkill, and that the pepper pot rate of 2,600 shells per km²/hr was enough to stop return fire.
3. *Complete collapse* was not evident in the Veritable fire plan, so Swann reverted to the rate and duration at Bauchem: 6,500 shells per km²/hr continued for four hours.[44]

To illustrate the wide variation between sources, Table 1 compares these rates with those described earlier in the chapter. The only pattern in this dataset is the repetition of 6,500 shells per hour, a figure that was entirely derived from the one attack on Bauchem and was close to twice the rate associated with successful 1918 attacks.

Table 1: Rates of Fire and Effects from Suppression Studies and Doctrine

Source	Shells/km²/hr	Duration	Effect
British 1918	3,840	Not stated	Attack successful
US inter-war	To 96,000	Not stated	Attack successful
Clipper 1944 observed	6,500	4 hrs	Complete collapse
Clipper 1944 proposed	4,300	4 hrs	Attack successful
Clipper 1944 proposed	5,800	30 mins	Considerable after effect
Swann observed	650	Not stated	Rear areas; in dugouts for duration
Swann observed	6,500	Not stated	Overkill; clear after effect
Swann proposed	2,600	Not stated	Prevents return fire
Swann proposed	6,500	4 hrs	Complete collapse

Swann's written report echoed the 1918 model, with successful attacks following a relatively light fire plan if assault troops hugged the barrage. However, this finding was not evident in his charts and tables, which only gave figures for the total fire supporting each attack, said nothing on the rate of fire, and only vaguely referred to the gap between fire and assault. Swann's data presentation included nine Veritable attacks where the assault was timely, three where the assault was considered so late that the results should be excluded from the analysis, and the four Clipper attacks. As the chart at Figure 3 suggests, once the three late attacks are excluded, the dataset shows a strong (and statistically significant) linear relationship between the number of rounds fired and the suppressive effect.[45]

Given the small sample size and the notoriously chaotic nature of combat, this is a remarkably strong correlation, and it is therefore not surprising that it has influenced operational research for decades. The observations on barrage hugging were forgotten because that strong relationship between fire and effect allowed gunners and analysts to predict the effectiveness of fire. The trend line can still be seen in classified doctrine publications and fire planning software tools that give figures for the number of rounds needed to suppress. However, closer analysis of the battalion battles on Veritable's D-Day has uncovered a problem with Swann's source data.

---

44 Swann, 'Veritable', pp.361–362.
45 When the late attacks are excluded Pearson's r -0.86 (p <0.05); when they are included r -0.32 (not significant). 21 AG, *Operational Research*, p.182.

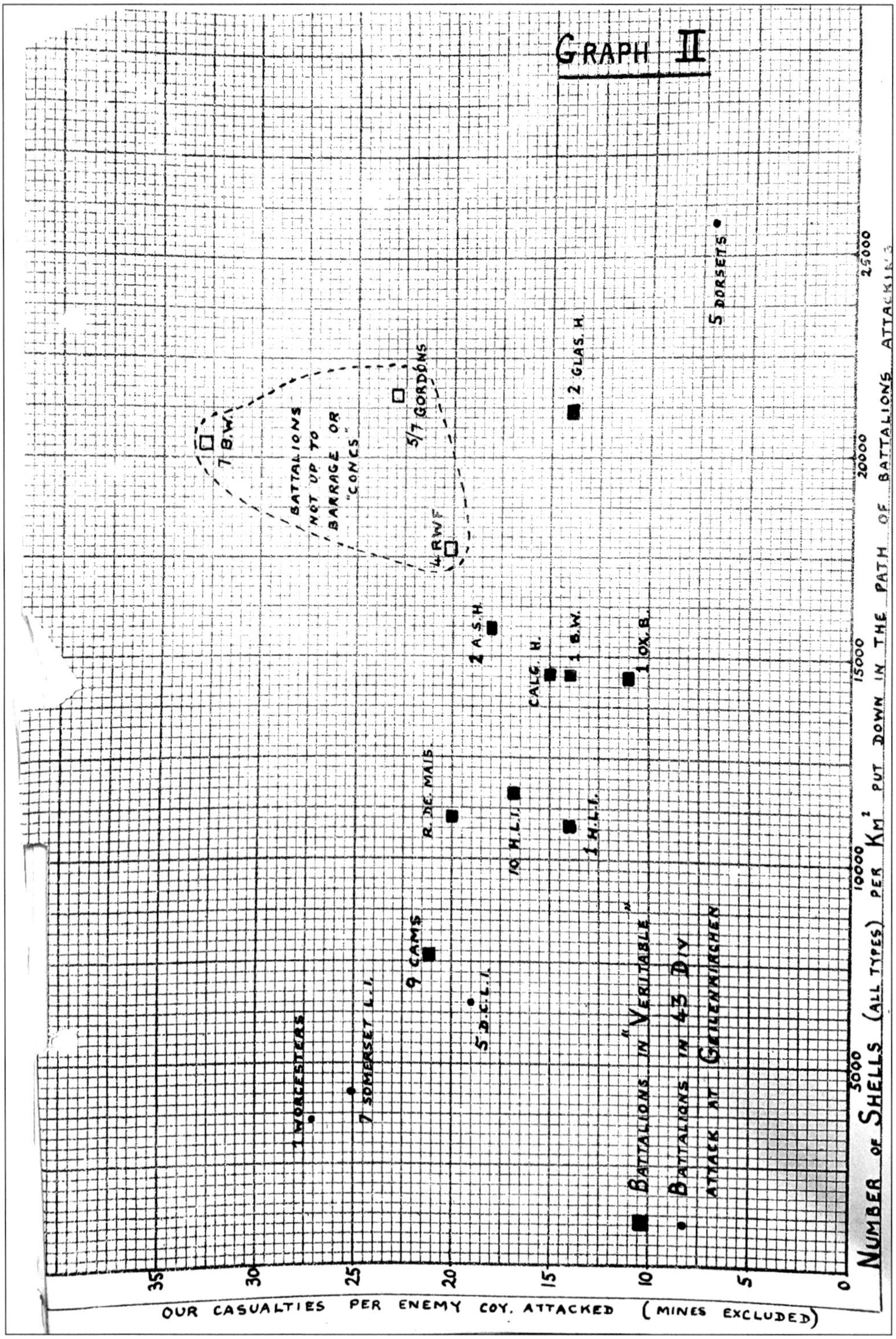

Figure 3: Swann's data on number of shells fired and attacker casualties per defending company, excluding losses to mines. (Swann, 'Veritable')

4 RWF and the Welsh Division

To illustrate the flaws in Swann's source data and the complexity of suppression, this chapter is focused on two battalions (Figure 4) with the other 10 attacks summarised to show context, variation, and commonalities.

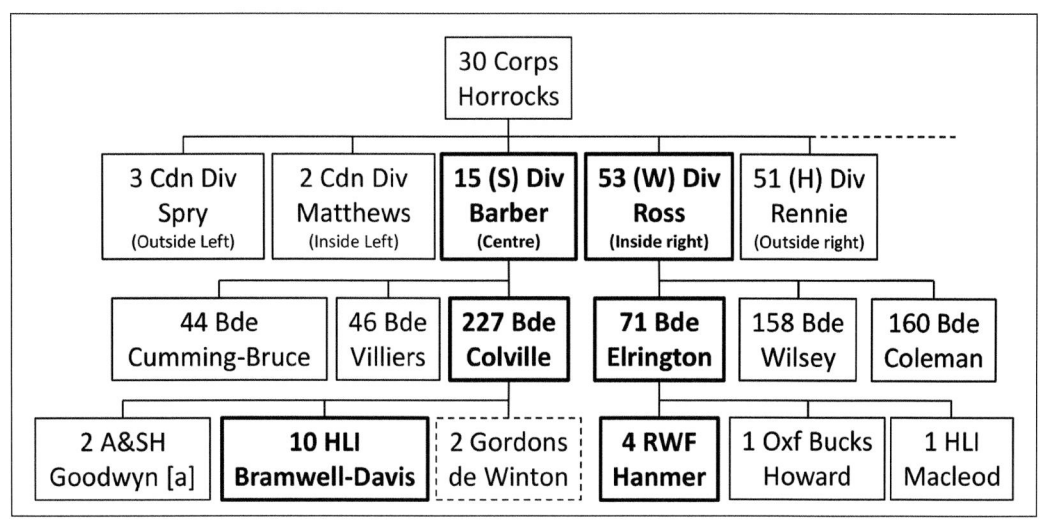

Figure 4: Abridged organisational chart for 30 Corps with focus organisations in bold.

The first battle of interest is the opening move by 53 Division as it demonstrates the value of suppression as a key component of combined arms tactics. The Welsh Division had to fight through the forward defensive line, then enter the Reichswald to protect the flank of 15 Division on the corps main effort. As Map 7 indicates, 53 Division advanced on a one-brigade front (71 Brigade) which launched its attack on a one-battalion front, so Fourth Battalion the Royal Welch Fusiliers (4 RWF) led the whole division and had the broadest but shortest advance of any battalion attacking that day.

Unlike the rushed preparation in some units, 4 RWF's platoon commanders got to see the ground from the Groesbeek windmill several days before their attack, they had plentiful air photographs, time to view them, and consulted with Canadian units who had patrolled into the *84. Division* area. So, it was only a slight exaggeration when the Division claimed that 'almost every house and tree was known to the men'.[46] The Battalion also had the advantage of prior training with their tank support, "A" Squadron, 147 Regiment the Royal Armoured Corps (147 RAC). Their training also involved cooperation with specialised armour in woods, to breach minefields and to flame bunkers. But as D-Day approached, the idea of a forest filled with pillboxes and dragon's teeth ebbed, because only one concrete structure was known to be on the Division's axis, a suspected HQ bunker just beyond 4 RWF's objective.

Despite capturing many men from *84. Division* in the Falaise Pocket (and having some of *84. Division*'s transport still 'working satisfactorily in 71 Brigade') 53 Division's staff were less bombastic than other formations: 'The morale of 84 Div has been rather written up; and probably the tps are not so bad, nor so affected by their winter in the snow and ice as one would like to think

---

46 C. N. Barclay, *The History of the 53rd (Welsh) Division in the Second World War* (London: Clowes, 1955), p.114; 4 RWF diary, (WO 171/5281); J. Riley, P. Crocker, and R. Sinnett, *Regimental Records of the Royal Welch Fusiliers*, Vol. V (2), (Warwick: Helion, 2018), p.743.

them.'[47] On 31 January it was expected that 'Except for small peaty areas, going must be considered as fairly good to good [but] In the predominantly wooded areas movement off the roads must be considered as most difficult.'[48] That summary was issued on the day of the thaw; by the final orders group on 7 February, 4 RWF knew the going would be 'indescribably bad'.[49]

Barrage hugging was the central pillar of the 4 RWF plan, with a three-up attack (three companies forward, one in reserve) to ensure troops could cover the entire front while, 'keeping close to the barrage and so be able to clear rapidly any buildings.'[50] Fifty-Three Division was unfashionably reliant on rigid artillery-infantry cooperation, employing a barrage much more often than 15, 43, or 51 Division, and giving greater attention to artillery in its orders. The 4 RWF plan also placed considerable emphasis on using the supporting squadron of Flail tanks to cross what was believed to be an extensive mine belt.[51] The RWF battalion group also included eight Crocodile flame throwing tanks, at least six AVREs (Armoured Vehicles, Royal Engineers, four carrying fascines, two carrying bridges) and the 16 to 18 Churchill tanks of "A" Squadron, 147 RAC. Additional firepower came from a troop of Achilles or Archer tank destroyers and forward observers for artillery, heavy mortars, and medium machine-guns.[52]

Each forward company would have Flails and a troop of Churchills in close support, while the other specialist armour moved with the reserve company. As soon as the barrage made its first 300-metre lift, the Flails would cut four lanes through the minefield, then companies would fight through the scattered houses and farms leading to the shattered village of De Horst (centre of Map 7), which had been an artillery target singe Market Garden.[53]

The 4 RWF objective was to secure Phase Line Ramillies, which followed a narrow north–south road that passed through De Horst about 1,500 metres short of the forest. Ramillies would be the start line for the next two battalions, so to secure it 4 RWF would have to clear De Horst of enemy and push troops out towards the line of the first barrage pause. The follow-on battalions would then attack in parallel, cross the *Leigraaf* (a stream playing the role of anti-tank ditch) then break into the treeline and capture the Brandenberg, a hill only 90 metres above sea level that nevertheless dominated the ground around it and was believed to be a hinge in the German defence.[54]

As 4 RWF moved from their forward assembly area around 09:00, they passed through the massed guns firing from Groesbeek woods, and any men who had forgotten their cotton-wool earplugs were deafened for most of the day. Their route also came close to an army historical team

---

47 71 Brigade, OO 1, diary (WO 171/4384); 71 Brigade ISUM 1, 1 HLI diary (WO 171/5202).
48 71 Brigade Veritable ISUM 1, 4 RWF diary.
49 4 RWF diary; 71 Brigade ISUMs 1-3; Barclay, *53rd (Welsh)*, p.114; P.K. Kemp and J. Graves, *The Red Dragon: The Story of the Royal Welch Fusiliers 1919–1945* (Aldershot: Gale & Polden, 1960), pp.242–243; 53 Division diary, 1–7 Feb.
50 Riley et al, *Regimental Records*, p.743.
51 4 RWF OO 1, diary. The minefield had been examined by Canadian patrols, but snow and German observation had made it difficult to determine how deep or thickly it was sown. All the mine clearing tanks deployed in Veritable were Sherman Crabs, but apart from their operators everyone called them Flails.
52 4 RWF diary; '147 Regt RAC Op Instr No. 1', 147 diary (WO 171/4721); 34 Brigade OO 27, diary; 34 Armoured Brigade, 'Seven days fighting through the Reichswald' (WO 205/961); 'Report on Operation "Veritable" fighting in the Reichswald 8–17 Feb 45', 34 Brigade diary, Mar 45. With very few exceptions, units always fought as battalion groups with attached artillery, armour, and engineers.
53 4 RWF OO 1.
54 4 RWF diary. Like most streams, the Leigraaf was marked as an anti-tank obstacle on the defence overprint maps issued to units. Units usually interpreted this marking to mean a deliberately constructed anti-tank ditch and were often surprised to find them full of water.

ARTILLERY AND EFFECTIVENESS 61

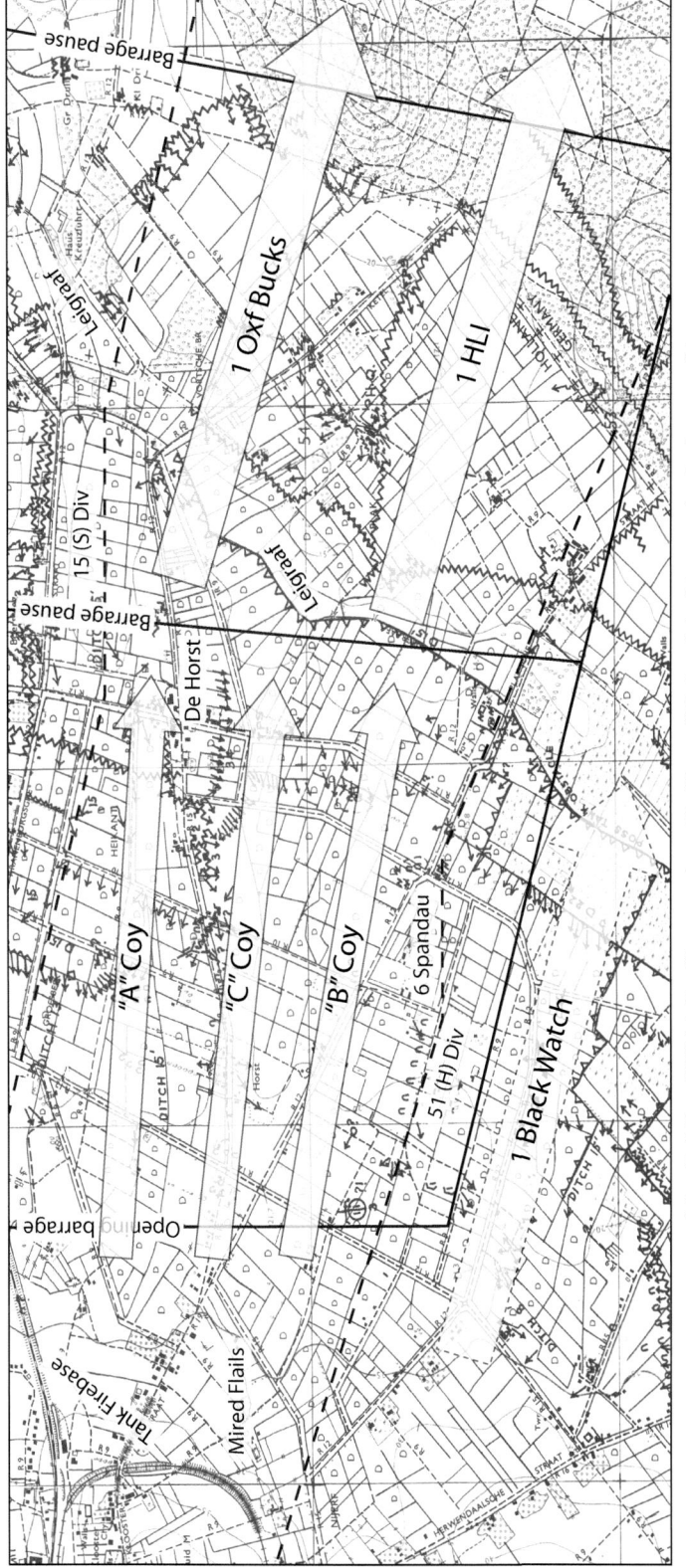

Map 7: 4 Royal Welch Fusiliers attack on De Horst. (National Archives, author's photograph)

whose fulsome account gives a good impression of activity at H-Hour, and (conveniently) the early shaping of the Veritable narrative:

> As H-Hr approached, if anything, the noise increased and a new note was added by the sound of armour moving forward and planes passing overhead. The combined effect produced a vivid picture of a war of machines – a war of calculated and terrible efficiency ... Carriers rattled by, with red cross flags prominently displayed, and a tp of "Cromwell" tanks that had been camouflaged with straw against the walls of a demolished barn added their guttural roar to the din of battle. "Churchill" and "Sherman" tanks began to move east along the draw in square 7556 [between 2 Canadian Division and 15 Division at Map 6], through the scattered debris of gliders that remained from the airborne attack of the previous September ... Besides the orthodox types of tanks, there were "Flails", "Crocodiles", A.Vs.R.E., all with their fluorescent panels (for identification from the air) glowing like red hot plates against the dull background. A tank officer enquired anxiously about minefields, but could not be satisfied. The armour lurched forward with all vehicles stripped for action – one tank still had a frying pan dangling from the back of the turret. An air O.P. flew slowly overhead, and smoke shells continued to drop a short distance in front, as the deafening noise increased. Some enemy rounds dropped about 300 yards distant and personnel took cover, but the armoured advance went on without hesitation. There was an air of urgency and tense expectation evident everywhere as H-Hr approached.[55]

This account was included in the Canadian post-operation report where it helped to hide the fact that 4 RWF, like most units, had considerable problems fitting into the 'war of machines' imposed by the 'terrible efficiency' of higher plans. To get close to the barrage before its first lift, the Battalion planned to cross the start line 10 minutes before H-Hour, but their Flails mired (western edge of Map 7). This only made the lead companies two minutes late, but given their keen appreciation of barrage hugging, this was concerning enough to be worthy of note in the 4 RWF diary. Most of the standard Churchills from "A" Squadron managed to avoid bogging due to their low ground pressure and low gearing, and so they led the way to the barrage line in place of the Flails, allowing the infantry to deploy just behind the tanks.[56] Six Churchills (possibly from another squadron) moved onto a railway embankment and added to the suppressive effect with direct tracer fire from their Besa machine guns: 'The din and noise was terrific and all the buildings were aflame or smoking.'[57]

When the barrage lifted at 10:30, one 25pdr failed to switch fire (itself exposing one myth of the Veritable narrative), but this was so obvious and regular that it was 'merely a case of walking round to avoid casualties.'[58] Given the Flail failure, it was fortunate for 4 RWF that the mine belt was much less dense than expected. As the intimate support tanks moved through the belt, 'Speculative fire was used freely to front and flank' and the infantry followed in the tank tracks until they were through the minefield.[59] One source has "C" Company (centre) suffering a handful of casualties to mines on the road into De Horst and troops had to work around this area until sappers could clear the road.[60] Then by staying close behind the barrage, companies picked up several groups of prisoners who put up no resistance. De Horst itself was expected to be a centre of resistance but,

---

55 Conacher and Harrison 'Operation Veritable', pp.26–27.
56 4 RWF diary; 147 RAC diary.
57 Kemp and Graves, *Red Dragon*, p.245. A 1:1 mix of 7.92mm ball-to-tracer ammunition was sometimes used for firebase tasks rather than the standard four ball to one tracer (4B1T). There is a chance these tanks were firing the less common incendiary rounds.
58 Kemp and Graves, *Red Dragon*, p.245.
59 147 RAC diary.
60 Kemp and Graves, *Red Dragon*, p.245.

in addition to the pepper pot and the barrage, it had been the target for a Mattress fire mission at 08:30, liberally hosed with tracer, and was set to be the target of Crocodile flame at 11:00.

A few Crocodiles made it forward but were forced off the road by the uncleared mines and then bogged just out of flame range of the defended buildings. However, the mass of firepower, the impending infantry assault and (it is assumed) a few speculative rods of liquid fire, seem to have discouraged resistance. The only noted opposition by defending infantry was when "B" Company was 'momentarily delayed' by fire from a farm on the extreme right, which killed two men and wounding three more.[61] The company commander quickly led the reserve platoon in an attack that retrieved the situation, capturing a German platoon of 23 men whose arms included six Spandaus.[62] The centre of the village was secured by 11:55 as infantry 'well under the barrage and supported by A Sqn' collected another batch of prisoners.[63]

By 12:15, 4 RWF had platoons all along Line Ramillies and Bren teams were being pushed to the Leigraaf. Here it was found that the bridge over the ditch had not been blown and so several of 147 RAC's Churchills crossed into the edge of the barrage without waiting for the AVREs, while others were able to ford the narrow stream. The Fusiliers had achieved their objectives on time, claiming 186 prisoners for the cost of only five casualties to defensive fire.[64] 'The opposition encountered by the assaulting Coys was not as stiff as was expected from this outpost of the Siegfried Line. Mines were met in very small quantities and enemy D.F. fire was light.'[65] Resistance was so slight that 71 Brigade recorded it as 'practically non-existent'.[66]

The next two battalions of 53 Division passed through and fought into the Reichswald, though no armour penetrated the forest to support them.[67] On the left, 1 Oxford Bucks hugged the barrage to a line of fighting positions dug into the raised track at the edge of the forest. These positions should have been proof against shellfire but were quickly overrun. One source has suggested that the viability of these positions was negated by the Allies 'secret weapon' of shells with 'Variable Timing' radar-activated proximity fuses exploding just inches above the ground, killing the occupants with shell splinters, but the tactical and technical details are unclear.[68] Once in the forest, and despite the ground being littered with trees that had been smashed by artillery, the Oxford Bucks quickly secured the Brandenberg. Although the Battalion suffered a small number of casualties, no count is given in their diary or histories; 115 prisoners were rounded up and these 'stated that the weight and duration of the arty sp had beaten the spirit out of them.'[69] In contrast, despite

---

61 Military Cross (MC) citation, Major Roberts, WO 373/53/392.
62 'Spandau' generally refers to the MG-34 and MG-42. This number of machine guns is an extreme example but reflects the late war organisation of German infantry. A typical British 37-man platoon had three Bren light machine guns. The likely impact of this imbalance is examined in Chapter 5.
63 147 RAC diary.
64 4 RWF diary (2 officers, 184 other ranks), 5 casualties from diary summary sheet. CWGC records no 4 RWF dead on 8 February.
65 4 RWF diary.
66 71 Brigade diary.
67 Oxf Bucks diary (WO 171/5253); 71 Brigade comms log (diary); 147 RAC diary; J. H. Roberts, *Enshrined in Stone: 1st Battalion (43rd) The Oxfordshire & Buckinghamshire Light Infantry in the Second World War* (Witney: Boldacre, 1994), pp.307–309.
68 Roberts, *Enshrined*, p.300 and the same author's *Welsh Bridges to the Elbe* (Witney: Boldacre, 2000), p.202, but the source is Spike Milligan's brother, D. P. B. Milligan, *View from a Forgotten Hedgerow* (Glebe NSW: Self-published, 1993), pp.27–28. Variable Timing was a codeword to obscure the fact that the fuses used radar. A. L. Pemberton, *The Development of Artillery Tactics and Equipment* (London: War Office, 1951), pp.259, 262, 281, 305.
69 Oxf Bucks diary and summary sheet; Roberts, *Enshrined*, p.309; J. E. H. Neville, *The Oxfordshire & Buckinghamshire Light Infantry War Chronicle*, Vol. IV (Aldershot: Gale & Polden, 1954), extracts taken from lightbobs.com. The latter mentions overnight losses to shelling. CWGC has one dead on 8 Feb. No sources mention losses to mines. Later analysis assumes 6 casualties excluding any lost to mines.

a similar pounding, 1 HLI described opposition as 'severe' and 'fairly heavy' but still suffered only two killed, 17 wounded, and claimed 162 prisoners.[70] To 71 Brigade's staff, the battle was over by 15:30 because resistance 'ceased altogether' once units entered the Reichswald.[71]

Planners had assumed that fighting into the Reichswald would be the more challenging task, so 71 Brigade's third phase was to have 4 RWF echelon through to secure the Frasselt road, but opposition was so unexpectedly light that 1 HLI did the job instead.[72] The next brigade then echeloned through, and in the early evening 4 RWF followed them into the forest. Unfortunately for 4 RWF, the Division's main supply route entered the Reichswald at an obvious chokepoint which, despite *84. Division*'s limited ammunition, was repeatedly under indirect fire. 'Owing to the general congestion in the area, cas were considerable' and 4 RWF lost far more men in their night move than during their attack.[73]

10 HLI and the Scottish Division

A few kilometres northeast of De Horst, Tenth Battalion the Highland Light Infantry (10 HLI, part of 227 Brigade of 15 Scottish Division) fought a quite different battle. It was a battle that shows the limitations of artillery suppression and how, contrary Horrocks's view, there was room for manoeuvre and scope for cleverness, at least at the tactical level.[74] The 10 HLI battalion group had a similar organisation to 4 RWF but with Churchills provided by Right Flank of Third (Tank) Battalion, The Scots Guards (3 Scots Guards) and extra Crocodiles to help with their more substantial urban objective.[75] An awkward dogleg in the Division's area forced 227 Brigade to lead with 2 A&SH (Second Battalion, The Argyll and Sutherland Highlanders) then move up 10 HLI onto their left flank during the first barrage pause. From there on, 10 HLI would advance to form a three-company front that was just 500 metres wide (Map 8).[76] Each forward company was to be supported by a troop of tanks, while specialist armour was held with the reserve company.[77]

A critical terrain feature was the 'flooded anti-tank ditch' of the *Groesbecker Bach*, a brick-lined stream fed by the Leigraaf that was wide enough to require at least a fascine to get a tank across, and deep enough to make any infantry crossing difficult (Figure 5).[78] A further complication was that Kranenburg's sturdy medieval buildings formed a town wall that had windows and loopholes offering protected firing points overlooking the Bach.[79] To augment the suppressive power of the barrage, Kranenburg was to be firebombed by the RAF just before H-Hour then hit with a Mattress fire mission at 13:00. Even so, a central pillar of 10 HLI's plan was to have armour forward to suppress those protected firing points and to use armoured bridging to quickly cross the

---

70 CWGC lists 4 dead. The 1 HLI diary gives no detail, and this is echoed in histories, e.g., L.B. Oatts, *Proud Heritage: The Story of the Highland Light Infantry (vol.4)* (Glasgow: Grant, 1963), pp.351, 355.
71 71 Brigade diary.
72 Oxf Bucks diary; 1 HLI diary; Barclay, *53rd (Welsh)*, pp.115–116; 4 RWF diary; 71 Brigade OO 1.
73 Oxf Bucks diary; Roberts, *Welsh Bridges*, pp.199, 208. K.G. Exham (CO 6 RWF), 'The Assault on the Reichswald', unpublished report chapter kindly provided by the RWF Museum. 4 RWF diary lists 26 casualties on the 9th and CWGC records three dead.
74 10 HLI diary (WO 171/5207): 1–8 Feb; Appendix D1A, summary of orders; Appendix G2, Memo 'Routine 7 Feb 45'; Movement Order No 2 and addendum.
75 10 HLI summary of orders. Right Flank was a tank squadron but has been an infantry company for most of its existence.
76 10 HLI diary.
77 10 HLI summary of orders; 15 Division OO 8.
78 10 HLI diary.
79 Anon, '*Denkmalbereichssatzung Orstkern* Kranenburg', (Unknown, 1991).

ARTILLERY AND EFFECTIVENESS 65

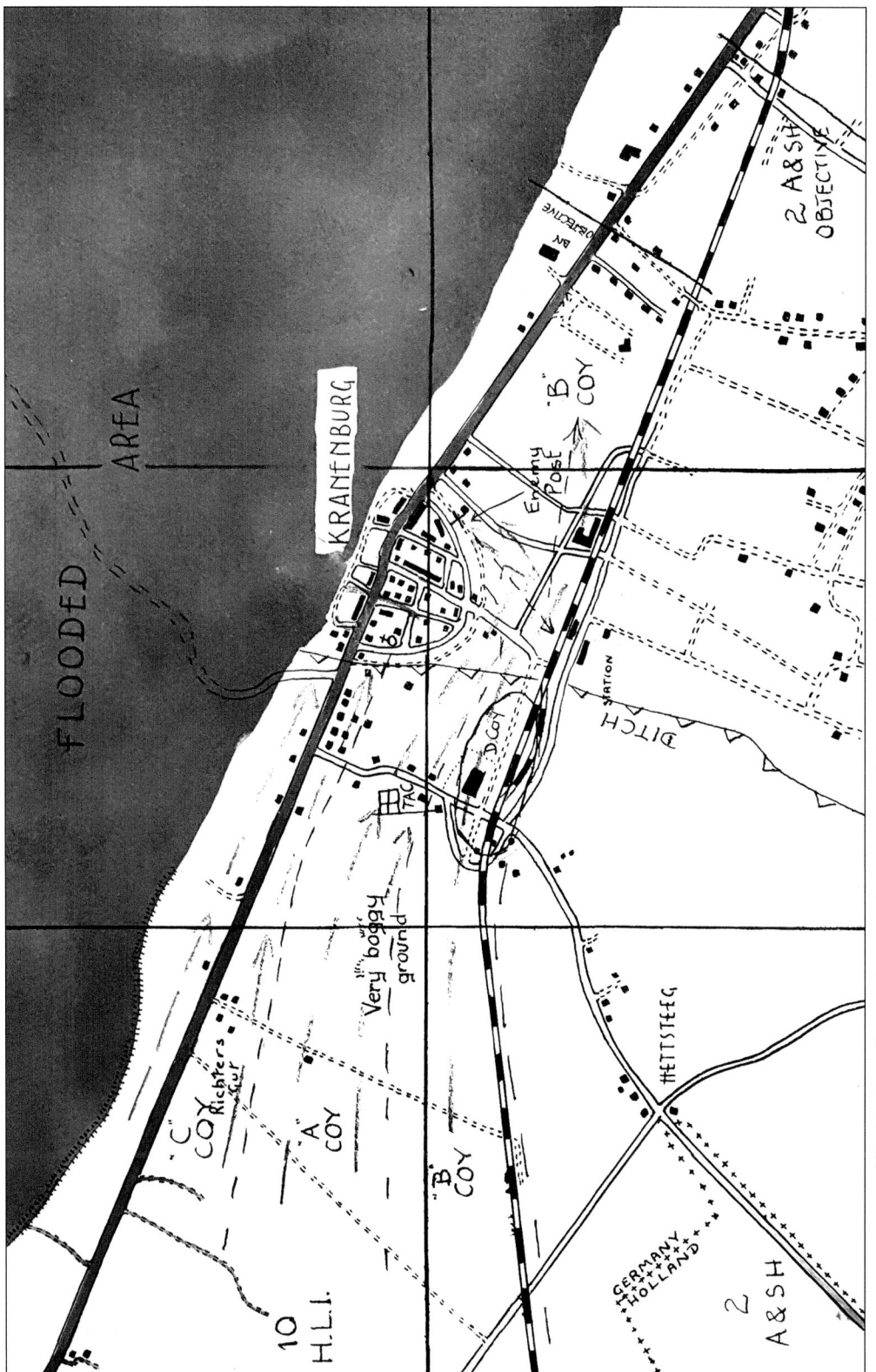

Map 8: 10 Highland Light Infantry schematic showing a mix of what was planned and what transpired. (National Archives, author's photograph)

Bach. When the barrage lifted at 14:15, "C" Company (left) were to assault astride the main road, force a crossing of the Bach, advance 200 metres to the north-centre of town then defend against any counterattack from the north. In the centre, "A" would cross the Groesbecker Bach, most likely using AVRE fascines, and secure the south-eastern half of the old town. On the right, "B" Company would cross the railway bridge (or near to it if blown), clear the station, then continue eastward. The Battalion would consolidate in town by 16:00 but were to be prepared to continue the advance overnight.[80]

Before 10 HLI could attack, they had to pass through 2 A&SH, whose advance was upset by bogging and congestion which held up specialist armour and the carriers that were hauling command radios and engineer stores. One of the A&SH companies had fallen about 15 minutes behind the barrage and was then badly mauled by defensive machine-gun and mortar fire before reaching the first barrage pause, where they were to secure the 10 HLI start line.[81]

The 10 HLI plan unravelled very quickly. The firebombing was cancelled at the last minute due to low cloud over the target.[82] Then, because 10 HLI were following 2 A&SH, the especially churned up ground exacerbated problems with bogging and traffic congestion, and so the HLI also attacked without their engineer stores, specialist armour, or the CO's carrier and radios.[83] The Battalion therefore no longer had the bridges, sappers and Crocodiles that were central to their plan for crossing the Bach and securing Kranenburg. The tanks that might have made up some of these firepower shortfalls were late (two tanks were damaged in the minefield, several others bogged) and the radio communication necessary for adjusting artillery fire seems to have failed with the loss of the Battalion commander's carrier.[84]

The leading infantry managed to keep pace with the artillery, and "C" Company 'took full advantage of the barrage' to launch a successful quick assault on Richters Gut farm, a kilometre west of town (marked '"C" Coy' at Map 9).[85] All companies caught up with the barrage pause before it lifted, but most needed to rush to do this. By this point all tanks were consigned to roads and sturdier farm tracks, which left "A" and "B" without armour support for the initial assault as all Right Flank's still-mobile tanks were headed towards the main road behind "C" Company.

Despite barrage hugging, "C" Company 'almost immediately came under heavy fire from a group of houses in front of the ditch' (C 2 at Map 9) but these were quickly cleared thanks to 'the opportune arrival of Lieutenant Scott-Barrett's Churchill troop'.[86] Then "C" found the bridge intact, crossed into town and started house clearing down the main road with one tank in close support

---

80 10 HLI summary of orders makes no mention of bridging for "A" Coy but is implied.
81 2 A&SH diary (WO 171/5153); 10 HLI diary.
82 P.D. Winslow and B. Brassey, *153rd Leicestershire Yeomanry Field Regiment R.A., T.A., 1939–1945*, (Uckfield: Naval & Military, 2015 [1945]), p.62, reports firing smoke indication for the bombers and hearing them fly overhead.
83 10 HLI diary; R. T. Johnston, D. N. Steward and A. I. Dunlop, *The Story of the 10th Bn. The Highland Light Infantry 1944–1945* (Uckfield: Naval & Military, 2020 [1945]), p.38; D. Erskine, *The Scots Guards 1919–1955* (London: Clowes, 1956), pp.401–402. Johnston et al report minefield casualties in the HLI "A" Coy, and this is repeated in H. G. Martin, *History of the 15th Scottish Division 1939–1945* (Smalldale: MLRS, 2006 [1948]), p.235. However, these losses are not mentioned in diaries, conflict with known losses from later in the battle and the account is remarkably like that given for "A" 2 A&SH, who preceded them through the minefield. As several hundred men would have passed through before "A" 10 HLI and (unlike the two mine-damaged tanks) infantry would have little motivation to go around churned ground in a minefield, it is assumed that Johnston et al are mistaken on this point.
84 There may have been some dismounted artillery observers, but most were in armoured vehicles to ensure reliable radio communication.
85 MC citation, Major Murray, WO 373/53/461.
86 Johnston et al, *10th Bn*, p.39.

Figure 5: Part of the Groesbecker Bach 'flooded anti-tank ditch' (on a much drier day) where "A" Company attempted to cross. Buildings on the left are part of the old town, those in the distance are post-war. (Author's photograph)

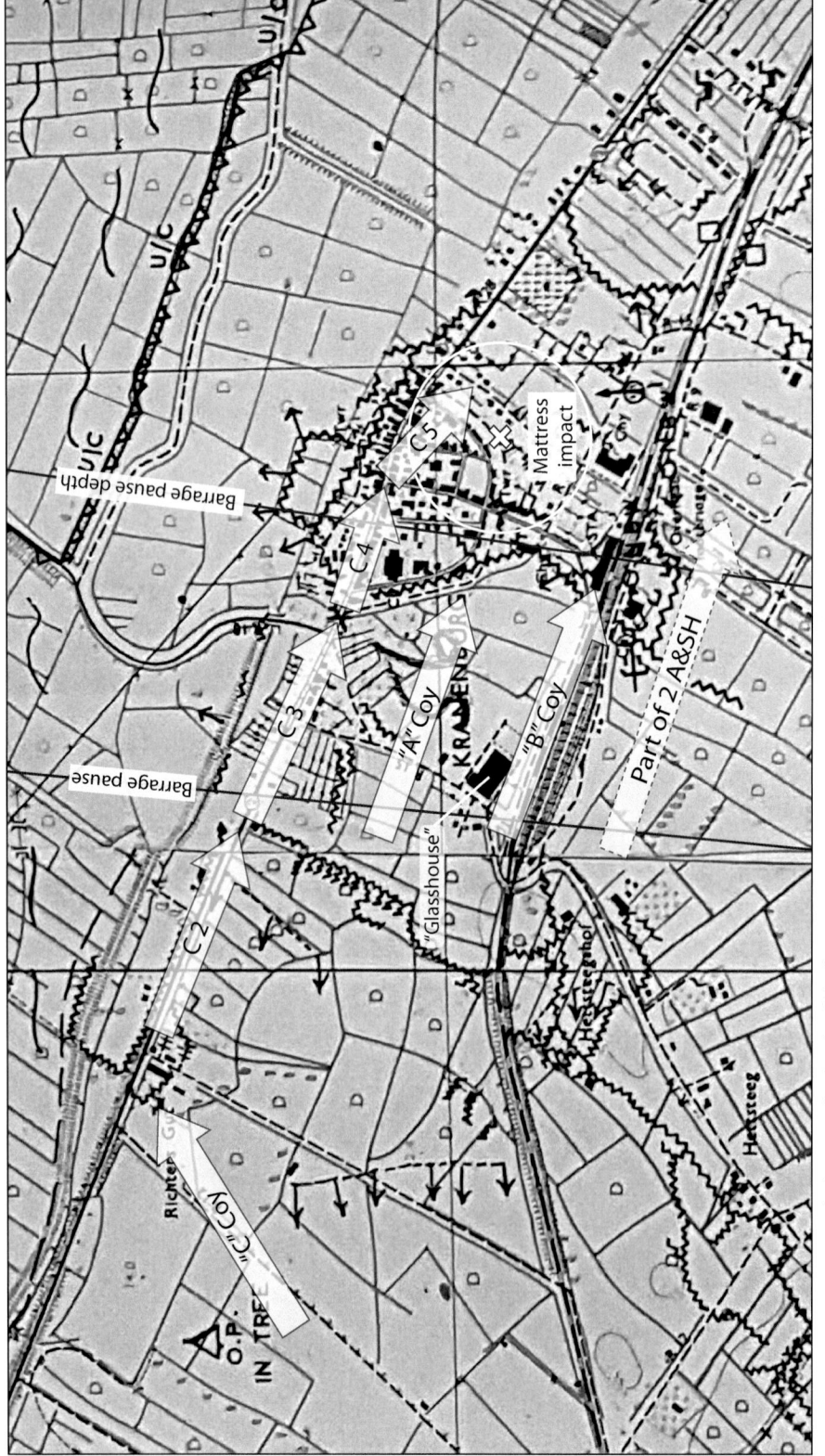

Map 9: 10 HLI attack showing the depth of the barrage pause area, mattress impact and company manoeuvre. (National Archives, author's photograph)

(C 3). Due to bogging at the chokepoint, eight Churchills backed up around the bridge where they were unable to support "C" or the other companies further south. Street clearing proved to be a difficult job but by 16:35, perhaps 45 minutes later than planned, "C" had reached their objective on the T-junction in the north-centre of town and went into all-round defence as ordered (C 4).[87]

At first, "B" Company (forward right) had similar success, clearing the 'glasshouse area' that had been bisected by the barrage pause, then crossing the rail bridge and securing the station without taking noteworthy casualties.[88] In the centre, "A" Company had a much harder time because, away from road and railway, they had no bridge and no hope of close tank support. The leading platoon attempted to cross the Bach under their own steam but ran into machine-gun fire from the buildings that formed the town wall; many men were killed or wounded, and the rest were pinned down in the Bach. The remainder of "A" Company hooked around to the right, chased by Spandau fire as they went, and followed "B" over the railway bridge. At that point, half of 10 HLI's fighting strength was in the station area and 'pinned down by accurate machine-gun fire for some considerable time'. The barrage had moved on, and without armour or artillery support, the infantry could not win the firefight to let them assault across the open ground between station and town. In addition to machine-gun fire, "A" and "B" suffered the unnerving experience of being engaged by a Nebelwerfer firing directly over open sights.[89]

The deadlock was eventually broken when some men from "A" Company' wormed their way into town and linked up with "C".[90] Major Murray, commanding "C" Company, then realised his subunit was the only part of the Battalion that could resolve the situation and at 17:30 he led a flanking attack on the remaining defenders (C 5 at Map 9). This was a risky move, as communication failures meant he had no idea whether friendly artillery was being called onto the area he was advancing into, but the risk paid off because once his men eliminated the Nebelwerfer crew, the German force quickly surrendered.[91] With the main threat defeated, "B" Company was able to resume its eastward advance and the town was secure by 19:00. This was three hours behind schedule, but 183 prisoners were taken at a cost of 46 friendly casualties and two damaged tanks.[92] Major Murray 'took over the consolidation of KRANENBURG until some stray Canadians arrived to announce that they had captured it!!!'[93]

Compared to the 4 RWF battle, artillery suppression had a much-reduced effect in the 10 HLI area because the town's sturdy buildings provided protected fire positions for the defenders. In the end Kranenburg fell to unsupported infantry manoeuvre, with junior commanders improvising despite being only dimly aware of their comrades' actions. This long and difficult battle was not

---

87 Johnston et al, *10th Bn*, p.39; Martin *15th Scottish*, p.236; 10 HLI diary; Murray citation. The 3 Scots Guards diary and Erskine, *Scots Guards* (p.402) claim a whole troop crossed the bridge. Note how Map 9 shows the "C" Coy bridge destroyed, which was likely a mistaken planning assumption.
88 2 A&SH and 10 HLI diaries, Johnston et al, *10th Bn*, p.40. On air photographs the glasshouse area appears a less substantial objective than is implied on maps.
89 10 HLI diary; Johnston et al, *10th Bn*, p.40; Murray citation.
90 Around this time Major Merrifield, commanding "A" Coy was killed while attempting to regain contact with 8 Platoon.
91 10 HLI diary; Distinguished Service Order (DSO) citation, Lieutenant Colonel Bramwell, WO 373/53/740. The Tac HQ was set up just outside town at 16:15 after its bulky radios were manhandled from the other side of the start line.
92 HLI diary had 13 killed, 28 wounded, five missing. CWGC has 12 killed and the names match the roll of honour in Johnston et al, *10th Bn*, p.74. The large proportion killed suggests few casualties to anti-personnel mines. L.B. Oatts, *The Highland Light Infantry* (London: Leo Cooper, 1969), pp.102–103, claims 'three officers and twenty-eight rank and file in killed and wounded' but is likely a mis-recollection from his more complete *Proud Heritage*, pp.349–351.
93 Johnston et al, *10th Bn*, p.40; Murray citation; Martin, p.236.

communicated in the summary offered by the Scots Guards, most of whom were outside town. The Guards described the defenders as being 'so overcome by the weight of the barrage and so surprised by the appearance of tanks in such bad going that they gave themselves up without a fight.'[94] Such misperceptions were repeated right across the Veritable front, with armoured commanders and Forward Observation Officers using their powerful radios to report their protected, often distant perspectives of the battle. They were unwittingly beginning to write the Veritable narrative of mines and mud being countered by powerful artillery and armour.

Meanwhile, 2 A&SH had resumed their long advance south of Kranenburg in what had been intended to be the most armour-heavy of all the break-in battles.[95] Their "B" Company struggled to keep up with what planners had consider a 'very slow-moving barrage' but did most of the Battalion's work on their own (Map 10). Having suffered heavy losses around the mine belt, 2 A&SH's "A" Company took no further part in the battle, and "C" Company was similarly 'disorganised' when they were caught by defensive mortar fire while mopping up behind "B". The next major obstacle was the Elsenhof strongpoint, which had been hit by preparatory fire, a strong dose of pepper pot, a Mattress fire mission, and then 'hammered for over half an hour by the full weight of the barrage.'[96] Yet even here barrage hugging was essential; "B" Company's leading platoon intercepted the defenders 'just as they were tumbling out of their deep shelters to man their defensive positions'.[97] The defenders were not so much eroded or shocked but caught at a severe disadvantage because they had been prevented from defending until 2 A&SH were almost on their position.

Hettsteeghof was the only objective where "B" encountered notable resistance, most likely because they were by then 15 minutes behind the barrage. From there on "B" were joined by "D" Company, breathless after rushing up from reserve. The attack then became a series of 300-metre dashes to catch the barrage lifts. This area was less strongly held and "B" 'were again lucky in being able to slip in close behind the barrage' but the final objective, Line Hot Dog, was secured two hours late, at which point a handful of tanks arrived to aid the hasty defence.[98] Despite suffering 43 casualties, mostly from defensive indirect fire, and having two tanks damaged by mines, 2 A&SH were 'in exceptionally fine spirits' and had collected 250 prisoners.[99] Most of the prisoners had been prevented from firing and were caught in cellars and troop shelters, but erosion and shock seem to have played a role too; instead of the expected counterattack when guns switched to support 3 Canadian Division on the left flank, 'a steady trickle of Germans with white flags came in to our forward platoons'.[100]

Just south of 2 A&SH, were two attacks by 15 Division's 46 Brigade. The first has the scantest record of any D-Day action, with just 45 words in the 2 Glasgow Highlanders diary and a similar treatment in relevant histories. The tanks were forced to follow the road but provided some support to the infantry who overran sheltering defenders 'on the tail of the barrage'.[101] The only reported island of resistance came when companies fell behind the barrage after an internal echelon change.

---

94   Erskine, *Scots Guards*, p.402; Scots Guards diary.
95   15 Division OO 8. 2 A&SH's advance was 6,000 metres, while 4 RWF's was only 2,500, but 4 RWF's 1,400-metre frontage was twice as wide.
96   W. L. McElwee, *History of the Argyll & Sutherland Highlanders 2nd Battalion (Reconstituted): European Campaign 1944–45* (London: Thomas Nelson & Sons, 1949), p.132.
97   McElwee, *Argyll & Sutherland*, p.133.
98   McElwee, *Argyll & Sutherland*, p.133.
99   2 A&SH diary and summary sheet. Many of the dead were collected the following day and counted for 9 Feb in the CWGC database. No other armour was damaged in this action but a tank and a tank destroyer following 2 A&SH were destroyed by anti-tank mines, most likely while trying to work around churned ground. No German casualties were recorded.
100 2 A&SH diary.
101 Martin, *15th Scottish*, p.232.

ARTILLERY AND EFFECTIVENESS 71

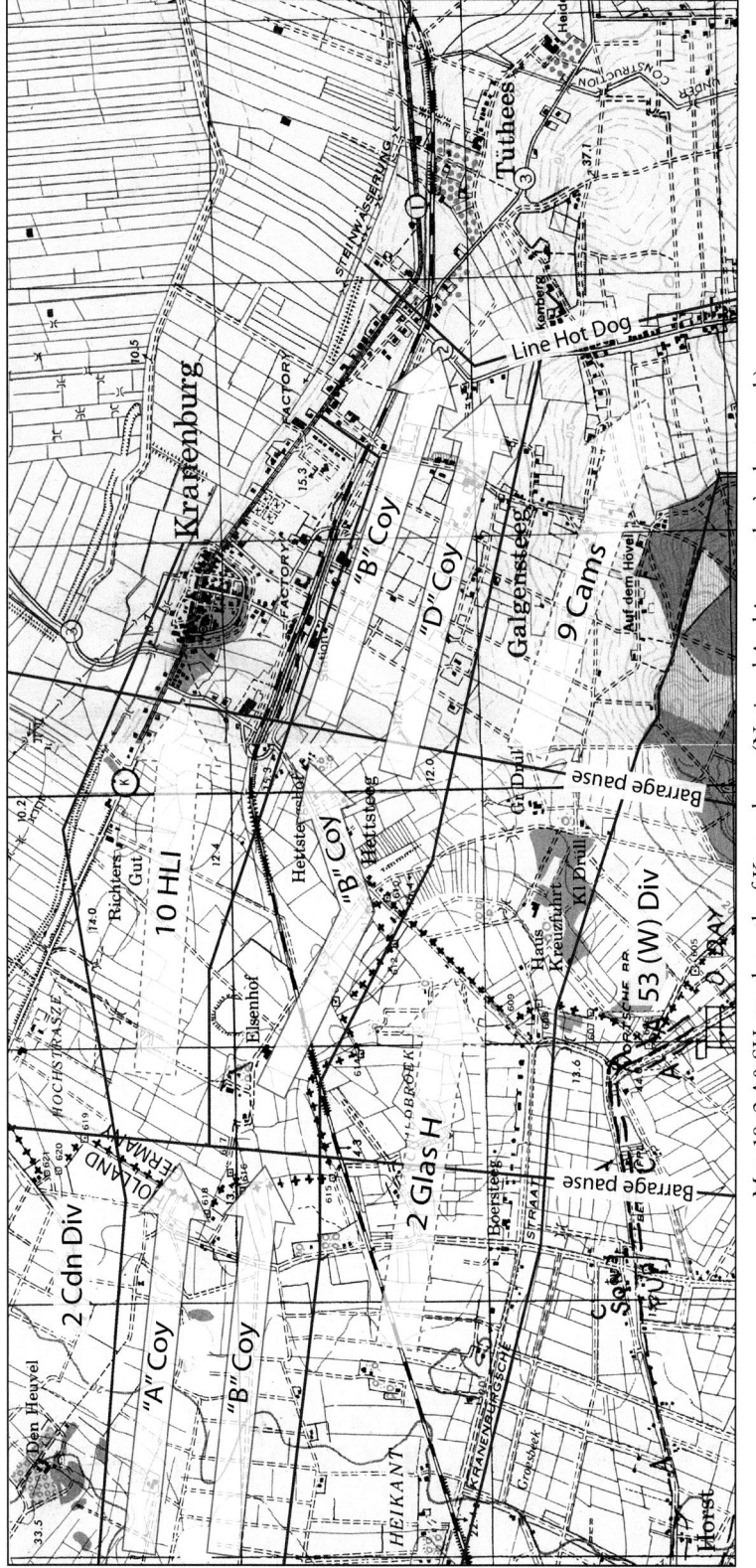

Map 10: 2 A&SH attack south of Kranenburg. (National Archives, author's photograph)

By 14:00, only half an hour later than planned, the Glasgow Highlanders had secured Haus Kreuzfuhrt ready for 9 Cameronians to continue the advance (Map 11).[102] Six men were killed and 35 wounded; 220 defenders were captured.[103]

In the next action 9 Cameronians passed through 2 Glasgow Highlanders but left their CO and armour support stuck in traffic near Groesbeek.[104] The Cameronians attack went smoothly at first, meeting some small arms fire from buildings along Galgensteeg ridge and finding an elaborate but unoccupied system of field works in the edge of the Reichswald (Unoccupied trenches at Map 11).[105] At that point, most sources have "B" Company (forward left) suffering heavy casualties from anti-personnel mines, but the Battalion diary makes it clear these losses were due to artillery fratricide.[106] This incident and the late armour stalled the second half of the Cameronians plan.

The final assault was at an angle to the main fire plan, with a single company due to be supported by Crocodiles and getting the suppressive effect from timed artillery concentrations moving north to south through Frasselt village.[107] These concentrations were all fired on the original timings and had to be repeated, but the delayed assault was successful, and many Germans were reported killed, despite showing 'little inclination to continue the fight' once Crocodiles began flaming houses.[108] The Cameronians achieved their objectives, capturing 115 defenders and three 105mm guns, but they lost 10 men killed, 47 wounded and eight missing, and were two hours behind schedule.[109] 'The village itself burned well – at least one out of every three houses, it appeared, was on fire, illuminating the surrounding country-side to no mean degree.'[110]

---

102 2 Glas H diary (WO 171/5193); 46 Brigade OO 18, (WO 171/4368); 15 Division comms log; 15 Division ISUM 198, Division diary; C.N. Barclay, *The History of the Cameronians (Scottish Rifles), Vol. III. 1933–1946* (London: Sifton Praed, 1957), p.179; Glasgow Highlanders Benevolent Fund, *Concise Official History: 2nd Battalion the Glasgow Highlanders* (Lubeck: Glasgow Highlanders, 1946), p.28; Martin, *15th Scottish*, pp.232-233; E.S. Snell, *The Scottish Volunteers* (Eastbourne: Menin House, 2009), p.149; Thompson, *Rhineland*, p.162; M. Howard and J. Sparrow, *The Coldstream Guards, 1920–1946* (Oxford: University Press, 1951), p.322. The 4 Coldstream Guards diary (WO 171/5142) is missing all of Feb.

103 46 Brigade 'casualty and strength state' (diary); CWGC records eight killed on 8th. Names are confirmed in the *Concise History* (p.28) and appear evenly spread among companies. Martin, *15th Scottish*, (p.232) has three 75mm anti-tank guns 'knocked out' by the Guards but Howard and Sparrow (p.322) make no mention of them, and they appear in no primary source.

104 E. Remington-Hobbs, 'Operation Veritable, Personal Account by CO 9 Cameronians', 9 Cams diary; 6 Assault Regiment RE diary (WO 171/5317). The 9 Cams diary has the main axis impassable but tanks 'still able to give support'. Later sources (e.g., Barclay, *Cameronians*) may have taken this to mean support for the Cams attack (despite being the wrong side of Kreuzfuhrt wood) but given the timing of this entry (13:00), it likely refers to the 2 Glas H attack.

105 Martin, *15th Scottish*, p.233 and Barclay, *Cameronians*, pp.178-9 assume the defenders had fled. Fiebig's comments (Ch 1) and prisoner identifications suggest this was a fallback position, but the unit intended to occupy it had been overrun in the forward defence line.

106 9 Cams diary, 14:40. The only other source found to mention this is Thompson, *Rhineland* (p.163), which states that 9 Cams: 'had time to curse their own artillery for falling short, while some said the gunners seemed to have forgotten about hill clearance after so much time in the flat lands of Holland'. Martin, *15th Scottish* (p.233) seems at pains to blame mines, even detailing the injuries. Several reported fire missions are contenders for hitting "B" and the late boundary change shown at Map 11 may have played a role.

107 9 Cams OO 2, diary; 46 Brigade Op Order 18.

108 Barclay, *Cameronians*, p.179; Remington-Hobbs, 'Personal Account'.

109 Timings from 46 Brigade OO 18 and 15 Division OO 8 compared to Division comms log and Martin *15th Scottish*, pp.229–230. Casualty data from 46 Brigade 'casualty and strength state'. Remington-Hobbs, 'Personal Account' and Bn diary give slightly lower figures; CWGC database has 12 dead on 8 Feb and one on the 9th, likely DOW. Prisoners from summary sheet and Remington-Hobbs. Martin (p.233) and others have three 88mm guns, which is unlikely.

110 Remington-Hobbs, 'Personal Account'.

ARTILLERY AND EFFECTIVENESS 73

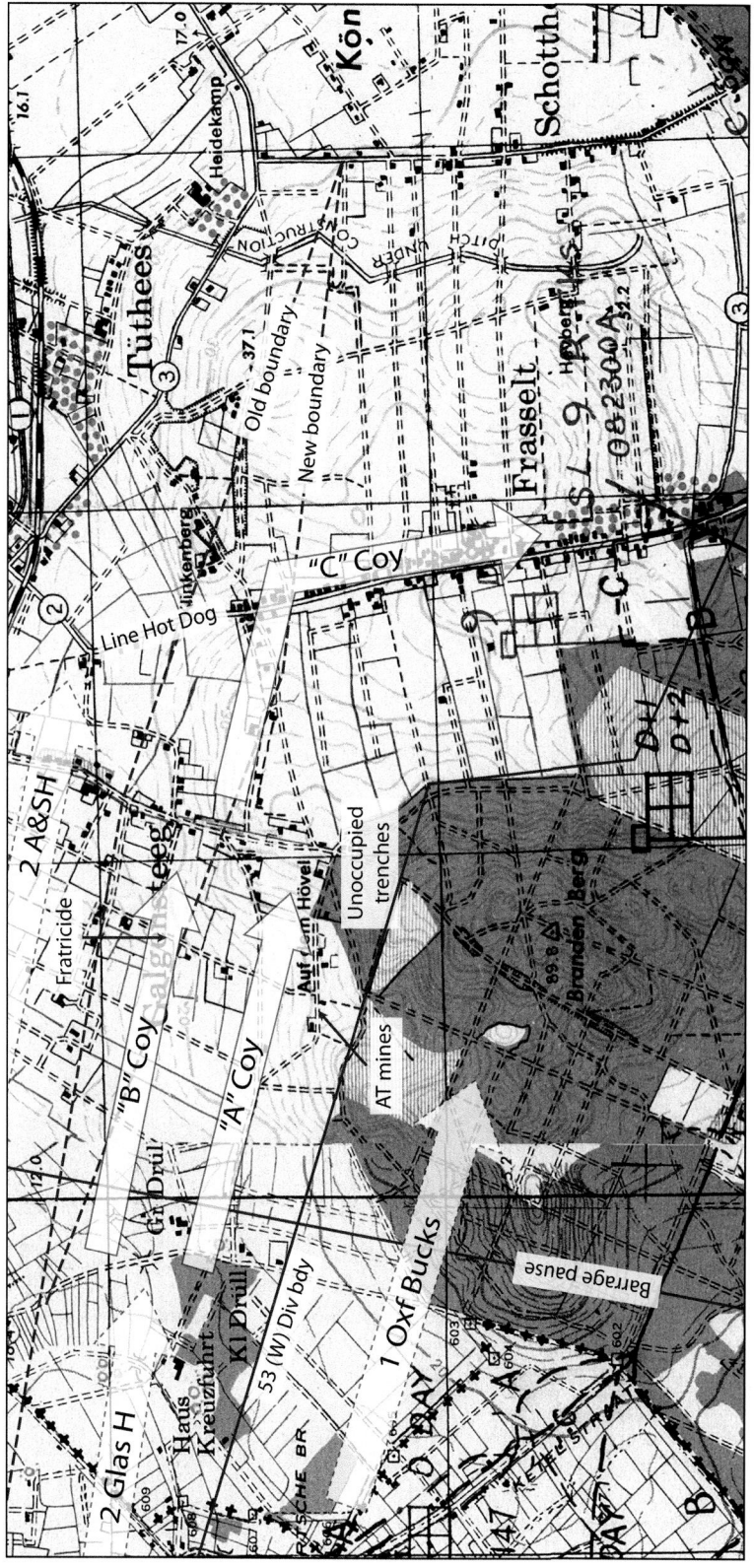

Map 11: 9 Cameronians Attack on Frasselt. (National Archives, author's photograph)

Canadians and Highlanders

The most northerly of all the daylight attacks involved the Calgary Highlanders of 2 Canadian Division, who faced many of the problems already described, but in an unfortunate combination.[111] Their target, the village of Wyler, was a tactical puzzle a little like Kranenburg but smaller and less dense. As with 9 Cameronians, their flanking approach went against the grain of the barrage and their armour arrived late, having been involved in the pepper pot until H-Hour. Then, where most units crossed their start lines early, the Calgaries were reportedly unconcerned about setting off 12 minutes late, by which time the barrage would have been falling 600 metres ahead of them.[112] As a result of falling so far being the barrage, the lead companies soon came under machine-gun and mortar fire. This happened while they were still negotiating the mine belt, without armour, and while turning away from the direction of the barrage.[113]

The Calgaries eventually managed to secure Wyler, but the attack had to be restarted, with a new fire plan and long-range fire support from the late-arriving tanks. Once this was launched, the encircled garrison quickly surrendered, yielding 287 prisoners, the best haul of the day. However, that came at least five hours behind schedule and at a cost of 74 casualties, the greatest loss suffered by any Allied battalion on D-Day.[114] Like the hidden fratricide of 9 Cameronians, the effect of attacking without artillery or armour suppression was subsumed into the mines and mud narrative. In the Calgaries case, the lessons were also hidden by an acrimonious debate over whether the initial failure was due to an 'ambush' in the minefield (a known obstacle covered by known defensive positions, so hardly an ambush) or a lack of aggressiveness in one company commander (an easy scapegoat for higher commanders).[115]

Between the Calgaries and 10 HLI, three companies of *le Régiment de Maisonneuve* hurried onto Den Heuvel farm, an outpost on high ground that threatened 15 Division's left flank, then they 'crowded the barrage' through a chain of smaller positions running eastward to the main road.[116] One depth position was subjected to a Mattress fire mission, but here the effect was bloodier and more dramatic than either 4 RWF's or 2 A&SH's experience following a rocket strike. Many defenders were killed, and the survivors were clearly subject to the shock aspect of suppression: 'Some reel drunkenly, others stare vacantly; some shamble along in tears, while others laugh hysterically.'[117] Despite the shocked defenders, the Canadian's barrage hugging, and the small garrison, the Maisonneuve casualties were quite high, perhaps due to flanking fire from

---

111 Assessment of the two Canadian attacks is largely based on secondary sources, which are detailed and seem thorough but must be treated with greater caution. For these two battles the author is especially indebted to "Stolpi" and other the members of WW2Talk.com (search 'Canadian attack on Wyler and Den Heuvel').
112 Zuehlke, *Forgotten Victory* (Kindle 3055) and others. D. J. Bercuson, *Battalion of Heroes: The Calgary Highlanders in World War II* (Calgary: Empire, 1994), p.203, claims the delay was only a few minutes. It is not clear why the Calgaries expected the suppression after effect to endure for so long but perhaps they were waiting for armour, Flails, et cetera
113 Bercuson, *Battalion of Heroes* pp.202–206; 13/18 Hussars diary; Zuehlke, *Forgotten Victory*, Kindle 3062-3159; Williams, *Long Left*, Kindle 2674-2694; Whitakers, *Rhineland*, pp.53–54; Copp and Vogel, *Maple Leaf*, p.28; Copp, *Brigade*, pp.176–178, 182.
114 Bercuson, *Battalion of Heroes* (p.206) gives the casualties as 13 killed and 61 wounded; CWGC has 15 killed, the two extra presumably DOW.
115 Bercuson, *Battalion of Heroes*, pp.206–207.
116 Conacher and Harrison, pp.27–28; Stacey, *Victory Campaign*, pp470–471; Whitakers, *Rhineland*, pp.53–54; Zuehlke, *Forgotten Victory*, Kindle 2915-3083.
117 Zuehlke, *Forgotten Victory*, Kindle 3045. The 'Rocket Regt' task list (53 Division HQRA diary) has Den Heuvel itself also due to be hit at 10:30 but this does not appear on a later overlay of confirmed targets and was probably cancelled due to the risk of fratricide close to the barrage lift.

positions around Wyler.[118] In addition to 35 prisoners, at least 46 defenders were killed, while the Maisonneuve suffered two killed and 20 wounded.[119]

On the southern edge of the 30 Corps front, 51 Highland Division had 1 Black Watch and 7 Black Watch (both from 154 Brigade) attack in parallel following timed artillery concentrations instead of a barrage.[120] In the first phase, 1 Black Watch had the easier task, attacking over open ground to seize a small, wooded area just short of the Reichswald (Objective Tomato at Map 12) then pushing on to Objective Tangerine, the northern half of Freudenberg ridge, just inside the Reichswald. In contrast, 7 Black Watch had to fight through Bruuk and Breedeweg, each a roadside ribbon of dispersed houses and farms that together made a larger urban target than Wyler. Being the outside right battalion of the outside right division, 7 Black Watch also attacked with an open flank, which was to be masked by smoke, artillery, mortars, and indirect machine-gun fire, but was still a threat. In expectation of difficulties from the open flank, 7 Black Watch were only expected to advance half as far as 1 Black Watch, then hand over to 5/7 Gordons who would assault into the forest to capture the southern half of Freudenberg.[121]

Both of the Black Watch battalions were held up by 'bogged cart tracks' to and from their assembly area, by sporadic defensive shelling, and by an Allied artillery round that dropped short onto 154 Brigade headquarters, causing three casualties.[122] The supporting armour was delayed, and both battalions appear to have waited before finally advancing with little or no tank support. The Flails and AVREs that should have been to the fore did not even leave the assembly area until 11:25. The first part of the 1 Black Watch advance was unopposed, with no casualties or prisoners reported until they approached Objective Tomato, where there was 'stiff resistance' because the timed concentrations had moved on.[123] This resistance was overcome with some difficulty, then by closely following their fire support 1 Black Watch secured Tangerine by 13:20, having suffered four killed, 17 wounded and two missing, but capturing 100 defenders.[124]

Although 7 Black Watch were 'careful not to push forward too quickly' and had to use 3-inch mortars to fill the gap between artillery lifting and their assault, their attack also began well, and 40 prisoners were taken in trenches on the outskirts of Breedeweg. However, the leading companies were soon pinned down and the left-hand company had its commander and two other officers killed by "snipers" on the edge of Bruuk.[125] Bringing up the rear of 7 Black Watch one of the Flails was trying to cut through mines along the road when bypassed defenders engaged and destroyed it with *Panzerfauste*.[126] Defensive fire from small arms and mortars increased but the delayed tank

---

118 Copp, *Brigade*, p.181; MM citation, Private Lefebvre, WO 373/55/616; Conacher and Harrison 'Operation Veritable', p.31.
119 Zuehlke (Kindle 3033, 3056); CWGC. Whitakers, *Rhineland* (p.53) has a tally of 46 German dead 'without examining slit trenches.'
120 First and Seventh Battalions, The Black Watch (Royal Highland Regiment) supported by "A" and "B" Squadrons, 107 Armoured Regiment, RAC (The King's Own). 154 Brigade, OO 5, Brigade diary (WO 171/4412); D.F.O. Russell, *War History of the 7th Bn. The Black Watch (R.H.R.)* (Markinch: Markinch, 1948), pp.122–123.
121 1 and 7 Black Watch diaries (WO 171/5158 and 5160).
122 7 Black Watch and 154 Brigade diaries.
123 1 and 7 Black Watch and 154 Brigade diaries. Russell, *War History*, p.123; 107 RAC diary (WO 171/4717).
124 1 Black Watch diary and summary sheet; CWGC has five killed on 8 Feb. Another three men were killed and seven wounded early on the 9th when "A" Company were sent to support 5/7 Gordons.
125 Russell, *War History*, p.123. The term "sniper" is used loosely in most sources and can mean any opponent taking aimed rifle shots.
126 107 RAC diary reports the Flail 'bazookered' at 12:50, while clearing the road after 7 Black Watch had passed but before 5/7 Gordons moved up. 154 Brigade diary, 00 No 5; W.A. Woolward, *A Short Account of the 1st Lothians and Border Yeomanry in the campaigns of 1940 and 1944–45* (Edinburgh: Publisher

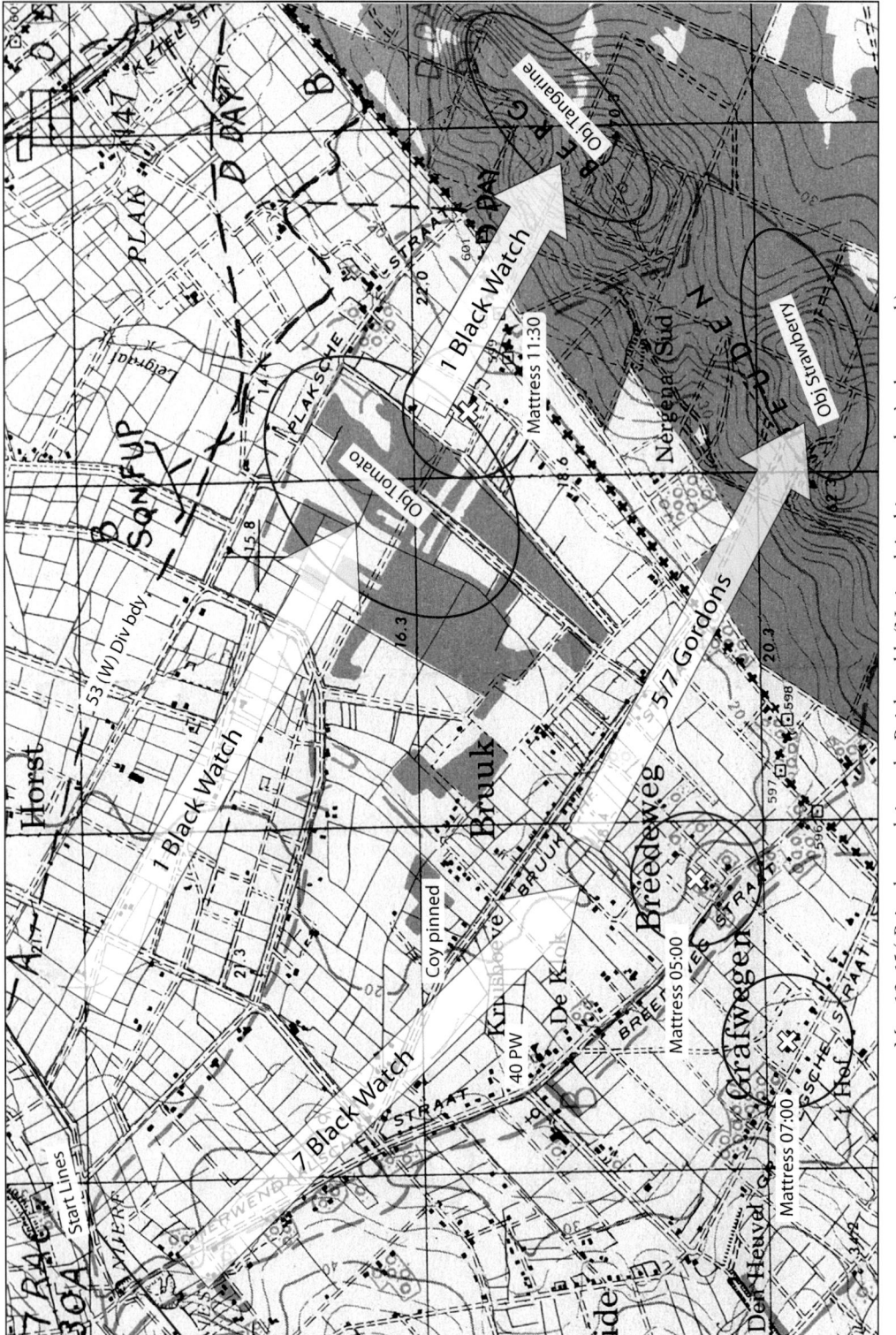

Map 12: 154 Brigade attack into the Reichswald. (National Archives, author's photograph)

support and an assault by the follow-on company got the battalion onto its objectives around 13:00, only an hour behind schedule.[127] Both of 7 Black Watch's leading companies then went into defence in the 'shattered remains' of the villages, the battalion group having lost one Flail, 11 killed, 26 wounded and one missing, but having taken 150 prisoners.[128]

The problems in 7 Black Watch slowed the takeover by 5/7 Gordons, who launched their attack two hours later than planned. Artillery, mortar, and indirect machine-gun fire missions were repeated to suppress the defenders on the flank, but it was dark before the Gordons broke into the Reichswald. Even with movement light, the advance was 'practically impossible' due to the difficulties navigating densely packed young trees that had been smashed by artillery.[129] The resulting confusion seems to have been even greater for the defenders who were caught midway through a relief-in-place, and a series of flanking engagements in the forest tipped the balance in the Gordons' favour.[130] The last of their flank attacks was launched in the early hours of 9 February, surprising 'several hundred Germans "milling" around in the area of the main track', and leaving 'many enemy dead … at a cost of only 1 man wounded.'[131] At 03:45, some 14 hours later than planned, 5/7 Gordons secured their objective and 164 prisoners at the cost of 49 personnel and two tank casualties.[132]

Reassessing Swann

Artillery suppression played a vital role in Veritable's initial success, but within the confines of the fire plan there was considerable variation between battalion group battles. Their aggregated experiences fit Swann's written report, with its emphasis on suppression preventing enemy movement and fire, but also on the need for a quick assault. Yet the critical caveat "as long as the infantry arrive quickly" is not reflected in Swann's charts and data tables, which suggest that once the three extremely late outliers were excluded, the number of rounds fired made all the difference in combat outcome.

The split between Swann's words and data become a concern when examining the 4 RWF attack which, of the 12 Veritable attacks examined, was easily the best fit to the template of "artillery conquers, infantry occupies". All sources but one describe a powerful fire plan with companies close behind the barrage and very few attacker casualties as a result. That one exception is the Swann Report, which describes 4 RWF as: 'mopping up, and did not keep up to the barrage. Encountered somewhat more opposition for this reason' and then lumps their attack in with those of 7 Black Watch and 5/7 Gordons as being so far behind the fire plan that it should be excluded from analysis.[133] In addition, where 4 RWF's records have only five men killed and wounded by defensive fire, and maybe a few more casualties to mines, Swann has the Battalion losing 20 men to defensive fire plus an unstated number to mines. Then, where intelligence summaries, histories,

---

unknown, 1946), pp.82–83.
127 154 Brigade diary; Russell, *War History*, p.123; 107 RAC diary.
128 7 Black Watch diary; Woolward, *1st Lothians*, p.82; CWGC.
129 154 Brigade diary.
130 As noted in Chapter 1, a battalion of *GR. 1222* was relieving part of *GR. 1062*.
131 5/7 diary (WO 171/5198); 51 Division ISUM 324. This prisoner total includes 16 wounded, usually omitted from accounts as they pass through the medical chain not prisoner cages.
132 54 Brigade, 5/7 Gordons and 107 RAC diaries and summary sheets: Eight killed, 33 wounded, 1 missing in 5/7 Gordons. CWGC lists six killed on Feb 8, two on Feb 9. Two tanks of "B" Sqn 107 RAC 'went up on mines' causing seven wounded.
133 Swann/Copp, 'Veritable', p.367.

and the Battalion's prisoner count have them fighting through two companies, Swann's data has 4 RWF opposed by only a single company.

These discrepancies seem to have been forced by Swann's reliance on third- or fourth-hand reports collected by 30 Corps staff. It should be remembered that Swann's team had a few weeks to compile and analyse the data and release the report, and during that time 4 RWF were in contact with the enemy, mostly inside the Reichswald, at the end of a tenuous communication chain. Swann's casualty figures appear to have included 4 RWF's overnight move into the forest and may even have been based on a weekly casualty report. It seems Swann was also misinformed about defence strength and relied on a 30 Corps schematic (the arrows and defensive "goose eggs" at Map 6) which has 4 RWF, 1 Oxford Bucks and 1 HLI getting an equal share of three defending companies.

There are discrepancies like this for all 12 attacks, and although many are trivial, the non-trivial differences have profound implications for both operational research and the Veritable narrative. A typical example is 10 HLI's attack on Kranenburg, which has only a minor discrepancy in the key figure of attack casualties per defending company, but the description of the battle is: 'Well up to barrage. Not much opposition', which fits the reports from supporting armour but is far from the reality of the infantry attack.[134] The Swann Report makes no mention of the long delay while most of the Battalion was pinned down when the barrage ran ahead, of the loss of armoured support, or of the difficulty in rearranging fire support due to lost communications. Kranenburg was effectively a fortress that reduced the power of artillery, but the Swann Report makes no mention of a town being in the way. Likewise, the 9 Cameronians attack, instead of being stalled for two hours and suffering considerable losses to artillery fratricide, is presented as proceeding according to plan against scattered opposition and some anti-personnel mines.

The differences between Swann's source data and the records of battalions mount up to alter the shape of the suppression chart: Figure 6 replicates the Swann Report data but with a trend line added; Figure 7 shows the reassessment using battalion level sources.[135]

The new chart (Figure 7) suggests four groups:

a) Clipper attacks, which should be excluded from analysis because they were not reassessed and may be subject to the same problems as Swann's Veritable data.[136]
b) Late attacks, including 1 and 7 Black Watch, 5/7 Gordons, and the Calgary Highlanders, where forward companies moved to assault more than 15 minutes after the fire plan lifted and therefore lost much of the suppressive effect.
c) Attacks with other degrading factors, including 10 HLI's dense urban target, 2 A&SH's long advance, and the Maisonneuves, who met a problem that is not clear from available

---

134 Swann/Copp 'Veritable', p.367.
135 Swann 'Veritable', p.367, and sources as detailed previously. Five ways of calculating strengths and casualties were examined, but for consistency Figure 7 applies Swann's methods to the data from units. Therefore, the highest reported losses in each battalion group, minus known mine casualties (or an estimate where sources are unclear) were divided by defence strengths. Defence strengths were estimated by adding five percent to the reported prisoner numbers to account for killed and wounded unless a specific number of casualties was stated in sources. It was assumed each German company comprised 110 men, as stated in the Clipper report.
136 Full analysis of the Clipper data would take about eight weeks and was therefore outside the scope of the current assessment, but there do appear to be problems with the dataset. For example, the attacking unit that suffered the most casualties had the longest advance, no tank support, and lost its carrier platoon to flanking SP fire, none of which appear in the suppression reports. Bauchem, the most successful attack, had been encircled by British and American forces. K. Ford, *Assault on Germany: The Battle for Geilenkirchen* (Newton Abbot: David & Charles, 1989), pp.65–79.

ARTILLERY AND EFFECTIVENESS 79

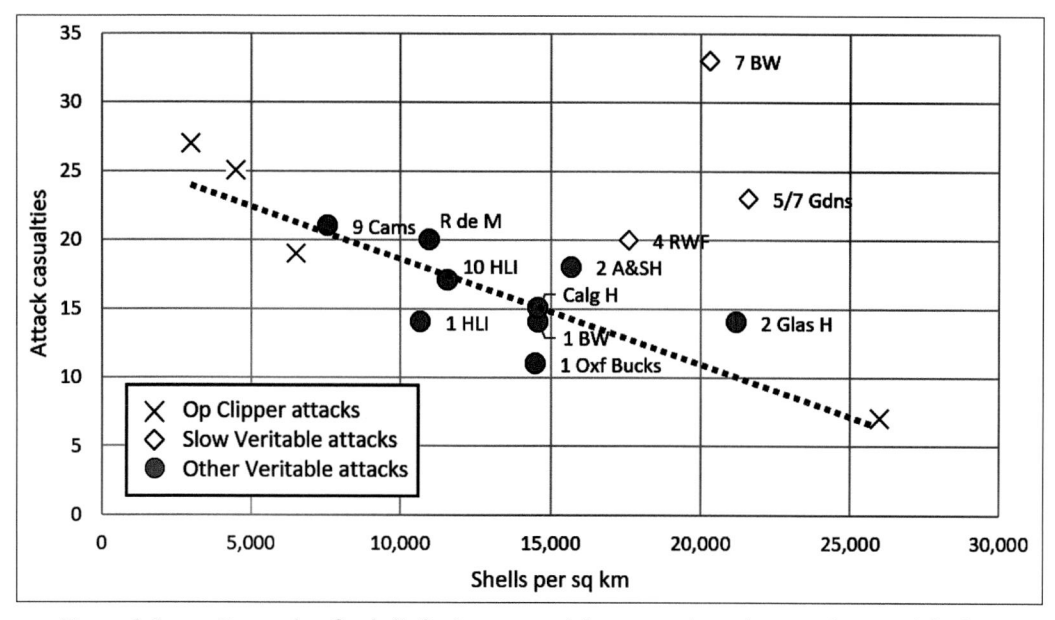

Figure 6: Swann Report data for shells fired per square kilometre and attacker casualties per defending company. Trend line excludes the three delayed attacks.

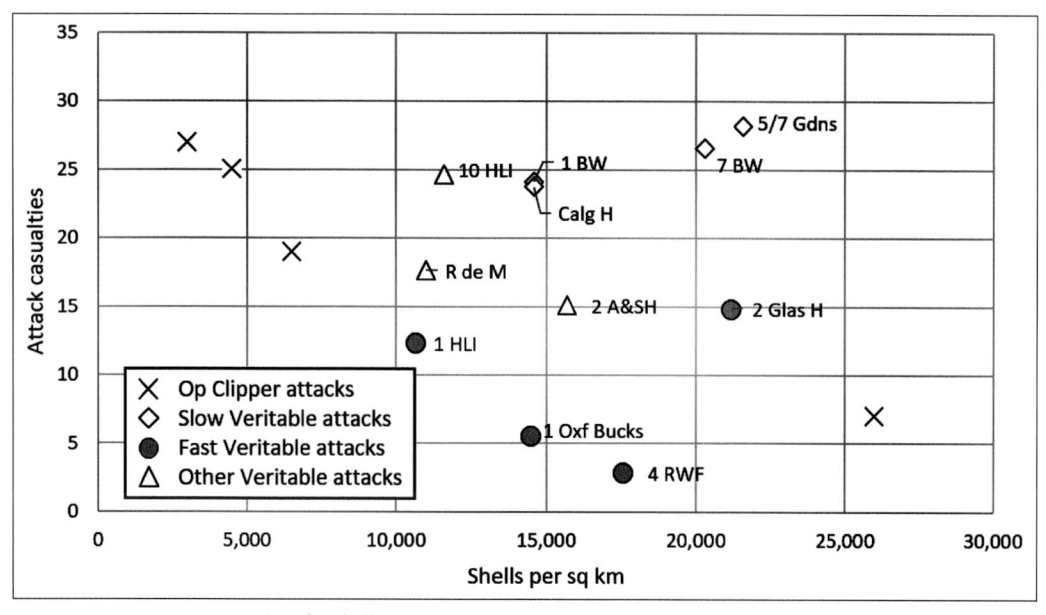

Figure 7: Swann Report data for shells per square kilometre and unit-derived data for attacker casualties per defending company.

records. The 9 Cameronians' losses to Allied artillery put their attack into this group, but with 50 casualties per defending company they were off the scale of these charts.
d) Fast attacks where almost everything went right, with short advances barrage hugging onto rural objectives.

These four categories are neither exclusive nor exhaustive, it being notable that all 51 Division's attacks were late, had no barrage, or lost much of their armour support, while two had an open flank and one fought into a smashed forest in the dark. Several other attacks could be considered urban or suburban, which has many disadvantages for the attacker (examined in Chapter 6), and there were many attacks where the barrage was lost for a short period. The Maisonneuve attack through Den Heuvel was one of the few where primary sources confirm the Swann Report claims that the defenders were 'green-looking', but the report missed the fact that this was a reaction to a depth position enduring a Mattress fire mission that caused heavy casualties.[137]

The most important finding of the reassessment is that something close to the 'complete collapse' at Bauchem (bottom right of Figure 7) could be achieved with around half the shells. That one finding makes the trend line disappear. With every combination of data preparation and analysis of the battalion level data trialled (including comparisons to weight of shell) the trend line only got its shape from the Clipper attacks. The loss of the trend line suggests that increasing the volume of fire above the minimum seen on Veritable's D-Day made little difference to attack casualties. Beyond that, other factors had a greater effect than the number of rounds fired.

With a larger sample it would have been tempting to exclude the flimsy accounts for 2 Glasgow Highlanders and the Maisonneuves, and the two open flank battles. Likewise, the Calgary Highlanders, 9 Cameronians and 5/7 Gordons battles could be excluded because they involved repeat fire missions, partly reversing the suppression relationship. (Rather than their casualties being a result of how many rounds they fired, they fired more rounds because they suffered casualties.) But historical analysis must make the best use of the available data. What this small, messy sample of battles highlights is the variety of tactical factors that undermine alluringly simple explanations like a linear relationship between fire and effectiveness. Despite its weaknesses, the reassessment of the dataset supports the idea that success was very much dependent on a ground assault closely following a fire plan that was just powerful enough to prevent defensive return fire.

Conclusion

Interactions of the elements of effectiveness are already evident in this chapter, with knock-on effects from Veritable's disjointed planning as outlined in Chapter 1, and hints of the logistic and infantry-armour cooperation difficulties that will be examined in later chapters. The flaws in the narrative dominated by the planners' post-operation reports and by commanders' memoirs has also been exposed, with the claim of not a single round falling short being shown to be worryingly false. Likewise, Horrocks's claim of there being no room for manoeuvre and no scope for cleverness has been shown not to apply at the tactical level, where even on this very constrained first day, battalion and company commanders repeatedly improvised to correct a flawed plan.

Exploring even this small dataset has pointed to suppression being far more dependent on rapid assault than on the number of shells fired. As *Slog or Swan* follows 30 Corps through Veritable, it will show how some units strove to closely coordinate fire and manoeuvre, while others naively

---

137 Swann, 'Veritable', p.367; Whitakers, *Rhineland*, p.53. The 46 dead around Den Heuvel is close to Swann's estimate of fatalities for the whole of *84. Division*.

expected a suppressive effect long after fire had lifted. Meanwhile, because barrage hugging did not reach Swann's tables and charts, it escaped the attention of subsequent operational research and artillery doctrine. Indeed in 1946, researchers doubled down on weight and rate of fire but almost ignored the timing of the ground assault.[138] Eight decades later, the problematic graphs from the Swann Report are now coded into fire planning software and units rarely practice assaulting close behind indirect fire.

The Swann Report's implications and weaknesses have also been homogenised by Veritable's historiography, which has bearing on the point where the two sides of the effectiveness debate align, namely the belief that the British Army was good at using artillery. Previous studies have shown that gunnery was well-handled and had a devastating effect in defence.[139] But in the attack, the tactical activity so critical for British Army effectiveness, it would be more appropriate to say that the army was fond of using artillery but only some organisations were good at using it. In Veritable, this inconsistency tended to promote artillery overkill which, as the next chapter will show, helped to undermine 21st Army Group's enormous logistic advantages.

---

138 Dorward and Strong, 'Current state of knowledge', passim.
139 Pemberton, *Artillery Tactics*, passim; Bidwell and Graham, *Fire-Power*, passim.

3

Tactics and Logistics

8 AND 9 FEBRUARY 1945 – BREAKING THROUGH THE WESTWALL – NON-TRADITIONAL LOGISTICS – THE PROBLEM WITH FLAILS – 44 BRIGADE'S "BLERICK JOB" – MYTHOLOGISING MINES AND MUD – MASS NOT VELOCITY – A QUART INTO A PINT POT

Movement and Supply

Historians have often referred to Veritable as an impressive logistical achievement but the history of logistics is as skewed as the history of Veritable, so their praise may be doubly misplaced.[1] The few sources that have examined Allied logistics in any depth have been stifled by the banality of the source material, making particular note of the reams of SHAEF documents, graphs, and tables that contain 'little of real informative value'.[2] The operational vagueness in logistic sources has forced later authors into broad assessments of only the largest organisations, where almost nothing happens below division.[3] The 21st Army Group administrative history is a prime example of operational vagueness, and it reads like a self-congratulatory list of material amassed, roads repaired, and soldiers replaced.[4] But it contains no measure of efficiency or waste, so it is impossible to say whether goods and people got to where they were needed in time or languished in storage and reinforcement centres. In the case of Veritable, the administrative history makes almost no mention of logistics forward of Groesbeek and the whole document reflects a strange detachment of the logistic machine from the fighting troops that it was supposed to serve.

---

1 Liddell Hart, *Second World War*, p.678; Ellis, *Brute Force*, p.426; Fennell, *People's War*, pp.587–598; P. Caddick-Adams, *1945: Victory in the West* (London: Penguin, 2022), pp.92–94.
2 M. Creveld, *Supplying War: Logistics from Wallenstein to Patton* (Cambridge: University Press, 2004), p.206.
3 For example, Dick, *Victory* breaks the logistic problem into four parts, with the final part being 'to deliver from ports or beaches what was needed where and when it was needed' (p.273) but then offers little assessment once material gets near to corps. On the German side, R.A. Hart, 'Feeding Mars: The Role of Logistics in The German Defeat in Normandy, 1944', *War in History*, 1996 3 (4) (pp.418–435) describes a supply chain that ends at divisions. The notable exception is A. D. Bolland, *Team Spirit: The Administration of an Infantry Division during "Operation Overlord"* (Aldershot: Gale & Polden, 1948) which covers logistics within 53 Division, which is inconveniently off the main effort for this chapter.
4 21 AG, *Administrative History*, pp.101–102, 121–122. Division primary sources (e.g., 15 Division Royal Army Service Corps diary, WO 171/4201) are very flimsy.

Veritable's historiography lists of the strength arrayed on D-Day: 268,000 men, 3,400 tanks, 30,000 other vehicles and over 3,000 guns, including anti-tank and anti-aircraft guns. Thirty Corps therefore outnumbered *84. Division* by 20:1 in men, 14:1 in guns, 200:1 in shells, and 3,400:0 in tanks.[5] That accumulation of combat power has impressed many authors, but the Canadian post-operation report is especially effusive: 'If the men assaulting for Phase I were shoulder to shoulder across a 6-mile front, there would be 3.7 men per yard, while Corps reserve would supply 1.1 men per yard. This excludes Artillery, Engineers, Services and Echelons.' These men were supplied with 350 ammunition types which, if 'stacked side by side and 5 feet high … would line the road from Toronto to Oshawa' (50km), while artillery allocation up to D+3 equalled 'a raid by 25,000 medium bombers.' Among the more mundane supplies that are bragged about is enough unnecessary winter camouflage to 'make a dress for every woman in the Province of Ontario between the ages of 20 and 24'. To get all of this into the Nijmegen area involved 446 freight trains transporting 'a tonnage equal to 89,200 three-ton army lorry loads which, if placed end to t ail, would stretch from London to Edinburgh' (530km).[6] To make sure the roads could carry all this material 'twelve formations of engineers, three road construction companies and twenty-nine pioneer companies' (perhaps as many as 15,000 men) were set to work on repairing and maintaining the routes into Nijmegen.[7]

Yet the delivery of troops, machines, and supplies to a corps hub is a relatively trivial matter, particularly for the Western Allies who enjoyed air supremacy and a supportive civilian population. The real difficulties lay in the "last mile" of the logistic chain, where the challenge was to get goods, services and (to use an awkward modern doctrine phrase) *effects* from the depot to the customer. To understand the interaction of logistics and tactics, this chapter extends a few concepts that were alien to Veritable's logisticians.[8] The first concept sees logistics as 'the movement and support of forces'; the second is that 'all elements of [a force] execute tactical logistics'.[9] Merging these concepts allows tactical logistics to become "the movement and supply of forces in contact with the enemy to enable the efficient achievement of operational goals." By this expedient definition, tactical logistics is an essential component of manoeuvre, rather than simple service provision. The definition demands logisticians and combat arms share responsibility for movement and supply in that last mile – and for ensuring the transport infrastructure in that "last" mile (and the next, and the next as the organisation advances) can support movement and supply of forces.

The definition comes close to expressing the way tactics and logistics overlap in the last mile, and stop being discrete entities studied separately by 'amateurs' and 'professionals'.[10] So, the definition is a long-winded way of including logistics in the age-old soldierly principle of anticipation, because tactical logistics requires combat arms to capture towns, roads, railheads, and bridges intact, or as intact as possible, and requires logisticians to avoid overwhelming this infrastructure with superfluous forces and supplies. The soldiers of 30 Corps were simultaneously providers

---

5   21 AG, *Administrative History*, pp.101–102; Johnson, 'Counter-battery'; Fiebig, '84th Infantry'; Conacher and Harrison, 'Veritable', pp.10, 14, Appendix E.
6   Conacher and Harrison, 'Veritable', Appendix E.
7   BAOR, *Tour*, p.33. No personnel data could be found for these groupings, so 15,000 is a conservative estimate that coys equalled their infantry equivalent and a 'formation' was battalion sized.
8   These concepts appear to be unknown to many twenty-first century organisations too, with repeated audits showing enormous waste along the last mile in Iraq and Afghanistan. K.F. Daniels, 'The Distribution Dilemma: That Last Tactical Mile', *Army Logistician* 40(5) 2008.
9   Joint Chiefs of Staff, *Joint Logistics* (Washington: Joint Chiefs, 2019), p.186; United States Marine Corps, Tactical-Level Logistics, (Twentynine Palms: USMC, 2016), p.12.
10 From the phrase "amateurs talk about tactics, but professionals study logistics", usually attributed to General R. H. Barrow, USMC, c1980.

and customers of tactical logistics, but it is also useful to consider the soldiers of *84. Division* as customers, for if those thousands of tanks, kilotonnes of ammunition, and hectares of camouflage material had no effect on *84. Division*, they were waste. Likewise, all the food, fuel, blankets, and rum (53 Division consumed nearly half its Northwest Europe rum ration during Veritable) were only of value if they supported the delivery of effect.[11] All the rest was waste, the bane of any logistic system.

Waste puts tactical logistics at the heart of the friction between concentration of force and economy of effort.[12] Concentrating at one point obviously weakens another, but concentration is also subject to diminishing returns. Environmental and tactical constraints (streams, woods, beaten zones of machine-gun fire) can make the extreme force ratios seen on Veritable's D-Day impractical, because attackers get in each other's way, become disorganised or bunch up in killing areas, and so yield worse results than the benchmark 3:1 ratio. Waste in this context is more than inefficiency because it increases attacker casualties and reduces the effect on the enemy.[13] Likewise, firepower and armour overkill damage the infrastructure needed for subsequent supply and movement.

By focusing on tactical logistics in the opening phases of Veritable, this chapter relates few traditional logistic problems, such as units running short of food or ammunition. Those problems will appear in later chapters, but the cause was seen on D-Day and the effect on the movement of forces was most evident on D+1. So, where the Veritable core narrative has a cunning concentration of force undermined by unfortunate mines and mud, this chapter aims to demonstrate how a failure to apply economy of effort caused Veritable's tactical logistic problems. In other words, this chapter will show how failing to address the impact of firepower and armour overkill on the known weaknesses of the Rhineland infrastructure *caused* Veritable to become more of an attritional slog.

Mines and Mud

Before the effect on movement of forces is examined, the causes need to be outlined, and these run up to and through Veritable's D-Day. The expected thaw and intelligence on the weak defence have already been noted, but evidence that the road network would fail had been plentiful for months, hence the vast effort directed on the roads to Nijmegen. Despite these efforts, Allied-controlled roads were 'rapidly going to pieces in the thaw, the edges crumbling away like toffee under the wheels of heavy vehicles.'[14] Then, long before the tide came in on 7 February, reports noted how floods in December had left the ground 'mucky and covered with scattered pools … abandoned channels, ditches, marsh and backwaters.'[15] This ground was boggier than that leading to Nijmegen, with fewer roads, but it was expected to supply and move the same force, and to do so while under fire.

In 15 Division, 2 A&SH bemoaned the fact that the routes from Nijmegen to forward assembly areas in Groesbeek woods had not been touched by engineers: 'It seemed fantastic that the

---

11   Bolland, *Team Spirit*, pp.26–27.
12   Principles of war from Directorate General of Development and Doctrine, *Operations* (Warminster: DGD&D, 1994), ii.
13   This is demonstrated in David Rowland's operational research, as outlined in *Stress of Battle*. To give local context, in personnel terms, "B" Coy 2 A&SH repeatedly succeeded by attacking with a force ratio little better than 1:1. "C" Coy, 10 HLI did the same in Kranenburg.
14   Blake, *Mountain*, p.149.
15   Conacher and Harrison, 'Veritable', p.17.

operation should have been jeopardised by the lack of foresight in making up the tracks to the FAA.'[16] Battalions predicted problems on these routes but could do little more than alter their orders of march to ensure lighter vehicles moved ahead of the heavy armour that would damage the tracks.[17] Battalions also had no control over the movement of units ahead of them, and the forward assembly areas had been occupied days earlier by multiple artillery regiments, each comprised of more than 100 vehicles. Even 2 A&SH, the centre-forward unit of the centre-forward formation, had to rescue bogged carriers on the way to their assembly area. Then, on the routes from assembly areas to forming-up places, many assets were stuck behind vehicles that mired while fording streams that had not been bridged, or behind Small Box Girder bridges (see Figure 8) that snagged in roadside trees that had not been cut back.[18] Follow-on units like 10 HLI had even worse problems because they were using tracks ploughed or blocked by the first traffic bow wave.

All of these logistic problems happened on ground that the Allies had controlled for five months. Forward of the start lines, tactical considerations put heavy armour ahead of lighter vehicles. From that point on, an essential part of the logistic plan was the established practice of separating wheeled and tracked movement, with wheeled vehicles using the existing road network, while tracked vehicles moved off-road to prevent damage to the wheeled routes.[19] This is where tactics and logistics most obviously collided because right across the front, tank crews were compelled to choose between moving off-road and risk bogging, or to ignore orders, use surfaced roads, and make later movement and supply more difficult.

The Flail tanks were the most obvious failure. Of the five Flail Squadrons deployed by the British divisions, only one vehicle was reported to have cleared a lane ahead of the assaulting infantry: a success rate of around one in 70. This debacle seems to have surprised 30 Corps, and while many sources mention trials between the thaw and D-Day to see whether the Flails could cope with the soft ground, none describe the result and most imply a successful outcome.[20] The important exception is the diary of the First Lothians and Border Yeomanry (1 Lothians), who ran those trials. Using only one Flail on ground that was not riddled with trenches or subjected to hours of artillery bombardment, and possibly on higher, drier ground than that crossed on D-Day, the Lothians discovered that they had to halve the revolutions of the flail drum to avoid it digging itself into a ditch.[21] This worrying finding was reported to 30 Corps, and should have generated warnings that the assault would have to rely on manual mine clearing or risk cluttering the battlefield with bogged vehicles. Instead, the near-useless Flails were pushed forward, trapping manual mine clearing stores behind them. And so most units were unprepared when they had to cross uncleared minefields, leading to unnecessary delays and casualties from mines and defensive fire.

Yet the trial results were themselves old news. The Sherman Crab was the last in a line of flail tanks that had evolved to operate in the North African desert. They were an excellent tool in dry conditions, where they were far preferable to manual mine clearing, but their limitations became apparent on the wet patches of the Normandy beaches and kept reappearing right through the

---

16   2 A&SH diary.
17   "Heavy armour" is used here for tracked AFVs except half-tracks, carriers, and armoured reconnaissance vehicles like the M3 Stuart/Honey. Inconveniently, the Honey was slightly heavier than the Archer tank destroyer.
18   Whether these essential preparations had been lost to the deception plan, to friction, or lack of forethought is not mentioned in any source examined.
19   15 Division HQRE diary (WO 171/4198).
20   For example, BAOR, *Tour*, p.33.
21   The flail motors usually ran at 2,000rpm to turn the drum at 180rpm, allowing the tank to advance at 2.6kph. The trial was able to run the motors at only 800rpm. D. Fletcher, *Sherman Crab Flail Tank* (Oxford: Osprey, 2007) pp.33–34; 1 Lothians diary (WO 171/4702).

Figure 8: An AVRE carrying a fascine (left) following another with a Small Box Girder bridge. In the distance between them is a turretless "Jumbo" bridge-layer. (battlefieldhistorian.com)

campaign. One of the lost lessons of the Scheldt was that the ungainly, heavy, and narrow-tracked Flails were a liability on soft ground, becoming mired in their own ploughed furrows or smashing the surface of paved roads.[22] It seems 1 Lothians passed the whole truth of the Flail trials to 51 Division, which they supported, because the Division directed them to stay on the roads and tracks from the outset, which reduced their bogging but damaged the paved surface.[23]

Beyond the minefields, the congestion problem was as much due to bottlenecking as sodden ground. Like the old joke where a city-dweller asks why farmers put their gates in the muddiest parts of fields, the resolution is that traffic at chokepoints creates the morass. The valley bottom between Groesbeek and the Reichswald was a series of chokepoints, the ground being criss-crossed with drainage channels that forced any off-road tank to hazard a small but slippery obstacle crossing every 100 metres. (Note the profusion of field boundaries at Map 6; each was a drainage channel.) The drainage system was then overlaid by *84. Division*'s field works, which comprised a network of zig-zagging damp ditches littered with camouflaged troop shelters and heavy weapon positions that were pitfall traps for tanks.

Laid across all of this was a fire plan that averaged an impact every five metres: 'it transpired that the ground, already soft from rain, had become quite impassable due to the concussion of the shells of the opening barrage'.[24] But of course, the fire plan concentrated on defensive positions, which

---

22 Phil Brazier of the Royal Engineers Historical Society ('The 79th Armoured Division in Operation Infatuate – Walcheren 1944', WW2TV, 16 April 2021) notes a historiographic gap, with post-operation reports, Fletcher's, *Crab*, BAOR, *Royal Engineers Battlefield Tour: The Seine to the Rhine* (Hanover: BAOR, 1947), and 79th Armoured Division, *Final Report* (Germany: 21 Army Group, 1945), all passim, underplaying the extent of Flail bogging. See also 21 Army Group 'Report on Operation "Blackcock"' (CAB 106/974), p.18.

23 1 Lothians diary. The late arrival of armour supporting the 51 Division attacks (Ch 2) may have been the result of pushing Flails forward, but records are vague on this point.

24 1 Oxf Bucks diary. Also J.R.P. Baggaley, *The 6th (Border) Battalion The King's Own Scottish Borderers 1939–1945* (Germany: Publisher unknown, 1945), p.78. This was a familiar effect in the First World War: Bidwell and Graham, *Fire-Power*, pp.113, 116–117. Five metre estimate based on Swann and excludes 81mm, 40mm and 7.7mm.

were thickest around road junctions, and these had drainage channels alongside them. These overlaid patterns of broken ground served to compound the effect of bogging in the very places where tanks were most likely to go.

Despite the dampness, the trenches, and the artillery pounding, the first handful of vehicles usually got through with little trouble, even fording some of the streams, but a few track spins or some vigorous turning made life more difficult for any following vehicle. Tanks were inevitably forced onto roads at the worst chokepoints but then the dilemma for crews was whether to stay on the road or repeatedly get on and off, each time riding over the fragile edge of the paved surface and performing a neutral turn. The frequency of drainage channels and trenches peaked around the Groesbecker Bach, but by that point it seems all the tanks were using roads all the time.

Chokepoint congestion was exaggerated for 15 Division which was due to be the main effort, and therefore had three Churchill regiments compared to just one in 51 Division. For 2 A&SH this meant attacking with 60 items of heavy armour and 40 lighter tracked vehicles, making them a battalion group with more armour than the whole of *1. Fallschirm-Armee*.[25] And so, after being pounded by artillery and the first wave of armour, their main supply route, the *Kranenburgsche Straat* was transformed into, 'one long traffic jam as the leading vehicles bogged down. Tracked vehicles cut ruts in the narrow road until they bellied, and recovery vehicles could not get forward to help.'[26]

The worst damage was where the Kranenburgsche Straat turned northeast towards Kranenburg, and it reached this state because the Churchills supporting 2 Glasgow Highlanders and 2 A&SH had followed the fire plan ahead of the 'lead vehicles' of the traffic jam. At least one of their Churchills kept up with the infantry by following the road far enough to fire into the Kranenburg railway station as 10 HLI attacked. There is no direct evidence that the bend in the road was subject to particular artillery attention, but it seems likely. Swann has the surrounding area subject to one of the heavier bombardments and defence overprints have a prominently marked mortar position right on the turn. In an effort to get around the traffic, 15 Division brought forward a pioneer company to lift the railway line into Kranenburg and make a route for wheeled vehicles, but congestion was so bad it took almost as long to get the pioneers forward as it did for them to lift a kilometre of track.[27]

By 13:00 most roads were unusable for anything but dismounted troops and the lumbering Churchills, which were generally the Allies' most capable off-road fighting vehicles. By 16:00 most infantrymen were attacking without any armoured support at all. To illustrate the extent of this failure, it is worth comparison with the first ever tank battle at Flers-Courcelette on 15 September 1916. Of the 49 tanks deployed for that battle, only 32 reached their start line, nine failed to marry-up with the infantry, nine more broke down, five bogged, and only nine contributed to the assault on the final objective: an 18 percent success rate. For Veritable's break-in battle, even a charitable reading of sources has only five of more than 80 Churchills reaching the final objectives in time to support the infantry: a six percent success rate. Excepting the Frasselt assault, which was held back for two hours to allow Crocodiles to catch up, no specialist armour was reported to have

---

25 2 A&SH OO 1, corroborated with 3 Scots Guards, 22 Dgns, 141 RAC and 10 HLI diaries. The full list of 2 A&SH heavy armour was two sqns of Churchills and part of the Regt HQ, two troops of Flails and Sqn HQ, a tp of Crocodiles, a tp of 17pdr tank destroyers, a pair of AVRE Small Box Girder bridges, a pair of standard petard-firing AVREs (likely carrying fascines), two armoured bulldozers, two Sherdozers and at least one armoured FOO. It seems 198 SP AT Battery (WO 171/4784, 2 Feb) was in transition between Valentine (Archer) and M10 (Achilles). The Guards diary mentions Valentines and M10s but no towed guns.
26 BAOR, *Engineers Tour*, p.169.
27 15 Division HQRE diary; Swann/Copp p.367; 3 Scots Guards diary.

reached any of the final objectives for that day.[28] The comparison with Flers-Courcelette is only an indicator (terrain, technology and weather being so different) but is instructive because Flers-Courcelette is presented as an example of how ineffective early tanks were. In Veritable's historiography, despite a much lower success rate, there has been no attempt to understand how ineffective the tanks were. Instead, 21st Army Group's logistic might is glorified by listing the thousands of tanks that had no effect on the enemy then lamenting the allegedly unrelated bogging.

Gilbert and Sullivan

As the barrage ended at 16:40 an operational pause began, and a large proportion of the field guns moved forward to support the Westwall breakthrough battle. Other guns turned their attentions to 3 Canadian Division's amphibious flank protection task.[29] The transition was hindered somewhat because every formation except 53 Division was late securing its objectives, although the only delay likely to have operational impact was in Wyler where the Calgary Highlanders had to secure the first section of the main road from Nijmegen.[30] The operational pause was due to end at 21:00 when 15 Division would renew its musically themed five-phase plan. In Chapter 2, the "Gilbert" phase had put 2 A&SH and 10 HLI from 227 Brigade through Kranenburg and onto the northern half of Phase Line Hot Dog (the north–south road on Maps 11 and 13), while 2 Glasgow Highlanders and 9 Cameronians from 46 Brigade had advanced through Haus Kreuzfuhrt to the southern half of Hot Dog at Frasselt. In the "Sullivan" phase, 44 Brigade would use Hot Dog as its start line, striking from there to pierce the main defensive line of the Westwall.

Breaching the Westwall was seen as a historic event by the men of 44 Brigade. Newsreel images of dragon's teeth and concrete gun emplacements had made the Siegfried Line a bogeyman to Allied troops. And for men whose fathers had fought through the Hindenburg Line, there was a feeling this would be the climactic struggle after which the *Reich* would collapse. Robert Woollcombe of Sixth Battalion, The King's Own Scottish Borderers (6 KOSB, the focus unit for this chapter) believed that: 'The Rhine may have stood for the mystique of our enemies, but the Siegfried Line seemed their brute embodiment. The Rhine was symbolic, the Rhine was Victory, but the Siegfried barrier had a grimmer significance.'[31] Woollcombe recalled gasps when Brigadier Cumming-Bruce introduced his plan: 'The other two brigades are going to reach the Siegfried Line, and then our Brigade is going to go through the Siegfried Line'.[32]

As with the Gilbert phase, there would be prodigious artillery support for Sullivan, but the armoured mass would be even greater and the attack frontage narrower. Anticipating a strong defensive belt, 44 Brigade planned to recycle a recipe it had used with remarkable success at

---

28 P. Harris, 'An Examination of the use of Tanks in the "Hundred Days Campaign" of 1918' (University of Wolverhampton PhD thesis, 2020). Bidwell and Graham *Fire-Power* (p.135) has a list of loss types at Cambrai but no figure for how many tanks reached the objective. Other references examined include, C.F. French, 'The 51st (Highland) Division During the First World War' (Glasgow University PhD thesis, 2006); J. Boff, J. 'Combined Arms during the Hundred Days Campaign, August-November 1918', *War in History*, 17(4) 2010, pp.459–478.
29 Winslow and Brassey, *Leicestershire Yeomanry*, pp.61–63.
30 30 Corps diary has Calgary Highlanders 'clearing up odd Germans' as late as 23:15.
31 Woollcombe, *Lion*, Kindle 2923.
32 *Lion*, Kindle 2930. Cumming-Bruce was: 'One of those insouciant types who might have been born for war, and a descendant of Robert the Bruce', Kindle 2926. Woollcombe appears to have been Company Second in Command at the time, but his account gets a little vague just before Veritable and he may have become an officer without portfolio. He was posted out of the battalion on a training course three days after this attack.

Blerick in December. The 'Blerick job' had been described in *The Times* as 'The Perfect Battle' and was arguably the birth of the modern armoured infantry concept.[33] But Blerick had been the product of extensive reconnaissance; for Sullivan there had been no chance to reconnoitre routes or forming-up places and 44 Brigade's commanders had seen their objectives only on maps and air photographs. As the Brigade's history recalled: 'it was not thought that the enemy had many troops in this second line, and if surprise was achieved, if the German defenders of the outpost line were overwhelmed, if the weather was dry and the going good, if few mines were encountered – then the attack should succeed. But there were many "Ifs".'[34]

The Brigade (Figure 9) would assault from Frasselt at 21:00 to punch through the main defensive belt in Schottheide, 1,000 metres to the east and just over a low hill. There was known to be an anti-tank ditch on the reverse slope (shown as under construction at Map 13), and the ground around it was expected to be heavily mined, registered for indirect fire and covered by pillboxes built into Schottheide's houses. This defensive system was to be penetrated by an armoured breaching force headed by two squadrons of Flails and two engineer companies with Kangaroos (turretless Ram tanks used as armoured personnel carriers), AVREs, Small Box Girder bridges, fascines, armoured bulldozers and Sherdozers. The fighting component of the breaching force would be two squadrons of Churchills from 4th (Tank) Battalion, The Grenadier Guards (4 GG), two armoured FOO teams and two infantry companies in Kangaroos. One of these companies would be drawn from Eighth Battalion, The Royal Scots, the other was 6 KOSB's "C" Company. These components would be split into five self-contained all-arms groups, each responsible for cutting its own lane through the minefield and across the ditch, then holding a small bridgehead just short of Schottheide.[35] The lanes were to follow tracks north of the word Frasselt at Map 13, using the method indicated at Figure 10.[36]

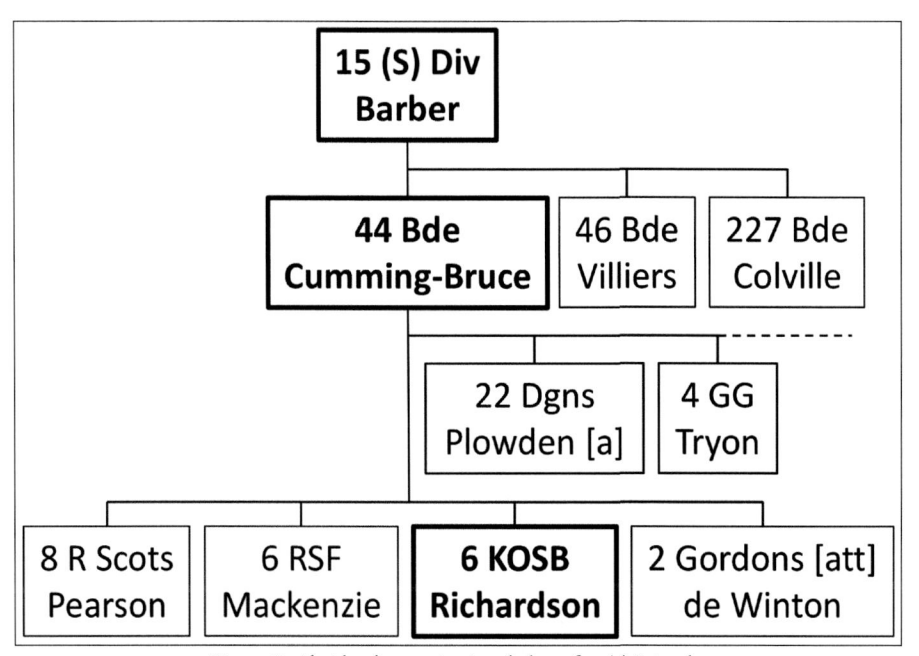

Figure 9: Abridged organisational chart for 44 Brigade.

---

33   Advocate, *From Normandy*, Kindle 1269.
34   Advocate, *From Normandy*, Kindle 1516.
35   44 Brigade OO 5 (WO 171/4366).
36   79 Division, *Final Report*, p.139.

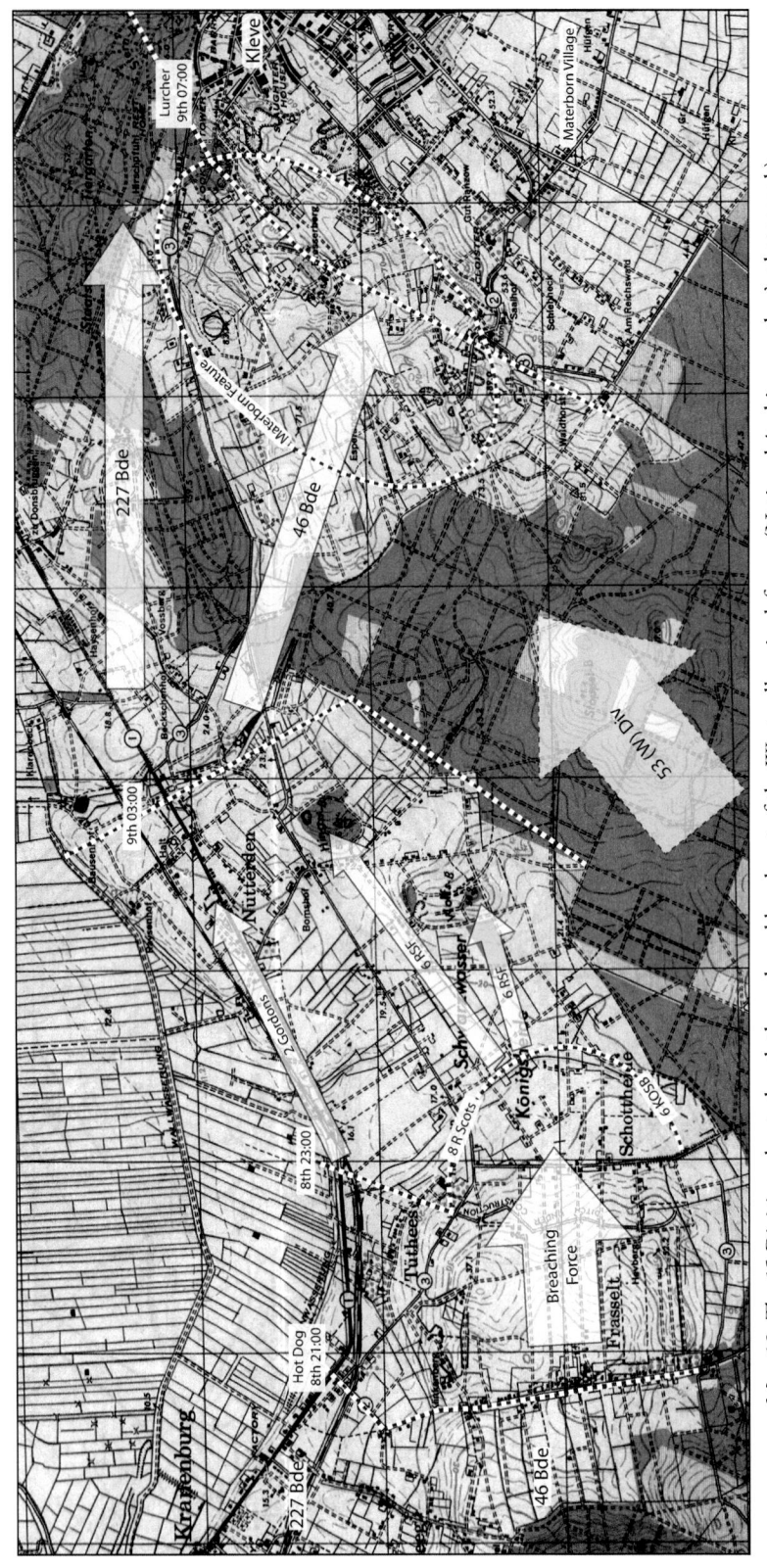

Map 13: The 15 Division plan to break through and break out of the Westwall main defence. (National Archives, author's photograph)

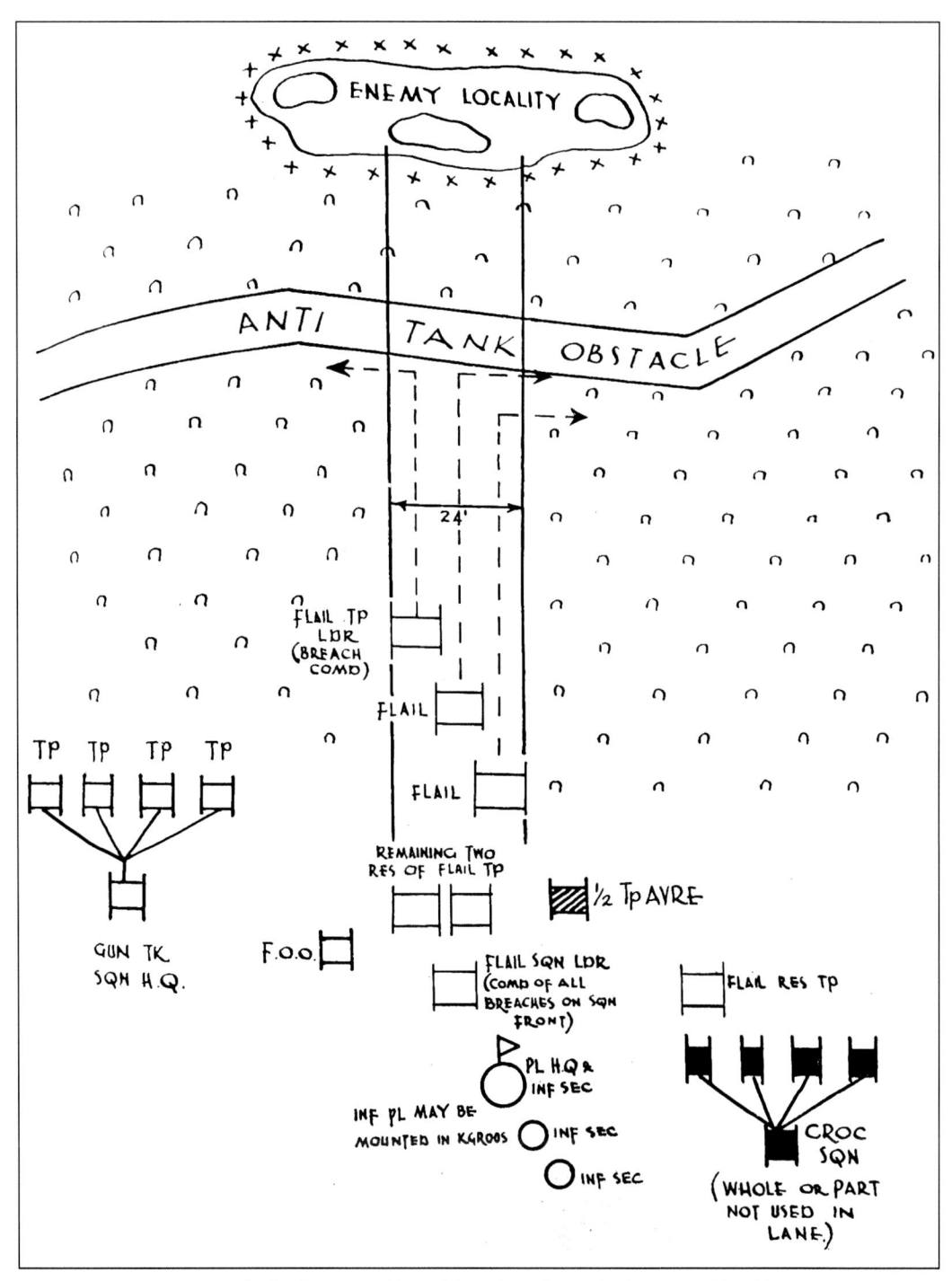

Figure 10: An idealised armoured breach based on the method attempted by 44 Brigade.
(79 Division, Final Report / battlefieldhistorian.com)

Once the bridgeheads were in place, the remainder of the infantry from 8 Royal Scots and 6 KOSB would secure the village with plenty of specialist armoured support. The AVRE petards would crack open pillboxes then Crocodiles would pour in rods of flame; all going well, the infantry would only need to debouch from their Kangaroos to sweep up prisoners and ash. To secure a more defensible lodgement, each battalion would push out 500 metres from Schottheide (marked as 8th 23:00 at Map 13) then Sixth Battalion, The Royal Scots Fusiliers (6 RSF) would assault depth positions on two knolls: Wolfsberg, 1,500 metres past the breach, and Hingstberg, another kilometre to the northeast.[37]

Meanwhile, just to the north but launching a little later than the main force, Second Battalion the Gordon Highlanders (2 Gordons, attached from 227 Brigade) were to attack up the main road to Nutterden. The Gordons' infantry would advance on foot with support from a Scots Guards tank squadron, a few troops of specialist armour, and an engineer platoon. The Nutterden defence was believed to be equal to that in Schottheide but was expected to collapse once the fast-moving armoured main force had punched through in the south.[38] As with Kranenburg, the Nutterden defence was to be degraded by firebombing early on D-Day, with Horrocks specifically requesting the use of 'liquid fire' (napalm) to maximise enemy casualties and shock without rubble and craters blocking the roads.[39] Having secured Wolfsberg, Hingstberg and Nutterden, 44 Brigade would have broken through the main Westwall by 03:00 and Sullivan would be complete (9th 03:00 at Map 13). At that point 46 and 227 Brigades would launch "Layton", the breakout phase to Phase Line Lurcher (9th 07:00).

An Open Door, but Narrow

The 15 Division plan had tight timings, several changes in task organisation and many moving parts, with at least nine parent units contributing to the battalion-sized breaching force. While movement light would help coordination, and rehearsals had tested radio nets and procedures, there were many opportunities for Sullivan to become derailed. Come the day, even getting to Frasselt proved extremely difficult because the road network that had collapsed under 200 heavy vehicles during Gilbert was expected to cope with another 300 for Sullivan. The narrow gap between these armoured waves was to be filled with the support vehicles for all the Gilbert assault battalions and by five field artillery regiments that were aiming to deploy around the traffic jam at the bend in the Kranenburgsche Straat.[40]

Forty-four Brigade had planned to move from Nijmegen by following the rest of the Division along the Kranenburgsche Straat to Haus Kreuzfuhrt but then leave the road and head due east to Frasselt along the muddy farm track that had already caused so much trouble for 9 Cameronians. Given the traffic and the state of the roads, most of 44 Brigade was diverted north to use the rubble-strewn main road through Wyler, and then through Kranenburg, which was choked with 227 Brigade's vehicles. The inevitable delays proved difficult to predict and work around.[41]

As traffic chaos mounted, so too did evidence that this massive force would not be needed: no concrete fighting positions had been found, all the minefields proved to be very weak (except

---

37   44 Brigade OO 5; Advocate, *From Normandy*, pp.86–87.
38   44 Brigade OO 5; Gordons (WO 171/5197) 8–9 February.
39   21 AG, *Veritable*, 17; Veritable Planning Note 5, 30 Corps diary.
40   HQRA 15 Division OO 4, lists five field regiments (86, 131, 147, 181 and 190) overlapping in the grid square just north of Haus Kreuzfuhrt. Two were self-propelled, each with 24 armoured gun mounts, 46 half-tracks, 13 armoured OPs, and dozens of wheeled vehicles. See 'Organisation' at nigelef.tripod.com.
41   15 Division HQRE diary; 15 Division comms log; Martin *15th Scottish*, pp.236–237.

perhaps at the Calgaries "ambush" site), and no enemy armour had been seen. Only one tank had been a casualty to defensive fire, and infantry casualties were much lighter than anticipated. Above all this, the huge prisoner haul showed that the main enemy force had been met, trapped, and defeated in the forward line.[42] Meanwhile, 15 Division's own units had pushed patrols out to the anti-tank ditch, where they found gaps through the minefields, that the main road bridge was intact, and little sign of defenders beyond.[43] Despite all this evidence, the mass of 44 Brigade was pressed forward because of the difficulties getting this intelligence back to a point where a decision could be made.

As the first battalion in 44 Brigade's order of march, 6 KOSB should have inched forward during the daylight hours, but instead they were held in Nijmegen until the road through Wyler was cleared at 21:00.[44] Their "C" Company were assigned to the breaching force, so they set off immediately, but 'found it impossible to get up to the start line in any sort of order.'[45] The rest of 6 KOSB moved an hour later, also using the Wyler route, on which they spent 'a hellish night of being banged and jerked about in open Kangaroos in continual rain, crawling and stopping and getting stuck, and interminably lurching forward again … soaked through and cramped and half asleep'.[46] Meanwhile the armoured engineers and Flails were still committed to the direct route using the Kranenburgsche Straat and farm track, where delays included a top-heavy Small Box Girder bridge overturning on rough ground. The resulting confusion caused five changes to H-Hour until, at 02:30 on the 9th, the forming-up place was moved to a more practical location and H-Hour was set at 04:00.[47]

Liaison officers were sent out into the night to inform the dispersed components of the breaching force of this change, but were only partly successful. The new H-Hour was met but the breaching force commander, the Flail troop leaders, most of the infantry, sappers and AVREs, and many of the Churchills were left behind.[48] Of the five lanes through the minefield, only two were cleared and one of these was soon blocked when a towed anti-tank gun became entangled in the bridge.[49] With the assault group at barely a quarter of its planned strength, its intentions clearly telegraphed to the enemy by the slow, noisy build-up, and then its approach silhouetted by movement light, the breaching operation had all the hallmarks of disaster.

Instead, the breaching force crossed unopposed. Churchills fanned out just short of the ditch and began firing into Schottheide, some Flails followed, finding no mines west of the ditch and perhaps only one on the eastern side. Despite all the armour deployed, dismounted sappers were needed to prove the routes east of the crossing. No Allied casualties were reported for this phase of the attack, and no source mentions defensive fire, so there may have been no active defence at all.[50] However, with only a few sections of infantry to hand, Schottheide could not be secured until 6

---

42   15 and 53 Divisions comms logs; 30 Corps diary.
43   9 Cams diary, SSVC/Dennis, *Rhineland*, part 1.
44   44 Brigade OO 5, 5 February; Report by 2 Canadian Division, 18:49 and phantom intercept, 18:15, 30 Corps diary of events (WO 205/954); 15 Division comms log; 6 KOSB diary.
45   Advocate, *From Normandy*, Kindle 1552.
46   Woollcombe, *Lion*, Kindle 2972.
47   15 Division comms log; 22 Dgns diary; P. Forbes, *Grenadier Guards*, p.194.
48   15 Division comms log; 22 Dgns diary; BAOR, *Engineers Tour*, pp.170–171; Forbes, *Grenadier Guards*, p.194. The breaching force commander seems to have sat out the assault in 15 Div's Tac HQ.
49   Four lanes were completed after the assault. It is an indication of the confusion that a towed gun, normally among the last assets deployed, was among the first over the bridge. The AT gun story appears in many sources (e.g., 'Entry in Germany', 81 Assault Sqn RE diary, WO 171/5325) but conflicts with BAOR, *Engineers Tour* (p.171), which claims a purloined German trailer wedged between girders.
50   BAOR, *Engineers Tour*, p.171; 44 Brigade and 6 KOSB diaries; BAOR, *Tour*, p.47. Advocate, *From Normandy*, (Kindle 1563) has the RSM hanging symbolic washing on the Siegfried Line.

KOSB's "C" Company HQ arrived two hours later. At that point, a composite force amounting to perhaps two infantry companies, a Churchill squadron and a handful of specialist vehicles set to work. They soon secured the village, an objective originally set for a force four times their size, and by 08:00 they were digging in, having passed 'through the Siegfried Line almost without noticing it'.[51]

With army, corps, and division all intensely focused on Schottheide, and constantly demanding progress reports, 2 Gordons (just to the north) were almost forgotten.[52] Temporarily attached to 44 Brigade for the Sullivan phase, they should have moved to Kranenburg around 17:00 on D-Day but had somehow fallen through the cracks and remained in Groesbeek woods until called forward at 02:00. By advancing on foot, 2 Gordons reached Kranenburg in 90 minutes rather than the nine hours it took the main body of 6 KOSB in Kangaroos. Then, after a nervous wait for support vehicles carrying their breakfast and rum ration, the Gordons married-up with their tank squadron and at 05:30 began advancing towards Nutterden, seemingly unaware that the planned firebombing (like that for Kranenburg) had been cancelled. Like 6 KOSB, 2 Gordons met negligible opposition. They found bridges and culverts not blown, demolition charges strapped to trees but unfired, and mines stacked neatly by the roadside. Despite a later H-Hour, 2 Gordons soon overtook 6 KOSB, and by 10:00 had captured Nutterden and 135 prisoners, all without a single friendly casualty being recorded.[53]

Back in Schottheide, after waiting four more hours for the other battalions to catch up, 6 KOSB were ordered to press on and capture 6 RSF's objectives at Wolfsberg and Hingstberg (Map 14).[54] The rising ground and improved going that came with it meant that 6 KOSB's companies could advance in Kangaroos with close tank support, although some chose to move on foot, and some drove along the cleared main road through Nutterden. One tank squadron advanced unsupported onto its objective where it was shelled by 25pdrs, but unharmed. By 14:00, 6 KOSB had cleared both objectives, captured 213 prisoners and suffered only 10 casualties, half of these from a 'Bazooka' attack on a Kangaroo.[55] As Woollcombe recalled: 'Once over the anti-tank ditch we debouched and advanced to our objectives, while whole bodies of enemy, their N.C.O.s in front, came doubling across the fields in perfect columns to give themselves up.'[56]

Unlike the men captured on D-Day, most of the prisoners on D+1 were not infantrymen who had been pinned down by fire then overrun by close combat; these were rear area troops who had been under intermittent but often intense fire for 32 hours and so they were likely suffering from

---

51 H. Gunning, *Borderers in Battle. The War Story of The King's Own Scottish Borderers 1939–1945* (Edinburgh: Martin, 1948). Forbes, *Grenadier Guards*, pp.194–195 describes a more spontaneous affair, with 4 Grenadier Guards struggling through the night then 'by a freak of chance' realising the Germans were not defending Schottheide and breezing across. Compared to primary sources, BAOR, *Tour* (p.47) has more lanes cleared, then all of 6 KOSB and most of the breaching force in place.

52 44 Brigade, 227 Brigade and 2 Gordons diaries. The 15 Division comms log makes no mention of 2 Gordons until 21:30, when 44 Brigade had to relay orders through Division and 227 Brigade.

53 2 Gordons, diary; 15 Division comms log; CWGC. On the evening of the 9th a shell scored a direct hit on Bn HQ, causing 11 casualties, apparently their only losses. The Scots Guards diary has the advance slightly later and the prisoners at 200, a number repeated in secondary sources but probably an overestimate.

54 44 Brigade, 6 KOSB and 8 Royal Scots diaries; Advocate, *From Normandy*, p.90. Curiously, 6 RSF diary, J. C. Kemp, *The History of the Royal Scots Fusiliers 1919–1959* (Glasgow: Maclehose, 1963) and S. W. McBain (ed.), *A Regiment at War: The Royal Scots 1939–45* (Edinburgh: Pentland, 1988) have no detail on this day's action. Though edited by Horrocks, A. M. Brander's *The Royal Scots (The Royal Regiment)* (London: Leo Cooper, 1975) sets this action in January.

55 Baggaley, *6th (Border) Battalion*, p.80; 15 Division comms log; 6 KOSB diary. The 'bazooka' was likely a *Panzerfaust*. Sources contain very few clear reports of the more capable *Panzerschreck*.

56 Woollcombe, *Lion*, Kindle 2994.

TACTICS AND LOGISTICS 95

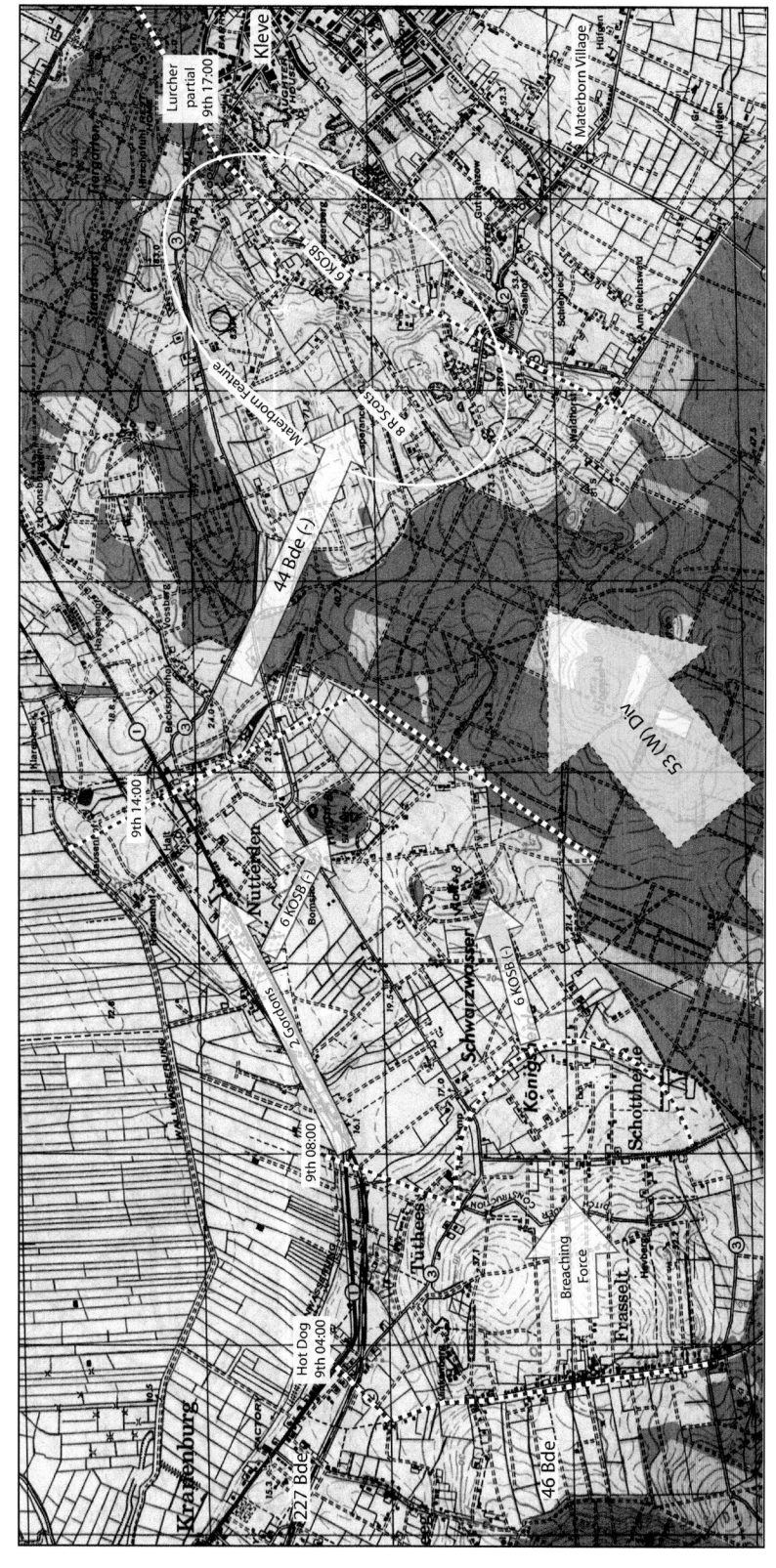

Map 14: Breakthrough and partial breakout by 44 Brigade, D+1 04:00 To 17:00. (National Archives, author's photograph)

the erosion aspect of suppression. They would have seen Frasselt put to the torch and Kleve was still smouldering behind them when they surrendered. Their timely surrender was also precipitated by an unforeseen and unreported benefit of British traffic chaos. As Map 14 indicates, when 6 KOSB resumed their advance in the centre at 13:00, the Wolfsberg and Hingstberg positions had already been outflanked, by 2 Gordons in the north at 10:00, and in the south by 53 Division at 09:00. Both arms of this impromptu envelopment had been held back to allow 44 Brigade's main effort to catch up, but being much lighter, had soon outpaced the armoured punch and unhinged the German defence.[57]

By capturing Nutterden, Wolfsberg and Hingstberg, 2 Gordons and 6 KOSB had completed the Sullivan phase. The ease with which they broke through the main defence line confirmed earlier assessments that 84. *Division* had been defeated, and captured German officers admitted there was no formed resistance further east. It was clear that 15 Division had kicked in an open door, but it was a very narrow door. With the roads clogged by 8 Royal Scots and 6 RSF, it would take too long to squeeze 46 and 227 Brigades through as planned, so 6 KOSB took on responsibility for leading the "Layton" breakout phase too. At 14:30, their leading Kangaroo-borne company and its tank support passed between the northern tip of the Reichswald and the parklike *Staatsforst Tiergarten* (the easternmost arrow at Map 14) and here they uncovered one of Veritable's critical intelligence failures. On reaching what had been judged to be a concrete road built to supply the Westwall, they found an unmetalled track surfaced with white sand. This track was intended to be the main axis for the thousands of vehicles in 43 Division and Guards Armoured Division, but it soon turned to mush once a dozen Kangaroos had passed under the dripping trees.[58]

Following a brief firefight with a small disorganised German force, the lead elements of 6 KOSB took up positions in Bresserberg, a hamlet two kilometres west of central Kleve: 'We arrived only just in time. As it was, there were some sharp engagements on the hill, but had we delayed, the enemy would certainly have had time to occupy it in strength.'[59] More prisoners were taken but this was harder work for less gain. As darkness fell, 6 KOSB were subject to a series of fierce local counterattacks and Churchills liberally poured tracer fire into likely enemy positions while Wasp flamethrowers torched buildings.

Woollcombe's first night in Germany was one of 'utter destruction and the crackling of fires', but he expressed a feeling common in Veritable memoirs: 'At last it was Germany: the thought never left you. Germany: it did not matter what damage you did.'[60] The men in 6 KOSB did not yet know it, but on the evening of the 9th they were facing the first trickle of *Fallschirmjäger* reserves that Schlemm had been throwing up the road to 84. *Division* since Goch and Kleve were bombed two nights before.[61] Behind the paratroopers came lead elements of *PzJgr 655*, with tank destroyers that would greatly reduce 30 Corps' armoured advantage.

The men of 6 KOSB were followed by 8 Royal Scots, who had finally made it through the traffic, mopped up a few bypassed defenders along the way and, after a short skirmish, dug in on the south-western end of the Materborn Feature around Esperance.[62] Still further back, 6 Royal Scots

---

57   2 Gordons diary; 4 Welch diary (WO 171/5286); 53 and 15 Division comms logs.
58   15 Division and 6 KOSB diaries; 15 Division comms log. H. Essame, *The 43rd Wessex Division at War 1944–1945* (London: Clowes, 1952), p.209, blames misleading air photographs and the ever-convenient Dutch underground for misinformation on the concrete road. No mention of concrete was found in any 15 Division documents.
59   Baggaley, *6th (Border) Battalion*, pp.80–81.
60   Woollcombe, *Lion*, Kindle 3025.
61   Baggaley, *6th (Border) Battalion*, p.81; 6 KOSB and 8 Royal Scots diaries.
62   Martin, *15th Scottish*, p.239, has 8 Royal Scots capturing Hingstberg then advancing to Esperance ahead of 6 KOSB but the sequence related here is a better fit to all other sources.

Fusiliers went firm on the Wolfsberg and Hingstberg positions. Meanwhile 2 Gordons, forgotten again, had not moved from Nutterden since the morning, and behind them a handful of battalions that could have been pressing the attack (including the uncommitted 7 Seaforth) spent the day digging out bogged vehicles that had made little or no contribution to Veritable's progress.[63] Further back engineers and infantry were repairing the roads ripped up by those same vehicles.[64] So, while there were a few units where men were missing meals or husbanding ammunition, the main tactical logistic problem was not the supply of forces but their lack of movement.[65]

D+1 (9 February) had been challenging for 30 Corps, but forward movement was going to become yet more difficult. The delays launching the breakthrough battle, coming on top of the failed deception plan, had allowed Schlemm's first reserves to meet 30 Corps in the bottlenecks of the Materborn Feature and Kleve, instead of further the east where Allied mass could have been deployed more effectively. Even as the Germans were trying to slam the door shut, the British side of the doorway was getting narrower. The next morning (10 February, D+2) the "tide" was lapping around Kranenburg, and sections of the main road were underwater early on the 11th. The competition between German and Allied engineers to raise and lower floodwaters was then in full swing and the main supply route was almost unusable to wheeled vehicles for at least four days.[66]

Conclusion

Instead of examining the tactical logistic difficulties in 30 Corps, the Veritable narrative excuses them. This is achieved, in part, by blurring the line between the mud that exacerbated problems on D-Day and D+1, and the flood that blocked the road from D+3. Many accounts bring the flooding forward by two days and no source mentions how it came after the tactical logistic battle had already been lost.[67] On the 10th, Montgomery's nightly cable to Alanbrooke set the narrative by reporting the road under water and implying that this had 'given the enemy time to SCRATCH up some units to oppose us …'[68] With this message, Montgomery changed the order of events to present the flood as the cause for a delay that had already occurred, while omitting the fact that failures in the Allied deception plan, and especially the unnecessary mass accrued for the attack, prompted both the flooding and the commitment of German reserves.

The subsequent historiographic focus on 53 Division's struggles in the Reichswald and 3 Canadian Division's amphibious actions in the flooded north (both relatively unimportant flank protection tasks) has also served to exaggerate the impact of weather on the main effort. Even Woollcombe's memoir repeated the myth of tanks sinking to their turret rings in the mud.[69] The

---

63   8 Royal Scots, 6 RSF and 2 Gordons diaries; 15 Division comms log.
64   15 Division HQRE diary.
65   For example, 43 Division comms log (WO 205/956, 9 Feb) has tight constraints on use of MMG (225 rounds per gun) and heavy mortar (14 rounds per gun).
66   The full duration and impact of flooding is uncertain. BAOR, *Engineers Tour* (p.164) has the road closed to wheels from 112300 but 15 Division RASC diary has DUKWs used from the 9th to 16th. The 30 Corps diary suggests intermittent road closures from 110715 to 151830.
67   Contrary to records made on the day, the Whitakers' *Rhineland* (pp.64–65) quotes 6 KOSB's commander recalling the efforts of their quartermaster on the 9th, bringing up 'the only rations we got that day because of the flooding', and has the road in Kranenburg under two feet of water.
68   Harris 'Rhineland I', p.29.
69   Woollcombe, *Lion*, Kindle 2961. 'On the right, in the grim depths of the Reichswald, tanks crashed through the trees while others bogged to their turrets in the heavy going.' Here Woollcombe was relaying a rumour from another Division axis, a rumour that seems to have its roots in BAOR, *Tour* (p.46) describing 147 RAC crossing the Leigraaf: 'fortunately the ditch was not so wide as thought and at certain places tanks were

core narrative also hid the collection of single-point errors (Flails, Small Box Girder bridges, engineer stores, unprepared routes, the supposed concrete road) that combined to produce a complex system failure. But the real problem with Veritable's narrative is that mud and flood are presented as unforeseen acts of God that were helped along by wily German sappers. In fact, these constraints, along with the mines, were foreseen and almost inevitable on a European floodplain in February. Blaming these near certainties for the failure to fully break out and transition to exploit/pursuit was effectively an admission of poor planning.

The plan had called for 15 and 43 Division, and perhaps part of Guards Armoured Division, to be well into the exploitation phase by the end of D+1, but 30 Corps struggled to get two battalions forward in that time. In contrast to the operational failure, 6 KOSB had a remarkable tactical victory, suffering fewer than 20 casualties to achieve most of the targets set for four battalions.[70] No previous assessment seems to have linked the wasted mass of the 30 Corps plan with the dramatic success of its lead battalion, a connection that makes it obvious that less mass and more velocity could have achieved much greater operational impact. For example, while questioning the unexpectedness of the thaw, the NATO Northern Army Group (NORTHAG) and SSVC video team make no explicit link between the mass of the attack and the congestion that undermined its velocity. As one of the NORTHAG team noted:

> From a German point of view this plan had every chance for a quick success because: first, it could and did achieve surprise; second, it succeeded in gathering a very favourable force ratio for the British; and third, it hit the German front at its weakest point. The only criticism I have according to the plan is that it depended very much on hard frozen ground, whereas in this part of Germany, and in this part of the year, frozen ground is rather the exception than the rule.[71]

This was a sound assessment given its source material, but missed the mark because the study group lacked access to the detail of the war diaries that showed how much mass was deployed and how little of it reached objectives.[72] Yet the NORTHAG/SSVC team, along with the Whitakers and Fiebig, concluded that a rapid advance on the evening of D-Day would have pushed 15 Division beyond the Materborn Feature and well into the pursuit/exploitation phase. The 2 Gordons attack on Nutterden would most likely have succeeded just as easily if they had set out at 18:00 on D-Day and the uncommitted 7 Seaforth could have seized Schottheide at the same time. Instead, battalions were set to digging out bogged vehicles as 30 Corps expended tactical assets to correct its logistical mistake.

Does this chapter say anything about 30 Corps logistics? Using the traditional concept, the answer would be 'no' because plenty of stores were amassed, and no units reported critical supply problems. But the chapter says much about the force movement aspect of logistics. By showing how velocity was reduced by mass-focused tactics, the chapter has also demonstrated the interactions underpinning tactical logistics. Traditional logistic problems will become more

---

　　able to cross unaided. One Churchill tank disappeared in the mud up to its turret.' The 147 RAC diary has several troops of tanks successfully crossing using this method, but taken out of context, one tank stuck in a stream has been used to imply deep mud across the whole Veritable area.
70　6 KOSB diary and summary sheet, 9–10 Feb; CWGC.
71　*Oberstleutnant* Berghard Franck, SSVC/Dennis, *Rhineland*, part 3.
72　The assessment also missed how mass stole Veritable's surprise. As an example of the power of the Veritable core narrative, Dennis/SSVC *Rhineland*, part 1 has, 'The speed of the advance was now aided by another Funny, the Kangaroo.' By focusing on the hour or so saved ferrying troops forward after Schottheide, this statement negates the Kangaroos' contribution to the congestion that made the assault seven hours late.

evident in later chapters, with days of delay for want of supplies and formations competing for resources. But those problems stemmed from the break-in and breakthrough battles that made the traffic chaos that prevented 30 Corps from breaking out and exploiting beyond the Materborn Feature.

There were three tactical logistical problems: amassing a force too large to fit the available infrastructure; battering that infrastructure with more artillery firepower than necessary; then pushing too much armour forward when there was ample evidence that doing so would be counterproductive. The first problem came from Allied logisticians being operationally pessimistic but tactically optimistic, with planners thinking a massive force would be needed and could then flow forward almost without friction.[73] It is no surprise that 21st Army Group had a weak conception of tactical logistics 70 years before the term was coined, but battalions and brigades knew about moving and supplying forces, and about the damage that artillery overkill and armoured mass would inflict. Yet army, corps, and perhaps even division headquarters did nothing to prevent the inevitable overloading of infrastructure. The total number of vehicles trying to use those fragile roads is not known but on 7 February (a whole week after the thaw) 30 Corps planners estimated that 12,461 vehicles might need to move forward on the 8th alone, with over 1,000 of these being heavy armour.[74]

Even the assumption that "Gilbert" and "Sullivan" would have succeeded in frost is questionable. The drainage channels and streams have banks that are prone to collapse under 40 tonnes of armour no matter how harsh the frost, forcing tanks onto cobbled roads that were especially fragile in icy weather.[75] Mark Henniker, 43 Division's Commander Royal Engineers, noted how just one heavy vehicle could ruin an icy road, while 'A regiment of tanks, driving along a frozen road, might do damage in a single pass comparable with the destruction of an earthquake.'[76] Even in mild weather, 21st Army Group operations were dogged by traffic congestion that came from trying to fit a quart into a pint pot.[77] For Veritable it was closer to tipping a gallon into a teacup.

The second problem came from the loss of the 1918 understanding of artillery suppression and therefore the recurrence of 1917 levels of overkill. All those extra rounds suffered from diminishing suppressive returns and made the assault more difficult, especially for armour. It is not possible to quantify the damage caused by artillery overkill but, as Chapter 2 suggested, perhaps half of the fire plan was waste. Those hundreds of thousands of wasted rounds must have made off-road and on-road movement considerably more difficult.

The third problem came from a complicated plan that had been set in stone by traditional logistics. Like A. J. P. Taylor's interpretation of the Schlieffen Plan, Veritable had a movement table with such tight tolerances and so many interdependencies that no single strand could be changed without upsetting all the others.[78] A simplistic "do the same but slower" appears to be the only concession higher command made to wet weather, reflecting the separation of logistics and tactics embodied by the division of labour in 21st Army Group. First Canadian Army seemed to see its

---

73 Paraphrase of Creveld, *Supplying War*, pp.202–230, which uses 'logistic pusillanimity' (p.215) and claims (p.210) that Normandy planners' 'greatest fault was that they did not allow sufficiently for the inevitable friction of war'.
74 30 Corps planning note 37 (WO 171/4076).
75 21 Army Group 'Blackcock', pp.19, 27.
76 Henniker, *Image*, p.213.
77 For example: G. Taylor, *Infantry Colonel* (Upton: Self-published, 1990), pp.24, 76, 79; Dick, *Victory*, p.172.
78 A. J. P. Taylor, *War By Time-Table: How the First World War Began* (London: Macdonald, 1974), pp.42–44. Creveld (*Supplying War*, p.210) noted the same phenomenon in Normandy.

main function as amassing stuff, with little consideration of operational or tactical manoeuvre.[79] Corps HQ, with its quite different operational concept, was responsible for operational manoeuvre and probably for the fire plan, but seemingly had no control over route preparation. Then the divisions were responsible for tactical movement but were slaves to the fire plan and movement table. Brigades and battalions were left to tweak their orders of march and hope for the best.[80]

Above all this hung the pervasive perception that more was better. There was time to collect all those rounds, so they were collected; then it seemed a waste not to fire them. There was time to collect all those tanks, so they were sent forward. Perhaps planners believed that throwing so many tanks onto such difficult terrain would increase the chances of some getting through, but on the day, like throwing a gallon into a teacup, it only made a bigger mess. Had the plan not been so focused on massing enough goods to stretch from London to Edinburgh and instead considered how those goods might cross the last mile to reach the German customer, it would have had more success.

---

79 Accumulating mass is the overwhelming consideration presented by Macdonald 'In search of Veritable' and post-operation reports. Note the ironic-prophetic quote in Ch 1 concerning mass – waiting to build up more when there was likely already too much to fit through the narrow corridor to the Materborn Feature. The only weather consideration mentioned in Macdonald's assessment of army level planning (p.202) is an expected 30 percent reduction in resupply *into* the Nijmegen area if there were a thaw. There is no mention of any effect forward of that.

80 Diffusion of responsibility and the lack of a satisfactory logistic history might have the same root. Forward of Groesbeek, responsibility passed through a profusion of inconsistently initialised roles like the Deputy Assistant Adjutant & Quartermaster General and Brigade Royal Army Service Corps Officer. Each level down had less understanding of the big picture and less power over action.

4

Command or Control

9 TO 11 FEBRUARY – HORROCKS'S MISTAKE – COMMAND ARCHETYPES – DETAILING THE FOG OF WAR – PLANS BUILT ON WHITE SAND – RADIO FREQUENCY ALLOCATION – SLIPPERY SCHWERPUNKT – TANK RIDERS PAY THE PRICE – COMMAND SYSTEM DESIGN

The Worst Mistake?

On the afternoon of 9 February (D+1), the Veritable narrative has 15 Division reporting that the German defence had collapsed, the Materborn Feature was secure, and one of its brigades was entering Kleve.[1] Then, as Horrocks recalled in both of his memoirs:

> This was the information for which I had been eagerly waiting. So I unleashed my first reserve, the 43rd Wessex Division, which was to pass through the 15th Scottish, to burst out into the plain beyond and advance towards Goch.
> This, however, turned out to be one of the worst mistakes I made in the war. The 15th Scottish had not reached as far as had been reported and one of their brigades had not been employed at all.[2]

This version of events is repeated in many histories, but primary sources suggest there was no misinformation from 15 Division and, given the information that reached Horrocks, he made no mistake by unleashing 43 Division. Indeed, diaries and communication logs suggest he might not have ordered it to be unleashed at all. Yet the failure to complete the partial breakout and to translate it into exploit/pursuit was definitely a fumbled pass, where 15 Division and 43 Division clearly dropped the ball of the 30 Corps main effort. It was a blunder that histories have blamed on Horrocks, 30 Corps staff, both divisions, their various subordinates, the RAF and, of course, on mines and mud.[3]

---

1   The order of events is sometimes confused. For example, Whitakers, *Rhineland* (p.66), has Horrocks launching 43 Division after he hears Grenade is postponed but the earliest report of the postponement (Harris, *Rhineland I*, p.14) came 90 minutes after 43 Division began its advance.
2   Horrocks et al, *Corps Commander*, pp.186–187. Relating this decision, Essame, *Wessex Division* (p.206) states: 'In the distant future, students of this history (if any) will infer that not the least attractive characteristic of the Corps Commander, Lieut.-General Sir Brian Horrocks, was his optimism.'
3   Warner, *Horrocks*, p.118; Horrocks et al, *Corps Commander*, p.184; Whitakers, *Rhineland*, pp.65–69.

The historiographic focus on 21st Army Group's performance in 1944, on the personalities of commanders and on national cultures has meant that the causes and effects of the ill-timed advance of 43 Division have never been examined in any detail.[4] This chapter argues that the root cause lay in the fundamental nature of the 30 Corps command system. The central functions of command are decision-making (working out what to do) and leadership (getting people to do it); a command system is the combination of technology, organisation, procedure, and people that support decision-making and leadership.[5] Command systems have been defined by the extent to which they rely on command-by-plan, command-by-direction, or command-by-influence; three interacting archetypes that were evident to varying degrees within 30 Corps but these labels need some clarification.[6]

The British Army has often been seen to epitomise command-by-plan, aiming to dictate the flow of battle with rigid schemes where multiple phases are dominated by barrage timings and movement tables.[7] Command-by-plan is notoriously vulnerable to enemy action and to friction, as has already been demonstrated in 15 Division's Gilbert and Sullivan phases. The obvious limitations of command-by-plan during the First World War encouraged the British Army's enthusiastic adoption of radio to enable command-by-direction, a more dynamic but still centralised approach, where the upward flow of reports informs the downwards flow orders.[8] Command-by-direction is limited by human and technological processing power (people and airwaves having limits to the amount of data they can accommodate) but it was clearly popular in 21st Army Group, with a profusion of radio nets and "directed telescopes".[9] The latter included the GHQ "Phantom" Regiment, which intercepted communications on subordinate radio nets and used liaison teams to give higher headquarters direct and unvarnished reports on subordinate actions.[10] In Veritable, the most obvious manifestation of command-by-direction was Horrocks's location on the morning of D-Day, overlooking the battlefield from a tree on the edge of Groesbeek woods while a team of radio operators relayed reports directly from divisions' radio nets. This arrangement cut out a layer of command, to speed the flow of information from bottom to top, but it increased Horrocks's information load, especially given the number of divisions in 30 Corps.[11]

The limitations of plan and direction have always required an element of command-by-influence, where subordinates act on their own initiative to achieve a higher objective. This decentralised approach, epitomised by the German *Auftragstaktik* and NATO's mission command,

---

4 This is no criticism of authors who have focused on personalities because that is where the weight of source material lies, but personalities are difficult to fathom, and it is doubly difficult for armies to ward against their limitations.
5 These definitions are an attempt to work around circularity in NATO terms, see C. McCann (ed.), *The Human in Command: Exploring the Modern Military Experience*, (New York: Springer, 2000) pp.163–184; J. Storr, *Something Rotten*, pp.147–169. Unlike command personalities or national cultures, command systems can be designed to avoid the weaknesses seen in historical organisations.
6 These archetypes are central to operational research on command systems but best defined in T. Czerwinski, *Coping with the Bounds: Speculations on Nonlinearity in Military Affairs* (Washington DC: Command & Control Research Program, 1998), passim.
7 M. Samuels, *Command or Control? Command, Training and Tactics in the British and German Armies, 1888–1918* (London: Cass, 1995), passim; G. Sheffield and D. Todman (eds), *Command and Control on the Western Front: The British Army's Experience 1914–1918* (Stroud: Spellmount, 2007), passim.
8 W. M. St G. Kirke et al, *Report of the Committee on the Lessons of the Great War (The Kirke Report)* (Upavon: DGD&D, 2001 [1932]), p.17.
9 J. Buckley, 'Montgomery: Command and Leadership in the 21st Army Group, 1944–45', presentation to Joint Command and Staff College, 2014.
10 P. Warner, *Phantom*, (Barnsley: Pen & Sword, 2005).
11 Horrocks et al, *Corps Commander*, pp.184–189.

has commanders stating what they want to achieve but then allowing subordinates to work out the detail of how they achieve it. While command-by-influence is presented as a paragon, it needs highly trained personnel and clear statements of intent, which are surprisingly difficult to compose. Command-by-influence also needs a high degree of internal predictability, with a common approach to solving tactical problems allowing each commander to be confident in the likely actions of their comrades, even when communications fail.[12] Command-by-influence had become more apparent in 21st Army Group since Normandy, with Montgomery giving greater freedom of action to his favoured subordinates.[13] Influence was evident at lower levels too, for example when Guards and Royal Engineers officers took over the Schottheide breaching force, but the competing pressures from plan and direction were also evident in the hours it took before that happened.

Command-by-plan having unravelled (as plans do) in Schottheide, this chapter will show how the subsequent attempt at command-by-direction was undermined by the limitations on human and technological processing power, and how 30 Corps' organisations and procedures prevented command-by-influence from filling the gaps. The most important tactical and operational effects of this failure are also examined. The chapter will focus on how the command system shaped the battle of Fifth Battalion, The Duke of Cornwall's Light Infantry (5 DCLI) and their supporting armour from 4th/7th Royal Dragoon Guards (4/7 DG, Figure 11) as they arrived at the point of main effort on the critical Materborn Feature and came in sight of the more open ground beyond it (Map 15).

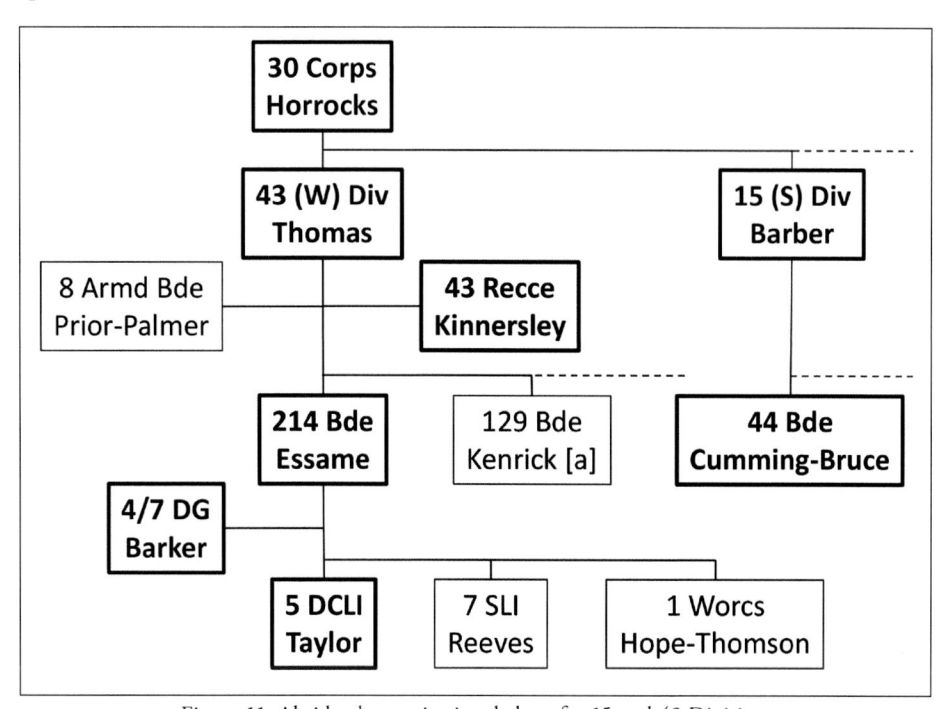

Figure 11: Abridged organisational chart for 15 and 43 Division.

---

12 Czerwinski, *Nonlinearity*, pp.238–241. A common approach tends to encourage external predictability too, with enemies coming to expect template tactics such as the German proclivity for counterattack and infiltration.

13 C. Forrester, *Monty's Functional*, passim. B.L. Montgomery, *High Command in War* (Germany: 21 AG, 1945), pp.21–23.

Map 15: Situation at 23:59 on 9 February (D+1). (National Archives, author's photograph)

The Fumbled Pass

Like the collection of single-point errors for tactical logistics (Flails, Small Box Girder bridges, et cetera) command system failures are usually born from complexity compounding a series of errors or 'normal accidents' that would be relatively harmless in isolation.[14] A chain of such errors was sparked by the arrival of 6 KOSB on the Materborn Feature but had its roots in 15 Division's complicated plan. The Gilbert break-in and the Sullivan breakthrough had worked towards Horrocks's intent of dashing for the Wesel bridges, but the Layton breakout should have ended with two brigades on Phase Line Lurcher. Once Lurcher was secured, the "Sousa" exploitation/pursuit phase was due to 'flood the country with armoured cars.'[15] Sousa included four sub-phases where Fifteenth (Scottish) Reconnaissance Regiment (15 Recce) and Second Household Cavalry Regiment (2 HCR) would move ahead of heavier armoured infantry groups, including 43 Division's southward advance through Goch and 15 Division's shorter strikes to Kalkar and Uedem.[16] The Uedem axis would then be used by Guards Armoured Division striking out to Wesel and Xanten, as shown at Map 5.

Sousa was to be conducted in parallel with a fifth phase, "Johnston", the fight to secure Kleve, which was a secondary objective for 30 Corps, the town having been bombed specifically to block movement through it. One of the failures to align commanding by plan and by influence was that, contrary to Horrocks's intent, 15 Division's plan listed Johnston ahead of Sousa, putting the clearance of a rubble-strewn town ahead of exploiting towards the bridges.[17] Fifteen Division's complicated plan also contained no explicit provision for handover to 43 Division, which was expected to happen where Route Club Red turned south, just above "To Goch" at Map 15.[18]

One of the last minute adjustments to account for D-Day's traffic chaos was that, instead of riding on the tail of 44 Brigade as originally envisaged, the two reconnaissance regiments were held back in Nijmegen.[19] However by 12:30 on D+1 (just as 6 KOSB were moving from Schottheide) 15 Division's commander, Major General Colin Barber, sensed an impending breakthrough, and ordered reconnaissance forward, effectively preparing for the exploitation before the breakout phase had started. It took two hours for this order to reach 15 Recce, by which time Barber was demanding his brigades open a clear route for the reconnaissance regiments.[20] An hour after that 15 Recce had still not set off, but then 44 Brigade staff relayed more news that appeared to confirm the wisdom of calling reconnaissance forward:

---

14   A considerable body of research stems from C. Perrow, *Normal Accidents: Living with High-Risk Technologies* (New York: Basic, 1984). For application to command systems see, Development, Concepts and Doctrine Centre, *Future of Command and Control*, (Swindon: DCDC, 2017), pp.35–46.
15   15 Recce diary, 8 February. Lurcher was itself a complication because Corps, Division and Brigade used different versions of the line.
16   15 Recce diary (WO 171/4199) suggests that 15 Div's plan to send a third column to Emmerich (as shown on Map 5) was abandoned on D-1 due to flooding.
17   15 Division's focus is echoed in subsequent events and histories, but blame does not sit squarely with the Div. For example, 30 Corps Op Instr 46, 3 Feb (Harris, *Rhineland I*, p.83) did not have Kleve on its list of objectives but later paragraphs introduced ambiguity: 'As soon as Commander 15 (S) Division is sure that he has effected an exit from the railway GOCH–CLEVE, he will pass through without further delay the whole of 2 HCR. [Household Cavalry Regiment]' As the railway looped southward (see south-east corner of Map 15), 15 Division may have assumed this required the capture of Kleve.
18   Route Club Red broadly coincided with 15 Division's Route Ayr, along Kranenburgsche Straat, through Haus Kreuzfuhrt, Frasselt and Schottheide but Club Red is used here for consistency with later accounts.
19   15 Recce diary, 8–9 February; 15 Division comms log, 9 February.
20   15 Division comms log, 091335; 15 Recce diary 091445.

> 15:45. 44 Brigade to 15 Division: Message for your SUNRAY [Barber] from my SUNRAY [Cumming-Bruce]. My SUNRAY is on his way back and says situation fwd is very satisfactory. Leading children have reached LURCHER (line WALDHORST 8653 – BRESSELBERG – Lookout tower 8855 – 893562 – rd and rly crossing 890570). We are now trying to get tpt up to fwd troops.
>
> 15:53. 15 Division to 44 Brigade: My SUNRAY says this might mean blocking the rd for Recce. This must NOT happen.[21]

As the delayed reply suggests, Barber and Cumming-Bruce were both cutting about the battlefield at the time, and only able to communicate via staff in their tactical and main headquarters. There would have been at least four people between the two commanders, with another handful of links down to the companies on Lurcher and yet more links heading back to reconnaissance regiments in Nijmegen.[22] These long communication chains presented many opportunities for information to be lost or misinterpreted. The long chains also meant there was no opportunity for Barber to ask what Cumming-Bruce meant by 'satisfactory', how many children of what type had reached Lurcher, or which points on Lurcher had been reached. Likewise, there was no chance for Cumming-Bruce to ask exactly what 'must NOT happen': blocking the road, sending transport forward or movement of combat forces?

It is not known whether 44 Brigade staff in Nutterden added the Lurcher grids to help clarify, or if 15 Division staff in Nijmegen gave Barber the impression that 44 Brigade had its troops all along that line, which dominated the outskirts of Kleve. That nuance is lost but subsequent events suggest Barber interpreted this much-relayed report as confirmation that Lurcher had been secured. In this context 'secured' would mean there were strong forces along the length of Lurcher and dominating the ground around it, not that a lone battalion had just arrived at one point on the line.[23] There is also uncertainty around how much Barber knew about the state of the roads forward of Nutterden, their suitability for wheeled reconnaissance, and the readiness of Recce to move forward. It is possible Barber only intended to keep logistic vehicles off the road for an hour, but his reply stopped all forward movement by his three brigades for at least 12 hours.

It is highly unlikely that Barber was prepared for a five-hour delay between his original order to release reconnaissance and that reconnaissance getting anywhere near Lurcher. At 17:15, when 15 Recce reached Nutterden, they were 'ordered to push on with the greatest possible speed to make the most of what little daylight was left.' Following Route Club Red, as planned, they reached the supposed concrete road around 17:45 and found a quagmire blocked by tanks and Kangaroos *returning* from 6 KOSB's Bresserberg position. The reconnaissance teams could also see indications of heavy fighting involving 'unidentified flamethrowers' on the Materborn Feature.[24] For the next three hours 15 Recce could make no headway, and after asking for higher direction, they were ordered to switch their attentions to Kleve and the railway at the far side of town. Even with movement light, entering a bombed-out town in the dark to reach a point four kilometres north of their original objective was a gamble and a considerable detour, but they took the chance as ordered.[25]

---

21 15 Division comms log.
22 For example, 'reached LURCHER' could have run from company command to battalion intelligence officer, to battalion command, to Cumming-Bruce, to staff in Brigade Tac HQ, to staff in Brigade Main HQ, to Division Main, to Division Tac, and then to Barber. This author has tracked communication chains in many digitised and analogue command systems, and chains this long, or longer, are common.
23 At 15:17, the Division comms log has a coy of 8 Royal Scots reaching Esperance, 400m short of Lurcher.
24 15 Division and 15 Recce diaries 091700-2100. The likely route of the concrete road is shown at Map 15.
25 15 Recce diary; 15 Division comms log 092113; 30 Corps diary 091910.

Meanwhile, radio nets across 30 Corps were filled with reports of 15 Division's progress and intentions, often relayed by third parties such as Phantom teams, who sometimes mistook intended destinations for current locations.[26] At no point was there a definite claim that Lurcher was secured, Kleve entered (other than by a few Recce cars after 43 Division had set off), or that the Sousa exploitation had been launched. Yet that is how all senior commanders recalled events, and how Montgomery presented the situation in his nightly message to Alanbrooke.[27] The cloud of incomplete information, accelerated by rumour and human cognitive "biases" (evolved heuristics that usually enable efficient decision-making) seems to have encouraged a perception that everything was more or less going to plan.[28]

These mixed messages might explain why an ill, tired, and overloaded Horrocks would order 43 Division forward as he later admitted to doing, but curiously there is no contemporary record of the order, only a message on the morning of the 9th directing the Division to raise its readiness state to one hours' notice-to-move at 18:00 that evening. Then, without any additional input from 30 Corps, the leading formation (129 Brigade) began to move at 18:00, intent on elbowing lesser formations out of their way.[29] The lack of a recorded "move now" order does not mean it was not issued, but as Horrocks was near the front and 129 Brigade well to the rear, any direction would have to travel by radio.[30] It is highly unlikely that this pivotal message would not have been recorded by any of the many headquarters and liaison teams that would have overheard it.[31]

In the 'good weather' plan, 43 Division's 1,000 tracked vehicles were due to move on Route Club Red, south of Kranenburg, then along the supposedly concrete road across the Materborn Feature.[32] But in the early hours of the 10th (D+2), having clogged the main road through Kranenburg to Nutterden, 43 Division's leading unit reached the quagmire under the trees. Here they took the advice of a 15 Recce squadron and paired up with them to head into Kleve. The rest of 129 Brigade followed.[33] Later that day, elements of 227 and 46 Brigades were also committed to Kleve and the ensuing battle well deserves the description "confused fighting", with units from one formation sent to clear objectives already occupied by units from another, and several instances of

---

26 For example, one Phantom intercept had elements of 8 Royal Scots going to Bresserberg at 091031, but they only came near there 18hrs later. Likewise, a corps liaison officer reported 8 Royal Scots in Materborn village at 091519 (repeated by 43 Division, 092130) which they never reached. 15 Division and 30 Corps diaries; 43 Division comms log (WO 205/956).
27 Harris, *Rhineland I*, pp.28–29. This included, 'I hope to be to have secured Goch by tomorrow.'
28 R. J. Heuer, *Psychology of Intelligence Analysis* (Langley VA: CIA, 1999).
29 43 Division comms log, 30 Corps, 43 Division, and 129 Brigade diaries, 9 February (WO 171/4207 and 4389).
30 At about the time this order would have been given, CO 6 KOSB recalled Horrocks arriving at the Bresserberg position and 'telling me that 6 K.O.S.B. had virtually won the war!' C. W. P. Henderson, 'Participation of 6th (Border) Battalion, The King's Own Scottish Borderers in the first phase of Operation "Veritable".' Undated file T1/34, KOSB Museum.
31 It is equally unlikely that Horrocks lied about giving the move order. This author has decided to shelve the 129 Brigade move as one of those "who knows?" incidents, but there is a chance Brigade staff simply mistook the notice-to-move time as the time to move and that Horrocks later misremembered giving the move order.
32 Estimate based on a generic order of battle. The 43 Division diary contains a 6 February movement instruction for 4,917 wheeled and tracked vehicles.
33 4 Wilts diary (WO 171/5290). Some authors (e.g., Elstob, *Reichswald*, p.108) claim 4 Wilts made a navigational error, but their diary is clear this was deliberate. However, the Wilts diary entry for 9 Feb summarises their orders as 'push on through CLEVE (E95) and capture the high ground 5½ miles SOUTH of the town (E9448)'. Kleve is not in grid square E95, and E9448 is 2km east of Forst Kleve; the notation and the error suggest the Bn was working from the 1:100000 Essen map, which does not include Kleve, which may explain some of the confusion.

artillery fratricide.[34] But Kleve was not the main effort, it was merely where all the combat power happened to congregate when command-by-plan and command-by-direction proved unworkable. In the struggle to untangle Kleve, the line of main effort through Materborn was forgotten, first by the commanders involved, then by historians who followed the lead of those commanders' memoirs.

The Tactical Effect

The fumbled pass gave the remnants of *84. Division* yet more breathing room. In the first two days of Veritable, Fiebig had lost most of his infantry in the outpost line, most of his supporting arms in the main defensive line and then his headquarters was nearly encircled in Kleve. His staff extricated themselves, re-established a defensive line and began absorbing the companies that Schlemm was rushing up from the southeast.[35] One of these ad hoc groups coalesced around remnants of *5 Companie* of *GR 1051*, who set up a defence around the cloister on the northwestern edge of Materborn village with an outpost in Saalhof, a hamlet maybe 500 metres south of 8 Royal Scots' forward positions. Despite this proximity, *5 Companie* seem to have prepared their defence without disturbance, as 8 Royal Scots remained static on the night of the 9th and through most of the 10th.[36]

As 129 Brigade became embroiled in Kleve, the next formation in the 43 Division order of march was 214 Brigade, which reached Nutterden at 05:30 on the 10th, making it ideally placed to echelon through 8 Royal Scots and 6 KOSB on the Materborn Feature. But then, in an echo of the blunder with 15 Recce the day before, the task of leading the advance through Materborn was handed to 43 Recce, who were near the back of the Division's column. Brigadier Herbert Essame, commander of 214 Brigade (later 43 Division's historian and co-author of Horrocks's *Corps Commander*) admitted: 'This was, as events turned out, an unfortunate decision.'[37] Quite how unfortunate is best viewed from the perspective of 214 Brigade's leading unit, 5 DCLI.

On the eve of Veritable, 5 DCLI's CO, Lieutenant Colonel George Taylor, issued an order that reflected Montgomery's anticipation of a climactic battle of manoeuvre. The order, which vowed revenge for an earlier Battalion defeat, ended with the exhortation: 'We will attack with great speed, dash and firepower. We cannot <u>and will not fail</u>.'[38] Taylor's men were keen for action when they left Nijmegen around 20:00 on the 9th, but by the time they reached Nutterden after a nine-hour "quick lift" perched on Shermans (Figure 12) in the rain and sleet, they were far less enthusiastic.[39] There was a long pause around Nutterden while senior commanders tried to work out what was happening, and junior commanders tried to get hot food to men who were spread

---

34   Essame, *Wessex Division*, p.207; 15 Recce and 4 Wilts diaries. 44 Brigade diary at 101745 has 6 RSF report: 'shelled by our own medium guns'.
35   Various ISUMs (e.g., 43 Division diary, Annex F5, 090111) mention a captured map showing *84 Division* HQ in western Kleve, which fits with Fiebig, '84th Infantry' and Essame, *Wessex Division*, p.208.
36   214 Brigade diary, 111615; 6 KOSB and 8 Royal Scots diaries.
37   Essame, *Wessex Division*, p.209.
38   G. Taylor, Order of the Day, 7 Feb, 5 DCLI diary.
39   5 DCLI diary. Taylor (*Infantry Colonel*, pp.164–165) recalled, 'the battalion had reached its zenith in efficiency' on the eve of Veritable but in Materborn, 'fighting spirit was at its lowest ebb' after 'that seemingly endless night'. Image at Figure 12 kindly provided by Bodmin Keep and battlefieldhistorian.com. This widely reproduced picture is sometimes attributed to units in 15 Division, due to the Tam O'Shanter on the officer beside the Jeep, but 15 Division had no Sherman Fireflies under command.

Figure 12: 5 Duke of Cornwall's Light Infantry in quick lift to Materborn on 4/7 Dragoon Guards' Shermans. (Bodmin Keep / battlefieldhistorian.com)

over five kilometres of crowded road. At 10:45, 214 Brigade issued orders for its part in the new 43 Division plan.[40] As Colonel Taylor recalled:

> Now, we were told, 5 DCLI would bypass the Reichswald Forest by moving along the axis of the Materborn–Goch road and capture Goch, some ten miles away, a tall order, we felt, as only a very small area of the Reichswald had been cleared of Germans.
>
> Air photos of the town [i.e. Goch] and its approaches were studied, and plans made for dealing with the hidden menaces of the forest on the way. A strong fire base consisting of 3in mortars and machine guns would be established among the hummocks just west of the forest, which, with artillery, would protect our right flank.
>
> The first round from a German gun would be the signal for the wood to be covered with fire and smoke.[41]

As with 15 Division, 43 Division's operational concept reverted to its original plan, which focused on a reconnaissance-led dash to distant objectives rather than the immediate problem of fighting through Materborn. The leading companies of 5 DCLI would ride on 4/7 Dragoon Guards' Shermans and follow 43 Recce along Club Red through Materborn village and 'Hau', then on to

---

40 214 Brigade diary. 5 DCLI diary puts Brigade orders at 11:00, with Battalion orders at 12:30.
41 Taylor, *Infantry Colonel*, p.166. The reliance on 3-in mortars and MMG is a concern as these would have been out of range soon after the Battalion passed Materborn village.

Goch and beyond.[42] Any enemy pockets that 43 Recce could not deal with would be subject to quick attacks from line of march by 5 DCLI and 4/7 Dragoon Guards. If strongly opposed, the battalion group would launch a deliberate attack then 7 Somerset Light Infantry (7 SLI) and 1 Worcesters would echelon through to repeat the process.

Like 15 Recce before them, 43 Recce's "B" Squadron took five hours to get near the Materborn Feature, where they too were surprised to find the concrete road was a rutted cart track. By that time vehicle crews from other units had been exploring alternative routes, spreading the ruts into the northern Reichswald and towards the boundary with 53 Division. It was 15:00 before "B" Squadron, who were navigating without the relevant route overlay, found their way out of the forest near Saalhof (Map 16).[43] Their advance was soon checked by the *5 Companie* outpost there, which "B" Squadron assessed as comprising 20 infantry and a machine gun, and therefore too strong for the few recce cars that could get forward, and so 43 Recce pulled back, reporting that 'Friends who were here before us are dealing with enemy.'[44]

By 17:00 the pause to bring 43 Recce forward had used most of the daylight hours and advanced 30 Corps no more than 100 metres. And so, perhaps eight hours after they could have first attacked Saalhof, 5 DCLI took over. An artillery and mortar preparation at 18:00 preceded an assault by "D" Company and 4/7 Dragoon Guards, "B" Squadron. Together they secured Saalhof shortly after 20:00, with no reported casualties but few if any prisoners, most defenders having withdrawn to Materborn village.[45] Then, with Brigade and Division keen for progress, Taylor sent "B" Company to bypass Materborn on foot, infiltrating along the edge of the forest and pushing on towards Hau. The rest of the Battalion was to join "B" after Materborn had been captured by a frontal assault in which "C" Company would ride into contact on 4/7 Dragoon Guards' tanks.

---

42   5 DCLI diary includes notes on the operation that emphasise studying maps of Goch but say nothing about Materborn or Kleve. 'Hau' on Allied 1:25000 maps was an area name close to the old St Antonius church, a kilometre southwest of the centre of Hau today.

43   43 Division diary; 43 Recce diary (WO 171/4215); Essame, *Wessex Division*, p.209; 'Op Veritable, Trace 'P' part 2', 227 Brigade diary. Compared to 15 and 53 diaries, 43 Division diaries have a notable shortage of maps and overlays: none of the Brigades having a route or boundary trace; 7 Hampshires diary (WO 171/5200) has an unlabelled route map that omits Club Red; 5 Dorsets diary (WO 171/5175) has a route overlay with general objectives around Goch, Weeze and beyond; 43 Recce diary has an orphaned and undated overlay focused around Uedem. Some guesswork was necessary for Map 16 because 15 Division, which routinely recorded all unit positions at midnight, did not do so between the 6th and the 11th. Also, 43 Division's surviving operational comms log does not start until noon on the 10th, by which time 129 Brigade was already being counterattacked in Kleve.

44   43 Recce intelligence diary, 101750. 43 Division Tac HQ log, 101505–102000; 43 Division diary. Elstob, *Reichswald*, p.109, implies recce losses from this action but the unit diary says not, as does A. Scott, C. Packer and J. Groves, *Record of a Reconnaissance Regiment: History of the 43rd Reconnaissance Regiment (The Gloucester Regiment) 1939 – 1945* (Bristol: White Swan, 1949), p.159. One troop from "B" Sqn did not withdraw but stayed to thicken the fire support for the first DCLI attack. 'Friends' could have been 5 DCLI but 8 Royal Scots were the closest unit. The 43 Recce diary suggests it was elements of 53 Division, despite Saalhof being outside their area.

45   Taylor, p.166; 43 Division Tac HQ log, 101721–102018. Timings for the start of the action are interpolated from fragments, e.g., 43 Recce diary has 'infantry passing through' at 17:50, and 43 Division comms log has '5 DCLI 2 children clearing up STAALOF' at 19:39. At this point Taylor criticises 53 Division for losing contact with the enemy and suggests this as the reason for 53's subsequent losses. In fact, 53 Division had been ordered to halt to allow 43 Division to catch up and suffered relatively few losses at this stage of the operation. Like many in 43 Division (see earlier footnote on 'Friends') Taylor may have confused 15 and 53 at this point.

Map 16: The Materborn salient before the 43 recce probe (front 9th 23:59) and just before the 5 DCLI final attack (front 11th 14:00). Note the cloister building, church and 'Tiger Corner'. (National Archives, author's photograph)

The long infiltration by "B" Company made good progress, reaching as far as Horstmannshof (southeast of Map 16) but, looking back, Taylor felt the frontal assault was doomed from the outset. One tank refused to start, blocking those behind it, then the advance came under artillery and machine-gun fire, forcing tank riders to 'make themselves as small as mice as the tracer and shrapnel flashed and crashed around them'.[46] The foremost Sherman, carrying 5 DCLI's Lieutenant Jones and some of his men from 15 Platoon, burst into flames following two *Panzerfaust* hits. Though Lieutenant Jones escaped unscathed, one of the tank crew was wounded and two others taken prisoner, suggesting they were engaged at very close range. It is not clear whether defensive fire was too great, the destroyed tank blocked the road or the men in "C" Company were too tired to press on, but the attack stalled. The tanks were pulled back and, like 43 Recce, were soon 'curling up … ready to move at first light'.[47]

This left the infantry with no armour support and, due to communication difficulties, little indirect fire, so a stealthy attack was attempted, with "C" Company providing an on-call firebase from Saalhof, while "D" hooked around to approach from the southwest. As their name implies, 5 DCLI had a tradition of infiltration, but the earlier actions had robbed this effort of surprise and although movement light was not considered sufficient to enable tank support, it was enough to make a clandestine approach near impossible.[48] Even had the Battalion's request to turn off movement light reached the responsible units, it conflicted with the requirements for light to support road repairs and the ongoing fight in Kleve.[49] As "D" Company began their attack around 01:00 (11th, D+3) it started to snow, and here the exhaustion over the last few days took its toll. Having travelled overnight on the 8th, then prepared for the advance the next day, Taylor's men were already tired when they left Nijmegen. They then spent 24 hours in quick lift, and another five hours trying to break into Materborn village. For "D" Company this involved wading through drainage ditches under fire, and after an hour of this, they were 'soaked to the skin and nearly dropping from fatigue'.[50]

As if further discouragement were needed, 5 DCLI could hear a group of tank destroyers from *PzJgr 655* moving up to support *5 Companie* in Materborn.[51] Colonel Taylor called off the attack around 02:00 and companies were ordered to get maximum rest in preparation for a deliberate daylight attack.[52] In the meantime, "B" Company's foray to Horstmannshof had captured an artillery officer and eight men, 5 DCLI's only recorded prisoners for the 10th. However, after waiting for a while at the rendezvous point, it became clear that the rest of the battalion were not going to join them. With no armour or anti-tank guns, and no reliable communications, there was a chance "B" would be cut off, so they headed back, reaching Battalion sometime between 01:30 and 03:00.[53]

---

46 Taylor, *Infantry Colonel*, p.167.
47 5 DCLI diary; J. D. P. Stirling, *The First and The Last. The Story of the 4th/7th Royal Dragoon Guards 1939–1945* (London: Art & Education, 1946), p.142.
48 The Regiment may have been "light" in name only but 5 DCLI had success with infiltration in Normandy (Taylor, *Infantry Colonel*, pp.58–60).
49 5 DCLI diary; 43 Division comms log, 102307. The main aim of "Monty's Moonlight" is unclear to this author. Although it helped armour deploy in darkness, tanks still tended to withdraw at night, suggesting its primary function was to enhance rear area administration. Anon, *Operations of Second Army*, p.459.
50 Taylor, *Infantry Colonel*, p.167. Fatigue in headquarters is evident in the high frequency of transposed numbers and unfinished sentences in communication logs at this time but must have been much worse in platoons.
51 43 Division ISUM 143 (11 Feb) and 147 (16 Feb).
52 5 DCLI diary; 43 Recce intelligence log; 43 Division comms log. Timing for end of action from Taylor (p.167) but other sources suggest the attack may have culminated a few hours earlier.
53 5 DCLI diary and summary sheet; 214 Brigade diary. A few prisoners are mentioned for the Saalhof action but only 9 were recorded in the summary sheet's total.

None of these events were at all obvious to 43 Division because, just as the command system had confused 5 DCLI by squeezing them onto overloaded roads, forcing them to wait for ineffectual reconnaissance, and fixating on Goch, the Battalion's actions were now confusing the command system. At 01:15, 5 DCLI were reportedly 'fighting on the Materborn Feature 8853' (part of the village is in that grid square but 5 DCLI were not); at 01:30 the Battalion were reportedly mopping up, implying a successful assault; at 04:45 they were said to be having difficulty getting through Hau, four kilometres beyond their actual position. Simultaneously, reports of 5 DCLI's opposition ranged from 80 infantry and four light tanks to 200 men, six tanks and two SPs.[54] Every radio net was telling a different story, and listeners filled in the blanks to make sense of the fragments. It was daylight before 214 Brigade realised (or admitted) that German forces had not been cleared from Materborn, but even then, the positions the brigade reported were nearly a kilometre further forward than the necessarily accurate grids given by artillery observers.[55]

While 5 DCLI was struggling on the edge of Materborn, the pressure on the command system had sparked confrontations between commanders. Essame admitted discussions, 'had been of a character which cannot justly be described as being noteworthy for their cordiality.'[56] Others reported the uncordiality as an enraged shouting match between Barber (15 Division) and Major General Ivor Thomas (43 Division) on the streets of Kleve.[57] The outcome of their altercation was an agreement that 15 Division would focus on the town, while 43 returned to the main effort through Materborn, even though that required 129 Brigade to reverse out of town. Thomas therefore ordered Essame, 'not without emphasis', to press on through Materborn and Hau.[58] Several options were examined, including sending 7 SLI to reach 5 DCLI's "B" Company at Horstmannshof, but "B" was already returning by the time this option was mooted. In the end it was decided to throw 5 DCLI at Materborn one more time.

Come daylight, Taylor and Essame went forward to see the tactical problem for themselves, and their reconnaissance confirmed the value of the Materborn axis as the Corps' main effort.[59] Route Club Red became a surfaced road again at Saalhof, and the road ran on through Materborn village to all points south and east. The muddy section was a problem but was already being worked on and was a clearer route than Kleve's craters and confusion, so Materborn had to be captured. The main centre of resistance was the massive three-storey cloister building. With its thick walls, many windows, and long sight lines, the cloister dominated the approaches to Materborn so any force holding it would be difficult to outflank, suppress or dislodge.

Three hundred metres past the cloister, the church tower was an obvious artillery observation post, with views up the Saalhof road and along any approach 5 DCLI might use. Beyond these

---

54 5 DCLI diary; 4/7 DG diary; 43 Recce intelligence log. 43 Division comms log (110740) includes an assessment with four Panthers and one SP. 43 Division ISUM 147 confirms the identification of a *Jagdpanther* disabled near Materborn but three-quarters of *PzJgr 655* armour was the light 75mm *Jagdpanzer IV*, which accounts for reports of light tanks in Materborn. Both vehicles were turretless and so fit the British definition of 'SP'. A *Jagdpanther*, with its track impression 'wider than a Tiger' (this from the "B" Coy foray to Horstmannshof) could simultaneously generate reports of Tiger, Panther, and SP. One of the most enduring misidentifications led to the label 'Tiger Corner' (Map 16 and Stirling, *First and Last*, p.142) following multiple sightings, despite the nearest operational Tiger being far to the south.
55 43 Division comms log, 110715–110740.
56 Essame, *Wessex Division*, p.210.
57 Whitakers, *Rhineland* (p.67) has Barber as 'six feet, six inches of towering rage' and Thomas 'more diminutive than Barber in stature, but not in anger.' Barber may have been 6ft 9in: see D.M. Henderson, 'Operation Enterprise. The Allied Crossing of the River Elbe 1945 – The End and the Beginning' British Commission for Military History paper, July 2007.
58 Essame, *Wessex Division*, p.210.
59 43 Division comms log, 110712–110820.

key buildings, the village was a matter of sequential house clearing tasks, but copses and orchards allowed covered approaches once the attackers got into the edge of the village. The armoured threat would have been a particular concern due to the widespread perception that the Sherman was outmatched, and because 5 *Companie* had likely set up tank destroyers to fire down the road from concealed positions.[60] However, southeast of Materborn, the ground was lower, flatter and more open, with a series of hamlets clustered around the long straight roads: this was the plain where Montgomery and Horrocks had expected 43 Division to burst out and fight a manoeuvre battle.

The situation on the flanks was unclear to Essame and Taylor, who omit any mention of flanks from their accounts, but there had been progress on both sides of 214 Brigade's stalled advance. On the left flank in Kleve, 129 Brigade had been ordered to hold its positions until relieved, but its main headquarters was barely 1,200 metres from Materborn and one of its units was almost overlooking the 5 DCLI objective. Despite this proximity, 129 Brigade could offer no support because of continuing counterattacks, unreliable communications, and the higher decision to pull the Brigade out of Kleve.[61] On the right flank in the forest, 53 Division had pressed on through mud and minor opposition to put companies a kilometre south of Materborn on the 10th. By the time 5 DCLI attacked on the 11th, 53 Division had troops on the eastern edge of the forest.[62] As with the Wolfsberg and Hingstberg positions two days earlier, 30 Corps had again accidentally outflanked the defenders on both sides of its main effort. This could have been of great assistance to 5 DCLI, but formation boundaries and lengthy command chains precluded a flank attack or even coordinated flanking fire.

Despite pressure from above, Essame was keen to avoid a repeat of the previous night's hasty failure and so took time to arrange a substantial fire plan. His 10:00 orders group outlined a deliberate linear phased attack in which 5 DCLI would hit Materborn at 14:00, 7 SLI would echelon through at 16:15 to capture Hau, and 1 Worcesters would follow an hour later to secure the roads and woods north of Hau.[63] At 12:30, Taylor's orders set out a two-up attack with the road as its axis. On the left, "C" Company would seize the cloister then press on past the church to the village centre, where they would hand over to "B". Their actions would be mirrored by "A" Company then "D" to the right of the road. An artillery preparation and a light pepper pot from mortars and machine-guns would begin at 13:45, then 15 minutes later, timed concentrations would move through the village followed by the rifle companies with a troop of close support Shermans on the road between them. Most of the armour was to give direct fire support from around Saalhof.[64]

The 14:00 H-Hour was met, but it seems 5 *Companie* had anticipated what was coming and pulled out, leaving a few men to slow the advance. "C" Company managed to cross the open ground but were soon pinned down on the edge of the cloister complex, and fell behind the fire plan (northwest of Map 17). In contrast, "A" Company had a more covered approach, including

---

60 Stirling, *First and Last*, pp.60–61: 'in a straight fight at anything over point-blank range, we were backing a loser every time.' This perception is briefly examined in the next chapter.
61 43 Division comms log; 214 Brigade and 5 DCLI diaries; Anon, *The Wiltshire Regiment in the Second World War – 5th Battalion* (Salisbury: Rifles Museum, 2011), pp.20–21; 129 Brigade summary sheet; 5 Wilts diary (WO 171/5291). There was an effort to use 129 Brigade's attached 4.2-in mortars on Materborn church prior to the attack but it is not clear whether this occurred.
62 53 Division SITREPs 238 and 239.
63 5 DCLI diary, especially intelligence log, ops log and 'Battle for Materborn' (these hereon called 'loose notes'); 43 Division Tac HQ log, 111230. Compared to actions on the 10th, Taylor is vague about the 11th and there is little detail in the main diary, so the timings presented here are an amalgam from the loose notes.
64 4/7 DG; 5 DCLI loose notes; 214 Brigade diary. The close support troop is this author's assumption. It would have been unusual for this not to happen.

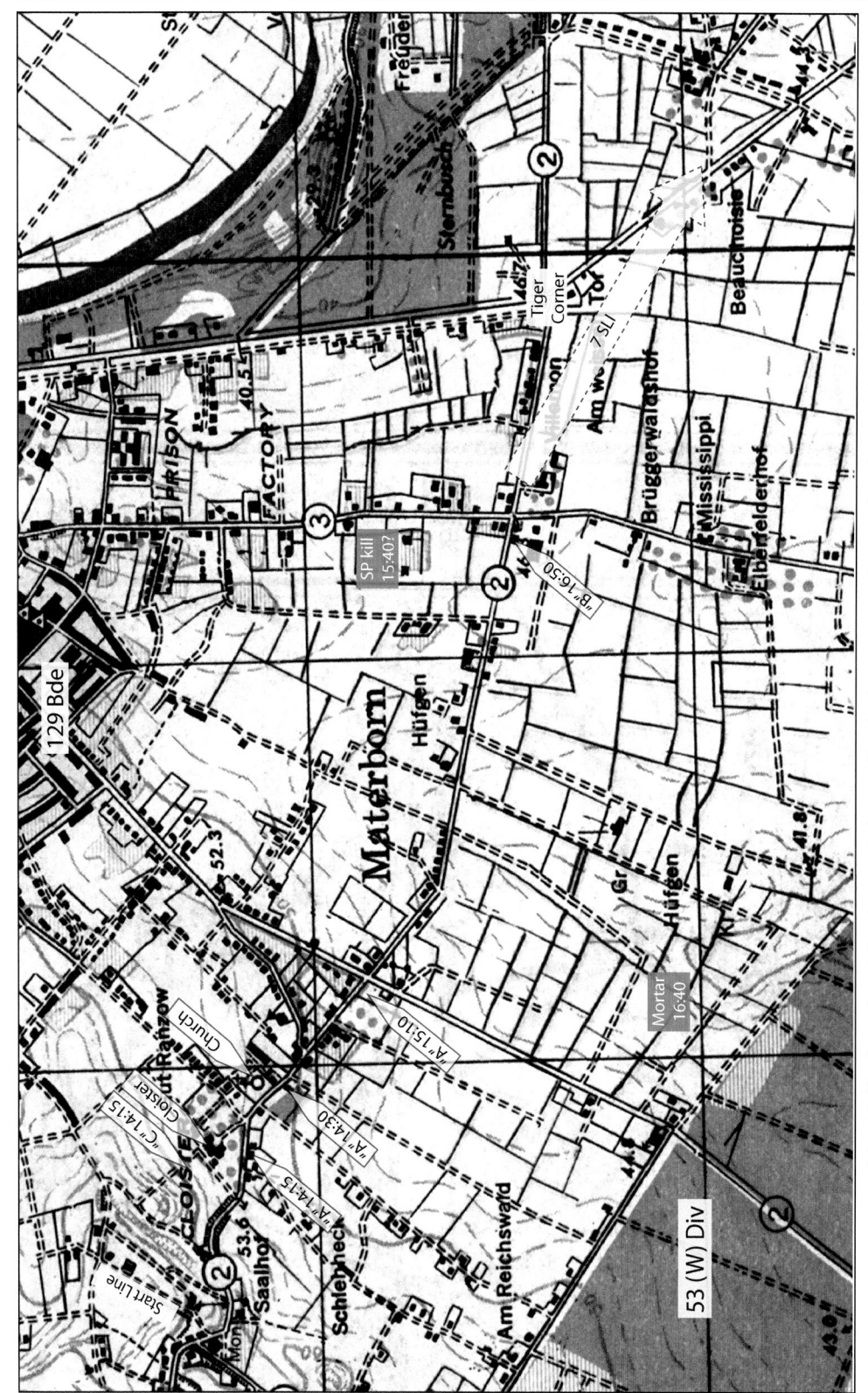

Map 17: Final attack on Materborn 11 February (D+3) 14:00 to 17:00. (National Archives, author's photograph)

a trench line that followed their side of the road, and within 15 minutes "A" were well ahead of "C", clearing houses south of the cloister. Ten minutes later "A" were approaching the church but being hit by the supporting fire plan and requesting it lift forward 100 metres. The lift took time to arrange but by 14:30 "A" Company were in the copse by the church and requesting permission to press on. The request was denied because "C" Company were still struggling to break into the cloister and Support Company were attempting to provide "C" with indirect fire.[65]

The 5 DCLI attack coincided with a general withdrawal by German troops from Kleve and Materborn, and "A" Company were not far behind them, reporting two enemy dead, no prisoners, and their belief that the rest of the village had been abandoned. Further requests to exploit were denied due to the difficulties of altering the fire plan. By 14:50 "C" had been overtaken by the follow-on companies who were approaching the church.[66] After some delay for adjustments, the fire plan was restarted at 15:25. Then, just after 15:30, "D" and "B" took over from "A". They met no opposition and at 16:50, "B" Company were consolidating a kilometre southeast of the village, having collected two German stragglers along the way.[67]

Although the second half of the Materborn attack was unopposed, Support Company, some 4/7 Dragoon Guards tanks and 43 Division's guns joined a deep battle against withdrawing German forces. At 15:35, an airborne artillery observer reported Tigers and Panthers a kilometre east of Materborn and a short while later a tank destroyer was 'brewed up' by a long shot from a Dragoon Guards Firefly.[68] The German force, including six to 10 tank destroyers from *PzJgr 655* (but not the Tigers or Panthers stated in some sources) was chased towards Hau and Bedberg by artillery directed by the air observer. The German departure marked the end of 5 DCLI's battle.[69]

At 16:30, 7 SLI passed through for a complicated fight that swung right at the junction that was already mislabelled as Tiger Corner, before losing a Sherman to a *PzJgr 655* tank destroyer. Then, with limited artillery support and their armour withdrawn for the night, 7 SLI struggled through an exhausting series of platoon attacks where 'Spandaus seemed to answer every move'.[70] After several hours of this, 7 SLI changed tack and, echoing the infiltration technique used by 5 DCLI's "B" Company the night before, they bounded ahead to reach the same location, Horstmannshof. In the early hours of the 12th (D+4) they dug in, and follow-on companies swung east to capture Hau. Later that day, just as 30 Corps was on the cusp of turning breakout into pursuit, 7 SLI were hit by the *47. Panzerkorps* counterattack.[71]

---

65 5 DCLI loose notes; 43 Division comms log.
66 5 DCLI loose notes; 214 Brigade diary.
67 5 DCLI loose notes and diary.
68 Stirling, *First and Last*, p142; 214 Brigade diary. Reported as a Panther and SP, so possibly two tank destroyers. There are other claims to these kills.
69 Artillery was also used to engage a mortar position south of Materborn after the village was cleared (Map 17, "Mortar 16:40").
70 J. L. J. Meredith, *From Normandy to Hanover: The Story of The Seventh Battalion, The Somerset Light Infantry (Prince Albert's)* (Hanover: Publisher unknown, 1945), p.115.
71 214 Brigade and 4/7 DG diaries; 7 SLI diary (WO 171/5272); 43 Division comms log. It is likely that this counter was supported Tigers of a sort, with the four to six *Sturmtiger* as artillery support for the failed attack on 53 Division in the Reichswald. These vehicles appeared a few more times in Veritable, launching their massive 380mm rockets against British and Canadian troops before being withdrawn around 2 March. L. Archer and T. Haasler, *Sturmtiger: The Combat History of Sturmmörser Kompanies 1001–1002* (Old Heathfield: Panzerwrecks, 2021), pp.91–92.

Conclusion

The Materborn salient did not collapse until the evening of D+3, which had been the best-case target for reaching Wesel, another 35 kilometres southeast. If Veritable had not been such an overlooked operation, historians might ascribe this failure to British commanders' caution or to British soldiers' lack of will, but examination of tactical level sources shows a more nuanced picture. Despite the difficulties of the Materborn fight, there were few casualties on either side. On the 10th, 5 DCLI lost four men wounded, 4/7 Dragoon Guards lost a tank and crew, and 43 Recce suffered no losses at all. The two failed attempts on Materborn therefore suffered a lower casualty rate than all but the most dramatically successful of the attacks on Veritable's D-Day. Perhaps counterintuitively, 5 DCLI's low casualties on the 10th reflected fatigue and disorientation, with troops stopped more easily than the men in D-Day assaults who were relatively fresh and knew their objectives.[72]

On the 11th, 5 DCLI lost one man killed and 17 wounded, mostly among "C" Company in front of the cloister, where they hit the same problem as 10 HLI attacking the large sturdy buildings of Kranenburg.[73] Except for "C" Company's losses, the Battalion's final attack could be considered a walkover, *5 Companie* having withdrawn but for a few delay teams. Although Taylor recalled 40 to 60 prisoners, a Panther and an SP destroyed, and one SP captured, the 214 Brigade diary records a more realistic eight defenders captured. A *Jagdpanther* was considered destroyed (Figure 13) and a *Jagdpanzer IV* was captured.[74] As with 6 KOSB's experience two days earlier, this tactical success masked an operational failure. Beside those factors covered in previous chapters, the weakness of wheeled reconnaissance in wet Northwest Europe played a part in this failure, as did the questionable tendency of armour to withdraw at night even when movement light was provided. However, the main factor in this failure was the fumbled pass between 15 and 43 Divisions, which was a direct result of a catastrophic command system failure.

The chain of 'normal accidents' from Cumming-Bruce's 'reached LURCHER' message is a familiar theme in military history and is evident in the many ifs involved surrounding this battle. If Barber and Horrocks had not been unwell, if some helpful person had not inserted the full description of Lurcher, if the ground was drier, if the road had been concrete, if everyone's radios had worked better, if there had been less armour on the roads, if everybody had got more sleep, if 43 Division had told 15 Division it was coming, if 5 DCLI had prepared to fight in Materborn instead of Goch, if movement light could have been turned off, or if 5 DCLI had walked from Nijmegen, then maybe Veritable would not have stalled on the edge of Materborn. But these single points of failure, so common in warfare, were not the problem. The problem was a command

---

72 The relationship between fatigue and motivation is the central subject of S. L. A. Marshall, *Soldier Load and the Mobility of a Nation* (Quantico: Marine Corps Association, 1950).

73 5 DCLI diary, summary sheet, loose notes, and Annex J21; Stirling, *First and Last*, p.142; 43 Recce diary. CWGC has three DCLI men died on the 11th, the two extra probably DOW. In addition to the wounded and captured in the 'bazooka' attack on the 10th, "B" Squadron 4/7 DG lost another man killed on the 11th.

74 Taylor, Battalion Order of the Day, 22 February, 5 DCLI diary, has a congratulatory tone and may include prisoners passed back by 7 SLI. The diary has only the 9 PW collected by "B" Coy on the 10th. 43 Division running total in ISUMs also suggests a lower figure. There is no consolidated figure for German casualties. Figure 13 Image Courtesy of the National Army Museum, London. The caption for this image reads 'A knocked out *Jagdpanther* south of Cleve' but thanks to the help of "Stolpi" from WW2Talk combining images and grids in ISUMs, it seems likely that this is north of Materborn, with the church spire on the left (later demolished) and the cloister's clock tower on the right. If so, it probably fell victim to armour supporting 15 Division.

Figure 13: A Jagdpanther from Pzjgr 655 north of Materborn village. (National Army Museum)

system that was not designed to cope with single-point failures, and indeed encouraged their proliferation.

It is remarkable that the capture of Materborn, on the designated main effort for the massive First Canadian Army (indeed the main effort for all three armies in 21st Army Group), was twice entrusted to a sodden, sleep-deprived infantry company, with one of those companies lacking any armour or artillery support. Despite commanders' talk of maintaining unceasing pressure on the *Wehrmacht*, there was a total of 36 hours of inactivity on the line of main effort. Historians may never know whether Cumming-Bruce misled Barber, whether Barber misled Horrocks, or even whether Horrocks gave a "move now" order to 43 Division. The multitude of lower-ranked links in this chain are also unknowable, but clearly each person in the chain would have acted differently if they had understood the tactical situation and the operational objective.

The pass was fumbled because the well-known limitations to command-by-plan hit home, then the radio nets necessary for command-by-direction failed too. Even on D-Day, despite long preparation, every battalion lost communications with its brigade for at least a few hours, and usually for most of the day. Links from brigades to divisions to corps fared better, but without information from battalions there was little worth saying. Much that was said was inaccurate, irrelevant, and consumed processing power. By D+1, 30 Corps signallers were complaining that divisions were hogging radio nets by repeating global situation reports to one another, and that half the paper despatches sent from 30 Corps were set at 'immediate', thereby overloading the despatch rider system.[75] It seems the system was ignorant of its own limitations.

---

75   Judging by reports from 214 Brigade, this continued until D+3.

Radio nets failed through the compounding interaction between reliability, usability, and training, which was most obvious with the man-portable No. 18 sets in battalion and company headquarters. These were the best technology available but like many tactical communication systems before and since, the No. 18 rarely performed to its advertised potential because it was bulky, fragile, low-powered, difficult to use, had a short battery life, and was an obvious target. Radios in vehicles and static headquarters were more likely to function but were often irrelevant because of the difficulty in getting vehicles forward to where the information was, especially when fighting in woods and villages. As a result, the infantry simultaneously owned command responsibility, the most valuable information, and the least reliable radios. Even when company sets did work, they were often drowned out by the more powerful radios of their supporting artillery and armour. When gunners and tanks stayed close to their infantry, they could sometimes relay information without too much delay, but in Materborn this failed too. Guesswork and rumour filled the void, as evidenced by the wide estimates of enemy strengths and friendly locations. Like mines, mud, flood, and congestion, the problems with radio communication were expected, but they were problems that the 30 Corps command system did not account for. It was a command system built around a command-by-direction ethos that required tactical radios to work better than they ever could.[76]

There were suspicions of German jamming, but the main problem was mutual interference from having so many Allied radios squeezed into such a small space.[77] The crude technology of the day meant frequencies overlapped and jammed one another far more than they do today, and while divisions deconflicted their own frequencies as best they could, the proliferation and size of networks made this difficult. In each division as many as 20 different frequencies were being used simultaneously, and while a division's command net had only eight official users, there were rear, main, and tactical duplicates of some call signs, semi-official extra call signs for artillery and armour, plus parasitic users like Phantom and the unofficial liaison teams.[78] Signal interference had been noted on previous operations and was expected to cause information loss on D-Day, but it continued throughout Veritable, peaking with the Materborn action when 43 and 15 Divisions passed through one another while sandwiched between 3 Canadian Division and 53 Division.[79]

It would be easy to blame technological failure, but the problem ran deeper than this. Command-by-influence should have cut through the clutter and saved the day, but the available information was too fragmented and organisational approaches (the different ways units and formations tended to solve problems) were too diverse for influence to succeed.[80] The inconsistent approaches can be seen in the very different army and corps plans, in the divergent intelligence assessments, in 15 Division's focus on Kleve, in 43 Division's intention to elbow lesser formations out of the

---

76 Radio signal interference was the subject of a massive effort at the strategic level, and is the main subject of Anon, *Report of Signal Division Supreme Headquarters Allied Expeditionary Force in Operation "Overlord"* (Germany: Publisher unknown, 1945), which runs to nearly 3,000 pages. At the tactical level signallers and commanders seem to have been left to muddle through.

77 15 Division Sigs diary, 090645.

78 One net for each of the nine battalions, three in each brigade, eight in division. 15 Division Sigs diary has a wiring diagram suggesting 20 sets monitoring 13 nets in the Main HQ.

79 Blake, *Mountain* (p.129) relates the experience in Op Blackcock: 'One odd and daunting result of the congestion was that the very air was crowded with messages on perilously close frequencies.' As in all armies there was constant competition between individuals trying to get more powerful radios (see Henniker, *Image*, p.232) thereby creating more interference.

80 Cultures in this context are the beliefs, values, behavioural norms, and basic assumptions that dictate how organisations approach problems: E.H. and P. Schein, *Organizational Culture and Leadership* (London: Wiley & Son, 2016), p.4. Military applications of organisational culture can be seen in McCann, *The Human in Command*, passim, and Storr, *Something Rotten*, passim.

way, and in the willingness of armour to curl up for the night. As noted earlier, command-by-influence needs internal predictability but where some units pressed on aggressively, others were extremely cautious; some took chances while others waited for direction. Influence also needs clear statements of intent, but these were lacking in the orders issued at every level and in verbal directions like Barber's response to the 'reached LURCHER' message.

One outcome of the confused command system was that battalion COs were subject to inconsistent micromanagement. In 15 Division, subordinates had been given considerable detail about what they needed to do to conform to the plan, then they were half directed to do something else when the plan failed, then expected to improvise once communications failed, then seemingly told to stand down and do nothing. In 43 Division, subordinates only had orders to get to Goch and were expected to improvise how they got there, but when they did improvise, they were told to stop and conform to new plans. Tired and stressed people are more susceptible to the cognitive biases that increase the salience of old information, such as those underpinning organisational approaches or the details of an outdated plan. To prompt a reassessment in such circumstances new information must be loud and unequivocal. It was not. Therefore, in line with the original plans and basic assumptions, reconnaissance regiments were moved to the fronts of queues, 5 DCLI stayed in quick lift for a full day, and 15 Division unnecessarily replaced 43 Division in Kleve.

The differing degrees of autonomy and initiative in 30 Corps were evident when forward movement was stopped across the whole of 15 Division; the crucial exceptions to that diktat were the dozens of Churchills and Kangaroos (attached from other organisations with different assumptions) that drove back to harbour areas, forcing 15 Recce off the road. In 43 Division, the approach seems more in line with command-by-influence, with 1 Worcesters advancing into Kleve and 5 DCLI sending "B" Company on their infiltration foray. But these examples of initiative could not survive for long in a system more focused on plan and direction; 1 Worcesters were eventually recalled, and "B" Company recalled itself. The fate of initiative in a centralised system is exemplified by 5 DCLI's "A" Company, eager to press on through Materborn and harry a fleeing enemy but stifled by a fire plan set in stone. Their attack had at least benefitted from time to rest and charge radio batteries, but with control directed through Support Company, then onto artillery nets and back to the guns of several divisions, the fire plan was resistant to change and this allowed German forces to withdraw in reasonable order.

Although it is not explicit in surviving records, excessive span of command probably contributed to the dysfunctional system. The limits of human processing power are reflected in the structure of military organisations, which typically limit a commander to three or four subordinate units. Horrocks was in command of seven divisions and his arboreal command post on D-Day fed him information directly from their brigades.[81] In such circumstances commanders are even more prone to being dragged into detail and, because they cannot be among all the detail at the same time, this creates inconsistent micromanagement. It is tempting to see a large part of the problem emanating from Horrocks, overloaded, unwell and sleep deprived, fixating on one division at a time, then on Kleve instead of Materborn.[82] However, the body of communication logs suggest Horrocks and his subordinates were so confused by fragmented situation reports that they were unaware of the Materborn problem until it was too late.

---

81   This potentially increased his span of command to 21 subordinates, but half the brigades were silent on D-Day. J. L. Marsden, 'Span of Command and Control in the British Army: an Initial Study' (Defence Evaluation and Research Agency report, 1996) puts the upper limit around five subordinate units.

82   There are other indications that Horrocks confused his objectives, having singled out Nutterden for napalm attack, then in memoirs and interviews repeatedly referring to the 'Nutterden feature' instead of the Materborn Feature. For example, Horrocks, *Full Life*, p.245.

Command-by-plan needs to create schemes that account for friction and enemy action, command-by-direction needs a reliable communication network, command-by-influence needs a clear and coherent chain of intention; none of these requirements were present in 30 Corps. Like most formations, 30 Corps did not have a designed command system but a disconnected collection of technologies, organisations, procedures, and people. Plan, direction, and influence were muddled, and so commanders and soldiers were too. That failure had a tactical effect in Materborn which then had a crippling impact on operational progress. The unnecessary pause meant 30 Corps was bottled up around Kleve when *47. Panzerkorps* counterattacked and another week of hard fighting was needed before the Allies reached Goch.

5

Infantry and Armour

16 TO 18 FEBRUARY – LOWLAND DIVISION AROUND AFFERDEN – CULTURE VERSUS ORGANISATION – THE MASTERPLAN REVISED – HOW TO PUSH OVER PINE TREES – COOPERATION, FAMILIARITY, AND CONTEMPT – ARTISAN HISTORY – OPPORTUNITY MISSED – SYMBIOSIS

Culture and Competence

One of the more influential criticisms of British Army effectiveness is Stephen Biddle's *Military Power*, which suggests that poor coordination of British armour and infantry in Normandy reflected a nationwide or army-wide mind-set that was unable to grasp the "modern system" of force employment. Biddle describes the tactical component of the modern system as 'a tightly interrelated complex of cover, concealment, dispersion, suppression, small-unit independent manoeuvre, and combined arms' and one of his three cases studies uses the example of Operation Goodwood to suggest that 21st Army Group did none of these things well.[1] However, it is evident from Biddle's assessment that the main problem in Goodwood was poor cooperation between infantry and armour. Armoured divisions launched 'dense, exposed waves' of tanks with extraordinarily little infantry support, suffered crippling casualties as a result, then left equally unsupported infantry units to be pinned down by pockets of bypassed defenders.[2] More balanced analyses have included other Normandy operations to show Goodwood to be more exception than rule, but this chapter uses one of Veritable's most obscured subordinate operations to show the extent to which cooperation between infantry and armour was still a problem in 1945.[3]

To get to that point we need to fast forward the Veritable story through four busy days where the phenomena examined in previous chapters were equally evident in British, Canadian, and German forces. When *47. Panzerkorps* struck on the morning of the 12th (D+4) it suffered many of the problems that had bedevilled 30 Corps; the *Korps* attacked late, slow, and piecemeal, with

---

1   Biddle, *Military Power*, p.3. Biddle's focus on force employment is a much-needed counter to assessments that fixate on mass and technology but involves a selective use of secondary sources and poor definitions. It has no definition of national culture, but the modern system requires: 'extensive independent decision making [that] for social and political reasons many states are unwilling to tolerate' (p.49). Two of the three case studies are of Britain failing to grasp the modern system.
2   Biddle, *Military Power*, pp.120–121.
3   For example: J. Buckley, *British Armour in the Normandy Campaign 1944* (London: Routledge, 2004), 33–37; Dick, *Victory*, passim.

little knowledge of its opposition and with the incredibly ambitious objective of recapturing Kleve. For two days, *15. Panzergrenadier* and *116. Panzer Divisione* launched assaults against a superior force in firm defensive positions. *Panzergrenadiere* repeatedly formed up in sight of Allied FOOs and died in their hundreds, but their actions halted the 30 Corps advance.[4]

A new front emerged and solidified. In the north, the amphibious flank protection of 3 Canadian Division secured the Kleve–Emmerich road. Just south of there, 15 Division launched its first mobile column onto *84. Division*'s new hard shoulder, initiating days of bitter fighting in Moyland woods. In the centre, 43 and 53 Divisions found their ammunition stocks so depleted that they could not advance against *47. Panzerkorps*. South of the Reichswald, 51 Division spent a week grappling with *FJR 2* and *GR 1222*, secured a series of towns and villages and opened a much-needed second supply route to Kleve but were only halfway to Goch, the Division's D+1 objective.

> Meanwhile on 16 Feb, 52 (L) Inf Div (less one bde) arrived in the battle area and took over the RIGHT hand sector of 51 (H) Inf Div. They were directed on WEEZE and were responsible for clearing the EAST bank of the MAAS. The leading bde, 157, started to clear the wooded area NE of AFFERDEN 8038 the same afternoon, and during the night secured AFFERDEN. The Recce Regt established themselves on the road AFFERDEN – REMPELD 8238, and in pursuance of their task of occupying GROOT HORST 8639, other elements closed on the fortified castle of KASTEEL BLIJENBEEK 8338. Further advances in this area were well-nigh impossible without special equipment. The leading tps of the Div were now faced with about 200 yds of deep flood water beyond which were strong enemy defences covered by an anti-tank ditch.[5]

This paragraph is the first mention of 52 Lowland Division in the 21st Army Group post-operation report, and it appears to describe events of little substance; a division arrives, quickly secures a wood and a village, then reaches an obstacle it was neither equipped nor perhaps expected to overcome. The opening 'Meanwhile' and the vague 'directed on WEEZE' imply triviality. As with the main Veritable storyline, this version of events was produced by 21st Army Group's planners and dictated the operation's subsequent historiography: the Official Histories have 52 Division engaged in ill-defined fighting around Afferden, Elstob and Zuehlke present the action as flank protection, and the Whitakers, Hastings and Buckley make no mention of it at all.[6]

Fragments of the Afferden battle feature in Division and unit histories, in White's classic memoir *With the Jocks*, and in some fundamental operational research.[7] However, there has been no attempt to corroborate these strands with primary sources or to combine them into a coherent assessment, and this has helped to perpetuate misconceptions about Veritable and about British Army effectiveness. In Stephen Hart's *Colossal Cracks*, British soldiers' fragile morale is countered by the 'crude techniques and competent generalship' of Montgomery's masterplan approach, and both were 'evident in "Veritable", which was continued inexorably day after day in accordance with the phases outlined in the original plan.'[8] In contrast, Charles Forrester's *Monty's Functional Doctrine*, contends that large parts of 21st Army Group had evolved an element of

---

4 Guderian, *Normandy to the Ruhr*, pp.374–386.
5 21 AG, *Veritable*, p.29.
6 Ellis, *Victory in the West*, p.266; Stacey, *Victory Campaign*, pp.482, 490; Elstob *Reichswald*, p.146; Zuehlke, *Forgotten Victory*, Kindle 4014.
7 Blake, *Mountain*, pp.146–158; Anon, *War History of the 4th Battalion, King's Own Scottish Borderers, 1939–1945* (Halle: KOSB, 1946), pp.130–138; White, *With the Jocks*, pp.182–195. Thornton and Watson 'Defence in Woods' (pp. D-17 to D-24) was the basis for the first draft of this chapter's battle description.
8 Hart, 'Montgomery', pp.22 and 119.

command-by-influence. Where Hart sees all British formations as 'pedestrian', Forrester directs this criticism only towards 52 Division (and that a month after Veritable) because its commanders failed to grasp 'the new understanding of the roles of armour and infantry in the changed conditions of combat.'[9] This would imply that rather than Britain being culturally resistant to Biddle's modern system, it might just be certain formations that failed to grasp the new understanding of infantry-armour cooperation.

This chapter will show that, contrary to Hart's suggestion of dogged adherence to a masterplan, 52 Division's deployment represented a considerable adaptation to Veritable's original schemes. The chapter will also show that 52 Division's overlooked operational failure was not due to its pedestrian commanders, or to any moral deficit in its soldiers. Instead, the chapter's primary aim is to use 52 Division's experience to highlight how Montgomery's 'functional doctrine' was dysfunctional in the critical area of infantry-armour cooperation. However, contrary to Biddle's suggestion that poor cooperation was due to a vague but potentially incurable nationwide or army-wide resistance to the modern system, the chapter will show that poor cooperation was due to specific and correctable features of 21st Army Group's organisation.

Cleverness and Manoeuvre

Afferden, a Dutch village east of the Maas, had no impact on Veritable's planning because it was in an area assigned to Second Army and Operation Ventilate (even some post-war mapping shows the boundary between 30 Corps and 8 Corps following the river Niers through Gennep, north of Afferden).[10] But as Ventilate expired, Veritable's boundary moved to the Maas, making 51 Highland Division responsible for an operational area three times the size of that assigned to other divisions. While Montgomery initially expected 51 to 'clean up area between Reichswald Forest and MEUSE [Maas] as far as AFFERDEN' within a few days, 51 Division's commander, Major General Tom Rennie, realised this was impossible and passed his concerns up to Horrocks.[11] The whole scheme for 51 Division had been predicated on German resistance collapsing once 15 and 43 Divisions began to exploit and pursue from Materborn, but with no breakout there was no collapse. As 51 Division's battles continued to be a slog, Horrocks asked Rennie to propose a solution, and on the 13th (D+5), Rennie recommended using a fresh division 'to bypass GOCH to the south by developing a thrust from the GENNEP area to take WEEZE.' Bypassing Goch would then allow a thrust on the *Schlieffen Linie* (Hochwald layback) encircling the main German force around Goch, Uedem and Kalkar. (If this scheme were laid over Map 5, the fresh division would strike down the eastern side of the Maas to Afferden then head due east to the point where Guards Armoured Division is shown swinging towards Wesel.) 'Once the HOCHWALD feature is ours we could dominate the approaches to the WESEL bridges and there would be a very good chance of seizing the crossings over the RHINE in this area.'[12] Rennie's bold scheme put cleverness and manoeuvre back on the table.

Rennie seems to have had Guards Armoured Division in mind for this operation, but his ambition was thwarted because the narrow road to Weeze crossed a floodplain where the soil was

---

9   Hart, 'Montgomery' p.91; C. Forrester, *Monty's Functional* (Kindle 3982) is centred on claims in M. Carver, *Out of Step: The Memoirs of Field Marshal Lord Carver* (London: Penguin, 1990) and related to a period when Craver's 4 Armoured Brigade was under command of 52 Division in April 1945.
10 For example, Diagram 3 of 21 AG, *Veritable*.
11 Harris 'Rhineland I', p.28.
12 51 Division diary: letter from Lieutenant Colonel Leslie (51 Div) to Brigadier Jones (30 Corps), 13 Feb, confirming earlier generals' conversation.

INFANTRY AND ARMOUR 125

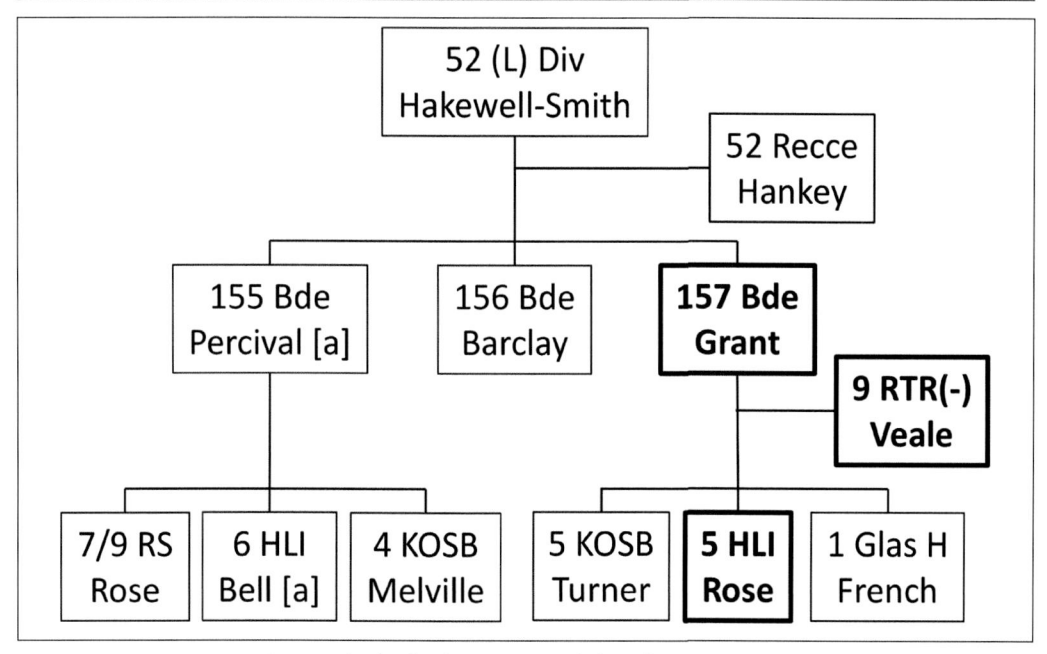

```
                    52 (L) Div
                    Hakewell-Smith
                         |
         ┌───────────────┼──────────────┬─────────┐
         |               |              |    52 Recce
         |               |              |    Hankey
      155 Bde         156 Bde        157 Bde
      Percival [a]    Barclay        Grant
                                        |
                                        ├──── 9 RTR(-)
                                        |     Veale
   ┌─────┬─────┐     ┌─────┬─────┬─────┐
 7/9 RS 6 HLI  4 KOSB  5 KOSB 5 HLI  1 Glas H
 Rose   Bell[a] Melville Turner Rose  French
```

Figure 14: Abridged organisational chart for 52 Division.

believed to have unusually high plasticity and water retention qualities.[13] However, a new shuffling of higher formations made it feasible to transfer an infantry division from Second Army, and so 52 Division got the job.[14] For weeks 52 Division (Figure 14) had been defending along the Maas and preparing for a quite different task: 'If the main attack under Canadian command had gone briskly from the beginning, then the Lowlanders would have crossed the Maas to cut through the retreating German forces in Operation Ventilate.'[15] The sudden switch from Ventilate to Veritable came on the 15th (D+7) and, in very un-pedestrian manner, 52 Division issued orders the next day.[16]

The plan had four phases. On the afternoon of the 16th, 157 Brigade was to clear the *Broederbosch* (point 1 at Map 18) and push patrols out to the line of the road between Afferden and Groote Horst. In parallel with that, 52 Recce would capture Afferden (point 2), cross the *Eckeltsche Beek* "anti-tank ditch" then protect the Division's flank by patrolling the triangle of roads from there to Bergen and Groote Horst (2a). On the morning of the 17th, 155 Brigade would launch the main thrust eastwards to secure the 'high ground about GROOT HORST 8639' (3). Finally, late on the 17th or early on the 18th (D+10) elements of the Division would press on to capture Weeze (4). There were some ambiguities in this plan (for example, whether the supposed high ground included the village of Siebengewald at 3a) but its biggest problem was that despite having thousands of

---

13 52 Division ISUM 68, 16 Feb. Veritable's mud helped spawn a branch of Cold War research into soil composition and ground pressure that continued into the 1980s, e.g., D. Rowland, 'Tracked Vehicle Ground Pressure and its Effect on Soft Ground Performance', undated conference paper c1980.
14 1 Glas H and 5 KOSB diaries (WO 171/5191 and 5216). It is not clear why the closer, readier 2 Canadian Division was not used.
15 Blake, *Mountain*, p.150.
16 Harris Rhineland I, pp.30–31; 52 Division diary SITREPs 141400–142330 (WO 171/4260); 157 Brigade diary (WO 171/4420) 11-15 February. Engineers were still examining options for crossing the Maas when 52 Division was ordered to stop planning for Op Ventilate on 12 February.

126 SLOG OR SWAN

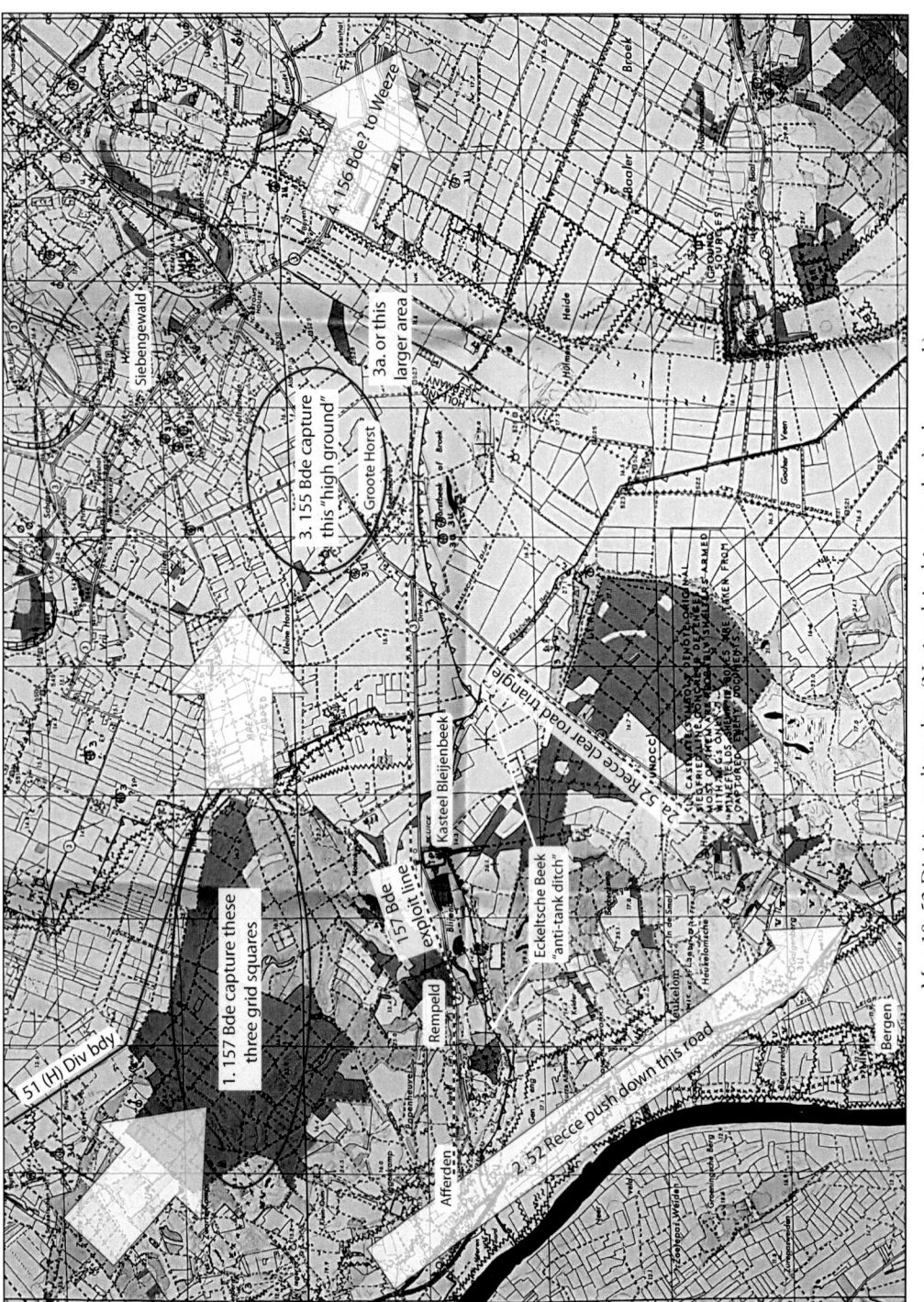

Map 18: 52 Division outline plan. (National Archives, author's photograph)

unemployed tanks, 30 Corps assigned no armour to 52 Division until 24 hours before the attack.[17] That role fell to "B" and "C" Squadrons of 9th Battalion, The Royal Tank Regiment.

Two days before joining 52 Lowland Division, 9 RTR had been supporting 53 Welsh Division in the Reichswald. The contrast between 9 RTR's battles under these two divisions is central to this chapter (and a little confusing due to the close numbering of these formations) so a summary of 9 RTR's earlier experience is necessary. From 1942, 9 RTR spent a year as an organic component of 53 Division in the "New Model" organisation, where divisions were comprised of two infantry brigades and an armoured brigade.[18] When the New Model was abandoned in 1943, infantry divisions lost their organic tank support and 9 RTR became part of the independent 34 Tank (later Armoured) Brigade. As part of 34 Brigade, 9 RTR were loaned to many formations but supported 53 Division on at least four occasions in Northwest Europe.

Immediately prior to supporting 53 in the Reichswald, 9 RTR spent a week in collective training with the Welsh infantry, which included mandatory social drinking events to encourage group cohesion. These technical and social preparations left 9 RTR's commanders 'full of confidence in [their] ability to remain with the infantry day and night' and 'determined, if necessary, to expend a complete squadron before giving up the attempt to lead the infantry into the edge of the Reichswald.'[19] Each squadron was assigned to a specific battalion throughout the Reichswald fighting and prior to H-Hour on 8 February, the tanks and infantry harboured together and moved to their start lines together. The result, despite notorious bogging, fatigue, and mechanical difficulties, was that 9 RTR stuck with 53 Division's infantry throughout their week in the Reichswald, even dismounting to stalk German armour with PIATs when necessary. Yet the close cooperation with the Welsh infantry meant 9 RTR lost only two tanks and eight personnel to enemy action that week.[20]

On the 14th, 9 RTR were withdrawn from 53 Division to rest and refit, but the next day they were assigned to 52 Division, a formation they had never worked with before. The units of 52 Division had limited experience with armour, having trained for mountain and air-landing operations but then being used in neither role. Parts of the Division had briefly fought alongside armoured units in the Arnhem corridor and in the Scheldt, but weather, terrain and training constraints meant they experienced little of the detailed cooperation needed in close country. Their most intense period working with armour came during Operation Blackcock but did not involve the Churchill tanks and crews designed and trained for close support work.[21] It seems the first meeting between the armour and infantry that were to fight together in the Broederbosch on the 16th was when a 9 RTR liaison officer attended 157 Brigade's orders group on the evening of the 15th.

The 157 Brigade plan was to assemble south of Gennep from 10:00 on the 16th, then move south to form up on a start line northwest of the Broederbosch (Map 19). H-Hour was not until

---

17 52 Division Op Instr 8, Division diary; 1 Glas H diary.
18 D. Crow, *British and Commonwealth Armoured Formations (1919–46)* (Windsor: Profile, 1972), pp.34–35.
19 P. Beale, *Tank Tracks: 9th Battalion Royal Tank Regiment at War 1940–45* (Stroud: Budding Books, 1995), pp.8, 168, 170–171; 34 Armoured Brigade diary; 9 RTR diary (WO 171/4713).
20 9 RTR summary sheet and diary; CWGC; Beale, *Tank Tracks*, p.179.
21 9 RTR diary; 21 AG, 'Report on Operation Blackcock' (pdf of 1945 document, possibly CAB 106/974), pp.17–22; Blake, *Mountain*, pp.126–145. Blake (p.136) has a 1 Lothians sergeant apologising for shooting a house occupied by 5 KOSB during Blackcock: '"You see, sir," he explained, "We are not used to working with your Jocks and have never seen infantry moving at such a speed ahead of the tanks."' S. Christopherson and J. Holland (ed.), *An Englishman at War: The Wartime Diaries of Stanley Christopherson, DCO MC TD, 1939–45* (London: Corgi, 2020), Kindle 7154, claims 52 Division had not worked with armour before December 1944.

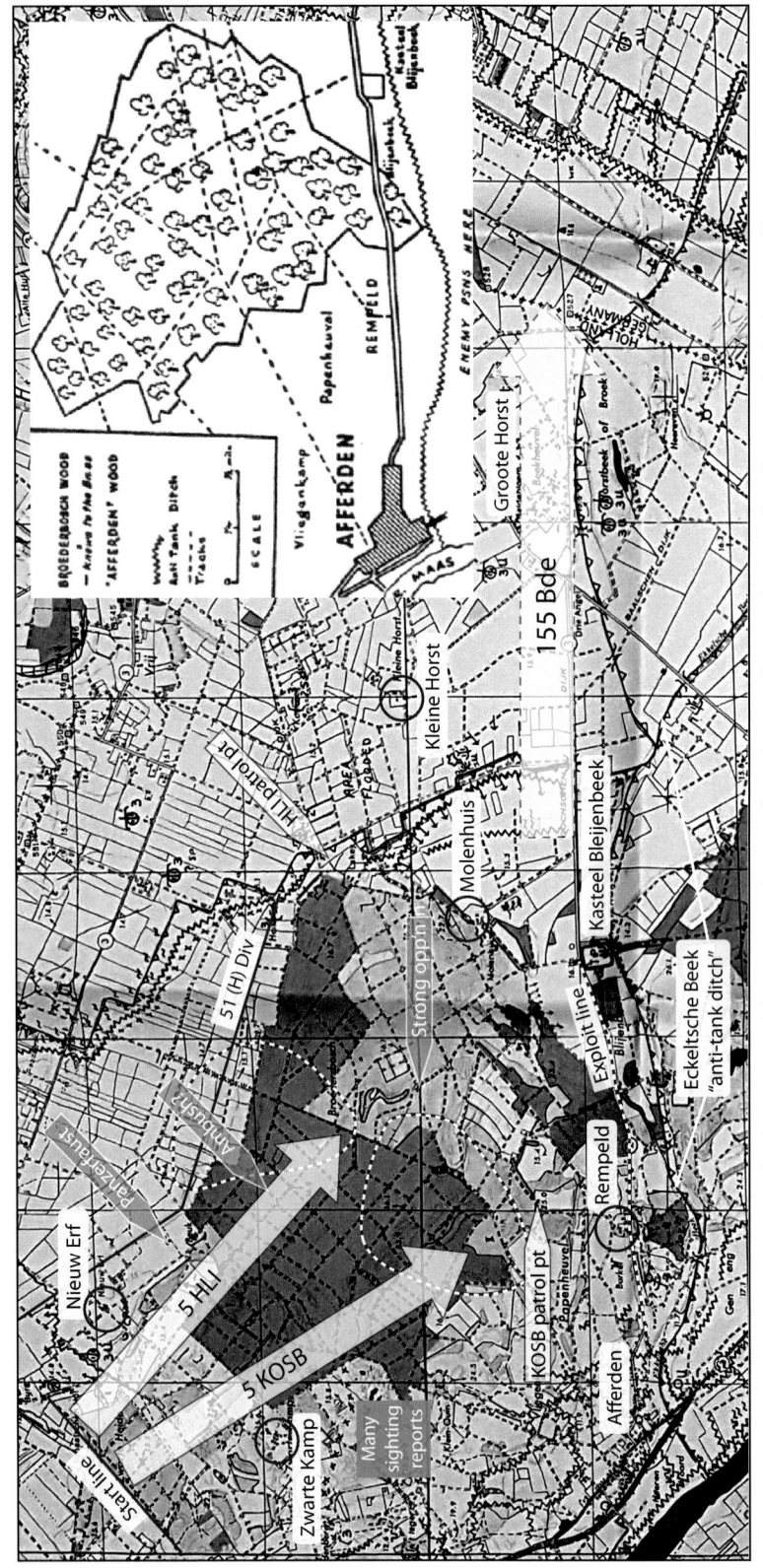

Map 19: 157 Brigade plan and notable enemy, with insert from 4 KOSB history. (National Archives, author's photograph)

15:00, suggesting the Brigade's priority was to get all the working parts through the bottleneck at Gennep then tie up details and study the ground.[22] The first phase of the attack had 5 HLI and "C" Squadron of 9 RTR forward left, with 5 KOSB and "B" Squadron forward right, with a troop of Archer tank destroyers bringing up the rear in each battalion group. Together they would capture the 'wooded area 8140 – 8240 – 8340 [the three grid squares in the middle of the Broederbosch] destroying all enemy wherever found' and, if possible, press on to the line of the road running from Afferden to *Kasteel Bleijenbeek*. Once the woods were secure, battalions would adopt defensive positions (the dashed goose egg shapes at Map 19) and deploy standing patrols to secure a start line for 155 Brigade and the third phase of 52 Division's plan.[23] Then, if 52 Recce had been successful in their advance through Afferden, 1 Glasgow Highlanders would exploit past 5 HLI and 5 KOSB; if not, the Highlanders would quickly attack Afferden.[24]

The attack was to incorporate the supposed morale-eroding lessons from the D-Day fire plan which were already being promulgated to all 21st Army Group's artillery units: 'Even before the arrival of assaulting tps, the enemy must be made to feel that he is overwhelmed. He must be convinced of the hopelessness of continuing the struggle.'[25] This new policy included no mention of the need for the fire plan to be closely coordinated with the infantry advance, and barrages were discouraged in favour of concentrations on observed enemy positions. Despite an emphasis on using 'all available guns', the policy was balanced against looming ammunition shortages. Victor fire missions would no longer use all the corps' guns at the observer's discretion but involve perhaps half the guns and only engage dense targets of at least 100 infantry or 20 armoured vehicles.[26] The 52 Division fire plan timings were also curtailed, with 30 minutes of counter-battery fire then 15 minutes of preparatory fire before H-Hour. If all the shells allotted to the attack were used, the intensity of fire would be around a third of that used on Veritable's D-Day but achieving that would require observed fire.[27]

The battle was to be dominated by the terrain of the Broederbosch, a small Dutch version of the Reichswald. The elevation and sandy soil were like the Reichswald, but with far fewer vehicles churning the tracks, bogging was to prove much less prevalent. Trees provided concealment, constrained vehicle movement, made digging difficult, and added the threat of artillery tree bursts. Unmapped undulations in the ground and unpredictable tree heights made it difficult to estimate artillery fall of shot, but the main gunnery problem would be getting observers close enough to

---

22   9 RTR diary; OO No. 9, 157 Brigade diary, probably issued at 160430, making timings tight for getting orders to companies moving at 160515. Timings may have been dictated by higher as Gennep was essential for the 2 Canadian Corps build-up.

23   Map 19 is an amalgam of 157 Brigade OO 9, 52 Division, 5 HLI (WO 171/5023) and 5 KOSB diaries; inset from Anon, *War History*, p.131.

24   Written in uncertainty and on the move, this is one of the most confusing collections of orders this author has seen. 157 Brigade OO 9 says little about 52 Recce or 1 Glas H tasks, which are inferred from Division and artillery orders (52 HQRA OO 10, WO 171/4264) and from diaries. Some diaries suggest 157 Brigade potentially securing Groote Horst with 52 Recce held back until dark or 17th, while 1 Glas H diary makes no mention of exploiting.

25   52 HQRA OO 10.

26   52 HQRA OO 10. A Victor target involved all corps guns; Uncle a division's guns; Mike a brigade's guns.

27   Estimate from 157 Brigade orders, 52 HQRA OO 10, 79 Fd Regt orders (WO 171/4824), the Swann Report and orders of battle at nigelef.tripod.com and BAOR, *Tour*, p.98. Each bn was to be supported by one of 52 Division's field regiments, with additional fire from 51 and 53 Division guns and three AGRAs. 52 Division brought forward 200 rounds per gun, so potentially 9,600; supporting field batteries limited to 80 rounds per gun, so potentially another 9,600. Remainder limited to 40 rounds per gun so up to 6,080 medium, 800 heavy and 960 3.7-inch rounds. The two battalion areas cover a little over six grid squares, making an average of 4,507 rds/km²; Swann reported 15,083 rounds on the average D-Day grid square.

confidently order concentrations. The accurately mapped rides aided targeting and navigation, but the loss of distant reference points (like church steeples) outweighed this, and the woods negated most of the effect of movement light for night actions.

A key concern when attacking into managed woods was long-range fire from concealed antitank guns and machine-guns shooting down the straight rides. This applied in the Broederbosch, but the undulating ground meant there were few places where shots could be attempted above 300 metres. Some of the trickiest tactical problems came from sudden variations in cover and movement, with recently harvested blocks of woodland creating open fields of fire that could be hundreds of metres across, while younger, denser planting was exceedingly difficult to move through. These variations would make it hard for subunits to keep pace and keep contact with one another.[28]

The Division seems to have had few air photographs and maps to work from, and the extent of the Broederbosch was not evident from the issued 1:25000 sheet (the main part of Map 19). That map was based on a 1930s German original and the paler part of the Broederbosch was labelled as brush, but was actually young planting that had grown considerably by 1945, as indicated by the insert to Map 19.[29] Mapping confusion may explain why, contrary to the Division's orders to secure grid squares 8140, 8240, and 8340, subordinate plans referred only to 8140 and 8240, and why 157 Brigade's defensive goose eggs did not cover that third grid square.[30]

Other tactical problems were expected at strongpoint farms, at Nieuw Erf on 5 HLI's left, Zwarte Kamp on 5 KOSB's right, and Molenhuis, on the south-eastern edge of the forest. Southeast of the Broederbosch were some long stretches of open ground that were dominated by concealed fire positions in the forest-covered higher ground south of the shallow valley of the Eckeltsche Beek.[31] The Eckeltsche was paralleled by the road from Afferden to Groote Horst, which was to be the main axis on the way to Weeze, and halfway along the stream lay Kasteel Bleijenbeek, which would later become a bastion of defence and a focal point for memoirs. Other features that were to become important were an unnamed tributary of the Eckeltsche (the north–south anti-tank obstacle down the middle of Map 19) and the road bridge across it. One element of uncertainty was the open left flank for 5 HLI, which 32 Guards Brigade (then under command of 51 Division) was to cover by fire but would not attack. These and other snags were worked over as troops approached the start line but were often unresolved, with personal accounts emphasising confusion and fatigue prior to contact.[32]

The 52 Division history colourfully described the defender as 'clinging by his eyebrows to a second-last bastion of the Reich ... The very desperation of his position spurred him into a frenzy of fantastic defence.'[33] The more sober pre-battle intelligence picture was dependent on reports from 51 Division, which had only seen the northern edge of the Broederbosch. On the 13th, 51

---

28 Paragraph compiled from walking the ground, following diaries. Beale, *Tank Tracks* (pp.183, 186) has trees from 1m to 6m tall and 'in need of an early thinning'.
29 There were also marked differences between the 1:100000 planning sheet and the 1944 US Geographic Survey that Veritable's defence overprints were based on. The only air photograph mentioned by sources is the image of Kasteel Bleijenbeek used later in the operation. Another "map recce" problem was the order to take Groote Horst 'high ground'. Everywhere near it was about 16 metres above sea level.
30 51 Division comms log (WO 205/957), 161005 has its LO report 52's intention to 'clear wood 8140 8240 entirely', suggesting that even at this late stage 52 Division thought the woods did not extend into 8340 or the three grid squares to the south.
31 White, *With the Jocks* (p.167) has the supposed anti-tank ditch 'unexpectedly flooded'.
32 Diary of J. W. Hendry (Sp/"D" Coy 1 Glas H) kindly provided by his grandson John Hendry via genealogy. com; Beale, *Tank Tracks*, pp.189, 190; White, *With the Jocks*, p.162.
33 Blake, *Mountain*, p.152.

Division had beaten off an armour-supported counterattack by *FJR 2* on Heijen (between Gennep and Afferden) and the following day RAF Typhoons attacked and dispersed German trucks and armour near Afferden.[34] Reports then speculated that the area had been abandoned or that there was only a company left holding Afferden, but just before 52 Division's attack a 'stop press' report included sightings of several infantry squads and a possible 88mm gun on the northwestern edge of the forest (Map 19's "Many sighting reports").[35] Intelligence compiled after the battle suggests the defenders of Broederbosch and Afferden were predominantly remnants of *FJR 2*, comprising around 400 infantry, along with mortars, infantry guns, and a few 75mm anti-tank guns. There were two or three tank destroyers or assault guns in the area, but these had most likely been withdrawn over the Eckeltsche before the battle.[36]

Into the Woods

Soon after 52 Division's fire plan started, 32 Guards Brigade's artillery began 'shooting up Bosche running away' on the open flank (just off the northern edge of Map 19).[37] German indirect fire was soon hitting the 52 Division start line, but the leading companies set off at 15:00 as planned. On the left, 5 HLI chose to attack with three companies up, each with a three-tank troop from "C" Squadron 9 RTR assigned to their axis. As with 4 RWF in Chapter 2, the three-up formation aimed to ensure a thorough clearance, but it also allowed forest rides to mark company boundaries for a large part of the advance. The fourth company, Battalion Tac HQ, and "C" Squadron's HQ followed 45 minutes later. On the open left flank "B" Company was soon being engaged by a group of defenders in Nieuw Erf. While this threat was dealt with, "C" Squadron Leader's tank was knocked out in a minefield where many infantrymen were also reported to be casualties.

At that point the infantry and armour were separated, and two troops of unsupported tanks were engaged with multiple *Panzerfaust* from another collection of buildings on the forest edge (Map 19, *Panzerfaust*). From 9 RTR's perspective, this was because 'the inf had passed on ignoring this obstruction'. From the infantry's perspective the obstruction was beyond their boundary, in danger of being engaged by Guards' artillery, and the tanks had failed to keep pace with the fire plan.[38] The *Panzerfaust* fire was high and wide, and the defenders were soon suppressed by tank fire, but the two troops continued unsupported for nearly an hour before catching up with the equally unsupported infantry companies.[39]

---

34 51 Division comms log 131520 to 141855; ISUMs 52, 53 and 325; Stimpel, *Fallschirmtruppe*, p.359.
35 There were no reliable sightings of towed 88mm in the area and this was likely one of *FJR 2*'s 75mm guns. 52 Division OO 10 (HQRA diary); 1 Glas H diary; 157 Brigade OO 9. Gunning, *Borderers* (p.174) claims the Broederbosch 'was reported to be strongly held' but may be applying hindsight.
36 52 Division ISUMs 172350, 69 and 70 list fragments of 11 coys from *FJR 2* and two from *GR 1222*. The SP in Division ISUM 69 and Gunning, *Borderers* (p.174) is not mentioned in diaries, suggesting it was an abandoned mechanical failure or knocked out by earlier Typhoons. A more specific sighting on the 21st (Division SITREP 211440) has an AFV with a Mk IV chassis. Thornton and Watson, 'Defence in Woods' (D-17 to D-24) used Division ISUM 68 (issued before the battle) and generic handbooks to estimate the defence comprised 450 men, two 75mm anti-tank guns, a dozen infantry guns, a dozen mortars (81mm and 120mm) and a tank destroyer tp. Their estimation methods are now opaque but later ISUMs and diaries (e.g., 7/9 Royal Scots, WO 171/5259; Derbyshire Yeomanry, WO 171/4696) suggest a more mixed bag with fewer men and mortars. No details on defensive artillery could be found.
37 HQRA SITREP, 162145; 32 Guards Brigade diary (WO 171/4357).
38 9 RTR diary. There is a chance "C" Sqn and 5 HLI never married-up. Their diaries have different start lines.
39 5 HLI diary; 9 RTR diary; HQRA SITREP at 162145; Beale, *Tank Tracks*, pp.185, 189.

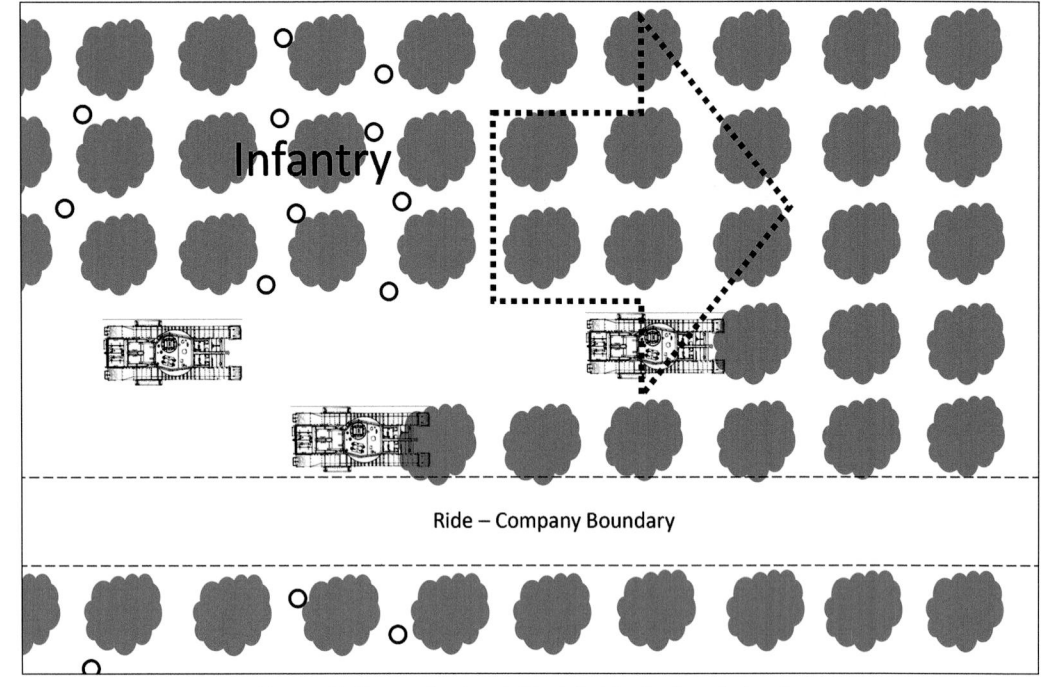

Figure 15: Forest-clearing drill trialled in the Broederbosch.

The two arms then briefly advanced together through the woods 'destroying occasional Spandau posns' but cooperation was still problematic.[40] Like some other Churchill units, 9 RTR had previously found that pine trees in managed forests tended to be thinned out enough to be driven between or they were small enough to be ridden down at walking pace. Both methods allowed the tanks to avoid ambush-prone rides. It was also believed that the sight and sound of falling trees had considerable effect on enemy morale. One method 9 RTR refined in the Reichswald had infantry advance 10 to 30 metres ahead of the tanks, thereby avoiding tree fall but keeping visual contact with the armour.[41] This approach did not seem to work in the Broederbosch, perhaps because trees were immature and tightly packed or because the infantry were wary of walking in front of unfamiliar tanks. A variation was tried where each tank troop advanced immediately to the left of a ride with infantry sections deployed to either side (Figure 15).[42]

The drill shown in Figure 15 was a new trick for Trooper Cyril Rees of "C" Squadron, who believed it was an expedient measure to avoid rides and gain surprise. Rees was himself surprised when splintered branches jammed in the Churchills' tracks, tore off the mud shields then wedged under turrets, prising them upwards and damaging turret ring gearing. Rees 'watched helplessly as the turrets swung first one way and then the other, quite out of control' and of little use for supporting fire or self-defence.[43] Once again, the tanks lost touch with the infantry and around 17:15 Rees's troop was ambushed by *Panzerfaust* teams and his tank was destroyed.

The ambush happened just as the left- and right-hand companies of 5 HLI were approaching their objectives, from which they had expected to overlook the brush to the southeast. Instead, they found more woodland blocks and more defenders. In the centre, the unsupported "A" Company

---

40 9 RTR diary.
41 9 RTR diary.
42 After Beale, *Tank Tracks*, pp.191–193.
43 Beale, *Tank Tracks*, p.193.

were held up by defensive fire just 30 metres short of their objective. The tanks played no part in dealing with this obstacle and "C" Squadron believed this objective was secure by 18:30. In fact "A" Company were stalled until 03:00 the next morning (17th), when they withdrew to allow a medium artillery shoot onto the target. When "A" returned in daylight, the surviving defenders had withdrawn but there was still another kilometre of forest left to clear.[44]

A comparable situation developed on the 5 KOSB axis, where infantry took casualties from their 'slow to lift' fire plan and German counter fire, then their right-hand company was engaged from Zwarte Kamp, which had to be reduced with close artillery support.[45] Many defenders were killed and 30 men from *FJR 2* were captured, but these were the last prisoners recorded by 5 KOSB. Despite early casualties, 5 KOSB's attack became easier once inside the forest, with companies soon on their objectives and pushing out patrols. The fragmentary accounts of the KOSB action include some incidents of tanks brought forward to provide support, and there were no overt claims of poor cooperation, but the differences between arms are evident in the content of histories and diaries, which read like separate battles.[46] As with "C" Squadron, there is no evidence that "B" reached the final infantry objectives.

Both actions were judged unsatisfactory by 9 RTR because the 'woods were not properly cleared by inf who were not familiar with tk cooperation.'[47] Although the two battalions had fallen short of a few objectives, and were still in the middle of the forest, they believed they had done all that was required of them. The HLI had suffered 36 casualties and captured 48 prisoners, while 5 KOSB traded 38 casualties for 30 prisoners, in each case the exchange was a little below average for a Veritable battle. In contrast, the two reduced squadrons of 9 RTR lost three tanks and five men to enemy action. Although this casualty rate was about the same as the infantry losses that day, it was almost as many casualties as the whole of 9 RTR sustained during their week in the Reichswald with 53 Division.[48] At 23:00, tank destroyers replaced 9 RTR, who withdrew to a laager near the start line. Both infantry battalions were heavily shelled overnight, although not as heavily as *FJR 2*. In addition to the Medium Artillery on 5 HLI's centre, two Victor fire missions were called onto suspected counterattacks and a distracting harassment fire plan was used in preparation for the assault on Afferden.[49]

Uncombined Arms

Poor infantry-armour cooperation in the Broederbosch was overshadowed by one of Veritable's most severe radio communication failures, with Brigade and Division unable to even monitor progress because it was 'impossible' to speak to battalions on the radio.[50] In this instance, the artillery net proved fragile too, making it extremely difficult to implement the on-call concentrations, leaving many of the allocated rounds unfired.[51] Trees blocked transmissions but it is likely that the main problem was, once again, interference between Allied radio nets. The Division, two of

---

44 5 HLI and 9 RTR diaries; Beale, *Tank Tracks*, pp.185, 191–193.
45 5 KOSB diary; Beale, *Tank Tracks*, p.185; summary of James McQuarrie's oral history at bbc.co.uk ww2peopleswar. Gunning, *Borderers* (p.174) is ambiguous about the nationality of the shells causing casualties.
46 Gunning, *Borderers* (p.174) relates two incidents of tanks being brought forward to give close support.
47 9 RTR diary.
48 5 HLI diary; 5 KOSB and 9 RTR summary sheets; CWGC.
49 HQRA SITREP, 171900.
50 157 Brigade diary.
51 As noted in Chapter 2, FOOs in vehicles often had trouble maintaining contact with infantry. Beale, *Tank Tracks* (p.190) has 52 Division FOOs in Valentines.

its brigades, 9 RTR and at least one battalion had their headquarters in Gennep, six kilometres to the rear of the battle. This was within the planning range of the various radio sets but call signs were huddled together near a large portion of 51 Division and on a road that was filled with units heading east.[52] Interference was likely exacerbated by 52 Division switching corps at short notice and therefore being last on the list for frequency allocation.

While 157 Brigade was fighting through the Broederbosch, 52 Recce's planned thrust through Afferden was stopped two kilometres north of the village at a crater covered by defensive fire. It took hours for the report of this holdup to travel the kilometre to 1 Glasgow Highlanders who had been standing by to take over the Afferden attack if needed.[53] By 17:30 half of the Highlanders had been committed to clearing stragglers and snipers behind 5 HLI and 5 KOSB. That task was cancelled just before it was due to launch at 20:00, when the Highlanders were redirected to Afferden, which had to be captured before phase three of the Division's plan could be activated. The difficulties of cancelling and restarting meant the H-Hour was eventually set at 05:00 on the 17th.[54] Despite communication problems, Afferden was secure by 09:45, with 1 Glasgow Highlanders suffering only four casualties while taking 41 prisoners, a much better result than the earlier attacks. This success was likely because the attack was launched stealthily, without armour support or a preliminary fire plan.[55] However, the Afferden attack was another example of a tactical success within an operational failure, the village being secured at least 12 hours behind the original schedule.

It took time for news of this delay to reach 30 Corps, which had already issued orders directing 52 Division to 'continue to operate on the axis cross roads 879403 – WEEZE'. This grid reference was southeast of Siebengewald (Map 18), at least four kilometres beyond the Division's easternmost patrol, suggesting that 30 Corps believed 52 Division was well into the third phase of the plan.[56] By the early hours of the 17th, it was obvious that a substantial part of 52 Division would have to cross the Eckeltsche to secure the woods that overlooked the route through Groote Horst to the crossroads and Weeze. But 155 Brigade was repeatedly stalled on its way through Gennep and its orders from Division kept changing as late information collided with changing priorities: 'Optimism succeeded pessimism and vice versa until no one quite knew where they were or what was to be done.'[57]

The ensuing battles repeated earlier cooperation and communication failures. The leading battalion of 155 Brigade, 7/9 Royal Scots, had been tasked with clearing across the anti-tank ditches on the morning of the 17th ("7/9 Obj 1" at Map 20) to provide start lines for the attacks by 6 HLI and 4 KOSB to east and south (black goose eggs).[58] Instead, the Royal Scots attacked at 16:00 to secure a more modest line through Molenhuis (7/9 Obj 2) in conjunction with an attack along the road to Groote Horst by 52 Recce and 9 RTR. Both attacks failed, and the follow-on battalions were held back until the 18th. The 18th attack failed too, and the attempt at a combined arms assault on the Eckeltsche quickly delaminated, though the failure was nothing

---

52 157 Brigade diary.
53 T. D. W. Whitfield *Time Spent, or The History of the 52nd Lowland Divisional Reconnaissance Regiment* (Hamilton: Publisher unknown, 1946), p.73; 52 Recce diary (transcript at chotiedarling.co.uk) has one man killed by fire from a German position just south of the crater.
54 1 Glas H diary. Another indication of confusion is that the 157 Brigade diary assumed Glas H had completed the clearance task.
55 1 Glas H diary makes no mention of using armour. Beale, *Tank Tracks*, p.186, claims the RTR Churchills were not deployed, and Crocodiles deployed but not used. The fireplan (HQRA diary) emphasised harassing fire on other targets to mask the approach rather than having infantry follow a barrage or concentrations.
56 Harris, *Rhineland I*, p.142.
57 Anon, *4th Battalion*, p.130.
58 This version of the 155 Brigade plan is from the 157 Brigade diary. Also 155 Brigade, 7/9 Royal Scots, 9 RTR, 52 Recce and 52 HQRA diaries; Anon, *4th Battalion*, pp.131–132.

INFANTRY AND ARMOUR 135

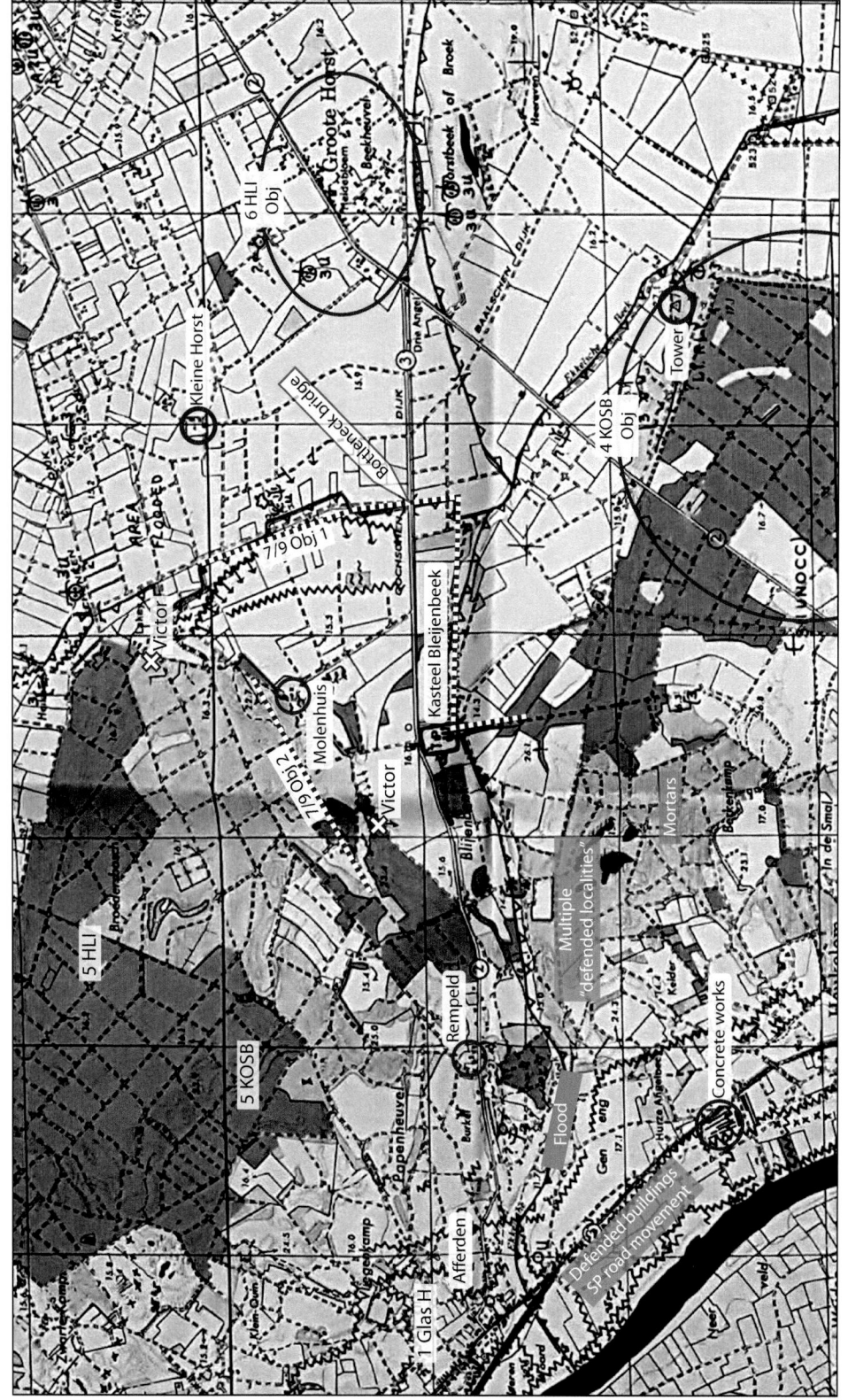

Map 20: Positions and intentions on the morning of 17 February. (National Archives, author's photograph)

like as dramatic as later claimed by one German source.[59] The tanks were late to the start line, then artillery fratricide and German tank destroyers, machine-guns and artillery dealt with British armour and infantry in isolation.[60]

Despite being outnumbered by as much as 8:1 on the 18th, *FJR 2* held off 52 Division and prevented any advance to Weeze. The German force had 'turned the KASTEEL and a concrete works South of AFFERDEN into small fortresses and deployed a number of self-propelled guns and mortars behind the crest to the south of the ditch … only a set-piece attack was going to make any further impression on him.'[61] The set-piece, Operation Sprat, was due to launch on the 20th, and German defences were mapped out, along with the two patches of flooding. (The largest flooded area is shown as "Flood" at Map 20, the smaller patch is just east, obscured by the word "Kasteel".) But Sprat was repeatedly postponed, and finally cancelled on the 28th.[62]

Sprat had in fact been rendered irrelevant on the 18th, when 30 Corps gave up on 52 Division and committed to attacking *through* Goch rather than bypassing it via Weeze. Rennie's scheme for an operational encirclement had missed its chance. Horrocks's disappointment was perhaps evident in the record of his conference on the afternoon of the 17th. Just 18 hours after the optimistic direction to continue from the Siebengewald crossroads to Weeze, the conference produced detailed directions for every division but 52, side-lined by its failure.[63] From that point until the very last days of the operation, 52 Division really was engaged in the mopping up and flank protection that became part of the Veritable narrative.

Like many of Veritable's problems, 52 Division's failure was hidden by the early narrative bias. In the paragraph quoted from the post-operation report, every sentence could be rewritten to reflect intentions, events, and outcomes more honestly. The Division did not 'take over the right hand sector of 51 (H) Inf Div … directed on WEEZE' and it was not 'responsible for clearing the EAST bank'; it *attacked through* 51 Division to *capture* Weeze then *encircle the main German defence*. Then 157 Brigade did not simply start to clear the wooded area; it failed to clear the woods as ordered. Granted, 52 Recce did establish on the Rempeld road as claimed, but they established late, tenuously, and almost irrelevantly. Further advances were not 'well-nigh impossible without specialist equipment' and there was not '200 yds of deep floodwater' with an anti-tank ditch beyond it; the supposed ditch *was* the flooded stream, and the flooding was localised, as shown in Map 20. And the Division had the equipment it needed to cross; what it lacked was a workable command system and the ability to employ infantry-armour cooperation.[64]

---

59 A translation error from British secondary sources has Bosch, *Zweite Weltkreig* (p.199) claim 7/9 Royal Scots was two battalions that suffered such heavy casualties they both ended the attack commanded by a private soldier. The 7/9 Royal Scots diary records a lieutenant killed and two captains wounded. Map markings from trace for 157 Brigade OO 10, 19/20 Feb and diaries listed.
60 52 Recce, 7/9 Royal Scots, 4 KOSB, 9 RTR and 52 HQRA diaries; 155 Brigade diary (WO 171/4413); Beale, *Tank Tracks*, p.186; White, *With the Jocks*, pp.163–164; Anon, *The History of Headquarters Royal Artillery, 52nd Lowland Division during the German War, 1939–1945* (Delbruck: Publisher unknown, 1945), pp.64–65.
61 Anon, *German War*, p.65.
62 HQRA diary; 156 Brigade diary (WO 171/4417). Anon, *German War* (p.67) claims Sprat was never formally cancelled but 'died a natural death and we all felt rather depressed'. The surviving documentation spends more words on the intricate planning for the aborted Sprat than the actual attacks on Afferden and Broederbosch.
63 Notes on 30 Corps Commander's conference 171430, Harris, *Rhineland I*, pp.142–143. Later orders (30 Corps diary, 172330) tasked 52 Division with holding Groote Horst and woods 3km south of the Eckeltsche that it had been expected to (and possibly claimed to) have already captured.
64 21 AG, *Veritable*, p.29.

Components of Cooperation

Infantry-armour cooperation played only a supporting role in this drama. If 52 Division's company groups had been coherent combined arms teams like those developed by 9 RTR and 53 Division in the Reichswald, they might have quickly secured the Broederbosch and Afferden, and maybe even put a bridgehead over the Eckeltsche, but command system problems made that outcome unlikely. The poor performance of 52 Division does not gel with Forrester's claim that 21st Army Group had developed effective infantry-armour cooperation because the causes were not peculiar to the Division. Perhaps 52 Division was pedestrian, as Forrester claims, but it was not appreciably more plodding than any other formation.[65] As with the 13/18 Hussars and Calgary Highlanders on D-Day (and other units in subsequent chapters) armour often hung back to provide only a distant firebase. In addition, as with 4/7 Dragoon Guards and 5 DCLI in Materborn (and other units in subsequent chapters) armour often curled up for the night, leaving the infantry to fight on alone. The fault did not lie with 52 Division, 9 RTR, or with any other fighting organisation, but with the structures, procedures and training that grew from an armoured doctrine that retained many longstanding flaws.

The root of the doctrinal problem has been traced to Fuller's "Plan 1919", which imagined the tank would always get through and, following a brief break-in battle, had infantry following an armoured assault merely 'to secure the administrative and engineer services from local annoyance'.[66] Most of Fuller's plan eschewed the original purpose of the tank as a tool for infantry close support and this spawned a dream of tanks as a single-arm manoeuvre force; a dream that was only dispelled through a painful process of trial and error.[67] When the Broederbosch was attacked, the doctrinal manifestation of that process was Pamphlet 63, *The Co-operation of Tanks with Infantry Divisions*, published in May 1944.[68] The pamphlet noted that the tank's primary task was to 'close with the enemy and destroy' and that to perform that task would need intimate cooperation with infantry. Pamphlet 63 also concluded that a common cooperation doctrine was indispensable, but then failed to provide that doctrine. Instead, it focused on dispelling Fuller-inspired, convenience-driven habits such as attacking with unsupported tanks, having the two arms attack on separate axes, and having tanks support infantry primarily as a distant and often indirect firebase.[69] To borrow Liddell Hart's famous dictum, Pamphlet 63 was focused on getting old ideas out of military minds, not on getting new ones in.[70]

Pamphlet 63 also aimed to dispel the custom of using Churchill-equipped tank brigades exclusively for break-in and breakthrough battles, while Sherman-equipped armoured formations performed only breakout and pursuit. Although Churchills were designed for close infantry support and Shermans were better suited to rapid road movement, experience had shown it was necessary for both formation types to do both jobs well. Just a week before Veritable was launched, Montgomery attempted to resolve, or maybe wish away, the difference between Churchill and

---

65 Forrester, *Monty's Functional*, Kindle 3982.
66 J. F. C. Fuller, *Memoirs of an Unconventional Soldier* (London: Nicholson & Watson, 1936). For the evolution and impact of Fuller's thinking see J.P. Harris, *Men, Ideas and Tanks: British military thought and armoured forces, 1903–39* (Manchester: University Press, 1995), pp.164–189, 203–208.
67 The most useful summary comes from combining Harris's *Men, Ideas and Tanks* Chapters 6–8 with Buckley's *British Armour*, Chapters 3–6.
68 War Office, *Military Training Pamphlet No. 63: The Co-operation of Tanks with Infantry Divisions* (London: War Office, 1944).
69 Such behaviours were still dominant in Normandy: Buckley, *British Armour*, especially Chapter 4.
70 B. H. Liddell Hart, *Thoughts on War* (London: Faber & Faber, 1943), p.115.

Sherman brigades by classifying them both as armoured.[71] As demonstrated by the fumbled pass in Chapter 4 (when the Churchill-supported 15 Division handed over to the Sherman-supported 43 Division) the difficulties of an echelon change usually outweighed the benefits of deploying the optimal tank design. However, the guidance in Pamphlet 63 and Montgomery's rebranding could not dispel years of habitual focus on specific phases and tasks.

Like most doctrine publications, Pamphlet 63 divides war into pre-planned intensive battles like Veritable's D-Day, and the 'more or less fluid' fights that were expected on the way to Weeze.[72] The pamphlet then presents detailed prescriptions for what to do in a long-planned break-in but gives only the scantest guidance on what activities could be safely ignored in fluid exploitation and pursuit battles. There is no guidance at all for the less fluid, intense but relatively quick battles that characterised Veritable's reality from D+1, and indeed dominated the campaign for Northwest Europe. Most notable are Pamphlet 63's directions for spending weeks getting to know the men of the other arm, directions that were useless when strangers were thrown together hours or minutes before battle, as with 5 HLI and 9 RTR. In such circumstances, statements like, 'The attack is the combined effort of a team, the members of which have trained together and know each other personally' were fatuous.[73] Pamphlet 63 sidestepped the obvious solution of advocating permanent associations such as those that had existed in the New Model divisions. Despite Montgomery's rebranding and Pamphlet 63's espousal of teamwork, 21st Army Group retained a modular "golf bag" approach that constantly broke up infantry-armour teams and sent the components to fight alongside strangers.[74]

Being formation-level doctrine, Pamphlet 63 omitted all the artisan activities essential for close cooperation, but there was no endorsed lower-level publication to fill the gap. The Directorate of Tactical Investigation (DTI) ran a project from 1943 that attempted to fill that gap by disseminating lessons learned by units, but surviving files trace an awkward, underfunded effort to identify best practice on matters ranging from target indication to tank riding.[75] There was disagreement on every point because units either ignored problems or developed workarounds specific to their local situation. The DTI project never reached a satisfactory procedural, tactical or technological solution and so doctrine continued to focus on the distant forms of cooperation, where armour and infantry fought in waves or on axes that were separated by hundreds of metres.[76] Distant cooperation is easy to understand and describe because it has few working parts. With companies and squadrons acting as discrete entities, coordination can, at least theoretically, be dictated by plan, by radio, or by obvious visual signals. The components are much smaller and the timings tighter in close support tasks, so coordination stops being directed by a few colonels or majors and devolves to dozens of corporals commanding the individual tanks and rifle sections.

---

71 In anticipation of the universal tank (Comet or Centurion) the armoured brigades became Armoured (Type A), and tank brigades Armoured (Type B). 34 Brigade became Type B on 2 Feb, Brigade diary. It could be argued that Goodwood (Biddle's focus) and Market Garden (where Guards Armoured Division was expected to break in, out, and through) were also attempts to dispel overspecialisation.
72 *Pamphlet 63*, p.9.
73 *Pamphlet 63*, p.11.
74 Although "golf bag" has been absorbed into twenty-first century jargon (e.g. Anon, 'Command and Control (C2) Agility', (NATO, 2014), passim), the term and the limitations of the approach were known in the British Army in the 1940s (e.g., Pemberton, *Artillery Tactics*, p.299), though no reference was found applying it to divisions.
75 DTI, 'Employment of tanks with infantry: operational reports; radio communications reports and trials' (WO 232/38). On tank riding, for example, responses ranged from never doing it to doing it until contact, like 5 DCLI and 4/7 DG, but most units used it only for administrative moves a long way from contact.
76 Harris, *Men, Ideas and Tanks*; D. Fletcher, *The Great Tank Scandal: British Armour in the Second World War: Part 1* (London: HMSO, 1989); M. A. Davis, 'Armor Attacks in Restrictive Terrain: is Current Doctrine Adequate?' (Fort Leavenworth: Command and General Staff College monograph, 1995).

In close support, the tank's role was much the same in 1945 as it had been in 1916: a mobile pillbox that helped infantry overpower defenders' machine-guns. The other side of the deal was that infantry provided flank protection for the tanks and usually scouted a short way ahead to find and neutralise anti-armour weapons. If anything, close cooperation was more necessary in 1945 because of the preponderance of German automatic weapons and the seemingly ubiquitous *Panzerfaust*. The often passionate debate over the relative merits of the Bren versus the MG-34 and MG-42, and the PIAT versus the *Panzerfaust* is still ongoing, but as noted in Chapter 2, the automatic weapon imbalance was as much about the number of weapons as their rate of fire, with a de facto German platoon in Veritable having around twice as many machine-guns as a British platoon, plus a considerable but unknown number of *Sturmgewehr 44* assault rifles.[77] For machine-guns and portable anti-armour, the attacker also had the disadvantage of having to carry weapons immediately before firing them, giving a less stable and more vulnerable platform.

But there were many barriers to close cooperation. For the armour, being near friendly infantry meant being near the enemy and those *Panzerfauste*, which turned a crewman's mind to his behemoth being a slow-moving, half-blind box full of fuel and explosives.[78] Troop leaders had additional concerns:

> Even in a relatively straightforward battle there are a hundred and one things a troop leader has to do. He has to guide his tank, make full use of the ground, keep in constant touch with his infantry, scan the landscape for the enemy, direct his gunner on to targets, position his other two [or three] tanks, pass messages back to the squadron leader over the air, and at the same time be on the alert for all the unexpected situations that might arise in modern warfare. It is even harder when he has to fight in woods, for the trees make ideal cover for snipers and bazooka-men, and he is suspicious all the time. Besides, the trees are natural obstacles for tanks, so he has to guide his driver with the utmost care. He has to protect his flanks and yet keep his gun from hitting the trees. He feels curiously alone and unprotected, even though his infantry may be all around his troop. It is dark and very frightening.[79]

On the infantry side, it was difficult to ignore the way tanks made stealth almost impossible, attracted enemy fire, crushed people by suddenly changing direction, or caused blast injury with main armament discharge. The detailed procedures to avoid these negatives and gain the positives of close support were a long way down a unit's training priorities (after driving, gunnery, field craft, et cetera), and so units developed close support skills in isolation, at varying rates and in different directions. This artisan level cooperation (like low-level logistics and signaller tasks) fell outside published doctrine, leaving little impression on the historical record.[80]

---

77 This author must bow out of the debate having developed a biased opinion from training exercises carrying and firing the Bren (in 7.62mm as the L4 Light Machine Gun) and the NATO reaction to the MG-42 (the L7 General Purpose Machine Gun), and from interviewing Sydney Jary, who said, 'we estimated one MG-42 to be worth nine Brens or three Vickers'. For a taste of the internet debate search YouTube for 'Bren vs Spandau part two – or Lloyd against the fan-boys'.
78 T. Greenwood, *D-Day to Victory* (London: Simon & Schuster, 2012) charts the development of this anxiety in a 9 RTR tank commander.
79 Forbes, *Grenadier Guards* (p.202) is describing a later Veritable battle involving 6 Guards Armoured Brigade (Type B).
80 There are mentions of artisan level cooperation in British-focused publications (e.g., Buckley, *British Armour*, pp.71–81, 93–102) but greater coverage of US experience, e.g.: M.D. Doubler, *Busting the Bocage: American Combined Armed Operations in France, 6 June – 31 July 1944* (Fort Leavenworth: Combat Studies Institute, 1988); H. Yeide, *The Infantry's Armour: The US Army's Separate Tank Battalions in World War II*

The use of tank telephones (fitted to the rear of some vehicles to allow nearby infantry to speak on the crew intercom) was patchy, even when these devices were fitted and working. As a result, radio communication was the doctrinal default, but the infantry's No.18 sets and armour's No.19 sets were unable to intercommunicate in tactical situations.[81] To resolve this, Pamphlet 63 demanded a few tanks in each squadron were fitted with additional No. 38 sets tuned to battalion nets, and 157 Brigade's orders for the Broederbosch followed that guidance. However, there was little time to test nets in the assembly area, where radio silence was rightly imposed.[82] In any event, companies' No.18 sets so rarely functioned in contact that this option was often irrelevant. Pamphlet 63 therefore strongly suggested that armoured squadrons 'as a matter of routine' provided infantry with vehicles carrying No.19 sets and that these should stick with company commanders 'dogging their footsteps throughout the battle.'[83] Few armoured units appear to have tried this during Veritable, and it was not used by 9 RTR, probably because it could have used up eight of their 22 available tanks.[84]

It was only after the experience around Afferden that 9 RTR produced their own subtly seminal "lessons learnt" paper. The paper incorporated pithy advice on many of the problems noted in the Broederbosch, plus recommendations on artillery liaison, resupply, overhead tracer fire for its morale effect, and how best to knock down trees. One of its main conclusions was that forest fighting 'should not be looked on as an entirely different type of warfare' merely an adaptation of core principles. Another was that pre-operational training with the supported infantry should fill one week as 'the absolute minimum'.[85] The 9 RTR lessons were born of trial and error, without reference to Pamphlet 63 or similar documents because so little of the published doctrine was relevant.[86]

Ultimately, Pamphlet 63 and Montgomery's rebranding failed because they did not address the way golf bagging undermined close association between arms and diluted unity of command.

(Mechanicsburg: Stackpole, 2010). The gap between pamphlet and practice is an enduring problem with doctrine authors having to guide and reflect operational developments while treading the line between readable blandness and unreadable completeness. The latter is epitomised by the notoriously wordy, 714-page, "pink pillow": Headquarters Doctrine and Training, *Generic Enemy (Mobile Forces) Part 1: Operational Art & Tactical Doctrine* (Upavon: HQDT, 1996).

81 A patient signaller spent half an hour explaining why, despite overlapping frequencies, the No.18 and No.19 sets were tactically incommunicado, but the author lacks the skills to condense it. For a glimpse into this complex world visit wftw.nl.

82 157 Brigade OO also suggested using Verey lights for target indication which was problematic in open country and almost irrelevant in woods. There were means to test nets without transmitting but these were convoluted, and beyond this author's comprehension. The No.38 set was noted for its tendency to drift off frequency: DTI, 'Employment of tanks with infantry'.

83 *Pamphlet 63*, pp.14–15.

84 This assumes one tank to each forward coy and one in each bn HQ. Despite a long association, the acting CO of 2 A&SH (see Ch 2) was denied a radio link by "S" Squadron, 3 Scots Guards: C. Farrell, *Reflections 1939–1945: A Scots Guards Officer in Training and War* (Edinburgh: Pentland Press, 2000), p.11. Using armoured cars was a partial solution but still had personnel and equipment costs, and the cars had poor off-road performance.

85 P. N. Veale, 'Lessons learnt from actions fought by Churchill tks in close sp of inf in forest country' 24 Feb 45, 9 RTR diary. More recent doctrine, e.g., UK MOD, *Army Field Manual 2/6: Operations in Woods and Forests* (MOD, Undated) includes several sections that echo the 9 RTR lessons.

86 Other units wrote their own doctrine too, often with satisfactory results, but this created the confusing inconsistency seen in the DTI files. One example of effective cooperation (unavoidably omitted from the current assessment) coincided with the Broederbosch assault, with 4/7 DG and 7 SLI in a daylight attack where 'Each forward section had its own tank'. Essame, *43rd Wessex*, p.218.

Close association has procedural benefits that surpass common doctrine because it allows infantry sections and tank crews to generate a tactical shorthand, to develop quick solutions to novel problems, and to anticipate each other's needs. Close association encourages fundamental but often untaught skills, ranging from simple hand signals to complicated street clearing drills. It involves subtle team working activities like predicting the other arm's actions when out of sight, and ingrained competencies like knowing which of the camouflaged blobs near a tank is the platoon commander. When hand signals and tank telephones proved insufficient, tank commanders would dismount, or platoon commanders clamber up behind the turret. Despite sounding simple, these skills involved individual risk and a spirit of reciprocation that could only be embedded through considerable shared experience.[87]

Perhaps the most important aspect of close association is that it breeds familiarity, and this brings the crewman and rifleman to care for one another as people. This, in turn creates the social cohesion and aggressive altruism that are essential to the moral component of fighting power. Familiarity therefore creates the motivation to aid comrades from the other arm, a symbiotic relationship that cannot be imbued unless people work, train, and fight together over weeks, preferably months.[88] Many methods were used to unofficially build and maintain close association: the former New Model divisions (including 15, 43 and 53) maintained a predisposition to reuniting with their former tank brigades, the Sherman brigades acquired their own infantry to protect the tanks, and the armoured divisions grew to pair battalions and regiments.[89] Having never met until immediately before action, the men of 52 Division and 9 RTR had none of this. Their experience was not unusual; after the first week of Veritable, half the actions involved battalions supported by squadrons they had not met until the eve of battle.[90]

If close association provided a rewarding "carrot" to encourage cooperation, unity of command was the threatening "stick" that could enforce cooperation. Unity is usually related to multinational or joint operations, where a clear command chain reduces the chance of a Montgomery and a Patton (or a Crerar and a Horrocks) pulling in different directions. But even in the same nation and service, unity was difficult for temporary organisations to achieve because the tactical commander was not the full-time boss of the attached subordinate. A temporary commander

---

87 One of the most coherent accounts of reciprocation in woods and the strain of close support is S. Dyson, *Tank Twins*, (Barnsley: Leo Cooper, 2004), pp.135–147, relating the experience of a 107 RAC troop supporting 51 Division in the first few days of Veritable.

88 Apart from *Pamphlet 63*, no contemporary reference was found relating familiarity to infantry-armour cooperation, but it underpins single-arm cohesion and is assumed to be universal. This author thought he was clever for using "symbiosis", but was beaten to it by M. Creveld, K. S. Brower and S. L. Canby, *Air Power and Maneuver Warfare* (Montgomery AL: Air University, 1994), p.205.

89 8 Armoured Brigade had three Sherman regts and a mechanised infantry battalion. This 3:1 organisation was designed to be an independent manoeuvre formation but was only briefly used as such after breaking out from Normandy. For the rest of the campaign the Brigade was loaned in parts, just like a Churchill brigade. Forrester suggests cooperation was solved because formations adopted a 1:3 structure by 1945 but closer examination of Veritable would have shown organisations varied from 1:9 when 107 RAC supported 51 Division (Chapter 2) to 1:1 in Guards Armoured Division (Chapter 7).

90 Other theatres were the same. Of the respondents to DTI surveys, Colonel R. J. Colwell, the CO of 6 Canadian Armoured Regiment, best summarised the phenomenon, noting that when infantry and armour had trained together beforehand there was: 'a minimum of misunderstanding, a mutual confidence and respect, and an unsuccessful action was accepted without any serious effect of morale'. But without prior training, there was more chance of failure and 'a strong tendency by both Arms to blame the "other fellow" followed by a serious decline in morale' – not unlike 53 Division and 9 RTR. It is telling that most DTI respondents seemed unaware of the close association problem, or any solution to it apart from blaming the other fellow.

might have the capacity to enact military law and pull rank in extreme situations, but he lacked the ability to compel cooperation more subtly with the permanent commander's power over careers, peer groups, and everyday living conditions.

The golf bag further undermined ability to compel cooperation because armour was explicitly "in support" of companies, battalions, and brigades rather than being "under command", as they usually were with divisions. The in-support relationship was a deliberate policy to avoid tanks being misused by the uneducated, thereby making the authority of a supported leader weaker and more ambiguous than it was with his commanded subordinates. In the Broederbosch, the in-support distinction meant every 9 RTR commander from troop corporal to lieutenant colonel was an adviser to the infantry commander above him and had the right to opt out of any scheme he judged inappropriately risky. The risk benchmark was always debatable, but would naturally have been lowered by unfamiliarity and lack of trust.

Conclusion

Far from Veritable following the original plan 'inexorably day after day' as suggested in *Colossal Cracks*, commanders in 30 Corps thought outside that box, made a considerable adaptation to the plan, and attempted a bold manoeuvre to break the deadlock. Aside from their cooperation with armour, 52 Division's soldiers fought well, with little indication of poor field craft or weak morale. They managed a creditable exchange of casualties for prisoners, notably when 1 Glasgow Highlanders exhibited tactical cleverness and manoeuvre by stealthily attacking Afferden. As with 15 and 43 Division, most of 52 Division's performance problems were due to operational level failings that were closer to Hart's 'competent generalship' than the fragile morale of its soldiers. The cooperation failure in the Broederbosch was less severe than it might have been because 52 Division was fortunate enough to be supported by a regiment that was trained, equipped, and expected to provide close support. It is notable that when the two arms became separated, "C" Squadron pressed on rather than loiter or withdraw, then unlike many Sherman subunits, they stayed near the forward companies long after dark.

The cooperation problem was imposed by the corporate expectation that strangers subject to different training regimes and command hierarchies could spontaneously form an effective team. Contrary to Forrester's claims, Monty's 'Functional Doctrine' was dysfunctional in the way it overlooked the need for collective training, unity of command, and close association between the two arms. It could still be argued that 52 Division failed because its commanders and men did not grasp Biddle's modern system. However, rather than a vague cultural deficit, 52 Division's lack of infantry-armour cooperation was due to specific shortcomings in organisational design, training and in the doctrine on which these were built. And unlike a vague national cultural blockage, these specific problems can be identified and rectified to avoid the repetition of failures like those around Afferden.

6

Urban Attrition

17 TO 21 FEBRUARY – GOCH GRABBED – VOLCANOES AND SCREAMING METAL – THOMAS'S GOOD BARGAIN – ANOTHER FAILED BLERICK – STEALTH AND SURPRISE – BLACK WATCH WIN THE DAY – ASKING THE AIRMAN TO GO ELSEWHERE – THE ATTRITION MYTH

A Battle of Two Halves

> All the approaches to the town were covered by dykes, anti-tank ditches, trench systems and pill boxes, and the whole area as the final attack opened was like the crater of a volcano in eruption. It seemed impossible that a single square foot of air could be free from screaming metal…[1]

Most sources lack Thompson's artistic flourish, but all agree the fighting in Goch was desperate, bloody, and confusing.[2] Goch was turned to rubble (Figure 16) in what was arguably the largest British urban operation in Northwest Europe and, although the battle is often overlooked, it still retains a foothold in British Army doctrine.[3] Even today, it is not unusual for training at Copehill Down (the purpose-built training village on Salisbury Plain) to include a showing of the army's 1980s video, *Fighting In Built Up Areas (FIBUA): Goch*.[4] The course leader will emphasise the video's anachronistic dumb bombs, flamethrowers, and lack of civilians (most were evacuated in October 1944), but the core lessons of the video match the dominant view of urban combat as an unavoidable attritional slog.[5]

---

1 Thompson, *Rhineland*, p.192.
2 Stacey, *Victory Campaign* (p.490) and Whitakers, *Rhineland* (p.130) use 'confused fighting' to describe the whole battle for Goch.
3 Goch was smaller than Caen, Nijmegen, Arnhem, Wesel, and Bremen but involved more unit-hours of fighting in town. L. A. DiMarco, *Concrete Hell: Urban Warfare from Stalingrad to Iraq* (New York; Osprey, 2012) for example, examines the more fashionable urban operations in Aachen, Inchon, Hue, Algiers, Belfast, Grozny, and Jenin. The civilian in the foreground of Figure 16 (battlefieldhistorian.com) gives scale to the rubble piles. Similar images were used as postcards and one on Flickr (search Robert Dorian Goch 1945) has a handwritten caption that reads: 'Our house where we were buried for 8 hours'.
4 Pearson, FIBUA video.
5 A. King, *Urban Warfare in the Twenty-First Century* (Cambridge: Polity, 2021), pp.1, 214.

Figure 16: Post-war image of Goch's market square and its main churches. (battlefieldhistorian.com)

The FIBUA video is based on a study by the Defence Operational Analysis Establishment (DOAE) that is often revisited when military interest cycles back to urban combat.[6] Historical study was particularly necessary in the most recent cycle because the skills developed over decades of peace enforcement are inappropriate for high-intensity urban battles.[7] Cities, technologies, and societies may have changed since the Second World War, but Fallujah, Mosul, and Mariupol were devastated just like Stalingrad, Manila, and Goch. The widespread perception that urban attrition is unavoidable has been encapsulated in the adage that armies must "destroy the city to save the city".[8] This chapter will push against that view to show how an omission from Veritable's historiography has helped generate some false impressions about urban attrition in Goch; an omission that may apply to other battles and to soldiers' core beliefs about urban combat.

The historiographic omission has its roots in Goch being bisected by the river Niers, which forced a battle of two halves, the northeast of town being attacked by 44 Brigade of 15 Scottish

---

6 R. D. Hanscomb, 'A Review of Urban Battles in Germany 1945', DOAE Working Paper, 662/5, 1983, centres on Goch, giving it 26 pages while the nine other battles (Kleve, Gennep, Xanten, Blerick, Aachen, Rees, Wesel, Bremen and Uelzen) have only 12 pages between them. Despite Hanscomb being the most complete source found, he admits 'GOCH is a complicated and difficult battle to analyse' and deliberately limits his focus to 44 Brigade in the north and 1 Gordons, one of the five bns deployed in the south.

7 UK MOD, *Future Operating Environment 2035* (Shrivenham: MOD, 2015), passim. One touchstone is the ubiquitous Battle Drill 6, a room clearing technique imported from law enforcement that has supplanted company and battalion tactics in some recent doctrine. Land Warfare Development Centre (LWDC), *Urban Tactical Handbook* (Warminster: LWDC, 2016), passim; R. D. Hooker, 'The Tyranny of Battle Drill 6' (Modern War Institute, mwi.usma.edu 2021). The cyclic nature of debate is evident among the entries in, Australian Army Research Centre, *Urban Warfare: A Practitioners Annotated Bibliography* (Canberra: AARC, 2021).

8 J. Spencer, 'Why Militaries Must Destroy Cities to Save Them' (mwi.usma.edu, 2018).

Division, while the southwest was attacked by 153 Brigade of 51 Highland Division (Map 21). The resulting compartmentalisation of accounts has been an obstacle to coherent assessment, but that is how the battle was fought. So, despite the difficulties of viewing Goch as unrelated brigade operations, this chapter will begin with those separate opening moves before uniting them for comparison with the existing historiography. Nine British battalions were directly engaged in the fight for Goch but the focus battalions for this chapter are 8 Royal Scots from 44 Brigade, and 5 Black Watch from 153 Brigade (Figure 17).

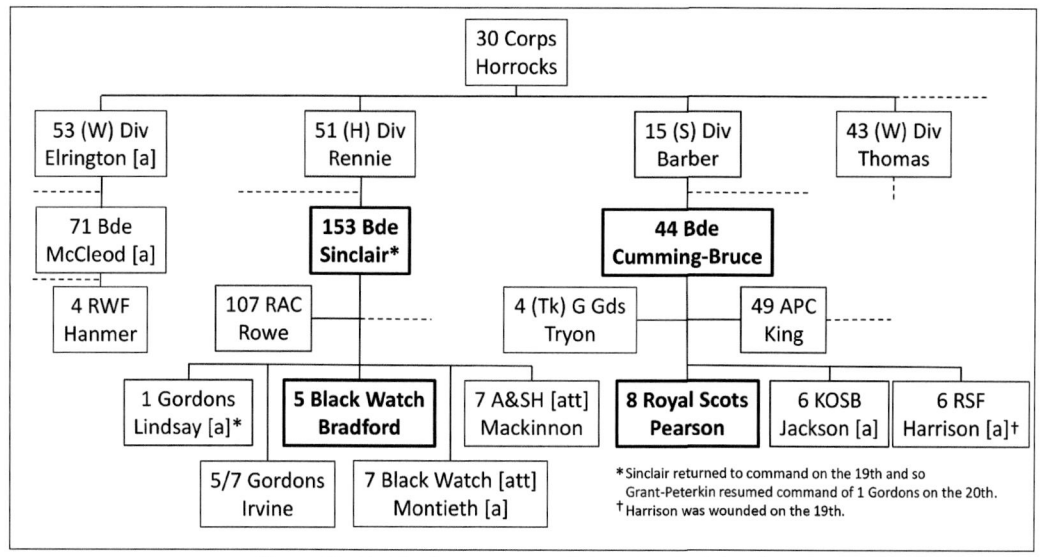

Figure 17: Abridged organisational chart for Goch battles.

Before its evacuation Goch had a population of 10,000 to 13,000 people. It was an industrial, commercial and communication hub, and a cornerstone of the German defence that was better integrated into the Westwall than any other town in the Veritable area. The concrete fighting positions west of Goch were well camouflaged and mutually supporting but they were outdated and outflanked, being built to accommodate the lighter anti-tank guns of 1939 and sited for an attack from the southwest.[9] Although the Goch battle started nine days later than anticipated, 30 Corps had succeeded in bypassing the town's defences, allowing 153 Brigade to slip between the Westwall and Niers, while 44 Brigade attacked from the rear.

The 464-bomber raid on 7 February caused most of the damage to the town but 'heavy smoke from the blazing inferno was causing meaningful control of the bombing to become impossible', so the raid was aborted after 155 aircraft had released their ordnance. The only recorded victims were 30 German civilians and 200 forced labourers from Russia, Italy, and the Netherlands.[10] Large parts of the town were destroyed, but between the bombing and the battle forced labour and German pioneers cleared usable routes through the rubble, one running north–south, the other east–west. Two bridges had survived the bombing, one near the centre of town (though sources disagree on which bridge this was) and the other 800 metres to the north, but it seems these could only bear light vehicles.

---

9   K. Margry (ed.), *After the Battle*, 2013, No. 159, p.36; N. Short, *Hitler's Siegfried Line* (Stroud: Sutton, 2002), pp.8–10.
10 *After the Battle*, 159, p.38; Middlebrook and Everitt, *Bomber Command Diaries* Kindle 12632.

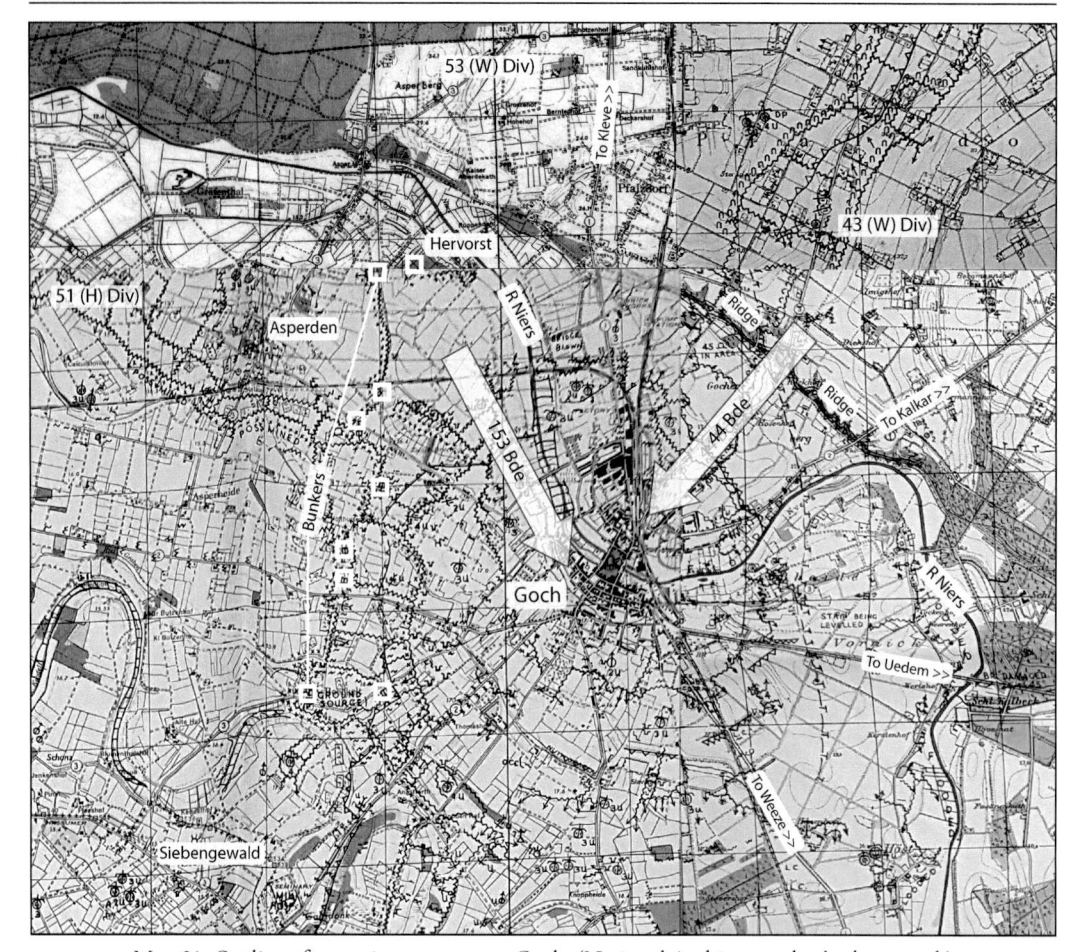

Map 21: Outline of operations to capture Goch. (National Archives, author's photograph)

44 Brigade

The Veritable plan had 43 Division rolling through Goch on 9 February, but after the fumbled pass at Materborn at least six more schemes were developed, generating a cycle of "order, counter-order, disorder."[11] On the 10th, 8 Royal Scots were directed to attack Kleve, on the 11th to mop up in Kleve, on the 12th, 13th, and 14th to counter *47. Panzerkorps* in various ways, on the 15th to support a dash southeast, and on the 16th to capture the Goch ridge. None of these plans were enacted, to the evident frustration of 15 Division staff. If anything, the confusion was greater in the armoured golf bag where, in the space of a few hours, 4 (Tank) Grenadier Guards was passed between 15, 53 and 43 Divisions, then went to 53 again and back to 15.[12] Forty-Three Division became trapped in a cycle of short advances south and east from Hau, hacking into the repeatedly reinforced *47. Panzerkorps* and often being forced back by counterstrokes. It was only on the 16th (D+8, the day the Corps main effort switched to Afferden) that 43 Division had any success. A chance combination of mild weather for air interdiction and excellent daylight cooperation

---

11   The root of the counterorder maxim could not be found but was used in C.S. Forester, *The Good Shepherd* (London: Four Square, 1955).
12   8 Royal Scots and 4 Grenadier Guards diaries.

between armour and infantry saw 43 Division advance over three kilometres and capture close to 1,000 prisoners. This success and 52 Division's failure around Afferden switched the main effort back to Goch.[13]

Fifteen Division issued orders on the 16th to exploit the 43 Division breakout towards the 'high ground dominating Goch from the north' (where 43 Division is marked at Map 21). These orders included three contingencies in case 43 was stopped short, achieved its objectives, or exceeded them to reach the ridge above Goch.[14] Each of these options required 44 Brigade (which fought the Sullivan breakout) to clamp an armoured cordon around northern Goch so 227 Brigade (which captured Kranenburg during Gilbert) could assault the town dismounted. Although these orders seemed to cover all bases, they were obsolete before being issued because much of 227 Brigade was being loaned to 2 Canadian Corps for the fight in Moyland wood.[15] However, by that time 44 Brigade had arranged enough armoured support to launch another Blerick job, and so it wrote the plan for Operation "Spider", an armoured assault on Goch.[16] Horrocks held a planning conference on the 17th that generated orders for two options: if 43 Division got the chance, it would seize the opportunity to attack the town that night and 15 Division would bypass to the east; if not, 15 would take responsibility for the Goch assault.

Unknown to Horrocks, the two divisions' commanders had already brokered a deal to go for the second option, using 44 Brigade's ready-made plan for Operation Spider.[17] On the afternoon of the conference, Thomas (43 Division) told Henniker, his Commander Royal Engineers: 'I have made a good bargain with 15 Scottish Division this morning. *We go as far as the first anti-tank ditch. 15 Scottish Division will then pass through us and will take on the very severe battle for the town which will certainly follow.*'[18]

As usual there were competing theories about how severe the battle would be. Goch was believed to be defended by remnants of *15. Panzergrenadier Division* and perhaps part of *7. Fallschirmjäger-Division*, but even after the battle started there was 'no definite clue as to who may be defending Goch'.[19] Most intelligence assessments erred on the optimistic side, suggesting *1. Fallschirm-Armee* had run short of fresh battalions and linking 43 Division's impressive prisoner haul with stories of troops 'pulled out of hospital and sometimes lacking sufficient rifles' to suggest Goch might lie undefended.[20] Post-war efforts to uncover German records admitted it was 'very difficult or even impossible to identify the commitment of German troops in this battle'.[21] However, hindsight

---

13   Essame, *43rd Wessex*, pp.214–221.
14   '15 (S) Inf Division Op Instr 50', 16 February 45. 'Dominating' may be another "map recce" failure, as with Groot Horst in Ch 5. The high ground mentioned was well behind the ridge and had no line of sight into Goch.
15   McBain, *Regiment at War*, p.286; 30 Corps, 15 Division, 46 Brigade, 227 Brigade and 10 HLI diaries.
16   141 RAC diary, 16 February. 44 Brigade, OO 6, 'Op "Spider"', 17 Feb 45. The name Spider seems to combine frustration with contradictory orders and Brigadier Cumming-Bruce's ancestor, Robert the Bruce, being inspired to 'Try, Try Again' by the tenacious spider in the Hickson poem.
17   30 Corps diary, 172330; Harris, *Rhineland I*, pp.142–143; 44 Brigade, 'Spider'.
18   Henniker, *Image*, p.236.
19   15 Division ISUMs 206 and 207 (17–18 February). Advocate, *From Normandy* (p.94) claims 'Once again the only uncertain element was the weather', this despite there being no clear picture of the enemy force and the weather being almost certain to be overcast and wet.
20   15 Division ISUM 16 Feb.
21   Quote in Hanscomb, 'Urban' (p.5) by *Bundeswehr Oberstleutnant* Bernhard Franck, part of the NORTHAG study and the SSVC/Dennis, *Rhineland* documentary. Hanscomb counted contributions from 21 units in 'loose battle groups' (p.29) and understandably made no attempt to write a German account. The Canadian Military Headquarters (CMHQ) 'Memorandum on Rhineland' (1956, CAB 44/312) reached similar conclusions.

shows British optimism was misplaced, with at least 1,000 men defending Goch on the 18th, and up to 2,500 committed before the town was captured, including at least three fresh battalions.[22]

The situation was just as uncertain for the men defending Goch, and considerably more threatening. The appearance of 52 Division around Afferden and the advance of 43 Division from Hau pointed to the British encircling the town, cutting off the defenders or assaulting from multiple directions. If Goch fell, the whole southern flank could collapse, and in response, *General der Fallschirmtruppe* Meindl (*2. Fallschirm-Korps*) was assigned to command the centre of the Veritable area, including Goch and its vulnerable flanks. However, this change of command was enacted just as the British attacked, and made for uncoordinated responses by Meindl and *Oberst* Matussek, the town commandant.[23]

Operation Spider relied on 43 Division securing crossings over the outer anti-tank ditch, then two armoured breaching forces under a 22 Dragoons officer would flail two routes through the expected minefields. On the left (south) Route Carter was a narrow, metalled road that would be the axis for 6 KOSB; on the right, Route Hiker was a track that would be the axis for 8 Royal Scots (Map 22).[24] The breaching forces would seize or build crossings over the inner ditch then push on into the edge of town, followed by Kangaroo-mounted infantry and tanks. Air reconnaissance had reported the cleared routes through town and the intact bridge in the town centre.[25] It was hoped, though perhaps only faintly, that the armoured onslaught would use the north–south route to take the town in a rush, quickly crossing the river and breaking out to the south.[26]

The immediate fallback plan was considered the most likely option, and this required 8 Royal Scots and 6 KOSB to debouch in town and have each of their company groups secure one of the named areas shown at Map 22. There was also a worst-case scenario should fighting continue until after dark, where each company group would occupy an 'overnight fortress' then secure the rest of their given area on the morning of the 19th. In the most likely and worst-case scenarios, the Kangaroos would return for 6 Royal Scots Fusiliers, who would force the crossing and exploit south on the 19th.[27]

Timings were critical for Operation Spider but soon became disjointed. The deal struck between Thomas and Barber required 43 Division's sappers to put six crossings over the outer ditch by first light, about 07:15 on the 18th.[28] However, 44 Brigade could only organise its armour and artil-

---

22 Hanscomb, 'Urban' (pp.29–30) counts three fresh battalions on the 18th and suggests 1,500 defenders. The higher figure is suggested by diaries and post-battle ISUMs that Hanscomb could not access.
23 Meindl and Matussek were both *Fallschirmjäger* with eastern front experience but Matussek's accessible history is currently internet fragments. 51 Division ISUM 57 has command of Goch 'extremely nebulous'. CMHQ 'Memorandum' (pp.34–49) and Bosch *Zweite Weltkrieg* (p.202) follow Meindl's interview (NARA FMS B-093, 12) with Meindl ordered to take over on the 18th and assuming command on the 19th. Meindl's interview (p.14) gives no tactical detail but repeatedly bemoans Allied material strength: 'The front became exhausted at an even faster rate than had been the case in Normandy'.
24 At least five more northern routes were marked on overlays or used in the battle, but the main events were on Carter and Hiker. 15 Division comms log 180120; C. G. Lawton, *Path of the Lion, 1944–1945*, (Ahrensburg: Publisher unknown, 1946), p.365. Map markings based on 15 Division HQRA, 'Spider' and 6 Royal Scots Fusiliers diary.
25 Henniker, *Image* (p.235) received air photographs on the 17th that showed 'the enemy had undertaken a considerable number of road and bridge demolitions', though most had been provided by the RAF.
26 This aspiration is not stated in any history or diary, orders clearly state the attack is on northern Goch, and no codewords were issued for features south of the river, but the fireplans of the 17th and 18th have phased concentrations running right through town and two kilometres past the southern outskirts. 44 Brigade, 'Spider'; 15 Division HQRA diary, 'Op "Spider". Notes on 15 (S) Inf Division fire plan.'
27 44 Brigade, 'Spider'; Martin *15th Scottish*, pp.256–257; 6 RSF diary, 18 February.
28 Henniker, *Image*, pp.234–235.

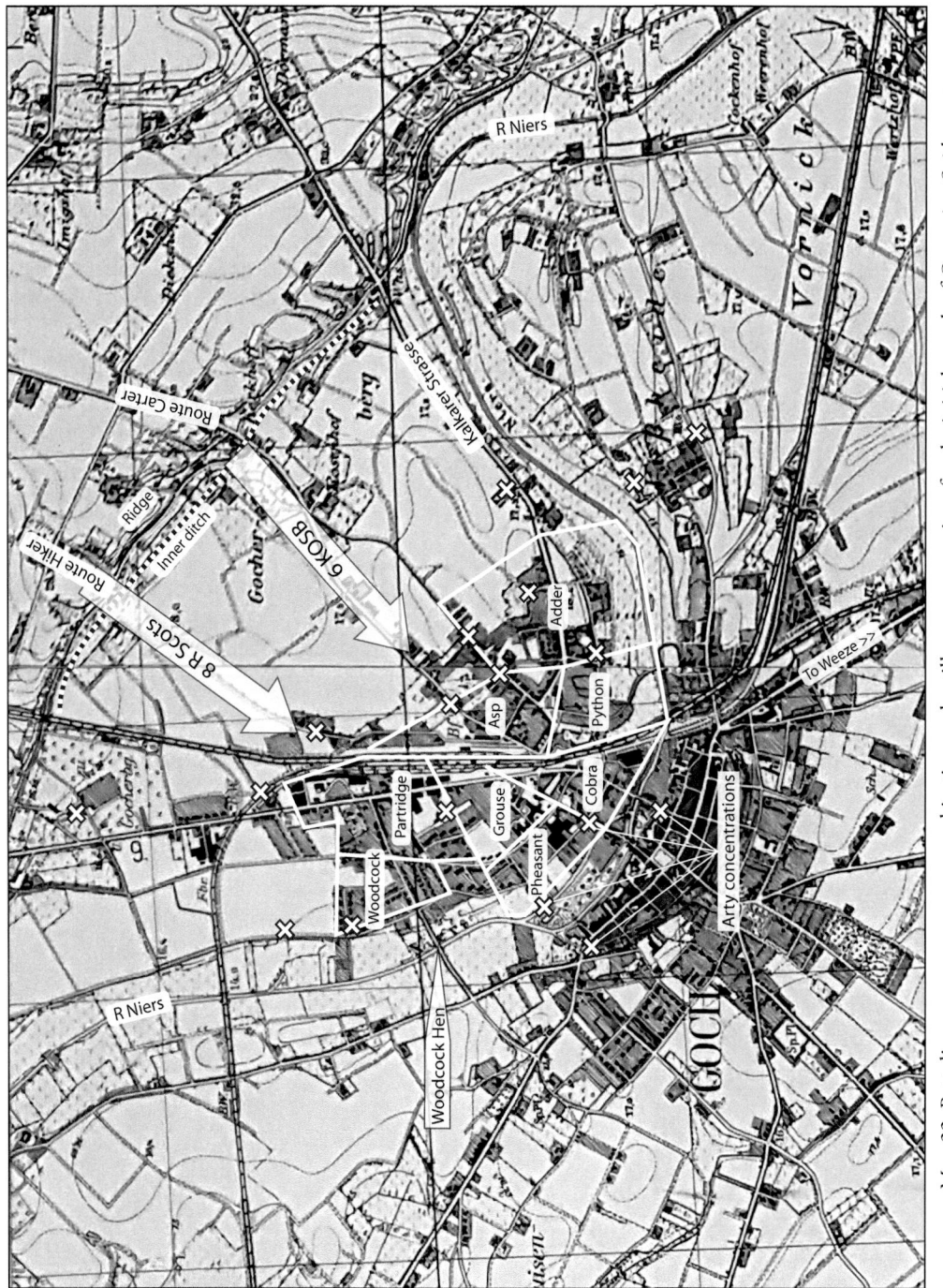

Map 22: Battalion axes, company group objectives and artillery concentrations for the initial assault of Operation Spider. (National Archives, author's photograph)

lery in time for a 15:00 H-Hour. The fire plan issued on the 17th was to involve 450 guns firing a two-hour preparatory bombardment to erode and misdirect defenders by repeatedly switching fire to every corner of town. Compared to the D-Day fire plan, this had a third of the artillery pieces firing for half as long but was still a considerable volume of fire as it focused on two battalions attacking on a front barely a kilometre wide.[29]

Come the 18th, the ammunition shortage (a combination of earlier profligacy, flooding, and smashed roads) had forced a sharp reduction to only 15 minutes of preparatory fire. The exception to this dearth was for Mattress rockets, which had been barely used in the previous week's close contact battles and were booked to fire for the full two hours. Efforts were made to fill the fire plan shortfall with a pepper pot using Vickers, 17pdrs, Bofors and mortars, but these weapons suffered similar shortages and there is no detail on what the pepper pot finally entailed. The remainder of the fire plan involved an on-call smokescreen and "off-call" concentrations, designed to achieve the suppressive effect of a barrage but moving at the pace expected of armoured infantry. Yet even with the reduced preparatory bombardment, gunners warned that some concentrations might have to be cancelled if the assault dragged on too long.[30]

At 09:30 on the 18th, the main body of 8 Royal Scots was en route to the assembly area while their company commanders and commanding officer, Lieutenant Colonel Pearson, were on the ridge getting their first look at Goch through the morning mist (north edge of Map 23).[31] A few kilometres further south, Brigadier Cumming-Bruce was on Route Carter conducting his own reconnaissance, reportedly getting to within 100 metres of the inner ditch.[32] Elements of 43, 51 and 53 Divisions had been engaged from Goch overnight, but reports suggested an exceptionally light defence. The only enemy Cumming-Bruce saw were dejected prisoners captured around the outer ditch, so the situation 'looked very much as if the enemy garrison, seeing the trap closing on them north and south, had decided to call it a day before worse things befell them'.[33] Cumming-Bruce therefore decided to send a company group into Goch straight away, dashing along Route Carter to seize the town and in a *coup de main*, thereby saving 'time and a great expenditure of ammunition'.[34]

It would be churlish to criticise Cumming-Bruce's decision, but tactical logistics and communication constraints meant the decision was slow to translate into action.[35] Orders reached 4 Grenadier Guards (the tank support) at 11:30 but did not reach the infantry until noon, while Flails and Crocodiles never got the order at all.[36] The coup de main also required the fire plan to be

---

29 15 Division HQRA, 'Spider'; 44 Brigade, 'Spider'. Guns were from 14 field, four medium and one heavy anti-aircraft regt, two medium and four heavy batteries. No usable figures could be found for rounds fired.
30 15 Division HQRA, 'Spider'; 6 Royal Scots Fusiliers and 15 Division HQRA diaries; BAOR, *Tour*, p.87. Where on-call missions were arranged before an action but not fired until called for, off-call missions were fired from a given time then called off by FOOs prior to assault by manoeuvre units, allowing guns to switch onto progressively deeper targets throughout the advance. This author might have accidentally invented the term "off-call".
31 The most coherent account of 8 Royal Scots action is by their adjutant, B.A. Fargus, 'Action of the 8th Battalion The Royal Scots during the Attack on Goch, 18th–19th February 1945', McBain, *Regiment at War*, pp.286–293.
32 284 Sqn RE diary (WO 171/5329).
33 Martin *15th Scottish*, p.258.
34 Advocate, *From Normandy*, p.94. Whitakers, *Rhineland* (p.127) considers this foray as a coup de main, Fargus (p.288) an effort to bounce the town, and the 15 Division comms log a 'recce in force'.
35 Even a cynical retrospective of evidence suggests a change from active to passive opposition in Goch but charitable sources like Martin underplay German activity, for example, ignoring a 15 Division comms log report of contact by 43 Division with a German platoon on Hiker at noon (Map 23).
36 4 Grenadier Guards, 141 RAC, 22 Dgns and 8 Royal Scots diaries. Neither Flails nor Crocodiles made the

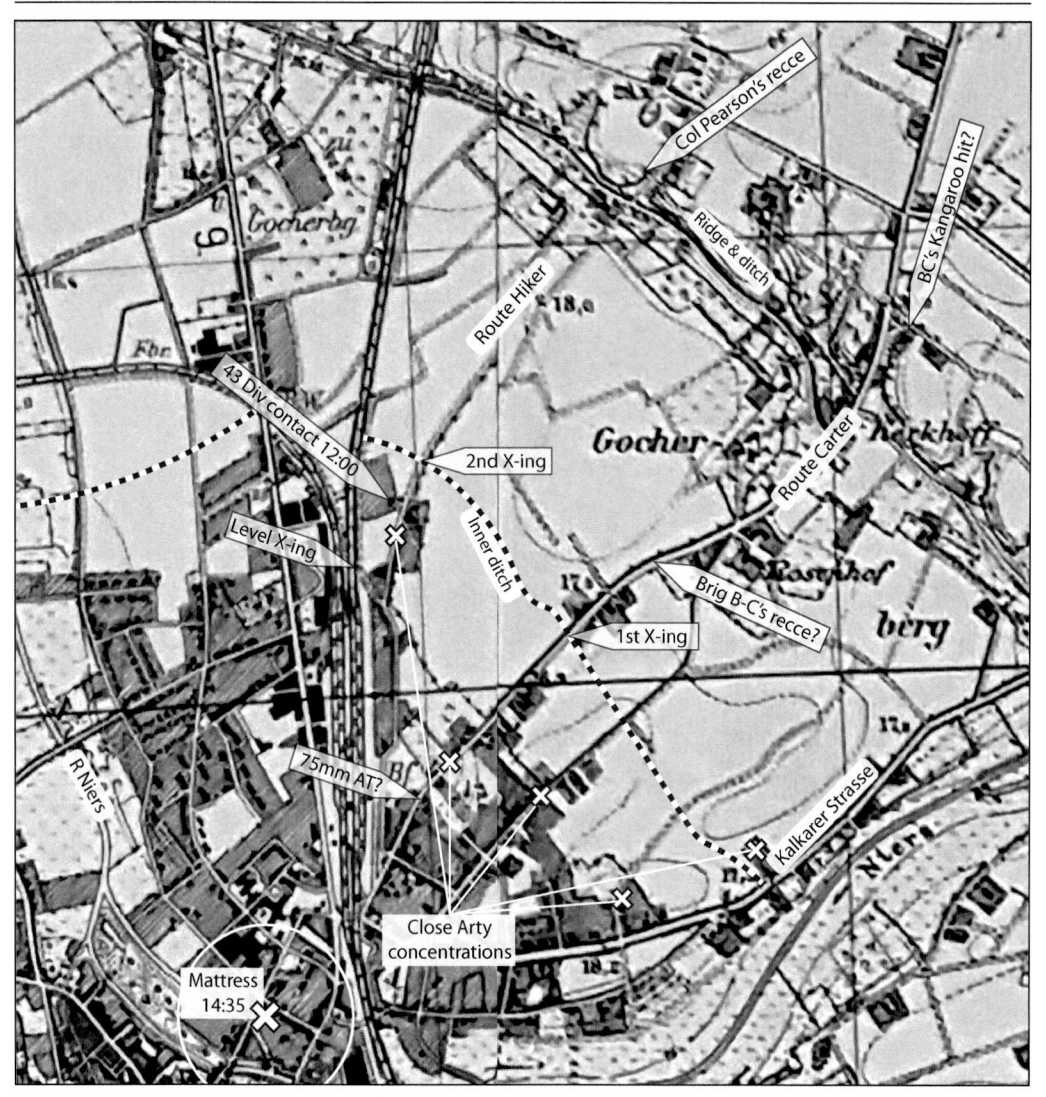

Map 23: Main events around the coup de main. (National Archives, author's photograph)

put on hold but there was difficulty contacting the artillery, particularly the Mattress commander 'whose apparatus was due to put down its dreadful missiles at certain fixed times'.[37] Then, although the coup de main was on 6 KOSB's axis, they were stuck in traffic, so Major McQueen's "A" Company, 8 Royal Scots, were given the job instead. It was 13:15, perhaps three hours after the Brigadier's decision, before all the available parts of the company group were married-up and heading for the crossing.[38]

The front of the column crossed the outer ditch at 13:30 but, as so often before, the AVRE-mounted Small Box Girder bridge had snagged in trees along the way. It seems this damaged the

---

15:00 H-Hr, and Flails are missing from most diaries. As with the Schottheide attack, much of the problem was in the complexity of the golf bag organisation, with seven parent units in the coup de main group.
37   Advocate, *From Normandy*, p.95.
38   284 Squadron diary; 15 Division comms log; Pearson, FIBUA video.

Figure 18: 'Small Box Girder Bridge in position over the anti-tank ditch north of Goch'. This picture was probably taken on the coup de main crossing on 19th. (battlefieldhistorian.com)

bridge release mechanism, so the AVRE could not detach when the bridge was laid, and therefore blocked the crossing to other vehicles (Figure 18).[39] Instead of waiting while another bridge was brought forward, the leading platoon crossed on foot, but were soon pinned down by machine-gun and *Panzerfaust* fire from buildings on both sides of the ditch. The rest of "A" Company debouched and secured the home bank with fire support from AVREs: 'OC 1 Tp fired 15 dustbins at bazookas in houses. Bazookas stopped.'[40] The home bank was secured, and 20 prisoners collected but the company was split up and mortar rounds were soon added to the incoming fire. British artillery support was hampered by the confusion of cancelling the fire plan, while tanks on the home bank were stuck on the line of the road and could provide little support.[41]

---

39 BAOR, *Tour*, plate 10. 15 Division comms log. There are variations of this bridge malfunction, with the release mechanism the most common but BAOR, *Royal Engineers Tour* (p.177) suggests an electrical problem.
40 284 Squadron diary. The 'dustbins' were 230mm spigot mortar rounds. No sources mention fire from the 4 Grenadier Guards tanks, though this may be implicit.
41 15 Division comms log, 8 Royal Scots, 4 Grenadier Guards and 15 Division HQRA diaries. This paragraph and the next two are the best fit to diaries and logs, but with multiple call signs close together in low ground, crossings are especially prone to confusion in primary sources so later accounts rely on memory and disagree on the sequence. Martin (p.259) has defensive fire before the first bridge laying attempt, Fargus (p.288) has it after. Perhaps protective of the Brigadier's decision, Advocate (pp.94–95) does not mention enemy contact, merely a bridge malfunction leading to the coup de main's cancellation. Fargus (p.290) and Martin (p.259) suggest the second AVRE was on site when the first bogged, but McQueen (Whitakers, p.127) is clear it moved up later. The FIBUA video also describes a counterattack by a *Fallschirmjäger* group moving along the anti-tank ditch.

At 13:55, a warning that "A" Company could be hit by Mattress fire used a wonderful example of veiled speech: 'Regarding the firing of the things you sleep on, our communications with these people have broken down. Unless you can stop it, the firing will come down between 14:20 and 15:00. Warn your chaps and keep them out of the way.'[42] This was the final straw for the coup de main, which was cancelled at 14:15 as Major McQueen set up a hasty defence around the houses and the stuck AVRE. "A" Company were digging in when, as Sergeant Cornwall, one of the platoon commanders, recalled 'our own artillery began to fall on us.'[43] This was not one of the feared Mattress missions but a preparatory concentration or heavier pepper pot. Only the first Mattress salvo was fired, and this at the centre of Goch, so "A" Company were well outside its danger area, see Map 23.[44]

As the potential for Mattress fratricide was being resolved, a second bridge-layer arrived, but bogged just short of the ditch. Then a German 75mm anti-tank gun began firing up the road from the edge of town, prompting one Churchill crew to reverse hard up the glacis of a Kangaroo, tipping their tank onto its side. The only other armour casualty that afternoon was a battery commander's Kangaroo on the ridge, apparently hit by a chance shot from the 75mm in town. By 15:00 the Kangaroos and tanks had withdrawn from the crossing site, leaving "A" Company largely unsupported until 6 KOSB could relieve them.[45]

The remainder of 8 Royal Scots re-launched their attack on Route Hiker at 16:00, an hour later than planned. The breaching force found an intact bridge over the inner ditch, but it collapsed as the first tank crossed. A Jumbo bridge was brought forward, and it seems this allowed "B" Company to cross in Kangaroos. However, "B" Company's armoured dash travelled barely 300 metres before the Kangaroo drivers baulked at the level crossing (Map 23), concerned that the railway lines would strip their vehicles' tracks. This curiously unforeseen circumstance forced the infantry to debouch in haste and darkness in an area overlooked by enemy-held buildings. After establishing a firebase in houses east of the railway, "B" assaulted across the tracks and into Goch's industrial area. The only armoured vehicle to cross the railway that night was an artillery FOO's tank. Once across the railway, "B" Company met stiff resistance in a mangled urban landscape but managed to secure part of a factory where, in line with the Brigade's worst-case plan, they went into defence for the night. Having lost their signallers and No. 18 set while debouching, they were reliant on the gunners' tank for communication.[46]

---

42   15 Division comms log.
43   Sergeant J. S. Cornwall, in Whitakers, *Rhineland* (p.128) and FIBUA video. There is a chance this was not friendly fire as some German guns could have been firing from the rear-left of "A".
44   None of the planned concentrations were near the crossing and the only mission reported to have not been cancelled was one Mattress salvo of 350 rounds on the centre of Goch at 14:35, after which fire was checked. This detail is from a part of a Canadian post-operation report, 1 Canadian Rocket Battery diary and a transcript of the British 102 Light Anti-Aircraft Regiment diary (WO 171/4952) which had a battery re-roled to Mattress rockets: all three sources kindly provided by "Buteman" from WW2Talk.
45   8 Royal Scots and 4 Grenadier Guards diaries; 15 Division comms log; Fargus, pp.290–292. The likely gun and battery commander's Kangaroo positions are marked at Map 23, making the engagement range close to 1,500m. Fargus estimates visibility at 400m, due to smoke. Hanscomb, 'Urban' (p.35), following BAOR, *Tour* (p.87), following Martin (p.259), claims a pair of SP guns fired on the crossing from south of the Niers but this critical information appears in no primary source. Given the visibility (400m) and range (c 1,300m) it is considered a spurious report.
46   BAOR, *Royal Engineers Tour*, p.176; 8 Royal Scots diary. As with the coup de main crossing, the order of events (but not the result) is debatable here, as primary sources (e.g., 15 Division HQRE, WO 171/4198) are vague and every secondary source presents a different version. Advocate (p.95) has "B" Coy crossing on foot, but the option presented here aligns with Martin (pp.259–260), Fargus (pp.290–291), and later events. Contrary to all other sources, the Brigade diary records '8 RS had three companies in the town' at 17:30. The 'had' suggests backfilling.

Behind "B" Company, the Jumbo bridge had fallen into the ditch and the crossing needed to be made good using fascines and bulldozers. Darkness and a rising mist hampered the work but also made German fire onto the crossing inaccurate. It was nearly 23:00 before the bridge was back in action at which point the Churchills and Kangaroos returning from "B" Company met those of "C", who were next in the order of march. Colonel Pearson had been to the rear to meet Brigadier Cumming-Bruce and at this point he returned to find a quagmire around the bridge and a hot dismount not far beyond it; he therefore ordered "C" and "D" to cross dismounted. It was 'intensely dark and misty' by the time "C" got moving, negating the effect of movement light, which was likely a benefit as the infantry had to advance unsupported over open ground on an axis known to the enemy.[47] A 'most unpleasant experience' occurred as "C" were strung out along the track when a German platoon, 'charged through the middle of the Company firing all their weapons and throwing grenades'.[48] Casualties included "C" Company's No. 18 set and two men captured. With little hope of coordination with the rest of the Battalion, "C" set up their defence on the eastern side of the railway and fended off small counterattacks throughout the night. As far as the Battalion was concerned, it 'was not until the next morning that the fate of this company was known.'[49]

Last in the order of march was "D" Company, who debouched on the ridge and advanced under harassing fire, which wounded their company commander and prevented them from reaching their intended objective (probably Woodcock or Grouse, Map 22) and so they joined "B" in all-round defence. Finally, back on the coup de main crossing, 6 KOSB relieved the Royal Scots' "A" Company who then attempted to re-join their Battalion in the early hours of the 19th. Sergeant Cornwall's platoon started to cross the railway line when they were challenged in English: 'Then they let go with everything they had. It was a German post, and they killed three or four of my men, including my young Bren gunner.'[50] Unable to cross the railway under fire, "A" Company backtracked, joined-up with "C" around 05:00, and remained there until daylight.[51]

Meanwhile, on Route Carter, 6 KOSB's line of Kangaroos and tanks had stacked up behind the coup de main force. A chain of miscommunications and stalled attacks culminated with their "D" Company crossing at 23:30. Having waited eight hours for a bridge that could support their armoured vehicles, "D" travelled a few hundred metres to the outskirts of Goch where a *Panzerfaust* ambush forced them to debouch and adopt all-round defence. This company also benefitted from the fog and darkness because a German gun in the edge of town (possibly the 75mm from earlier) repeatedly fired blindly down the road but scored no kills. To the left (south) of Carter, 6 KOSB's "B" Company attacked dismounted and endured a four-hour fight along a trench line 'manned by paratroopers for its entire length'.[52] Their advance began 400 metres short of the ditch and at 03:00 it ended perhaps 300 metres beyond it. Having captured a few houses in the outskirts of Goch, this company also adopted a hasty defence and engaged in a

---

47 4 Grenadier Guards and 8 Royal Scots diaries; MM citation of Lance Corporal Whittaker, WO 373/53/483.
48 Fargus, p.291.
49 Fargus, p.291; 8 Royal Scots diary; BAOR, *Tour* pp.87–88.
50 Whitakers, *Rhineland*, p.128.
51 BAOR, *Tour*, p.87; 8 Royal Scots diary; MC citation, Major Fife, WO 373/53/761.
52 Baggaley, *6th (Border) Battalion*, p.85; 6 KOSB movement order, 18 February; 6 KOSB, 4 GG, 49 APC and 15 Division diaries; 15 Division comms log; MM citations, Sergeant Campbell WO 373/53/787 and Private Lindie, WO 373/53/813; Advocate, p.95; Gunning, *Borderers*, pp.172–173; Martin, p.261. Most of these events never reached the Division radio net, with optimistic reports from 44 Brigade not corrected for four hours.

'grenade-slinging match' with defenders just 30 metres away.[53] The other two KOSB companies did not attempt to cross the ditch.

The overnight attack by 44 Brigade had culminated. All of 8 Royal Scots and half of 6 KOSB were holding out until daylight in the hope that tank support would resolve the situation. The rest of the brigade was still behind the inner anti-tank ditch. Except for one artillery observer's tank, none of the armour had got further than the outskirts of town before withdrawing.[54] Although later assessments would obscure the fact, 44 Brigade had fallen short of achieving even its worst-case objectives, with a toehold in only three of its eight overnight fortresses.[55]

153 Brigade

Since breaking into the southern corner of the Reichswald on D-Day, 51 Highland Division had fought a difficult series of actions south of the forest. These were tied to various plans for the capture of Goch, but the last few plans are sufficient to illustrate the constraints facing 51 Division and help explain why its tactics were so different to 15 Division's (see outline at Map 24). On the afternoon of the 15th (D+7) 51 Division's orders had 152 Brigade attacking Goch from the northwest by advancing straight down the main road through Asperden, following the dashed arrow marked "152 Bde plan A". While that attack went in, 154 Brigade and 32 Guards Brigade would continue to apply pressure in the centre and 153 Brigade would rest after handing over to 52 Division near Afferden ("153 Bde plan A"). As a clearer understanding of local resistance developed, 152 Brigade was directed to change its axis, shifting east through Hervorst, and by doing so allow 153 Brigade to move across the Division's rear to attack Goch from the north.[56]

Changing the axis turned the Asperden attack into a feint by 5 Seaforth, who promptly 'dug deep, lay low, and for two days watched that already shattered village being reduced to utter ruin around us.'[57] The feint had attracted German fire aimed at battering the battalions that would have echeloned through in a traditionally linear British attack. Instead, the fire was wasted because the rest of 152 Brigade moved behind Asperden to open the new route for 153 Brigade.[58] The assault on Goch could not be launched until the night of the 18th/19th because 153 Brigade needed to follow a winding route through recently captured villages, and initially had only 20 trucks to do it. Yet despite the delay between attacking on one axis then another, 2 Seaforth from 152 Brigade managed to erect a Jumbo bridge north of Goch without attracting much German attention (see Map 25).[59]

---

53 Martin, p.261; Distinguished Conduct Medal (DCM) citation, Sargeant Telfor, WO 373/53/398; MC citation, Major Tinniswood, WO 373/53/764; Gunning, *Borderers*, p.173.
54 Baggaley, pp.86–87; Whitakers, p.128; 15 Division comms log 200242. The 4 Grenadier Guards diary ends at 17:35 with No 1 Squadron providing fire support to an attack.
55 The FIBUA video, for example, has 8 Royal Scots achieving all their objectives at this point.
56 51 Division Op Instr 28 and 29; 152 Brigade Op Instr 21 and 22, diary (WO 171/4406); 2 Seaforth diary (WO 171/5267).
57 A. Borthwick, *Battalion: A British Infantry Unit's actions from El Alamein to the Elbe. 1942–1945* (London: Baton Wicks, 2001 [1946]), p.250.
58 2 Seaforth, 5 Cam H (WO 171/5164), 5 Seaforth (WO 171/5268) and 107 RAC diaries; J. Sym (ed.), *Seaforth Highlanders* (Aldershot: Gale & Polden, 1962), pp.297–298; Borthwick, *Battalion*, p.250. These actions developed into mopping up activities behind 153 Brigade, clearing the concrete positions northwest of Goch ("Bunkers" at Map 21) with clever and often bloodless use of Crocodiles and AVREs attacking from the rear. Histories tend to roll these rural actions into the Goch account, giving the false impression that the town itself was filled with bunkers and flamethrowers.
59 152 Brigade, 153 Brigade, 2 Seaforth and 107 RAC diaries.

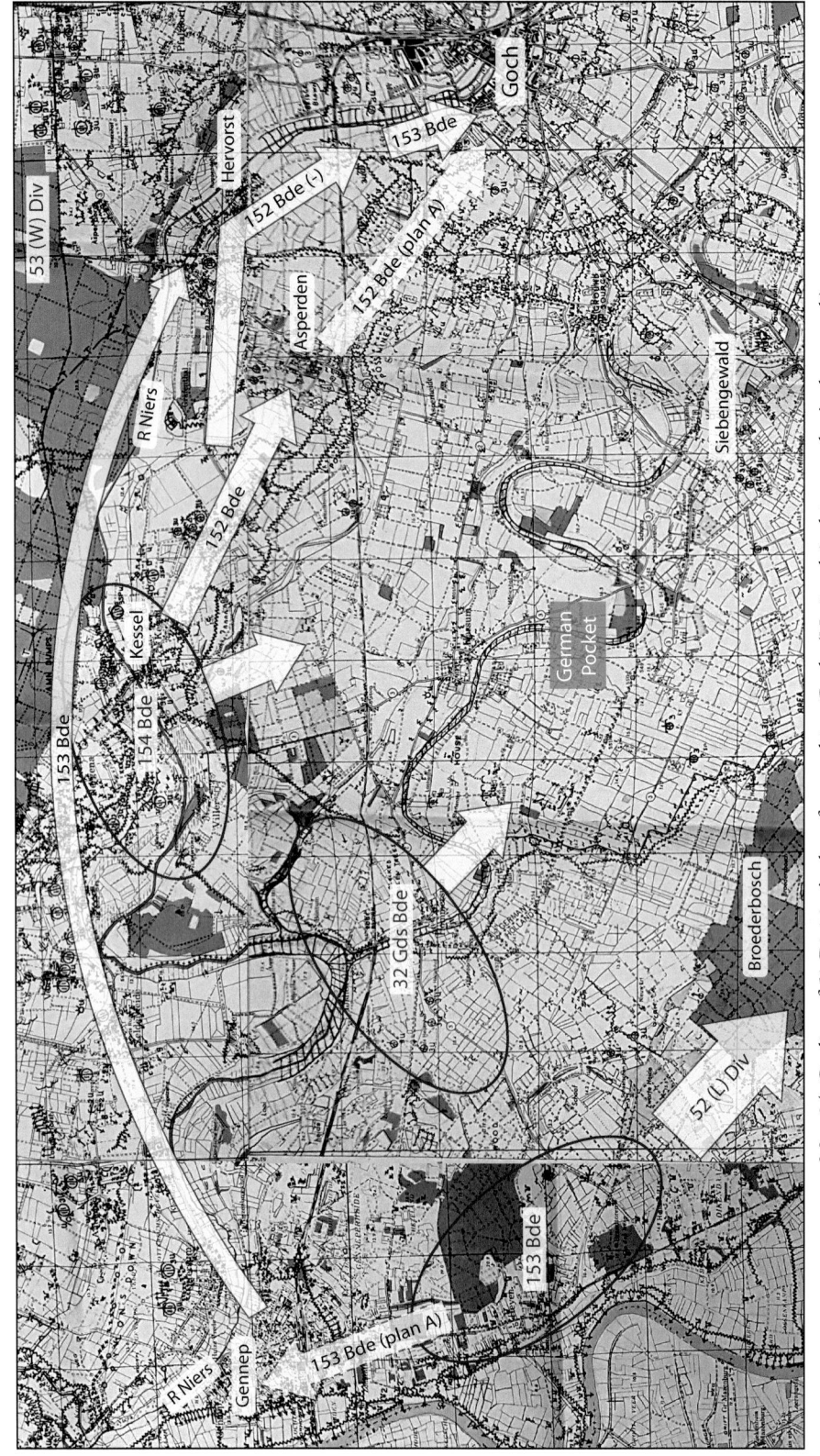

Map 24: Outline of 51 Division's plans for attacking Goch. (National Archives, author's photograph)

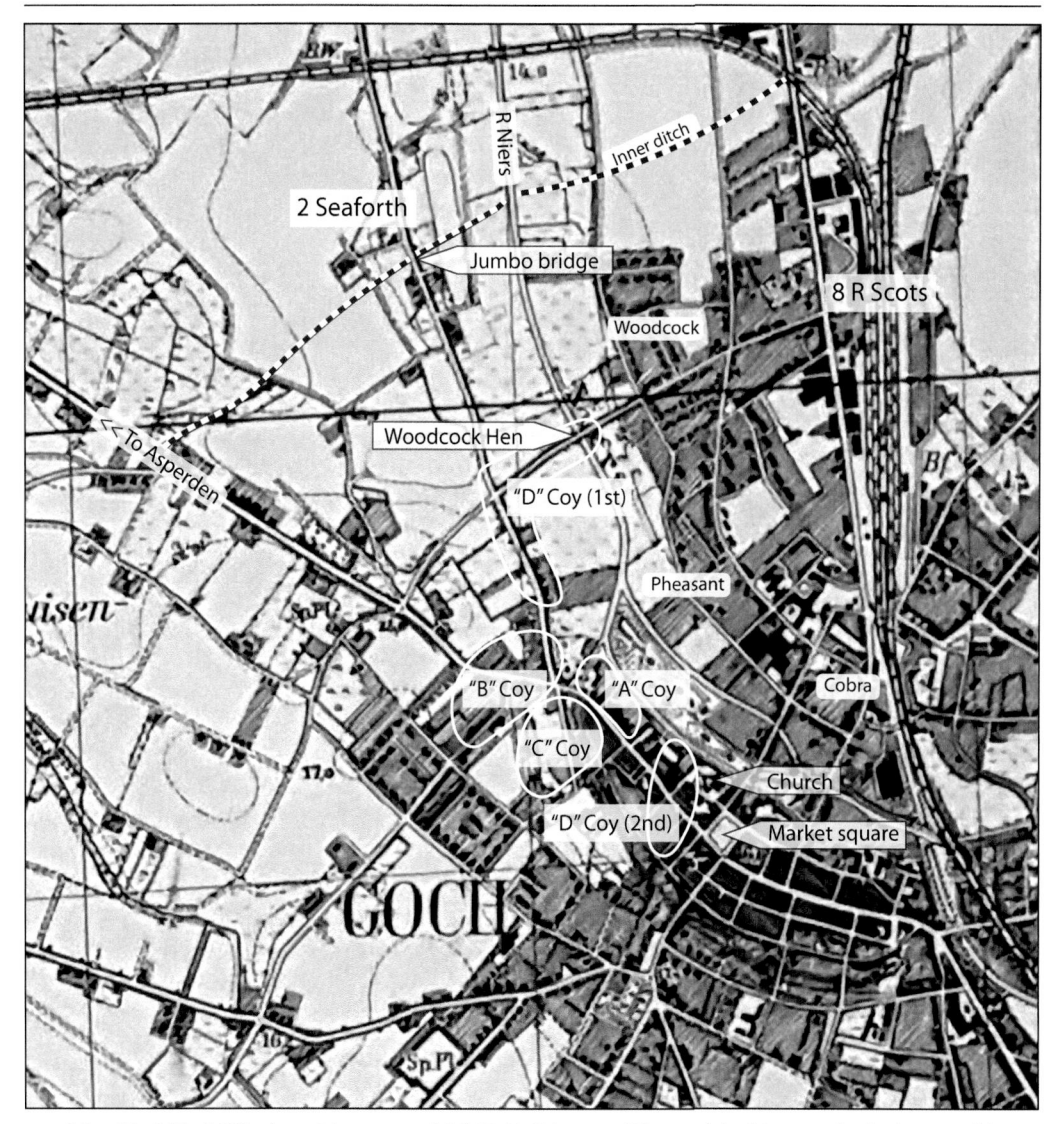

Map 25: 5 Black Watch positions around 06:00 19 February. (National Archives, author's photograph)

The first 153 Brigade unit over that bridge was 5 Black Watch, who were driven to Asperden on the afternoon of the 18th, then marched to Hervorst and formed up just north of the anti-tank ditch around midnight. Their fire plan started at 00:45 on the 19th, and 15 minutes later, "D" Company led the battalion through the small bridgehead and headed south towards Goch behind a series of timed artillery concentrations. As Major Brodie, "D" Company Commander recalled, 'It was a very dark misty night, and there was a terrific bombardment before we started, so the Boche were rather dazed.'[60] Resistance was 'slight as the enemy were still cowering from the barrage' and so "D" quickly overran the small collection of German positions along the road before going firm in an unnamed hamlet a few hundred metres north of town.[61]

---

60 Letters of Alec Brodie quoted in V. Schofield, *The Black Watch: Fighting in the Frontline 1899–2006*, (London: Head of Zeus, 2017) Kindle 7013. 5 Black Watch diary (WO 171/5159).
61 5 Black Watch diary. The use of 'barrage' likely in its generic sense. No barrage plan was found.

At that point "B" Company took the lead and had similar success, 'shooting up and capturing a few enemy' before going firm in the outskirts of town around 02:00.[62] The next phase of the advance involved "C" Company clearing buildings on the left of the main street, closely followed by "A" who did the same on the right. As planned, both companies advanced a few hundred metres then shifted to defence around 02:30, sending patrols to the edge of the market square, and reporting the area clear of enemy. However, there were minor engagements behind these patrols as bypassed defenders emerged from buildings and exchanged fire with the forward companies. Further back, part of "D" Company had captured the small intact bridge over the Niers (Woodcock Hen, Map 25) aiming to contact 8 Royal Scots.[63] Even further back, there was an undefined problem with the Jumbo bridge that made it impassable to the Jeeps carrying the Battalion Tac HQ. But, except for Battalion Tac, 5 Black Watch was now in position waiting for 5/7 Gordons to arrive and continue the attack. The difficulty moving units meant this was not due to happen until 07:30.[64]

Brute force and a few spare planks got Battalion Tac over the bridge around 04:00, allowing Lieutenant Colonel Bradford to set up a command post in one of the cellars along Goch's main street, the Mühlenstrasse.[65] It then seemed there was a chance to press on, dominate the town centre and the surviving bridge and, just like the 44 Brigade coup de main, save much time and ammunition. Unfortunately for 153 Brigade, the chance was fleeting and coordination was complicated. At 06:45, the 5/7 Gordons fire plan was cancelled and 5 Black Watch's "D" Company advanced towards the market square, only to find that German troops had started to reoccupy the area in the three hours since patrols gave the all-clear.[66] German sniping and shelling had increased, making it more difficult for troops to advance, and "D" drew fire from the church and hospital, which they assaulted. The wounded *Oberst* Matussek and his staff were captured in the hospital cellar, but it is not clear whether "D" Company even reached the market square given the delay, darkness, and destruction (Figure 19).[67]

When 5/7 Gordons came through, they lacked 5 Black Watch's advantages of attacking in the dark on an unexpected axis with a heavy fire plan. Daylight also meant 5/7 Gordons had armour, but this could not get into town due to rubble and craters and served only to advertise the Battalion's approach.[68] The infantry therefore had to advance under indirect fire then fight their

---

62   5 Black Watch diary.
63   In R. Grant, *The 51st Highland Division at War* (Shepperton: Ian Allan, 1977), p.120, Brodie claims capturing the bridge was an unplanned task suggested by a platoon commander: 'I suppose everyone from [CO] Bill Bradford downwards had been too tired to notice this bridge on the map in the poor light and so nothing was arranged.'
64   51 Division comms long; 5 Black Watch and 30 Corps diaries. 5 Black Watch moved their Tac HQ in Jeeps rather than the carriers that were the norm at the start of Veritable. The reduced weight, maintenance, and resupply burden of the Jeep may have compensated for losing the protection of carriers.
65   51 Division comms log has a more robust crossing completed at 07:15.
66   5 Black Watch, 153 Brigade and 51 Division diaries. The original 5 Black Watch task was to remain at the edge of town rear protection for 2 Seaforth who were to mop up along the road to Asperden. Additional support for cancelling the 5/7 Gordons fireplan came from a PW statement (Division comms log 190325) that 'most of the enemy already withdrawn to WEEZE'.
67   J. McGregor, *The Spirit of Angus* (Chichester: Phillimore, 1988), pp.171–173; Grant, *51st at War*, pp.122–123. 51 Division diary puts the time at 09:10 and this delay suggests communications difficulties. The same message has 5/7 Gordons about to attack from 200m east of the market square. The hospital is not shown on any contemporary maps but a best guess is shown at Figure 19 (Eddie Worth / Associated Press / Alamy Stock Photo). Putting HQs in hospitals was common, and still is. There are conflicting stories around Matussek's capture but McGregor has it ending with the wounded *Oberst* saluted by "D" Coy men as he was carried on a stretcher, a gesture which prompted further surrenders.
68   M. Lindsay, *So Few Got Through: The Diary of an Infantry Officer* (London: Collins, 1946), p.208. The 5/7 diary makes no mention of armour in contact. W. Miles, *The Life of a Regiment: History of the Gordon*

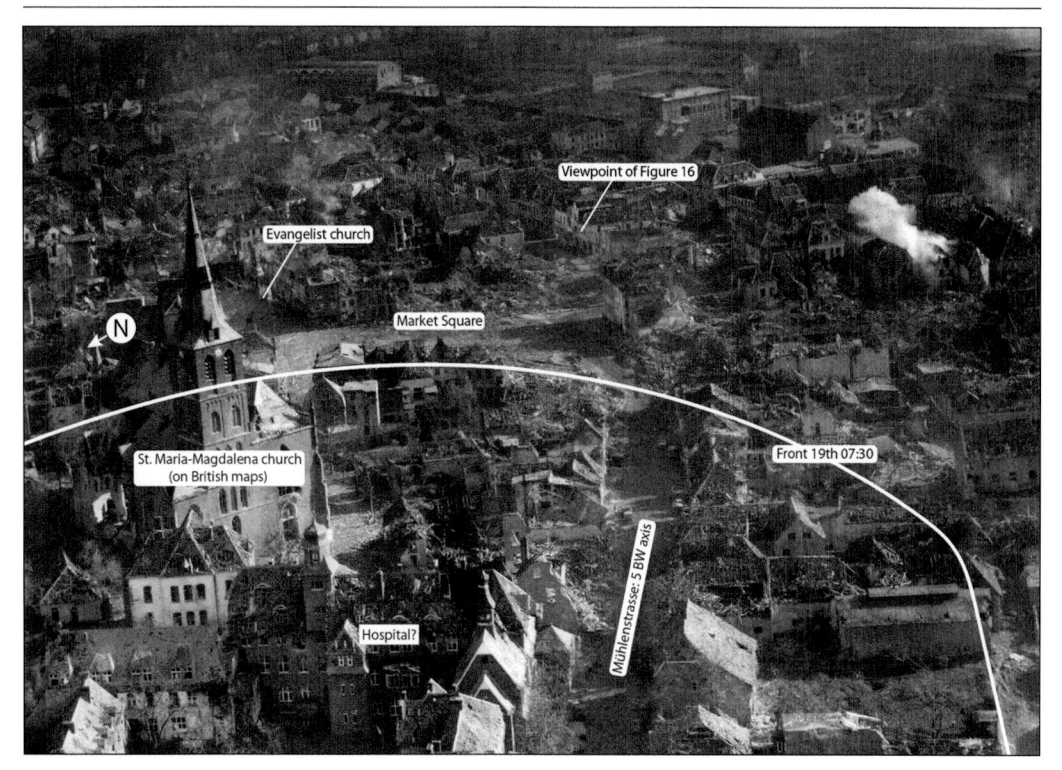

Figure 19: Aerial view of central Goch on 23 February, with overlay showing British front at 07:30 on 19th. (Associated Press)

way forward before they even reached the market square. On reaching the square they found that the power of urban defence lay in having multiple protected firing points overlooking an open killing area. Their casualties were not severe, but it proved exceedingly difficult to move men forward. Where 5 Black Watch had advanced close to 1,000 metres through town in the first two hours and claimed 160 prisoners, 5/7 Gordons struggled all day to advance 200 metres and made no reports of German prisoners.[69] Another difference between the two battalions' battles lay in the composition and motivation of the defending force, with 5 Black Watch fighting Matussek's confused rear area troops, but 5/7 Gordons colliding with some of Meindl's combat-ready reinforcements who had been given clear direction to hold onto southern Goch for as long as possible.[70]

The main reasons for the new defensive vigour can be seen by joining the two halves of the Goch battle, something that has been absent from Veritable's historiography. Although there is scant information on German tactical decisions, prisoner information suggests 44 Brigade's slow and

---

Highlanders. Volume V 1919–1945 (Aberdeen: Publisher unknown, 1961), p.338, records: 'The assistance of tanks and flamethrowers, which could not get forward through the choked and cratered streets, would have been invaluable.'

69 Miles, *Life of a Regiment*, p.338; 51 Division comms log; CWGC. 5/7 diary says they advanced 200m beyond the start line and suffered 25 casualties, many to indirect fire on the approach. Similarly, 7 Black Watch suffered 12 casualties in their approach on the 20th: Russell, *War History*, p.126.

70 51 Division ISUM 192330 includes the interrogation of Matussek and his adjutant, who emphasised poor coordination, the lack of a suitable defensive plan and the desertion of four *Volkssturm* companies who 'apparently managed to filter home at the last moment'. CMHQ 'Memorandum' (p.37) has *21. FJR* despatched to southern Goch on the 18th, presumably arriving as Meindl took command on the 19th.

noisy approach on the 18th had drawn the garrison into a hasty defence north of town. Then, as indicated by the forward line shown at Map 26, 5 Black Watch struck into the heart of Goch early on the 19th, closing a noose around the main defending force and threatening their escape route over the surviving bridge. The risk of the northern defence collapsing would have been clear to Meindl, and so every effort was directed to blocking the British in the south, allowing the northern defenders to withdraw across the river. This was, however, already too late for many of the northern garrison. Their perception of the overnight battle would have been dominated by the sound of British artillery pushing round their flanks, then the distinctive bark of the MG-42 being replaced by the thudding Bren as communication with friendly forces went dark. In such a situation, the chance of withdrawing would have looked very slim indeed.

Northern Success

At first light on the 19th, 8 Royal Scots' "B" and "D" Companies had a strong position in the factory area but were still reporting 'very stiff opposition' with 'enemy on every side'.[71] The balance of force shifted when a Grenadier Guards troop arrived, having driven along the railway line behind dismounted guides. Then, as the Churchills 'hotted up each house in turn, the enemy's morale began to crack. Soon there were white rags in every doorway.'[72] By one account, "D" Company and its armour killed four defenders and captured 230 for the cost of one killed and five wounded.[73] The results were less dramatic for the other Royal Scots companies but followed a similar pattern as infantry groups with a few supporting tanks mopped up around their overnight positions. By noon, 8 Royal Scots had cleared all but stragglers from the Woodcock and Partridge areas and linked up with 15 Division at Woodcock Hen, but they had to hand responsibility for Pheasant and Grouse to 8 Royal Scots Fusiliers. All told, 8 Royal Scots suffered 45 casualties and took 320 prisoners. Most of the cost (35 of the 45 casualties) was incurred breaking into the outskirts overnight and nearly all the reward (300 of the 320 prisoners) was reaped in town the following day.[74]

North of 8 Royal Scots and notably absent from the existing Goch narrative, 53 Division's 4 RWF (who captured De Horst in Chapter 2) had another successful barrage hugging attack, suffering few casualties, and taking a little over an hour to collect 168 prisoners in the edge of town.[75] South of 8 Royal Scots, records grow murkier, but progress was slower and the prisoner haul more modest. Once they received tank support, 6 KOSB captured isolated groups of defenders, usually after firing a few rounds of high explosive into buildings.[76] The KOSB reported

---

71 Fargus, p.292.
72 Martin, p.262.
73 Martin, p.262. Fargus (p.292) has tanks merely approach the main strongpoint for 160 defenders to surrender.
74 15 Division comms log and diary; 8 Royal Scots diary; Fargus, p.293. Casualties from 8 Royal Scots summary sheet and CWGC.
75 53 Division and 71 Brigade comms logs and diaries; 4 RWF diary and summary sheet; Riley et al, *Regimental Records*, pp.754–755; CWGC. The summary sheet lists 29 casualties, but the diary and 71 Brigade comms log have most of these to snipers and indirect fire during reorganisation. The timings and log entries indicate a high chance of fratricide during reorganisation.
76 Baggaley, p.86: 'After the first two rounds, twenty-five scared Germans came out to surrender, one of fine physique, being literally caught with his trousers down to be greeted with roars of laughter from "B" Company.'

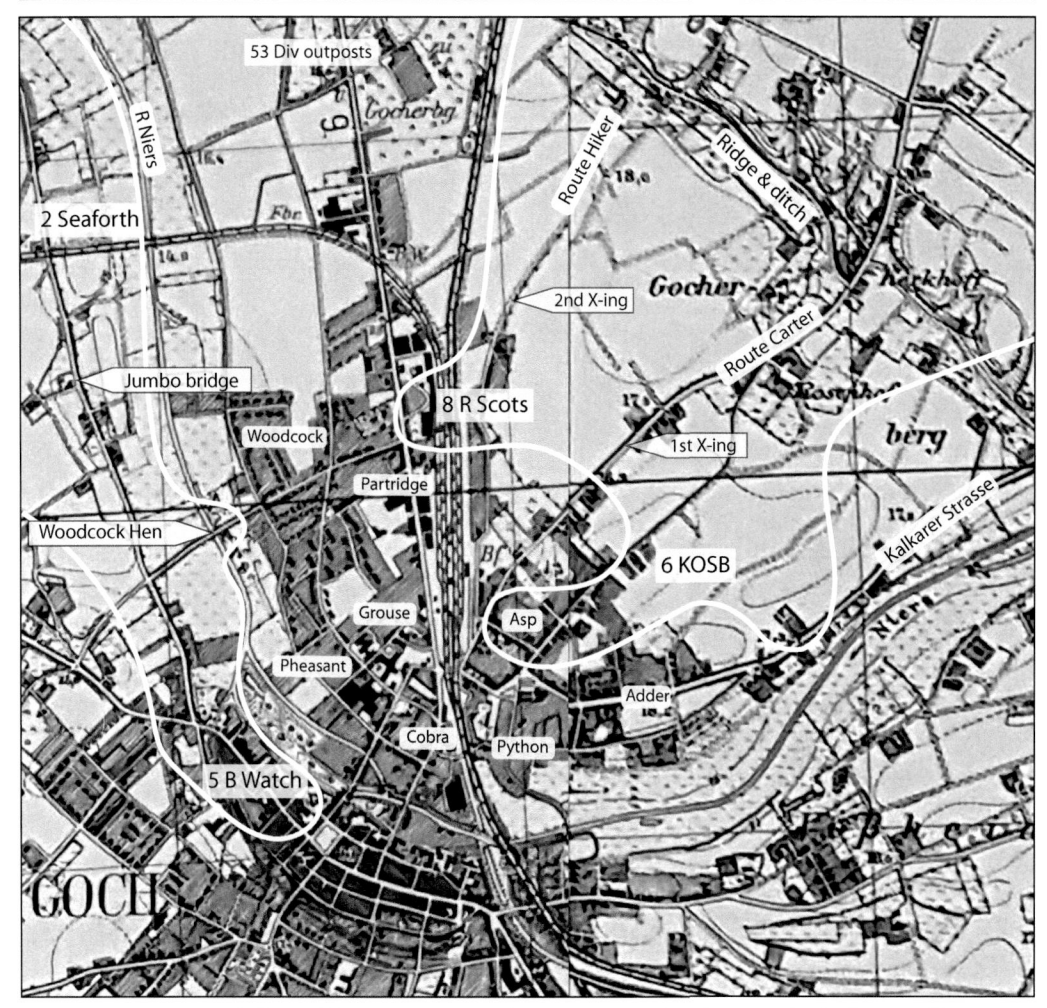

Map 26: British forward line at 06:00, 19 February. (National Archives, author's photograph)

126 prisoners for the cost of two casualties to add to 29 casualties recorded on the 18th, but companies were unable to reach the river before reverting to defence at nightfall.[77]

Meanwhile, 44 Brigade's third battalion group, 6 Royal Scots Fusiliers, had begun moving into Goch at first light on the 19th to secure the areas Pheasant, Grouse, and Cobra. They advanced on a 'southern route', most likely Route Carter and probably on foot, and seem to have been spotted by defenders south of the river because they came under heavy accurate fire from German artillery and mortars, suffering considerable casualties with one being their acting commander.[78] As 6 Royal Scots Fusiliers came closer to the town centre, indirect fire was joined by small arms. The advance and communications broke down, but once again it seems most of the casualties came in the open areas on the edge of town, while the greatest movement difficulties involved getting men forward once in town. The Battalion suffered 30 casualties to gain 92 prisoners.[79] By nightfall, 6

---

77 6 KOSB diary.
78 6 RSF diary; J. C. Kemp, *Royal Scots Fusiliers*, p.308.
79 6 RSF diary, summary sheet and CWGC suggest two killed on the 19th and one on the 20th.

Royal Scots Fusiliers had not entered Cobra, but the last pockets of defence withdrew south of the river overnight, and by noon on the 20th northern Goch was judged to be clear of enemy.[80]

Southern Victory

While 44 Brigade started mopping up on the 19th, 153 Brigade continued its struggle in the south, repeatedly attempting to bash through or work around German strongpoints. At 11:00, an hour after 5/7 Gordons stalled at the market square, the first two companies of 1 Gordons arrived and tried to advance on the right (south) of 5/7. They were soon pinned down 'by snipers and spandau fire from individual enemy posted in windows, craters and heaps of rubble, commanding X-rds [crossroads] on axis of advance from side streets.'[81] It was about this time that British armour was used for the first time in southern Goch, but this was unsuccessful, a 107 RAC troop leader's tank being destroyed by *Panzerfaust* in the edge of town. The next two companies from 1 Gordons arrived that afternoon and launched a successful flanking attack a few hundred metres further south with some Churchill and Crocodile support, but this attack lost momentum by 16:00.

On the 20th, 1 Gordons continued to push south of Goch. After a day-long struggle where one company was overrun by a German counterattack, they secured the Thomashof manor farm, threatening the escape route of a larger pocket of German forces between Goch and Afferden. However, rather than unhinging the defence, this encouraged Meindl to redouble the effort in the southeast corner of town, with the apparent aim of delaying the British while the Afferden–Goch pocket (centre of Map 24) was emptied to form a new defensive line north of Weeze.[82]

Once Thomashof was secure, 51 Division committed to a three-pronged assault on the night of 20/21 February (Map 27). This involved 5/7 Gordons renewing their push from the town centre while 7 Black Watch (attached from 154 Brigade) attacked to their right. At about the same time, 5 Black Watch would launch a wide right hook through Thomashof to secure positions around Slavanien, another farm complex south of town. Grouping these three actions together gives an illusion of structure, when in fact they resulted from expedients forced by logistic constraints and tactical events. The initial intention was for 5 Black Watch to launch a daylight attack, but this was shelved due to a shortage of smoke rounds and the long struggle for Thomashof. At one stage 5 Black Watch were set to rescue 1 Gordons. The final scheme was only decided at 16:00 on the 20th when General Rennie visited 5 Black Watch to emphasise the importance of the Battalion cutting Goch off from the south.[83]

The 21:00 H-Hour for 5 Black Watch followed a 15-minute preparatory bombardment then "B" and "C" Companies assaulted a pair of farms 800 metres east of Thomashof (Map 28). Hugging the fire plan got companies into these two positions but once in the buildings there was 'fierce close-quarter fighting' and 'Germans were knifed and hit over the head, and dealt with in every

---

80   Kemp, *Royal Scots Fusiliers*, pp.308–309.
81   1 Gordons diary.
82   107 RAC diary; J.M. Cowper, *The King's Own: The Story of a Royal Regiment, Vol. III. 1914–1950* (Aldershot: Regimental Association, 1957), p.465; Lindsay, *So Few*, pp.207–215; 5/7 Gordons, 153 Brigade and 1 Gordons diaries. Latter includes 'Account of the operations carried out by the 1st Battalion The Gordon Highlanders 8 – 23 February 1945' (1 Gordons post-operation report). Omitting a detailed account of the Thomashof action from this assessment was a difficult decision but 5 Black Watch's later action had much greater effect.
83   McGregor, *Angus*, p.173; 5 and 7 Black Watch diaries; 'History of 154 Infantry Brigade in North West Europe' extract at 51hd.co.uk.

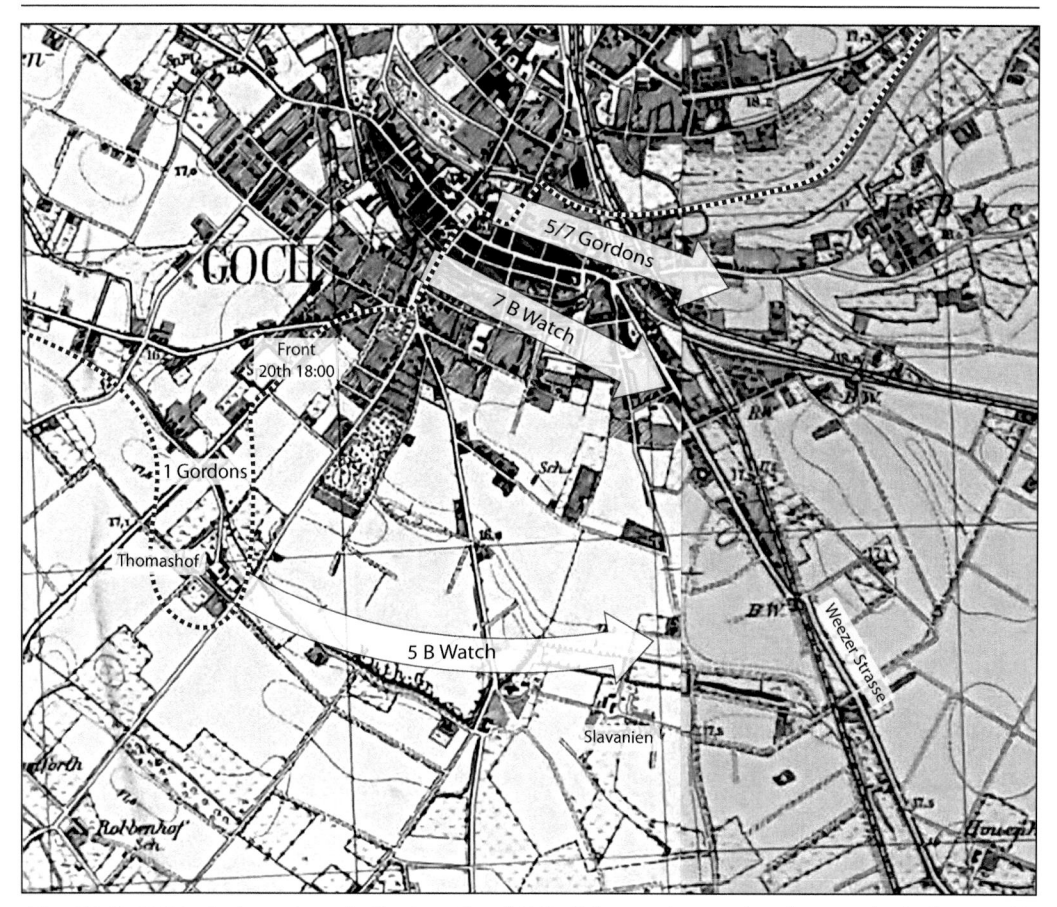

Map 27: 51 Division's planned attacks for the night of 20/21 February. (National Archives, author's photograph)

way.'[84] Both companies were soon counterattacked by German infantry from north, south, and east, and the fighting drew in the leading sections of "A" Company, who were preparing to attack Slavanien. The counterattacks were beaten back with the assistance of the fire missions intended to precede the "A" Company attack, delaying that action until 23:00.

The Slavanien farm complex was surrounded by a network of trenches and earth shelters built to protect an artillery battery.[85] "A" Company managed to get into the earthworks but not the buildings then, with some buildings burning and others stubbornly defended, a stalemate developed that lasted several hours. Further advance by "A", who lacked armour and anti-tank guns at this time, may also have been discouraged when they heard tracked vehicles moving north up the *Weezer Strasse* around midnight. By 02:00 on the 21st, 5 Black Watch had captured 60 prisoners, but Slavanien was not secured until 06:00.[86]

In the meantime, "D" Company set off at about 02:00 to secure the final objective, a small farm north of Slavanien. They attacked without artillery support, reportedly 'because of the close proximity

---

84 5 Black Watch diary; McGregor, *Angus*, p.173.
85 Defence overprint 14 February 45. No guns were reported on the position, but the location and layout suggest Slavanien was built to house a battery to fire across the Maas.
86 5 Black Watch diary; McGregor, *Angus*, p.173; 51 Division comms log, 210135.

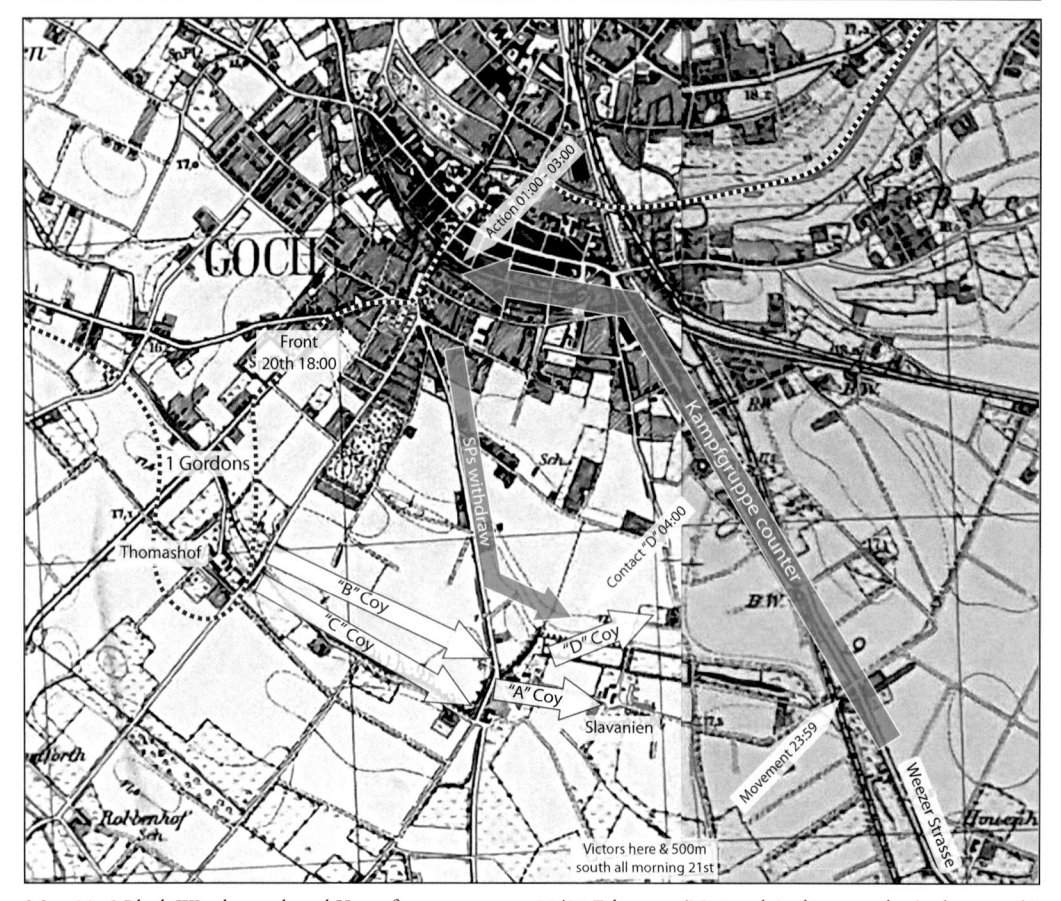

Map 28: 5 Black Watch attack and Kampfgruppe counter 20/21 February. (National Archives, author's photograph)

of the other companies', but perhaps more due to communication difficulties.[87] After being pinned down briefly by 'withering fire from several Spandaus', Major Brodie and the lead platoon dashed in, eliminated two machine-gun teams, surrounded the first building, then lobbed in grenades and captured 12 defenders.[88] The other two platoons fought through to clear an orchard behind the farm and the Company then dug in. For the rest of the night, 5 Black Watch were engaged from all sides, but these encounters were piecemeal, even accidental, involving seemingly confused German troops.[89]

A much greater threat to the Battalion came from those armoured vehicles that "A" Company heard at midnight. This was the first substantial commitment of German armour to Goch and appears to have been a *Kampfgruppe* that included a few companies of infantry, four SPs, a tank, and up to 10 light armoured vehicles – a mix of half-tracks and armoured cars.[90] After moving up the *Weezer Strasse* the *Kampfgruppe* swung west into Goch, stalled 5/7 Gordons advance, then hit the 7 Black Watch attack on its northern flank. This vigorous counter split

---

87 McGregor, *Angus*, p.174. The nearest friendly force was 200m from the objective.
88 McGregor, *Angus*, p.174.
89 McGregor, *Angus*, p.174; 5 B Black Watch diary; MC citation, Major Brodie, WO 373/53/738.
90 30 Corps, 153 Brigade, 154 Brigade, 5 and 7 Black Watch diaries and 51 Division comms log give different figures, so the total given here is based on 51 Division ISUM 59. Despite inflationary tendencies, the heavy armour count seems reasonable given the opportunity to identify vehicles after the battle, but the light armour count may have been swollen by including kills to later artillery fire missions.

one of the 7 Black Watch companies, causing heavy British casualties and derailing the whole attack before 'rumbling off' while British armour was still waiting for daylight before coming forward.[91]

Perhaps realising their escape route was closing, part of the *Kampfgruppe* headed south into the area 5 Black Watch had just captured. Unlike the two battalions in town, 5 Black Watch had been fortunate enough to have a troop or two of Archer tank destroyers follow their advance despite the darkness.[92] It was a struggle to get the Archers forward and they arrived at company positions in ones and twos so at 04:00, when a pair of German SPs approached "D" Company from the rear, they were mistaken for friendly vehicles. These SPs and their infantry then launched an attack that separated "D" Company from the Battalion. The only information to reach Battalion Tac came from a runner who reported the SPs 'pumping shells into the Coy' from 50 metres away. The leading SP disabled an Archer then withdrew; the second was hit by a PIAT round, which did not detonate but prompted the crew to bail out and surrender. The rest of the *Kampfgruppe* had started to withdraw down the *Weezer Strasse* covered by another series of uncoordinated attacks on "D" Company, who were 'shot up at close range by bazookas etc.'[93]

Dawn on the 21st gradually revealed the impact of the 5 Black Watch attack. Across the countryside east and south of Goch, large parties of German troops became visible, variously attempting to withdraw, counterattack, or simply find cover. By then, the Black Watch companies had been joined by artillery observers and more tank destroyers. Throughout the Goch operations, the German force had held the advantage of dominating flat open ground from buildings, but now the tables were turned, and with devastating effect. A tank destroyer with "D" Company knocked out two SPs withdrawing down the *Weezer Strasse* but most of the killing was by indirect fire:

> When it was light enough, enemy could be seen in every direction round the Battalion, but particularly to the South and South-East, where some three or four hundred could be seen. A counter-attack appeared imminent, as they were advancing on us. Luckily communications were through and for the next two hours the gunners had the time of their lives. Shells were crashing down on enemy in the open, some only 400 yds in front of our positions. Some enemy were digging in mortars a short [way] off also. Soon the mediums were firing too, and then Victor targets began, and the enemy were in a state of chaos. The F.O.O. could hardly contain himself, and was rushing about so as to see all directions in turn, while calls for fire continued to come in from "A" and "D" Coys. A great many casualties were caused, and bodies could be seen lying about everywhere.[94]

The German defence was shattered. By noon on the 21st, 5/7 Gordons and 7 Black Watch found their forward movement unopposed, and soon reached the railway line that had been the Gordons' objective for the last two days. In the evening, 7 A&SH passed through to occupy positions east

---

91   Russell, *War History*, p.126; CWGC. 7 Black Watch diary has 44 casualties but includes at least 12 from earlier artillery. The 107 RAC diary, Cowper, *King's Own* (pp.464–465) and Dyson, *Tank Twins* (pp.157–160) reflect limited involvement of tanks in southern Goch, a greater role outside the town but no record of any Allied tank action in darkness in Goch.
92   5 Black Watch diary: 'One S.P. gun slipped into the ditch, and the track was blocked and impassable to anything except a carefully driven Jeep'.
93   5 Black Watch diary; McGregor, *Angus*, p.174; Division comms log 210135; 7 Black Watch, 107 RAC and 153 Brigade diaries.
94   5 Black Watch diary.

of Goch. Although German artillery continued harassing fire throughout the day, there was little formed resistance on the 30 Corps main effort, which now pointed southward, to Weeze.[95]

Conclusion

Goch is a prime example of "confused fighting" being more an artefact of research constraints than the fighting itself. Combatants' perception, communication, and coordination were hampered by the enclosed environment, and there are gaps in surviving records, but the historical confusion comes from the sheer volume of source material. With two divisions engaged, and two more on the margins, 60 sources had to be cross-referenced to create this chapter. Even so, the presentation of the assessment was inevitably abridged and biased towards 8 Royal Scots and 5 Black Watch, neglecting the other seven battalions that fought in Goch and yet more units that contributed on the flanks. Despite these constraints, the chapter has presented the main strengths and weaknesses of the British approach to urban combat in Goch, and the implications for historians and soldiers.

Contemporary assessments blamed the RAF for most of Goch's problems, summed up by the statement that 'the infantryman would ask the airman to go elsewhere, particularly as he does not kill or even frighten the defenders the infantryman is going to meet.'[96] Yet, with the notable exception of the Whitakers, sources play down the fact that 30 Corps requested the town to be smashed on the 7th while expecting to drive through it on the 9th. Despite the lessons of Cassino and Caen, planners failed to appreciate the negative effects of heavy bombing. Then, disregarding the more immediate lessons of Gilbert, Sullivan, and Kleve, 44 Brigade ignored the inconvenient bogs, buildings, rubble, and Germans to justify recycling the Blerick formula. It was perhaps fortunate for 44 Brigade that tactical logistics and a stiff defence made it so difficult to reach the outskirts of town. Had 44 Brigade managed to ferry battalions into central Goch as planned, the result could have been a disaster on a par with the first battle for Grozny.[97]

The only positive from the armour-heavy assault was that it gave two companies protection from small arms and shell fragments across 300 metres of open ground. Those companies suffered fewer casualties than some dismounted subunits, but this was a poor exchange for hours of delay and telegraphed assaults, factors that greatly increased those dismounted companies' casualties. Then the Kangaroos and Churchills were quickly withdrawn by in-support commanders who judged the threat of stripped tracks and hidden *Panzerfaust* to trump the requirement to move and support the infantry, and so 44 Brigade failed to achieve its worst-case objectives. The stunning transformation in daylight on the 19th was due to infantry and small packets of familiar armour giving one another close support, but this was enhanced by defenders having no armour of their own and being encircled by the southern battle. That encirclement was provided by 5 Black Watch attacking dismounted, which proved to be a far more cost-effective approach than the Blerick template that dominated post-war doctrine.[98]

---

95 Most British daylight casualties on the 21st were caused by a Dutch squadron of RAF Mitchell bombers that hit Goch instead of Weeze. Casualties included four killed, 17 wounded from 7 A&SH, and 51 Division's Commander Royal Engineers. 7 A&SH diary (WO 171/5154); letter to Horrocks from 84 Group RAF, 51 Division diary.
96 Anon (possibly Martin Lindsay), Annex C to 21 AG, *Veritable*, p.88.
97 Using what looked a lot like 44 Brigade's best-case plan, one Russian Brigade lost 700 men and 140 armoured vehicles in Grozny. T. L. Thomas, 'The Battle for Grozny: Deadly Classroom for Urban Combat' *Parameters*, Summer 1999, pp.87–101.
98 This will be familiar to any soldier since the 1950s and still has echoes in doctrine publications such as Land Warfare Centre, *Formation Tactics* (Army Field Manual Vol. 1 Part 1) (Upavon: LWC, 2007).

Infantry-armour cooperation was inadequate in the south, and though 153 Brigade's post-Goch report politely blamed radios and insufficient collective training, the frustration is clear: 'co-operation did not, perhaps, reach the level it should have [with] considerable delay in the tks being made ready to fight after reaching fwd Bn areas.'[99] It is noteworthy that 153 Brigade did not blame craters and rubble as armoured sources did, but perhaps overlooked the effect of fatigue on 107 RAC, who were the only gun tank regiment supporting the enlarged and widely dispersed 51 Division.

On both sides of the Niers, the defence only collapsed when outflanked, an effect that could have been achieved by bypassing the town entirely. From the German perspective, 43 Division's advance on the 17th was stopped by British lethargy. Had 43 Division pressed on, or been promptly overtaken by a lighter force from 15 Division, 'Goch would have fallen that evening and the [British] enemy would have had the opportunity from there to pierce through to the South and roll up the Maas front.'[100] The British delay ran contrary to Horrocks's intention to assault or bypass quickly and was prompted by 44 Brigade convincing Barber to sell a ponderous echelon change to Thomas, who was only too keen to pass on the risk. That a brigade dominated the corps plan is no surprise to experienced staff officers, but in this case, it undermined operational effectiveness and post-war objectivity.[101]

Contrary to the dominant perception of urban attrition favouring the defence, there were few attacker casualties once men were in buildings, and defenders readily surrendered in close contact. Most British casualties were suffered during the break-in battle or moving into town as a second echelon. Once in town, the main difficulty was moving troops forward, with organisational and psychological frictions enhanced because urban terrain broke companies into small packets that had difficulty coordinating their actions and lacked training in independent manoeuvre. An additional psychological aspect was that the suppressive effect of defensive fire was enhanced by there being multiple protected firing points. The other major source of British casualties was German counterattacks, which is contrary to the accepted view of defence having the advantage in urban areas.

Many of the British problems in Goch reflect the immaturity of an urban doctrine designed around intact villages rather than large towns smashed by aerial bombing. As 153 Brigade later noted: 'if the town is badly cratered, battle school drills cannot be applied.'[102] Much of the doctrine was detailed and relevant, emphasising night infiltration and decentralisation, but it said little about investing or bypassing a town, clearing large buildings, or crossing open spaces. Doctrine said next to nothing about infantry-armour cooperation, which was understandable given the lack of corporate experience before the doctrine was written in 1943, but it seems 21st Army Group was slow to absorb lessons from other theatres where platoon-sized combined arms teams achieved remarkable success.[103]

---

99 'Op Veritable', 153 Brigade diary.
100 CMHQ 'Memorandum', p.37.
101 Author's communications with serving and retired staff officers.
102 'Op Veritable', 153 Brigade diary; Annex C to 21 AG, *Veritable*, p.88.
103 War Office, *Fighting in Built-Up Areas: Military Training Pamphlet No. 55* (London: War Office, 1943) is more relevant than some current urban doctrine. Its principles were compared to lessons from Ortona in DTI 'Employment of tanks with infantry' and described as 'sound as far as they go'. See also: War Office, *Infantry Training, Part VIII.- Fieldcraft, Battle Drill, Section and Platoon Tactics 1944* (London: War Office, 1944), pp.86–95 (Annex C to 21 AG, *Veritable* (p.87); S.J. Cuthbert, *We Shall Fight in the Streets* (Aldershot: Gale & Polden, 1942) looks like the source for much pamphlet content, and drew on "EGYPTFORCE", *Street Fighting for Junior Officers*, (London: Publisher unknown, 1919) which discussed the problem of open spaces like market squares.

As with essential collective skills like hugging a fire plan or infantry-armour cooperation, the constant pressures on training meant urban skills were inconsistently acquired, and generally inadequate. Major Brodie recalled 'some lectures and sand table exercises' from 1943 and an impromptu exercise in a bombed barracks in 1944, 'but once a battalion gets into an operation, there is no time or opportunity to practise rather specialised forms of battle, and all one can do is to bash on.'[104] As with 9 RTR in the Broederbosch, units in Goch had to improvise, effectively writing doctrine as they went. One improvisation was attributed to Sergeant Maxie of "D" Company who, finding it 'messy' to clear cellars with grenades used large stones instead, 'which invariably had the desired effect of producing a scramble of Germans anxious to surrender'; a version of this drill is still taught today.[105] The Goch battle was won by combining improvisations like this with sound extant doctrine like 5 Black Watch's combination of artillery and infiltration on the 19th.

Few of these observations have made their way into Goch's patchwork historiography, which focused on 44 Brigade's worst-case plan of occupying overnight fortresses. As with the broader treatment of Veritable, omitting key aspects of 44 Brigade's planning and execution has made the two seem to overlap much more neatly than the reality, and this has devalued the impact of aggressive improvisation by junior commanders and private soldiers. A similar omission afflicts the DOAE study, which correctly noted that 44 Brigade suffered only a third of the casualties of 153 Brigade but mistakenly attributed this to 153 using a flawed plan that did not 'exercise the tight control and methodical approach necessary' or the 'all-arms mix' of 44 Brigade's assault.[106] As this chapter has shown, there was little method or control in 44 Brigade, and its notable successes came when small groups improvised. The criticism of 153 Brigade also ignored its larger operational area and stronger opposition, which in each case was around double that faced by 44 Brigade. The DOAE study and the FIBUA video also make no mention of German armour and counterattacks, or the southern encirclement's impact on the collapse of the northern defence.

Although the 44 Brigade history presents events in northern Goch with some candour, it makes the preposterous claim that the Blerick formula was 'a complete and overwhelming success' in Goch.[107] Martin's *15th Scottish* followed 44 Brigade's lead, as did the BAOR *Battlefield Tour*, the DOAE study, the Whitakers' *Rhineland*, and German secondary sources.[108] Yet even 51 Division's histories underplay the operational impact of 5 Black Watch's victories. This was partly due to 1 Gordons' influential post-operation report, which framed the narrative within days of the battle and then was popularised in Lindsay's *So Few Got Through* just a year later. It also seems 153 Brigade's statement that the garrison was metaphorically 'coming to life' prompted the author of the 1 Gordons post-Goch report (12km away in Gennep at the time) to claim the cowering defenders were 'presumably asleep'.[109] Lindsay, and Salmond's *History of the 51st Highland Division* concur, as do all those authors who followed the 44 Brigade history.[110] No doubt fatigue and

---

104 R. Grant, *51st at War*, pp.121–122, 124. Brodie had to give a platoon commander a hasty summary of his own scant experience when directing the platoon to secure Goch hospital. He also suggests the 1 Gordons company in Thomashof was overrun because they had not been taught to clear cellars and attics.
105 McGregor, *Angus*, p.171. LWDC, *Urban Tactical Handbook*, p.96.
106 Hanscomb, 'Urban', pp.40, 47; FIBUA video.
107 Advocate, *From Normandy*, p.94.
108 The Goch chapter in Whitakers' *Rhineland* is heavily influenced by the FIBUA video, has northern Goch captured before 152 Brigade secured the bridgehead for 153, then confuses the actions of units (p.128). Bosch *Zweite Weltkrieg* (p.209) seems to follow BAOR, *Tour* but is disjointed; Stimpel, *Fallschirmtruppe*, has next to nothing on Goch.
109 Division comms log, 190740; 1 Gordons diary and post-operation report.
110 Lindsay, *So Few*, p.208, 'all the Huns were asleep at the time in cellars.' Salmond, p.224. Hanscomb 'Urban', p.41. Likewise, Matussek, wounded in the attack becomes a figure of fun, captured in bed or at breakfast: P.

fear meant there were some Germans sleeping despite (or because of) the intense bombardment, but like so many soldiers overrun by attackers hugging their fire plan, the majority would have been awake yet prevented from defending.[111] Astonishingly, Salmond goes on to describe 5 Black Watch's pivotal Slavanien battle as 'attacked some buildings on a road' and 'cleared up some other positions around Thomashof.'[112]

The FIBUA video is still passing on these historiographic flaws to soldiers, helping to teach new generations that infantry stealth and mobility have little value, that defenders have the advantage in town, especially at night, that higher commanders need tight control, and that urban battle is decided by attrition rather than cunning. The flanking effect in Goch, despite being evident in more famous urban battles in Stalingrad, Aachen, and Mariupol has been missed by the resurgent interest in urban combat. That interest is belatedly looking up from peace enforcement drills to reconsider how companies can cross open areas and how brigades can capture towns. Likewise, the lessons of infantry infiltration that were central to the 1943 doctrine and 153 Brigade's post-Goch report have been overwhelmed by the focus on destruction.[113] There is a gulf between the early 2020s focus on section-level room clearance and the higher skills needed to save a city without destroying it. A larger historical sample would be useful, but Goch provides valuable lessons that could help fill the gap.

    Elstob, *Reichswald*, p.158; Whitakers *Rhineland*, pp.219–130.
111 Phil Neame (Second in Command of 2 Para in 1982) reported a 'sleep of fear' among Argentine defenders in the Falklands: 'The Challenges of Leadership During the Falklands War by a Veteran', speech at Royal Military Academy, Sandhurst, 19 November 2022.
112 Salmond, *51st Scottish*, p.224.
113 War Office, *Built-Up Areas*; 'Op Veritable', 153 Brigade diary.

7

Manoeuvre Warfare

24 FEBRUARY TO 6 MARCH – WEEZE TO BÖNNINGHARDT – FORCE DESIGN – 53 DIVISION'S SLOG – A CHURCHILL CUCKOO – 8 ARMOURED'S SWAN – THE CRATER COMPETITION – GUARDS ARMOURED BARGES IN – TANK DESIGN WITH APOLOGIES

The Components of Lethargy

If "Veritable" had gone according to plan and the Germans had not flooded the entire northern half of the battlefield, the Guards Armoured Division would almost certainly have played a brilliant part in the operation; they might even have captured the bridge at Wesel and saved the Allies from having to fight their way across the Rhine later. But the narrow, bog-infested front to which the battlefield was soon reduced by the flooding was no milieu for an armoured division, and they were left milling around in Tilburg until the 20th, the day the 4th Battalion [Grenadier Guards supporting 44 Brigade] captured Goch.[1]

The debate on British Army effectiveness has been hottest when focused on manoeuvre warfare, morale, and their interactions. It is a relationship epitomised by the scene of British soldiers stopping for tea after crossing the Nijmegen bridge in the movie *A Bridge Too Far*. The scene is debated by historians but still underpins the popular view of British forces lacking the aggression needed for high tempo operations. And, whether historians hold critical or charitable views on 21st Army Group, they use anecdotes like the Nijmegen tea break to suggest a collective weakness, as if the British Army or nation lacked the genes or culture to generate operational tempo.[2]

Charles Dick's otherwise balanced and authoritative assessment of the Allies' Northwest Europe Campaign has the Nijmegen tea break central to his assessment of British caution, referring to US 'incredulity, incomprehension and fury' while presenting the lack of British infantry as an 'excuse'

---

1 Forbes, *Grenadier Guards* (p.202): a typical example of Veritable's historiography exaggerating the effects of flooding that conveniently inflates the effectiveness of armour in Goch too.
2 Hastings, *Armageddon* (Kindle 1389) is predictably critical. Buckley, *Monty's Men* (pp.224–225) appears to accept British lethargy but argues that sending a 'scratch force of a handful of tanks and infantry' towards Arnhem would have been a rash move. Despite a personal stake, Roy Urquhart's *Arnhem* (London: Pan, 1960), is only mildly critical (p128) and Cornelius Ryan's book *A Bridge Too Far* (Bungay: Richard Clay, 1975) echoes that restraint (pp.358–359).

for not pressing on to Arnhem.³ Dick also suggests the British morale problem was partly an excuse used by generals to hide their own shortcomings. However, he then reflects the dominant view that 21st Army Group and its commanders were 'blinkered, unimaginative', 'plodding', and 'over-conservative' with a 'lack of aggressiveness', and a 'tendency to over caution'.⁴

Dick's interpretation occasionally goes beyond personalities to hint at 'doctrinal inhibitions on exploitation' but, like Biddle (outlined in Chapter 5), he presents these as symptoms of cultural and personal weakness. For Dick, one manifestation of culture and personality is that Montgomery 'refused to form a *corps de chasse*' in Normandy because doing so would have been risky, but not doing so ensured British battles 'remained essentially attritional and therefore indecisive.'⁵ Dick's other judgements relate operational failures to more concrete factors but then he attributes these specifics to personal-cultural deficits: traffic congestion, over-reliance on firepower, and (referring to Operation Bluecoat) 'an inflexible plan and a lack of initiative in its execution, not to mention indifferent tank-infantry cooperation – common British vices.'⁶ This list is a close match to the main components of the current assessment, but Dick's corps-focused sources give him little opportunity to see how these British vices might have causes that were more tangible and repairable than an entrenched cultural deficit.

In Goch, British effectiveness was hindered by negative interactions between planning, artillery effectiveness, tactical logistics, command systems, and infantry-armour cooperation, but the combined effect could be attributed to 21st Army Group's limited experience of urban combat. This chapter and the next will show how those tangible and repairable problems identified earlier in the book shaped the ability to conduct manoeuvre warfare, something 21st Army Group was designed to do. Then, where most historians have emphasised the way low morale stifles manoeuvre (which it surely does), these two chapters will show how the British inability to conduct manoeuvre operations undermined morale. This reversal of perspective is of greater value to soldiers and analysts because, instead of rooting the problem in the imponderables of culture, personality, and morale, it points to means of repairing tangible faults and by doing so enhance manoeuvre and morale.

The interacting components (planning, artillery effectiveness, et cetera) can be seen as products of force design. Like suppression, tactical logistics, and command systems, force design is a modern and poorly defined concept.⁷ It is an apt concept nonetheless, as it expresses how an organisation combines the moral, physical, and conceptual components of fighting power in greater detail than doctrinal publications allow. It is axiomatic that a well-designed force would have a plan, structure and command system that could win a break-in battle by efficiently using artillery and armour to suppress, thereby allowing infantry to assault without overwhelming tactical logistics. Such a force would then allow this process to be repeated in the face of friction and enemy action through breakthrough, breakout, and exploit/pursuit. To show how 21st Army Group was not designed to fight the battles it faced, these chapters step outside Veritable's core narrative, into the two weeks

---

3   Dick, *Victory*, p.255.
4   Dick, *Victory*, pp.58, 61, 66, 135, 151, 156, 185, 326. Robert Citino (quoted in Buckley, *Monty's Men*, p.6) claims Britain lacked 'officers who could recognise such momentary opportunities when they arose and a military culture that encouraged them to seize those golden moments.'
5   Dick, *Victory*, p.63.
6   Dick *Victory*, p.152.
7   Marine Corps, *Force Design 2030* (Arlington VA: USMC, 2020) describes a collection of project teams focused on organisation, logistics, weapons, communications, and training but there is little consideration of how the components combine. Likewise, L. Retter, Z. Hernandez, B. Caves, M. Hughes and A. Knack, *Global Mobility: Force Design 2040* (Cambridge MA: Rand, 2021) defines force design as 'the exercise of conceiving and producing a plan for Defence capabilities' but examines components broadly with few links between them.

172   SLOG OR SWAN

of 30 Corps action that go unmentioned in Horrocks's memoirs and are barely summarised in post-operation reports.[8] The two chapters focus on the actions of 53 Welsh Division, 8 Armoured Brigade, and Guards Armoured Division to demonstrate how the interactions between planning, firepower, tactical logistics, command systems and infantry-armour cooperation severely constrained the ability to conduct manoeuvre operations and by doing so undermined morale.[9]

Operation Leek

At the end of the Goch battle, 5 Black Watch were crying out for units to exploit the carnage along the Weezer Strasse: 'Urgent requests were made for something to pass through us and complete the rout of the enemy in front, as there was obviously great disorganisation but unfortunately nothing was available.'[10] In fact, there were three under-employed battalions in 51 Division, whole divisions inactive north of Goch, and the quick deployment of even a fraction of this force would, most likely, have chased the shattered defenders right through Weeze and dislocated the whole German defence. Instead, in an echo of the self-inflicted confusion following the *47. Panzerkorps* counter-attack, the planned breakout and pursuit were allotted to 15 Division, then 51, then no division, then back to 15. Finally, the day before Goch fell, 30 Corps issued a planning note for 53 Division to strike through Weeze on the 24th, three whole days after Goch fell.[11]

A top-down history would present this gap as a classic example of British lethargy, but a closer inspection shows the delay grew from the logistic constraints imposed by Operation Blockbuster, which, after its own confusions, was due to launch on the 26th. In preparation for Blockbuster, 43 Division had transferred to 2 Canadian Corps, 15 Division was pushed east to protect the Canadian flank, and 53 Division was forced to wait. It is not clear whether 53 was waiting for a bridge that could support the Kangaroos it was due to use, or waiting for the Kangaroos themselves, for traffic in Goch to clear, for artillery ammunition, for armoured support, or for its soldiers to recover from fighting in the Reichswald. However, the focus on preparations for Blockbuster magnified all these constraints.[12]

On the morning of the 22nd, 53 Division was nominally allocated all the assets to equip its own "Blerick job" and later that day it issued orders for Operation "Leek", a Kangaroo-borne dash supported by two Sherman regiments from 8 Armoured Brigade.[13] The Division was to advance across what was assumed to be good tank country, secure bridgeheads over the Ottersgraben waterway just north of Weeze, then capture the town itself: 'if the situation is favourable' by coup de main; if not, by set-piece assault (Map 29).[14]

---

8   *Full Life*, p.254.
9   The actions of these formations overlap those of 3, 15, 51 and 35 (US) Divisions, which are regrettably barely covered. 3 Division was another difficult omission from this assessment, as it seemingly developed a solution to the armour-infantry cooperation problem and its Veritable operations have a detailed history (T. Colvin, *The Noise of Battle: The British Army and the Last Breakthrough Battle West of the Rhine, February-March 1945* (Solihull: Helion, 2016)).
10 5 Black Watch diary.
11 30 Corps tasks for 20 and 21 February and Corps planning note 39, Harris *Rhineland I*, pp.161–163. The directive of the 20th also has Guards Armoured Division preparing for later exploitation through Weeze.
12 30 Corps, 15, 51 and 43 Division diaries 18–23 Feb; 30 Corps planning note 43, Harris, *Rhineland II*, p.188.
13 53 Division OO 31, Division diary; 160 Brigade OO 15, diary (WO 171/4428). In addition to most of 8 Armoured and 49 APC Regiment Kangaroos, half of 141 RAC (Crocodiles), most of 284 Squadron Armoured Engineers, a troop 82 Squadron Armoured Engineers, a 1 Lothians' Flail squadron, and a tactical air contact car were attached to 53 Division.
14 30 Corps planning note 41, Harris, *Rhineland II*, p.187. Map overlay from 1 HLI diary.

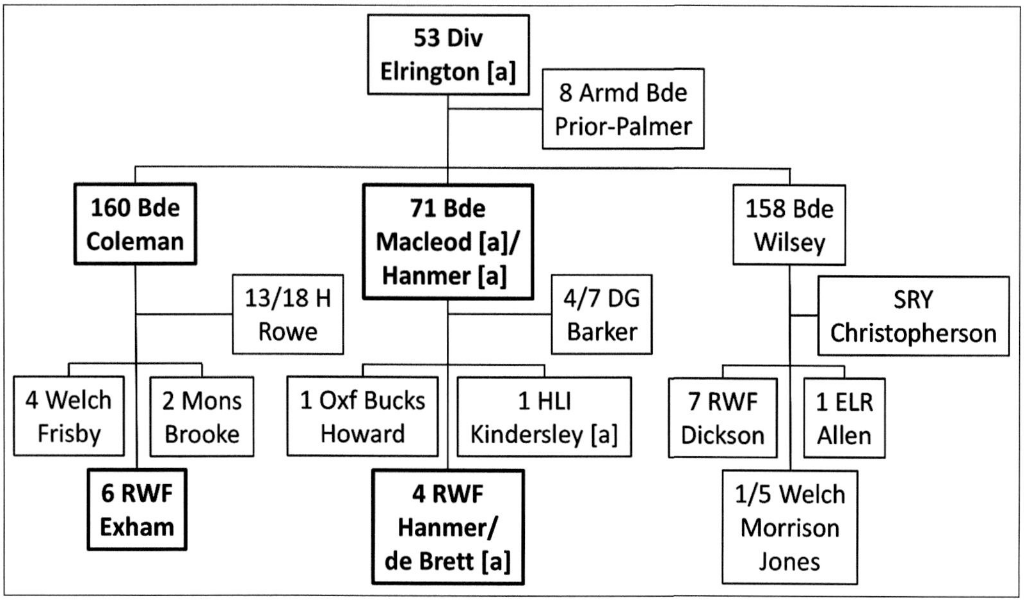
53 Div
Elrington [a]
8 Armd Bde
Prior-Palmer
160 Bde
Coleman
71 Bde
Macleod [a]/
Hanmer [a]
158 Bde
Wilsey
13/18 H
Rowe
4/7 DG
Barker
SRY
Christopherson
4 Welch
Frisby
2 Mons
Brooke
1 Oxf Bucks
Howard
1 HLI
Kindersley [a]
7 RWF
Dickson
1 ELR
Allen
6 RWF
Exham
4 RWF
Hanmer/
de Brett [a]
1/5 Welch
Morrison
Jones

Figure 20: Abridged organisational chart for 53 Division.

On the night of 23 February, fighter-bombers were to harass Weeze and the woods north of it, woods that had previously been pummelled by 5 Black Watch's Victor fire missions on the 21st. A four-hour artillery preparation would be followed by two deception barrages that aimed to fool defenders into expecting attacks from the west and northeast, then the real attack would be preceded by a series of deep artillery concentrations. Finally, a barrage would cover the crossing of the Ottersgraben while 53 Recce and a continuous smokescreen covered the exposed right flank.[15]

One curious feature of this plan was that after capturing Weeze, 53 Division was to leave the straight main road that ran on south through Kevelaer and Geldern and sidestep two kilometres west onto a woodland route via the hamlet of Hees. This move had its roots in the expectation that Blockbuster's inevitable success to the northeast would create an expanding torrent requiring 30 Corps to budge westward and give 2 Canadian Corps manoeuvre space.[16] Another curiosity of the plan was that it listed no objectives or fire missions for the three kilometres between the start line (where 153 Brigade ended the Goch battle) and the Ottersgraben, but then included considerable detail on objectives beyond Weeze.[17] The plan assumed negligible opposition between Goch and Weeze, which may have been appropriate on the 21st but was far less so when the defenders had been given three days to recover.

The plan was based around an assessment that the main opposition would be *FJR 21*, which was sorely depleted after the Goch battle, with a weak battalion in Weeze and few outposts north of the Ottersgraben. However, an intelligence update arrived late in planning which suggested the main defence had moved north, putting 600 men, six anti-tank guns and six SPs between Goch and Weeze. This update appears to have been a compromise between the earlier estimate and a wild

15 53 Division HQRA Arty Op notes, diary; 53 Division OO 31. Fire support included 13 field regiments, two heavy anti-aircraft regiments, 90 medium guns, six 7.2-in guns, a counter-mortar radar detachment and the air observers.

16 3, 53 and Guards Armoured Division diaries (WO 171/4103 and 4104). In the event, Blockbuster bogged down and its scope narrowed, allowing 53 Division to use the straighter and clearer southward axis.

17 For example, the 7 RWF diary details which company would exploit to which copse west of Hees.

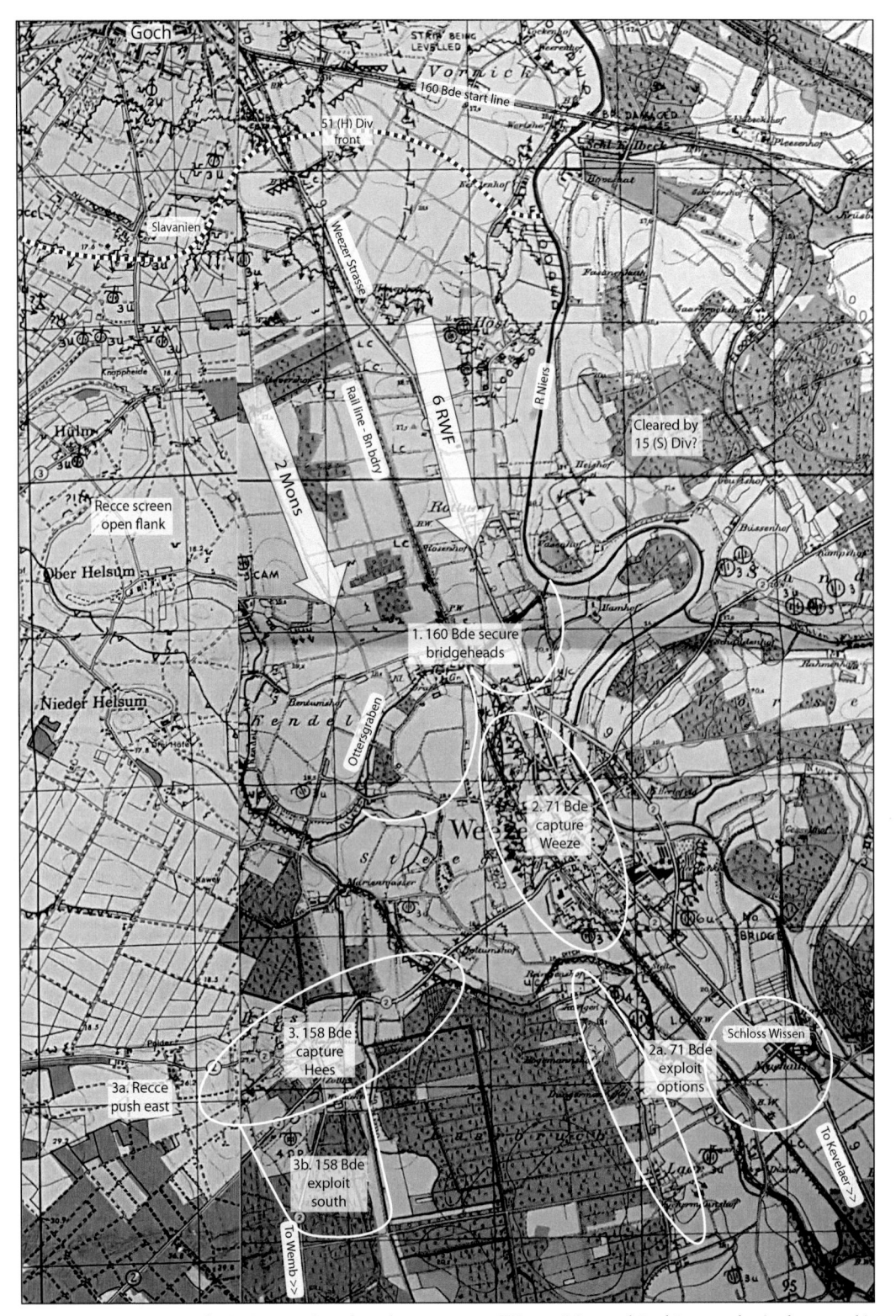

Map 29: Operation Leek, 53 Division's earlier plan to capture Weeze. (National Archives, author's photograph)

guess from 51 Division, in which up to 15 SPs were supporting *FJR 21* and the *Fallschirmjäger* right flank was protected by the imagined presence of the elite-but-battered *Panzer-Lehr-Division*.[18] Despite its dubious origin (*Panzer Lehr* was nowhere near Weeze), the compromise assessment was not too wide of the mark, with post-battle intelligence showing the defence comprised five SPs and 900 men in three composite battalions based around *Panzergrenadier Regiment 104* and fragments of *FJR 19* and *GR 1223*.[19] Arrayed against this, 53 Division had a fighting strength of 4,500 men and 200 heavy armoured vehicles but, as so often in Veritable, the first obstacle would be getting this mass through a congested rear area then down a few narrow roads.

Several late changes were made to the plan, the most profound being the loss of the Kangaroos. Battalions were told this was because 15 Division had not yet cleared the area northeast of Weeze, so there was danger of flanking fire from woods across the Niers, but the real reason may have been traffic congestion in Goch.[20] In any event, the absence of Kangaroos transformed the armoured dash into a two-bite dismounted advance to contact, with intermediate objectives on a possible German line through Höst, Houenhof and Rectangular Wood (Map 30). The two-bite scheme retained the earlier optimism however, with 6 RWF expected to fight all the way to and over the Ottersgraben, then other parts of the Division ending the day in Weeze and Wemb, four kilometres southwest of Weeze, and at one stage even Winnekendonk, five kilometres southeast, on the opposite side of the Niers.[21]

The Division was also told that 160 Brigade's intended armour support, the Sherwood Rangers Yeomanry, had to refit after losing a squadron's worth of tanks north of Goch the week before. Their replacements, 13/18 Hussars, who had suffered similar losses, were unable to marry-up with the Brigade until dusk on the 23rd and so had no time for rehearsals or familiarisation.[22] It is unclear whether the full preliminary bombardment survived the ammunition shortage, but low cloud prevented air strikes on the woods and delayed a planned cab rank for close air support until noon. Then, with too little time to replan fire support onto the first bite objectives, 160 Brigade aimed for a "silent" attack, like 5/7 Gordons entering Goch, with armour but only calling on guns after being engaged by defenders.[23]

---

18   INTSUM 190; OO 31; 160 Brigade comms log (in diary) 22–24 February; Guderian, *Normandy to the Ruhr*, p.394; 'STOP PRESS' amendment 51 Division ISUM 61. The *Panzer Lehr* rumour came from a misinterpreted report of the far less formidable *Fallschirm-Lehr-Bataillon* (parachute training unit) near Weeze. *Pz Lehr* had been active further north against 2 Canadian Corps around Xanten and Uedem and was moved south on the 24th to counter Operation Grenade. F.P. Steinhardt, *Panzer Lehr Division 1944–45* (Solihull: Helion, 2010), p.300. The rumour persisted until at least the 26th when 160 Brigade reported being counterattacked by *Pz Lehr*: 6 RWF diary.
19   53 Division ISUM 192 included what it called reliable information that the most effective of *PGR 104*'s two battalions had a fighting strength below 250. *FJR 21* seems to have withdrawn south to refit.
20   49 APC Regt diary (WO 171/4722) and L. V. Scull, *49th Unparalleled: The Story of the 49th Battalion Royal Tank Regiment Later Designated as an Armoured Personnel Carrier Regiment, 1939–1945* (Bovington: Tank Museum, 2002), p.33, Division and Corps sources describe repeated cancellations. 153 Brigade 'Op Veritable' complained: 'Tpt in the British Army is getting more out of hand as the days go by. The scenes in GENNEP and GOCH even before they were clear were really terrible and why more vehs were not "brewed up" is amazing.' Congestion worsened when Goch became the secondary supply route for Blockbuster.
21   30 Corps, 15, 51, and 53 Division diaries and comms logs. Bosch *Zweite Weltkrieg* (p.210) mistakenly has 160 Brigade attacking in Kangaroos.
22   53 Division, 8 Armoured Brigade, SRY and 13/18 Hussars diaries (WO 171/4327, 4704 and 4691). The SRY diary and Lindsay, *Sherwood Rangers* (p.151) have 31 personnel and 14 tank casualties, then refitting from 16 to 28 Feb, so this was not a sudden change as suggested to 53 Division.
23   53 Division comms log (WO 205/958).

176 SLOG OR SWAN

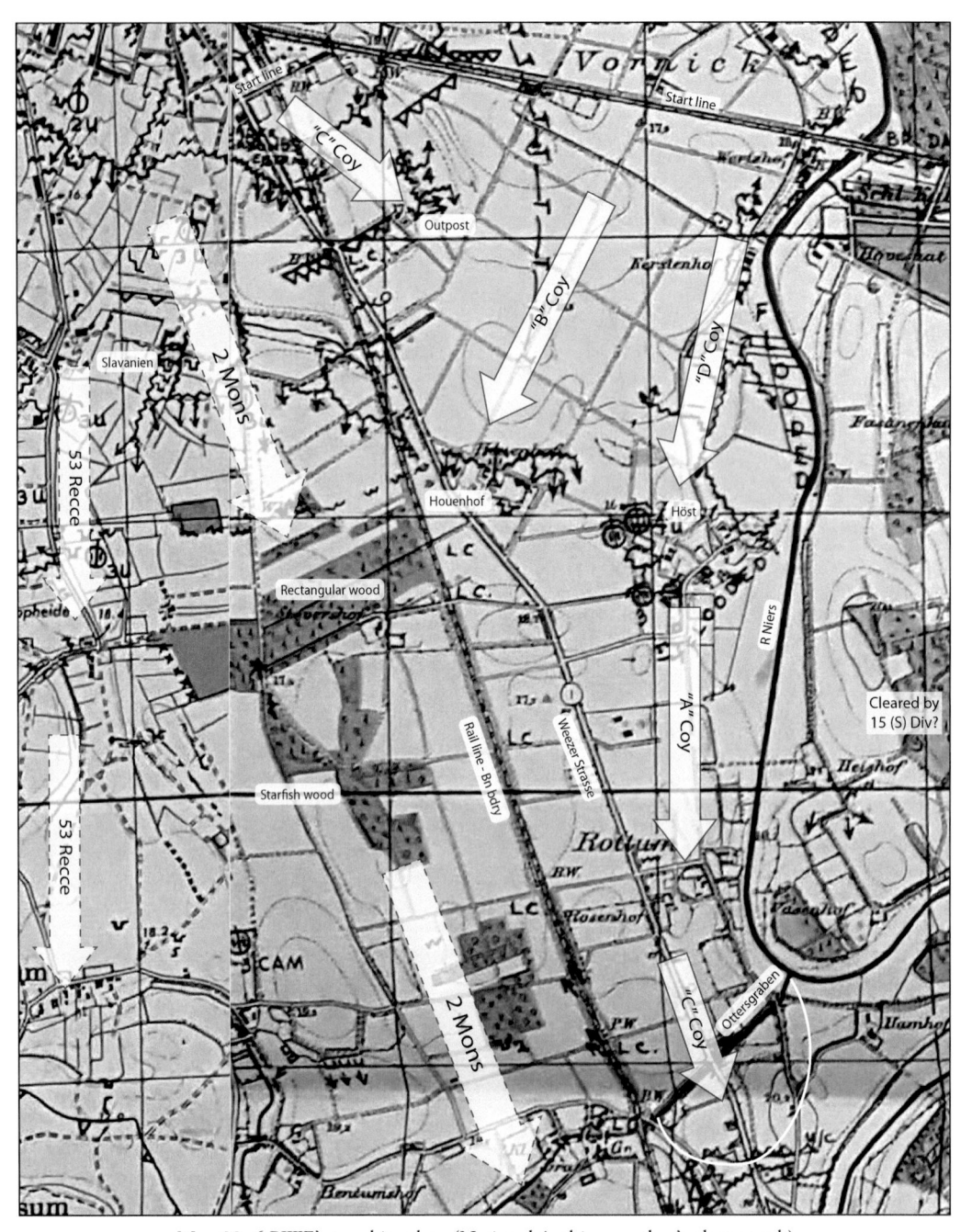

Map 30: 6 RWF's two-bite plan. (National Archives, author's photograph)

Only the very first steps of the attack went to plan, with an infiltration by 6 RWF's "C" Company capturing five prisoners ("Outpost", Map 31) and the main attack launching on time at 06:00 despite the late arrival of armour. On the left (east), "D" Company moved along a riverside track until they were pinned down a few hundred metres north of Höst by small arms fire from the hamlet and from woods across the Niers ("Possible enemy", Map 31). Mortars joined the defensive fire and casualties mounted. As the assigned Sherman troop tried to catch up, one tank bogged, and another was damaged by a mine. It was full daylight when the other two tanks arrived and by 08:15 one of these had its main gun jammed by machine-gun fire. None of the tanks had suffered damage from enemy armour or anti-tank weapons.[24]

Artillery coordination also proved difficult. The leading platoon was pulled back so Höst could be shelled, but the full concentration did not materialise and so "D" was 'kicked on to' the objective at 09:00 with mortar smoke and fire from the reserve tank troop. This attack also failed. The company commander and company sergeant major were wounded, and "D" held on as best they could in the abandoned German trenches north of Höst. The situation was 'not quite clear' at 10:40 and at 11:05 the battle was 'complicated by snipers from across the Niers' some of whom were believed to be from 15 Division.[25] Higher coordination was further undermined by aircraft reporting friendly forces in woods just over the river ("Possible friendly", Map 31) while radio nets were clogged with efforts to get air or artillery to engage a reported German counterattack from Rottum ("Counter massing?"). To cut through the confusion, 53 Division issued a revised plan, part of which required "A" Company to pass through "D" and clear Höst from 13:50. This attack also failed, leaving half of 6 RWF exposed just north of Höst.[26]

The Battalion had achieved more success on the right, where "B" Company, also lacking armour, surprised the defenders and captured one of the two main buildings of Houenhof farm by 06:50. However, "B" then spent several hours in a firefight with defenders in the second building, while being sniped at from Höst, and from buildings near the boundary with 2 Mons ("Fire from rear?").[27] "B" Company's problems were eventually solved by "C" Company and a tank troop clearing down the Weezer Strasse around 09:30. Then, having formed up along the railway line, "C" launched a flanking attack on Houenhof, which soon secured the remaining buildings and collected 71 prisoners. Despite this success, 6 RWF's attack had culminated with heavy losses, having advanced barely a third of the way to their final objective.[28]

Further west, 2 Mons began their attack with infantry separated from armour by a crater, which was unexpected despite being reported days previously ("Crater", Map 31).[29] The attempt to screen the open right flank with smoke and reconnaissance cars also failed when the shell-starved smokescreen dissipated, and defensive fire forced 53 Recce to dismount. Defenders around

---

24 160 Brigade comms log; Royal Welch Fusiliers diary; Anon, *A Short History of the 6th (Caernarvon and Anglesey) Battalion the Royal Welch Fusiliers, North West Europe, June 1944 to May 1945* (Caernarvon: Evans, 1946), pp.96–97. Latter suggests "D" surprised the defenders then the Battalion fought a rapid series of actions but is a classic example of a secondary source compressing time.
25 160 Brigade comms log; RWF diary. *Caernarvon and Anglesey*, p.96–98.
26 160 Brigade comms log 241125–241345; 6 RWF diary; 53 Division ISUM 191. Supposed friendly on the eastern flank were reported to be a pair of carriers. One indicator of the lack of preparation for any defence on this first bite was that the "A" Coy attack needed a new set of codewords, none having been issued for objectives north of the Ottersgraben.
27 The fire may have been from 2 Mons delayed on the right, who were themselves hit by overs from Houenhof.
28 53 Division ISUM 191; 160 Brigade comms log; 6 RWF diary. Anon, *Caernarvon and Anglesey* (p.97) claims over 100 PW from Houenhof.
29 51 Division and 160 Brigade comms logs. Map 31 shows the only reported crater, spotted by 51 Division on 21 Feb and reported to 160 Brigade on 23 Feb.

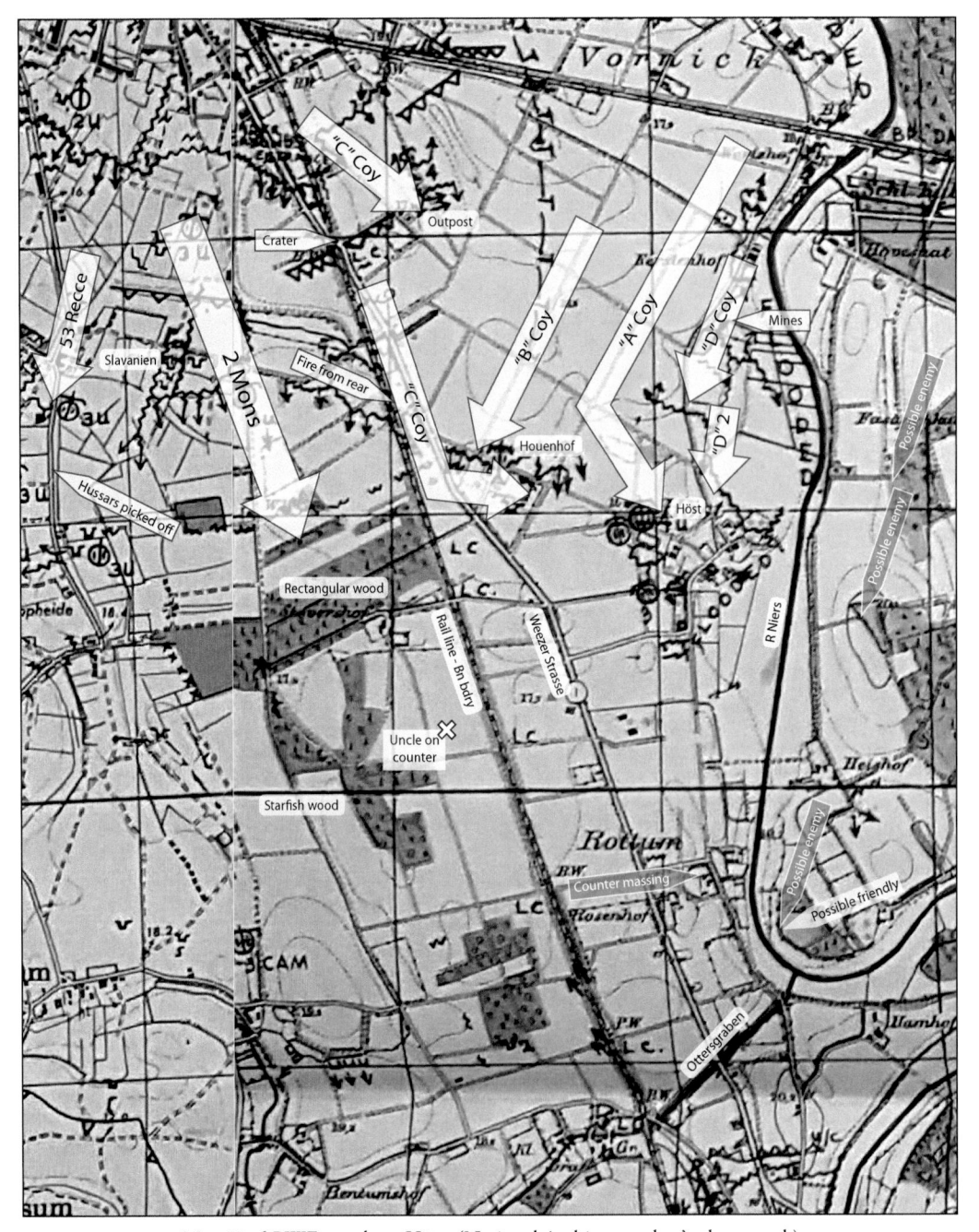

Map 31: 6 RWF attack on Höst. (National Archives, author's photograph)

Rectangle Wood engaged the leading Mons' companies as they advanced past Slavanien, then fractured communications with mounted FOOs stuck behind the crater made it difficult to call artillery concentrations. As the Hussars' Shermans began to catch up, they were picked off by tank destroyers concealed on the exposed flank. The 'greatly depleted' forward companies managed to reach Rectangular Wood and the reserve company was moved up to bolster their hasty defence.[30] At 10:30, 2 Mons called an Uncle fire mission onto a counterattack force near Starfish Wood but the threat endured for at least an hour before it was broken by fire. As with 6 RWF, 2 Mons had suffered heavily and secured only half of their first bite objectives.[31]

The final 160 Brigade unit, 4 Welch, had originally intended to cross the Ottersgraben, but their objective was adjusted to take only Starfish Wood. At 16:30 they assaulted through heavy indirect fire, only to find the wood unoccupied. The adjusted plan had 71 Brigade take over the second bite, but this quickly unravelled too (Map 32). As 1 HLI advanced on Rottum, they took casualties from defenders holding out in Höst. Crocodiles were brought forward and by 18:25 these were squirting rods of flame into the hamlet before issuing the third mistaken claim that Höst was secure.[32] Two hours later, 1 HLI had bypassed Höst but were then pinned down by fire from front, flank, and rear. Their forward left platoon eventually crept into Rottum with a flanking move along the river line, but it was not until after midnight (25th) that patrols were sent towards the Ottersgraben.[33]

In the next phase, 1 Oxford Bucks with Sherman and Crocodile support were to follow 1 HLI, then turn right near Rottum and attack the two small woods south of 4 Welch. Confused by insistent shelling, false reports of Rottum being secure, and by attacking well ahead of their infantry, the Crocodiles turned right too soon and flamed 4 Welch in Starfish Wood, inflicting considerable and horrific casualties.[34] The correct woods were attacked at 02:00 but found to be deserted.[35] The Oxford Bucks were to be followed by 4 RWF (who captured De Horst in Chapter 2 and northern Goch in Chapter 6) in an assault crossing the Ottersgraben, then by 158 Brigade taking Weeze, but the leading companies of 4 RWF had to be redirected onto a fourth attempt at clearing Höst.[36] By the time Höst was finally cleared it was mid-morning, a full 24 hours after it should have been secure, 4 RWF needed to reorganise, artillery ammunition was getting low, and six battalions had been engaged. However, the critical problem was that accumulated delays

---

30 2 Mons diary (WO 171/5245); 53 Division diary and comms log.
31 160 Brigade diary describes air support as 'accurate and plentiful' and several successful engagements are reported in the comms log, but targets were kilometres ahead of forward troops and effects are unclear.
32 4 Welch diary, notes on orders 231400; 7 RWF and 1 HLI diaries. 141 RAC diary has flame 'used extensively and with great success, the inf being put in and the village captured in approx 20 mins.'
33 1 HLI diary. The Battalion was also bombed in or near Höst around 18:45 and 71 Brigade comms log (250040) suggests 15 casualties caused by one bomb. Barclay, *53rd (Welsh)*, p.134, has Rottum captured by 21:00. A recollection in Bosch, *Zweite Weltkrieg* (p.212) has a farm somewhere near Rottum surrounded by British tanks but then abandoned by both sides until the following night.
34 J. H. Roberts, *Enshrined in Stone*, p.325. Oxf Bucks, 4 Welch, 4/7 DG and 160 Brigade diaries; 53 Division comms log; *First and Last*, pp.153–154. Division direction was to attack 'wood 9239' but both the target wood and the bottom of Starfish Wood are in this grid square. Most sources brush over this incident. The 141 RAC diary blames the Oxf Bucks liaison officer, mistakes the victims for RWF, and is more concerned with bogged vehicles.
35 Shelling is the only defence mentioned in diaries, even so the Oxf Bucks summary sheet lists 11 casualties on the 24th and 36 on the 25th; CWGC has one man killed on the 24th, but this was an officer on detachment to another unit (MC citation, Lt. Hands, WO 373/52/698).
36 71, 158 and 160 Brigade diaries and comms logs. With so many changes, the planned sequence is unclear. This version seems most logical, but 4 RWF's bridgehead is implied by 158 Brigade's aims. 71 Brigade 250100 claimed 25 prisoners; 160 Brigade 251015 'pulled out 50 dazed Boche from cellars at Höst.'

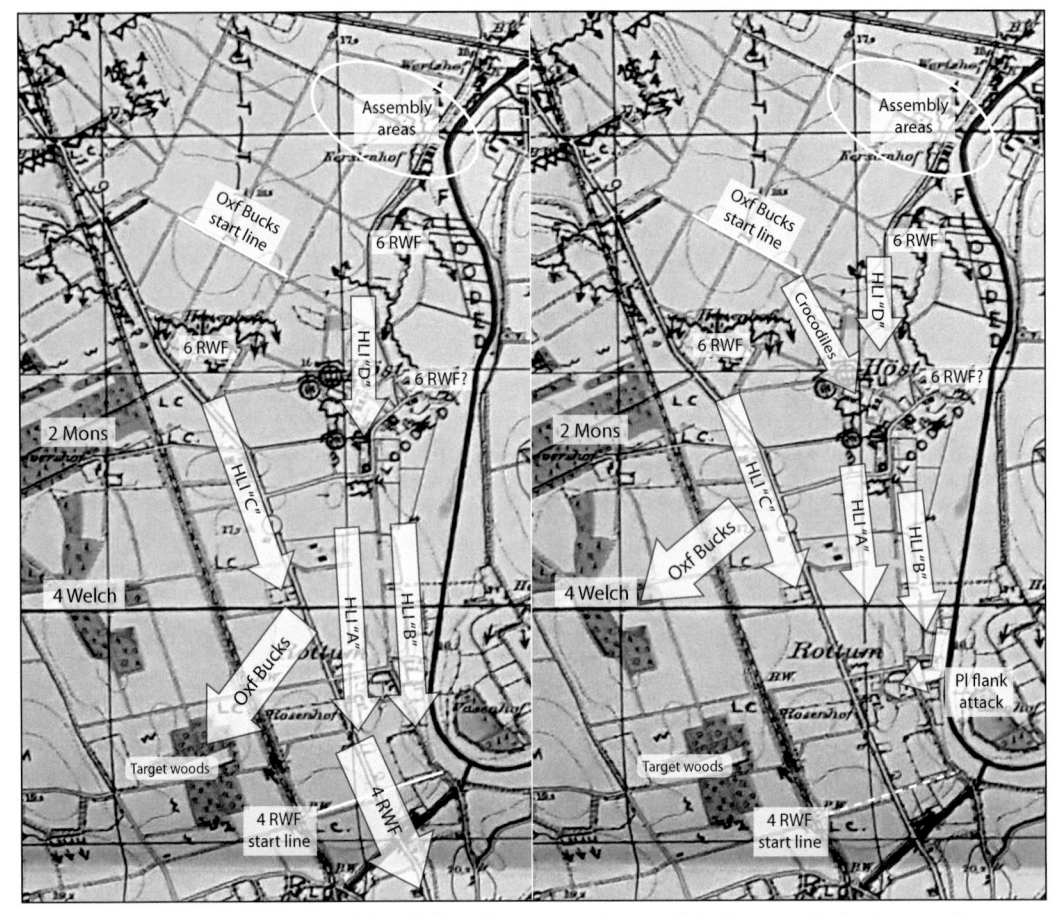

Map 32: 71 Brigade's second plan (left) and execution. (National Archives, author's photograph)

had stranded 158 Brigade north of Goch, the wrong side of 'extreme congestion' and 3 (British) Division, which had control of the roads as it advanced to take over the flank protection task for Blockbuster.[37]

Operation Leek was called off. Although no source uses the word, it was a failure; even the Division's initial objective of a bridgehead over the Ottersgraben had not been achieved. The acting commander of 71 Brigade was quietly replaced.[38] Yet at the tactical level, the result was a close-run thing. Despite suffering around 250 casualties, 53 Division had defeated the main enemy force and collected 500 prisoners, leaving just a few stragglers north of the Ottersgraben and 200 mostly rear area troops holding Weeze.[39] As with Schottheide on the 8th, Materborn on the 9th or Goch

---

37 53 Division log 242005; 3 Division diary (WO 171/4129 and 4130). Regarding Blockbuster priority, Essame, *Wessex Division* (p.225) has it supported by 'All but a few of the guns of 30 Corps, 2 Canadian Corps and First Canadian Army and the whole air effort of 21 Army Group'.

38 ISUM 190 ignored the original aims and claimed the Division had achieved its objectives by having patrols reach the planned 4 RWF start line (bottom of Map 32). As Figure 20 indicates, Lieutenant Colonel Macleod (1 HLI) was commanding 71 Brigade while Brigadier Elrington stood in for the Division Commander, Macleod was replaced on the 25th but did not return to his battalion. No source gives any reason for this.

39 By 18:00 6 RWF lists 80 casualties, claims 150 defenders killed and 150 PW; 2 Mons suffered nearly 100 casualties, claims 60 defenders killed and 148 PW; 4 Welch diary mentions no enemy and gives no casualty

on the 17th, operational disorganisation made tactical success less likely then prevented one more push that, if launched quickly, might have achieved operational success. Operationally imposed logistic constraints prevented any chance of turning defeat into victory.[40]

Operation Daffodil

It was three days before 53 Division could activate its next scheme to capture Weeze, which aimed to take advantage of 3 Division's advance east of the Niers and so outflank German defences on the Ottersgraben. Operation Daffodil was a complicated five-phase plan due to launch early on the 28th (D+20), with 160 Brigade taking over a 3 Division bridgehead over the *Kervenheimer Mühlenfleuth*, a stream that fed the Niers ("1" at Map 33). In the afternoon, 158 Brigade would clear the eastern side of the river bend (2), then early on 1st March, 71 Brigade would cross the Ottersgraben in a feint to fix German attention to the north (3). Once the feint was in place, 158 Brigade would launch the real attack to capture Weeze (4), then 160 Brigade would exploit to Hees (5).[41] The need to flank the Ottersgraben was emphasised in 30 Corps orders: 'Direct attack on WEEZE from the NORTH is NOT to be carried out'.[42]

In addition to its convoluted logistics, Daffodil was hampered by pure bad luck. On the 27th, 6 RWF, still recovering from its losses around Höst, sent a team to liaise with 2 East Yorks, the 3 Division unit holding the Mühlenfleuth bridgehead. The 6 RWF liaison team was hit by German artillery which cost the Battalion their mortar officer, anti-tank officer, signals officer, two company commanders, and meant the Battalion advanced almost blind.[43] Then, instead of taking over a secure bridgehead as expected, they stumbled into the epic battle of Yorkshire Bridge, where 2 East Yorks suffered 147 casualties and repeatedly called fire onto their own positions to prevent them being overrun.[44] The 158 Brigade clearance action therefore slipped into the early hours of 1 March, when ineffectual tank support due to it being dark, meant the presence of three German armoured vehicles held up the Brigade well short of the Niers. German armour withdrew before British tanks arrived in daylight, but the attack could not be restarted.[45]

With 158 Brigade stalled, 71 Brigade's feint, with its timings dictated by the fire plan, had morphed into the main assault. The attack was to begin with Crocodiles and Wasps flaming over

---

figures but CWGC lists 12 dead, suggesting 70 total casualties; 13/18 Hussars lost 10 men, with six tanks lost to direct fire, five to mines, one to indirect fire and two mired; 12 KRRC (8 Armoured Brigade infantry protecting 13/18 Hussars tanks) reported two casualties. CWGC concurs. ISUM 192 claims 550 prisoners but lists only 450 by unit. The higher figure exceeds the number in unit diaries and a cautious reading of Bolland, *Team Spirit*, p.50. PW included the CO of II Bn *PGR 104*.

40 Devine, 'British Way' (p.264) recognises tactical success but not the operational failure and does not explore the reasons for the attack stalling. Due to the time and space constraints on Devine's longitudinal thesis (following 53 Division since before Normandy) the last week in Veritable is summarised in just a few paragraphs.

41 Summary composed from OO 32 (Division diary) with variations from other sources as the plan evolved. One variation (53 Recce diary, 27–28 Feb) has 160 Brigade forcing the Mühlenfleuth rather than taking over from 3 Division.

42 Harris, *Rhineland II*, p.205.

43 6 RWF diary, 271800.

44 Colvin, *Noise of Battle*, pp.52–133; Scarfe, *Assault Division*, pp.207–214; T. Craggs, 'An "Unspectacular" War? Reconstructing the history of the 2nd Battalion East Yorkshire Regiment during the Second World War', (Sheffield University PhD thesis, 2007) pp.166–171. K. G. Exham, 'The Battle of Weeze' (unpublished, RWF Museum), p.17, has the bridgehead 'only slightly larger than a football pitch'.

45 53 and 158 Brigade comms logs; 7 RWF diary.

Map 33: The five steps of Operation Daffodil, 53 Division's later plan to capture Weeze.
(National Archives, author's photograph)

the Ottersgraben, then 4 RWF following a barrage that crept over the waterway and into the north of Weeze (Map 34). The barrage had fewer shells, fewer serviceable guns, and shorter pauses than that which gave 4 RWF their D-Day success, but it probably matched the barrage they successfully hugged into northern Goch on the 19th.[46] However in this instance the tight timings unravelled, with the shock of the flame attack (from which a few defenders 'ran as flaming torches') coming long before the barrage, then the 4 RWF infantry were held up by logistic frictions that included manhandling assault bridging over ploughed fields.[47] Despite efforts to delay the barrage, it soon left the men behind on open ground, where they were exposed by movement light, a brilliant

---

46 The barrage had six field regiments and a medium regiment on an 1,100-metre front but up to 25 percent of guns out for maintenance, versus D-Day's five field and four medium regiments on a 1,400-metre front. 53 HQRA, 4 RWF and Oxf Bucks diaries.

47 Stimpel, *Fallschirmtruppe* (pp.369–370) skims the Weeze battles with Crocodiles attacking only after 4 RWF cross the Ottersgraben, a sequence that conflicts with primary sources.

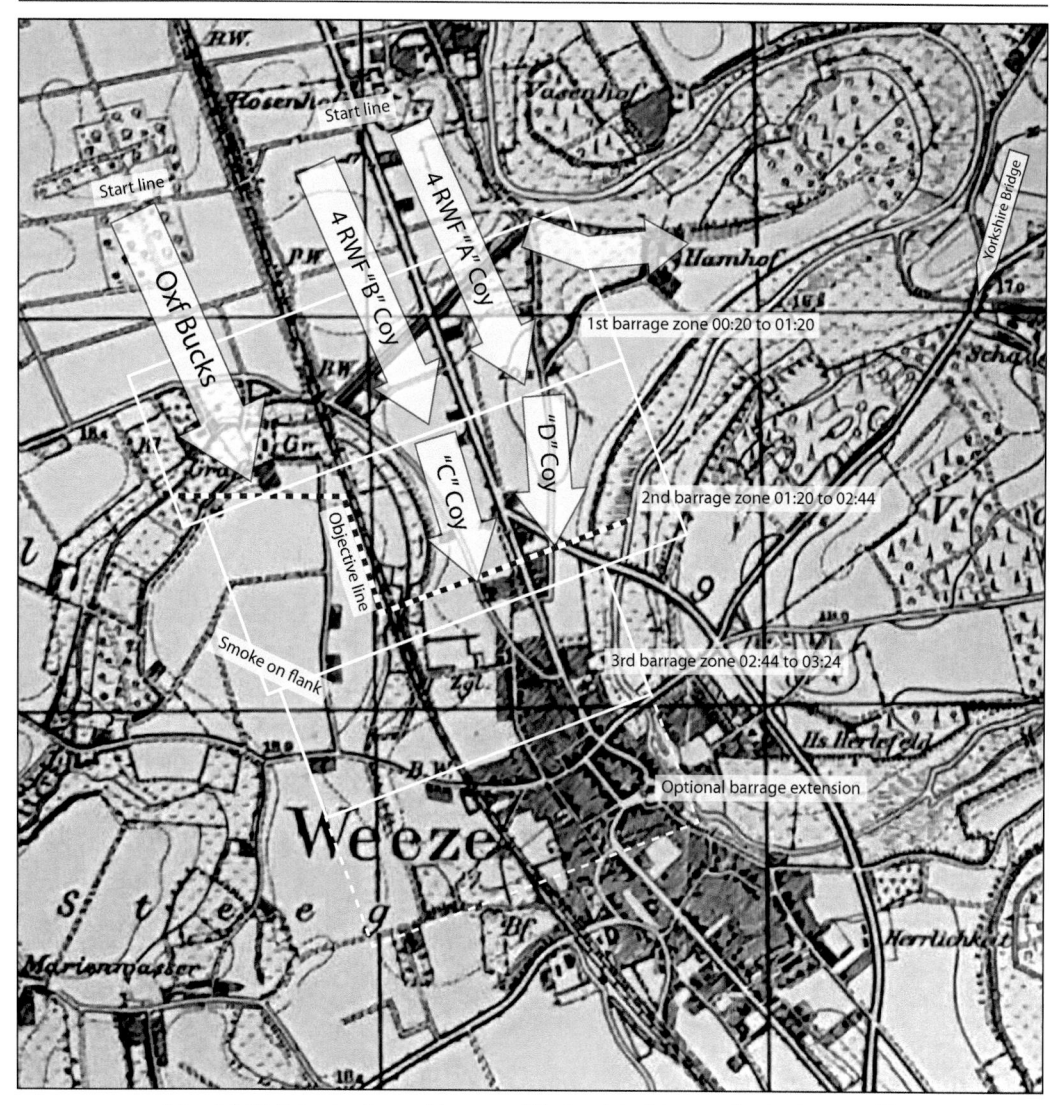

Map 34: 71 Brigade plan and barrage. (National Archives, author's photograph)

moon, flaming buildings and the shortage of smoke shells. Inexplicably, and despite the plan emphasising close tank support, it was an hour before 4/7 Dragoon Guards' Shermans arrived to silence the most troublesome machine-guns. The Sherman support allowed the infantry to force the crossing but difficulties putting in a tank bridge and then getting tanks across it meant 'Bren and Spandau fought it out' in the outskirts of Weeze for another few hours.[48]

By dawn on 1 March a few 4 RWF platoons had found an intact bridge over an inner waterway, 400 metres south of the Ottersgraben, defused the charges on it, and were covering the crossing with the help of two Shermans. At that point, there was a German counterattack with two infantry companies supported by the armour that had stalled 158 Brigade earlier. This counter, which included a captured Churchill "cuckoo", dislodged 4 RWF's forward company, destroyed the

---

48 Roberts, *Welsh Bridges*, p.223; MM citation, Fusilier Henderson (WO 373/53/810).

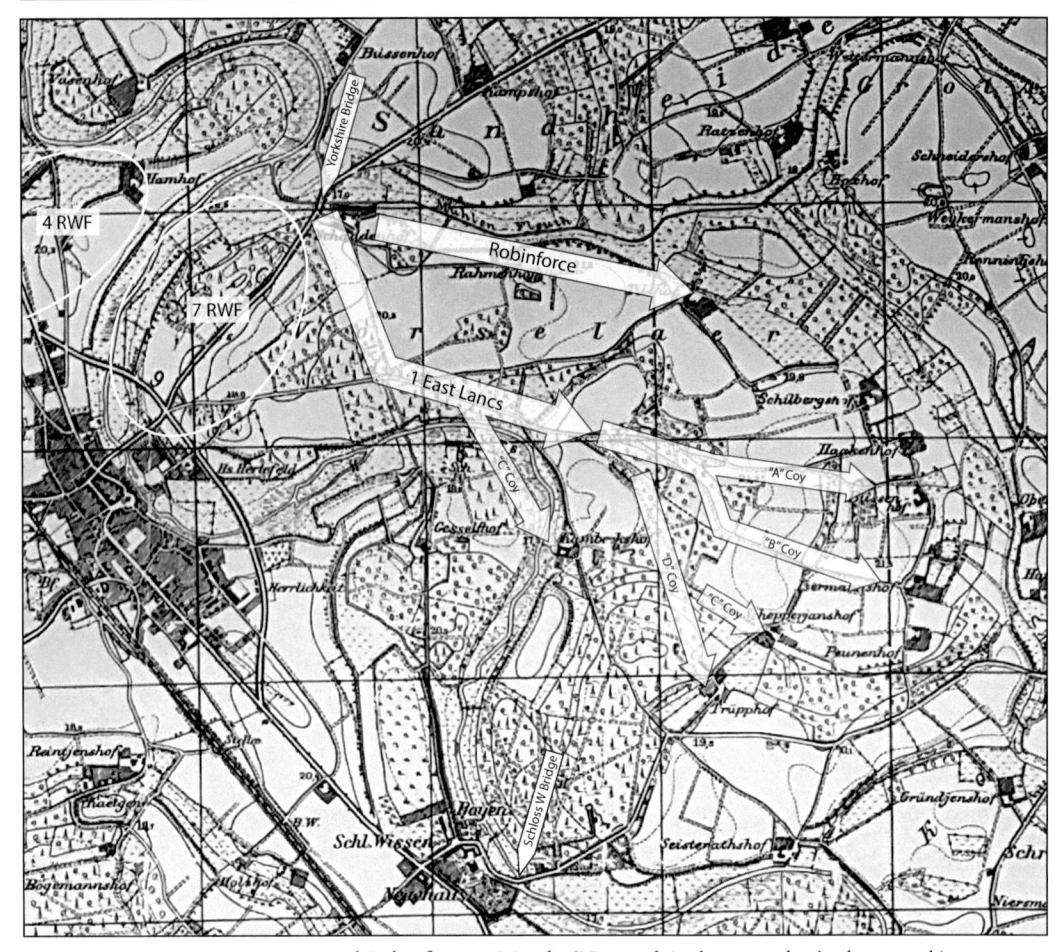

Map 35: 1 East Lancs and Robinforce, 1 March. (National Archives, author's photograph)

two Shermans and captured as many as 30 British troops, including the company commander.[49] Although the counter petered out, 4 RWF had lost up to 154 men, 30 percent of its fighting strength. The remainder dug in just forward of the Ottersgraben. For the captured company commander, 'The worst shame was being taken prisoner on St David's Day'.[50]

By 09:30 it was clear that all the attacks on Weeze had failed, and so 53 Division pinned its hopes on a longer left hook, with 1 East Lancs (First Battalion, The East Lancashire Regiment) and an armoured reconnaissance group, "Robinforce", heading southeast from the Mühlenfleuth bridgehead to attempt a crossing near Schloss Wissen (Map 35). Robinforce was comprised of a Sherwood Rangers squadron, a 53 Recce squadron, and a 12 KRRC company in half-tracks, but

---

49 53 Division ISUM 196. Riley et al, *Regimental Records* (p.761) imagines 'three Royal Tigers' in the counterattack. Stirling, *First and Last* (p.155) attributes the Sherman losses to a German tank that engaged them from the rear, having 'lain doggo all night' among buildings that the infantry failed to clear, another example of blaming "the other fellow". Given the insistence on fire from the rear, it is possible the Shermans were destroyed by friendly fire. There is no mention of *Tiger*s or a doggo tank in any other source.

50 Riley et al, *Regimental Records*, p.761. Loss figures are contradictory. The summary sheet lists 116, including 15 taken prisoner by the counterattack, while Riley et al has 28 killed, 93 wounded and 33 missing (total 154) but has the captured coy commander recalling only 10 captured. CWGC lists 23 dead.

being road-bound they had difficulty making headway. In contrast, 1 East Lancs made timely progress by moving dismounted with another Sherwood Rangers squadron following them along woodland tracks. This allowed a day-long series of at least seven quick attacks that did not reach the Schloss Wissen but ate through the German defences, held off combined arms counters and came close enough to the Schloss to threaten the Weeze garrison's escape route.[51]

Breakout

The threat to the Weeze escape route prompted a hasty German withdrawal around 19:00 on 1 March.[52] British overnight patrols into town found blown bridges, abandoned equipment and no German troops, but news of the withdrawal spread through the command system slowly and unevenly.[53] So, when 1 HLI advanced to secure Weeze around noon on the 2nd, they found a handful of Royal Engineers had accidentally captured the town ahead of them. Part of the confusion might have been because 53 Division had been due to be relieved on 3 March but Horrocks (having learned from the delayed Materborn and Goch breakouts) 'did not wish to relax the pressure by carrying out a major relief', so 53 Division was obliged to fight on.[54] Perhaps Horrocks was justified because the Weeze transition to breakout was much quicker than earlier attempts, but it was still nearly 24 hours behind the German withdrawal. Allied movements over the following days are shown at Map 36, with circled numbers indicating the position of 53 Division's leading unit at 18:00 each evening from 1 to 6 March.

The slow transition in Weeze was due to a combination of convoluted command chains, German demolitions and the damage caused by Allied firepower, including the collapsed *Sankt Cyriakus* church blocking the main road. Exhaustion and emotional fatigue also played a part. For the infantry battalions the shock of losing up to 30 percent of their fighting strength so soon after their trials in the Reichswald was considerable. When 6 RWF Weeze battles ended, 'a very tired band of officers gathered at the Battalion Command Post to make their reports to the CO. The reaction to the long slogging days of battle was beginning to become apparent, and it was clear that the Battalion badly needed a proper period of rest. This was, however, not yet to be…'[55] Fatigue and grief permeated 53 Division, increasing friction in an organisation that already had many barriers to smooth operation.

Another component of the apparent lethargy was that 53 Division chose to turn 8 Armoured Brigade into a corps de chasse (the very thing Montgomery dared not risk in Normandy) with over 100 tanks and 2,000 men from six different units. With its reconnaissance group, vanguard, and intention to attack from the line of march, this was a very Soviet-sounding organisation, and was followed by the main body of 53 Division ready to mop up bypassed enemies or launch deliberate attacks if needed.[56] At 17:30, a kilometre south of Weeze (point 2 at Map 36) the reconnaissance

---

51   1 East Lancs and SRY diaries; Division comms log.
52   In another indication of the weakness of German sources for tactical assessment, Oberst Ernst Blauensteiner (probably *2. Fallschirm-Korps* staff in Veritable) recalls Weeze being captured on 27 Feb: 'II Parachute Corps (19 September 1944–10 March 1945)', NARA FMS B-262, 1950. His account, recorded five years after the event, includes other dates that conflict with contemporary records.
53   ISUM 197; 53 HQRA and 4 Welch diaries; 160 Brigade comms log.
54   Barclay, *53rd (Welsh)*, p.138; 160 Brigade and 53 Division diaries.
55   Anon, *Caernarvon and Anglesey*, p.99.
56   4/7 DG diary reflects the complicated hasty administration, with no warning before the brigade conference, then needing to bring subunits from north of Goch across the dominant eastward flow of traffic. Diaries make no mention of Soviet influence, but the jargon fits Cold War publications like Department of the Army, *FM 100-2-1 The Soviet Army: Operations and Tactics* (Washington: Army, 1984).

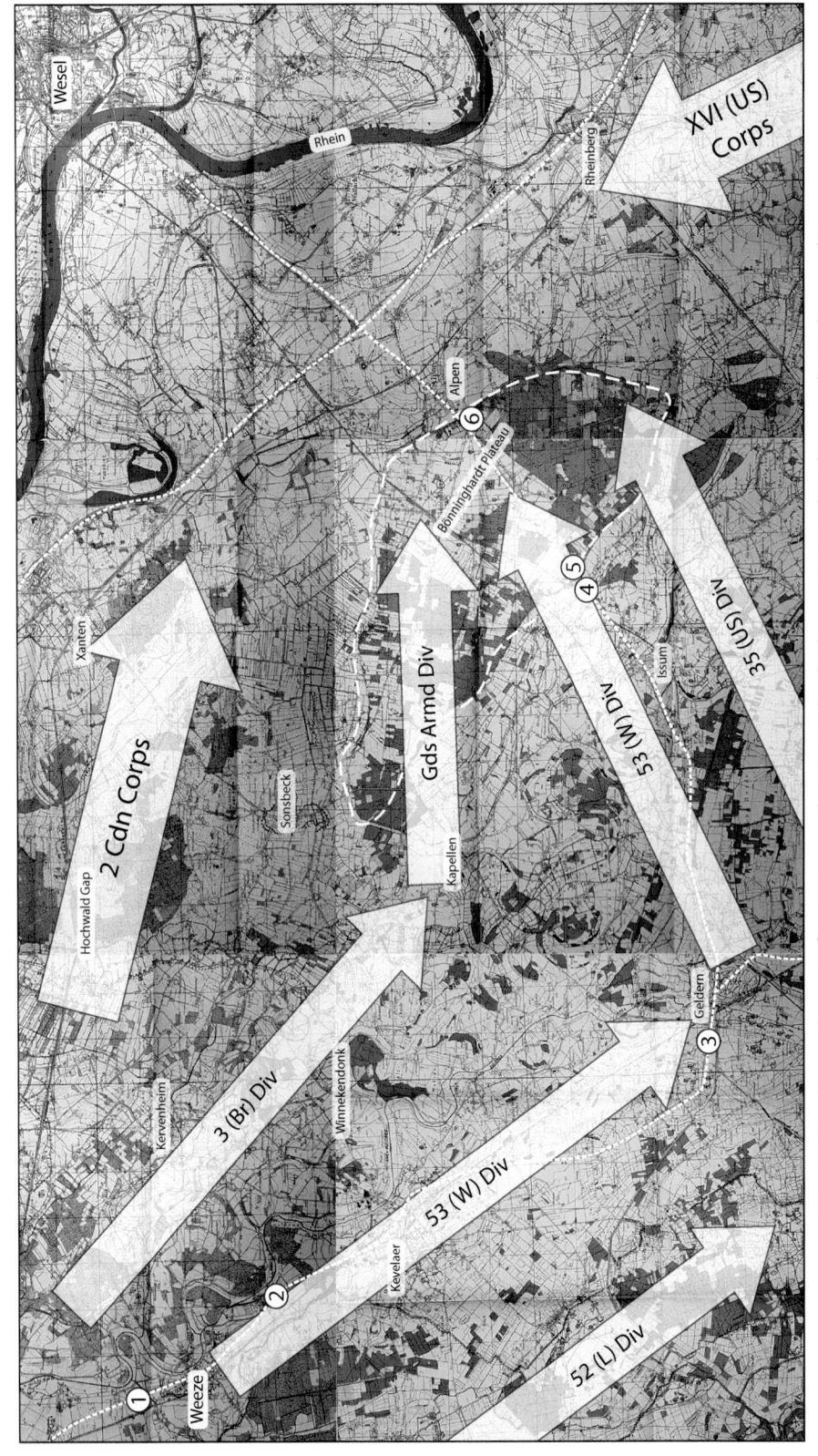

Map 36: Breakout and pursuit from Weeze to the Bönninghardt Plateau. (National Archives, author's photograph)

group reached a mined crater where two vehicles were destroyed by a German anti-tank gun firing from woods to the south. The gun was battered by a series of artillery concentrations then 1 Oxford Bucks debouched and cleared the woods of a few German machine-gun teams. The next morning the Oxford Bucks captured Kevelaer unopposed, 'the first town to be entered in Germany which was not a complete ruin'.[57]

Over the next few days, the advance was repeatedly delayed by craters that German pioneers made by detonating 250-kilogram aerial bombs in culverts under the road. Most craters were partly flooded and over 10 metres across, a gap that was too wide to be spanned by the standard armoured bridges, causing a considerable engineering problem that often had to be solved under fire. The culvert craters were part of a military engineering arms race where British sappers countered using "push Bailey" bridges, composed of long bridge sections dragged then pushed into position by AVREs. This and other ingenious solutions to wider craters (such as multiple spanning backed up by fascines and bulldozers) were much slower to arrange and more damaging to the road surface than a Jumbo or Small Box Girder bridge.[58]

The next town, Geldern (point 3, Map 36) was a similar problem to Kevelaer but compounded by a brief exchange of fire with US forces moving up from the south, then an awkward division of labour between American and British units.[59] The next day, 4 March, 8 Armoured passed through Geldern and Issum, both essentially undefended, German units having escaped encirclement while British and American formations redrew their boundaries.[60] A thousand metres east of Issum the corps de chasse found a blown bridge over a two-metre-wide stream (the *Spandicker Ley*) beyond which were, 'at least four spandaus ... and the track marks of a Tiger tk' (point 4, Map 36).[61] This opposition was considered sufficient to halt an armoured brigade, and so one of the infantry brigades was called forward to take over. This decision was more than mere Tigerphobia on 8 Armoured's part, but understanding it requires an examination of the concurrent actions of Guards Armoured Division.

Guards Armoured

British uncertainty over how to conduct manoeuvre warfare is reflected in the varied organisational structures developed to conduct it.[62] The enduring problem was a shortage of infantry, and in retrospect the evolutions to address this seems painfully slow. For example, 8 Armoured Brigade's 3:1 structure proved too clumsy for Northwest Europe, and apart from the "great swan" of August 1944, its regiments and squadrons were detached to serve other formations.[63] Guards Armoured Division usually retained its integrity, in part because since Goodwood, the Guards aimed to fight as three 1:1 armour-infantry groups: the Grenadier Group, the Coldstream Group, and the Irish Group. There were many adaptations (like that shown at Figure 21) but the 1:1

---

57 Anon, *The 8th Armoured Brigade, 1939–1945* (Hanover: Publisher unknown, 1946), p.28.
58 Roberts, *Welsh Bridges*, pp.219–223.
59 53 Division comms log, Op Instr 48, 4/7 DG diary and after-action reports of US 134 Regt and 35 Division (coulthart.com) give four quite different outlines of the plan. In the end British units walked into Geldern unopposed mid-morning on the 4th (1 East Lancs diary) capturing 30 stragglers. Much of the engineering problem was caused by Allied bombing on 14 Feb.
60 Stimpel, *Fallschirmtruppe*, p.364.
61 Oxf Bucks diary.
62 Buckley, *British Armour*; Harris, *Men, Ideas and Tanks*; Fletcher, *Tank Scandal*, all passim.
63 Anon, *8th Armoured*, pp.19–21.

structure could be repeated down to troop-level/platoon-level.[64] This approach addressed familiarity and unity of command problems and went some way to address the shortage of infantry, but it did not reduce the unwieldy mass of the Division.

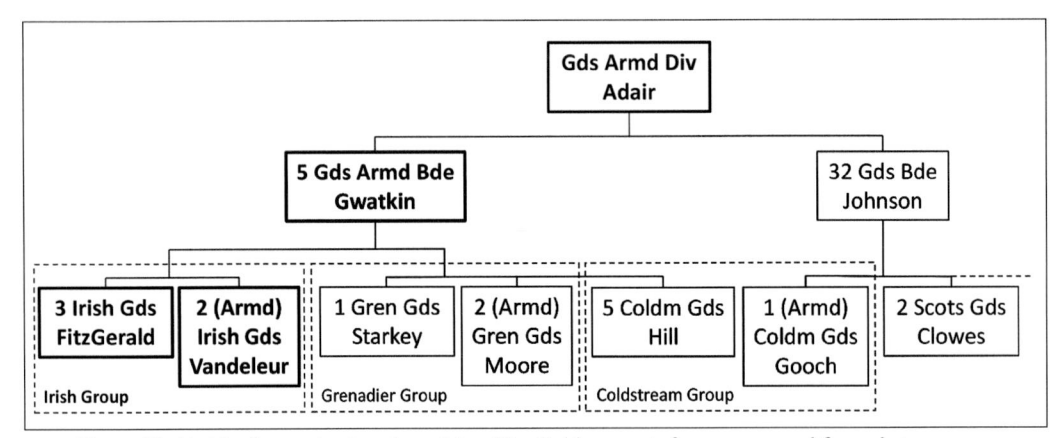

```
                        Gds Armd Div
                           Adair
                   ┌─────────┴─────────┐
           5 Gds Armd Bde          32 Gds Bde
              Gwatkin                Johnson
     ┌──────────┬──────────┬──────────┬──────────┬──────────┐
  3 Irish Gds  2 (Armd)  1 Gren Gds  2 (Armd)  5 Coldm Gds  1 (Armd)    2 Scots Gds
  FitzGerald   Irish Gds   Starkey   Gren Gds     Hill     Coldm Gds      Clowes
               Vandeleur              Moore                  Gooch
   Irish Group          Grenadier Group          Coldstream Group
```

Figure 21: Abridged organisation chart. Note The Coldstream infantry separated from their armour.

As 53 Division attacked Weeze, Guards Armoured began to concentrate for what would be its first time fighting as a division since Market Garden, nearly six months earlier.[65] In an echo of the disconnected army and corps plans at the start of Veritable, Guards Armoured was ostensibly taking over the flank protection of 2 Canadian Corps but actually formed another corps de chasse that aimed to overtake Blockbuster and seize the Wesel bridges.[66] Once again, the core problem was how to get thousands of vehicles down a few fragile roads already clogged with traffic, in this case the armour, artillery and support vehicles of 53 and 3 Division. Unlike the impromptu activation of 8 Armoured Brigade, the Guards breakout was arranged days in advance, so multiple schemes were developed and abandoned, with at least six convoluted routes planned to get the Division around and through the other divisions to reach the edge of the plateau near Kapellen (centre of Map 36).

Striving to make room for Guards Armoured on 3 March, 53 Division ordered 8 Armoured Brigade to move most of its vehicles off the road so 158 Brigade 'with minimum transport' could take over the advance between Kevelaer and Geldern.[67] The resulting complicated movement of Welsh bridges and radio batteries around Weeze proved a wasted effort because the Guards spent that whole day in 'conferences and cancellations' and 'rather annoyed by these constant postponements.'[68] Finally setting off just past midnight, the Grenadier Group led the Guards

---

64 Earl of Rosse (L.M.H. Parsons) and E. R. Hill, *The Story of The Guards Armoured Division* (London: Geoffrey Bles, 1956), Ch 2. By repurposing 2 Welsh Guards Armoured recce, the Division had four 1:1 groups. Just before Veritable the Division acquired 2 Scots Guards, briefly giving a 4:5 structure. 2 Scots Guard diary (WO 171/5149) January–March.
65 Rosse & Hill, Chs 7–9.
66 53 Division comms log, 1–5 March. 2 Welsh Guards, 'Operation "Veritable": brief summary of events' includes a plan to get ahead of 53 Division and cut the road between Issum and Wesel. The story sold to First Canadian Army was that 3 Division needed to rest in preparation for the Rhine crossing, but 3 was far fresher than 53 or the Guards infantry, and was never used in the crossing. Scarfe, *Assault Division*, pp.217–220.
67 53 Division comms log 030810; 158 Brigade diary 030900.
68 5 Guards Armoured Brigade diary (WO 171/4318).

through Weeze and Kevelaer before turning off the main road halfway to Geldern. By 06:00 on 4 March, the Grenadiers were stacked up on the back roads that wound eastward to Kapellen when they learned that German pioneers had converted a bridge ahead of them into a 30-metre crater that would take 16 hours to span.[69] This created a dilemma that staff could not resolve; they could wait and write off another day or follow an unproven route back through 53 Division, then 3 Division, with which it had no direct communications. The dilemma was resolved when Horrocks arrived at noon and ordered the bulk of Guards Armoured back north through Winnekendonk, but even this route needed three hours of repair before it could bear the weight of the Division.[70]

The Irish Group took the lead, and at 18:00 launched an attack from Kapellen through Hamb aiming to seize the high ground northeast of the hamlet (Map 37). Following a Victor fire mission (the fourth that Hamb received that day) an armoured squadron led the assault and found the hamlet undefended.[71] However, the subsequent advance (arrow 2 at Map 37) was halted when a German tank destroyer disabled one of the Shermans, blocking the lane running north out of town, and the following infantry were soon pinned down by machine-gun fire. Map reconnaissance had suggested Hamb as a good forming-up place for an assault, but it sat in a natural amphitheatre, a shallow bowl overlooked by camouflaged German positions. To attack from Hamb, armour would have to use a narrow lane that could be engaged from both flanks, while infantry would need to cross a kilometre or more of open ground. Nevertheless, the Irish Group gathered in Hamb that night while the disabled tank was forced off the lane. Meanwhile at least one more tank and a dozen men fell victim to fire from German mortars, *Nebelwerfer* and assault guns.[72]

The Division's intention was that before dawn on 5 March, the Irish Group would press on with the attack from Hamb, penetrate 'the crust which they had encountered', and then be followed by the Grenadier Group.[73] These orders made it clear that formation planners were ignorant of the tactical situation around Hamb, so an Irish officer was sent to suggest that the Grenadiers Group might have greater success using the more covered approach from Kapellen to Point Lobster, while the Irish Group distracted the defenders with a limited attack up the lane from Hamb. This proposal was accepted, and the Irish Group sent a troop-platoon up the road at 06:00. Two of the tanks 'somehow got bogged and also went off the air' but by first light the objective, a farm and wood halfway to the ridge line, was reached by nine infantrymen and one or two tanks (arrow 3 at Map 37).[74] However, it was full daylight before the rest of the squadron-company group tried

---

69   3 Division comms log (in diary); Forbes, *Grenadier Guards* (p.205).
70   The Rosse & Hill (p.205) credits BrigadierGwatkin (5 Guards Brigade) with the decision but 5 Brigade diary has Horrocks giving the order. Gwatkin likely had the idea but needed Horrocks's authority to get 3 Division's compliance. See 3 Division diary, 051800-060001.
71   The Guards preferred a hasty attack from line of march (like 4/7 DG and 5 DCLI first Materborn action) or, if defence was stiffer, this slightly slower attack where tanks then infantry advanced in separate waves.
72   Guards Armoured log and 'Part played by Guards Armoured Division in Operation "VERITABLE"', 2 (Division diary); 3 Division diary and log; 5 Brigade, 2 and 3 Irish Guards diaries (WO 171/5147 & 5148); Rosse & Hill, p.205. 2 Irish Guards diary suggests the German gun was an obsolete 50mm SP, which seems unlikely, and one account suggest a 50mm towed gun. All later reports suggest the SPs were 75mm tank destroyers and 105mm assault guns, which Stimpel, *Fallschirmtruppe*, Ch 9, suggests were from *FJ-Stug-Brigade 12*. Two other tank losses were reported to Division at 042030 'owing to spandau and shell fire'. D.J.L. Fitzgerald, *Irish Guards* (p.558) contradicts diaries, with no losses but the leading tanks bogging.
73   'Part played by Guards Armoured', p.2.
74   2 and 3 Irish Guards diaries; Fitzgerald, *Irish Guards*, p.559; MM citation, Guardsman Veale, WO 373/54. The suggested objective and culmination of this attack (arrow 3) are a compromise between vague accounts and grids in 5 Brigade diary. The troop-platoon was possibly halted at the earlier farm (300m SW) or reached the wood 300m further NE. The latter may explain subsequent artillery fratricide.

190 SLOG OR SWAN

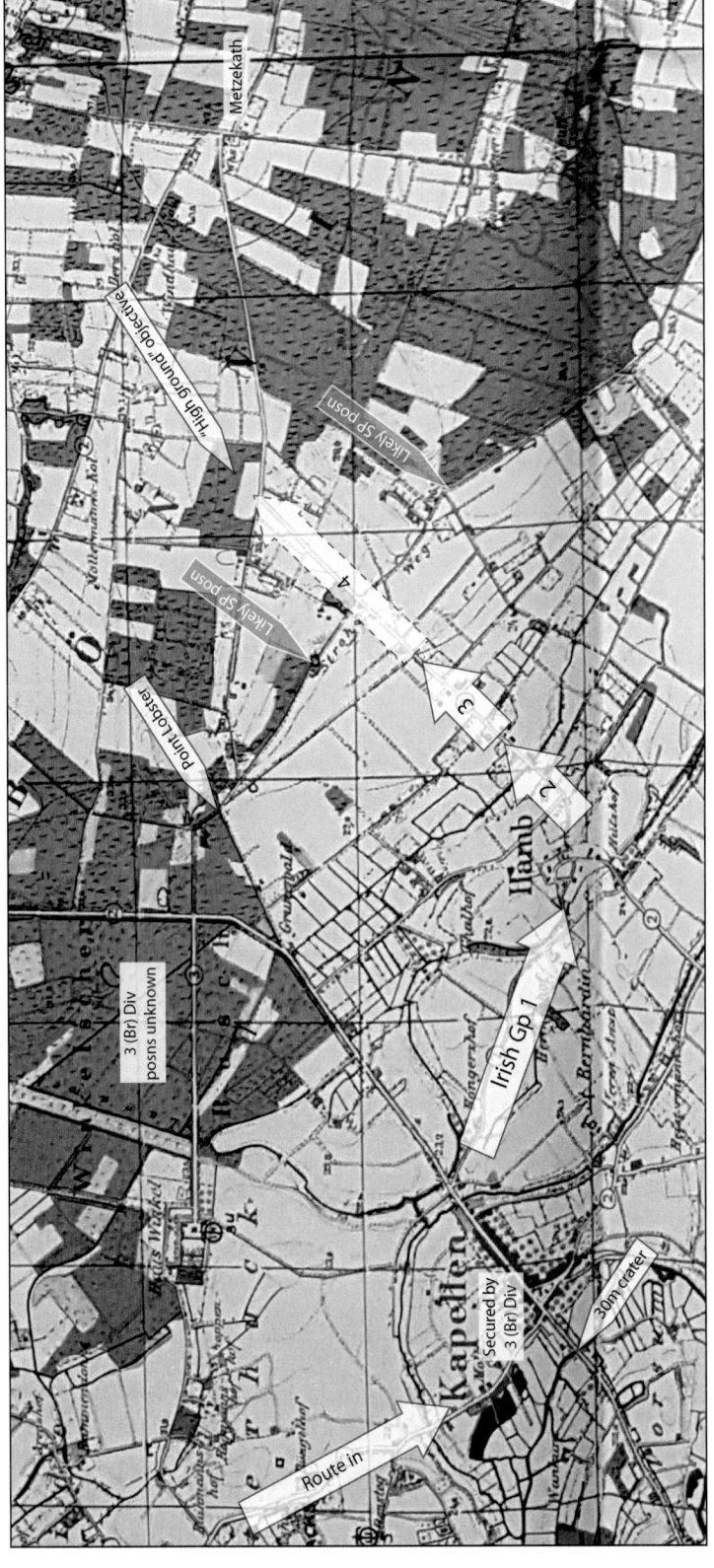

Map 37: Irish Group actions 4 and 5 March. 1. Unopposed Battalion Group attack. 2. Unsuccessful Company Group attack. 3. Successful Platoon Group attack. 4. the original planned attack. (National Archives, author's photograph)

to join them, and a handful of SPs in the woods knocked out seven of the Guards' tanks while indirect fire and machine-guns suppressed the infantry.[75]

The main attack by the Grenadier Group did not leave its harbour area northwest of Kapellen until 07:30, then the leading squadron-company fought a slow but successful wood clearance to Point Lobster ("Gren Gp 1" at Map 38) which, like Hamb, had been abandoned the night before.[76] Another squadron-company was due to head east immediately to secure the Metzekath road junction, but the advance was halted (arrow 2) when the leading tanks met and destroyed two of the SPs that had just mauled the Irish Group. There was then a delay while 2 Grenadier Guards spent 45 minutes trying to call air onto SPs that were 'milling around' in the woods before giving up and using artillery instead. Although this was also unsuccessful, it caused the German armour to withdraw.[77]

Perhaps sobered by the Irish losses, the Grenadier Group arranged a deliberate attack, bolstered by a strong fire plan and by the infantry of 5 Coldstream Guards.[78] The first phase of this attack (arrow 3) suffered only light casualties to German delay teams, but its fire plan involved 'a certain amount of stonking' of the Irish Group. In the final phase (arrow 4), the fire plan hit the Coldstreams' start line, 'killing and wounding several men', then Grenadier tank crews cheered on the Coldstream infantry but seem to have provided no physical support on the advance to Metzekath.[79] The woods contained only a few outposts that were easily overrun, but Metzekath was stoutly defended by elements of *FJR 22* and *GR 1062*, plus a collection of anti-tank guns, and two SPs, although the latter withdrew before the assault.[80]

The capture of Metzekath marked the end of 5 Guards Armoured Brigade's contribution to the breakout, it had suffered around 120 personnel casualties and 10 tank casualties, but captured 200 men and three guns, destroyed two 75mm tank destroyers, and inflicted perhaps 100 casualties.[81] The next morning (6 March) 32 Guards Brigade passed through and secured Bönninghardt but by the 7th, the Guards had still not drawn level with 53 Division, which had made more headway using fewer resources. Although the Guards inched closer to Wesel over the next few days, their breakout attempt was over.[82] The Irish Group had suffered the most. 'After "*l'affaire Hamb*," which

---

75 2 and 3 Irish Guards diaries. Former has SPs jockeying between fire positions to 'nose forward under cover, fire a shot or two, and disappear again.' Guards Armoured diary tank states; CWGC. Rosse & Hill mistakenly has 5 March activities and casualties on the night of the 4th.

76 1 and 2 Grenadier Guards diaries (WO 171/5144 & 5145); Division comms log & ISUM to 060100A. 1 Grenadier Guards diary mentions no losses in this phase of the attack with 24 PW mostly *GR 1062*.

77 Division comms log.

78 The 5 Coldstream Guards diary has five field and three medium batteries. Concentrations were likely linear and perpendicular to the advance.

79 2 Irish Guards diary; Howard and Sparrow, *Coldstream Guards*, p.356; Forbes, *Grenadier Guards*, p.205; 5 Brigade diary; 5 Coldstream Guards diary (WO 171/5143); Division comms log. There is a dearth of information from Grenadier diaries here and a gentle conflict between sources, but this description hinges on the order of events suggested by Forbes. 2 Grenadier Guards diary has two killed, four wounded, 30 PW; 1 Grenadier Guards has five killed, 13 wounded, 14 Germans killed, 46 PW. CWGC concurs.

80 5 Coldstream Guards diary; 109 prisoners claimed but neither diary nor history record losses. CWGC has six or seven dead. Division ISUM 060100 has one PW claiming four assault guns defended the area attacked by 5 Brigade, which suggests the 'milling around' SPs were the two that were later seen to withdraw from Metzekath.

81 Brigade diary and Fitzgerald, *Irish Guards* (p.559) claim 250 prisoners, with the diary stating, 'mainly from 22 and 24 Parachute Regt' and Fitzgerald 'all young parachutists.' Division ISUM 060100 gives a more sober 148 prisoners, half from *FJR 22*, the remainder *GR 1062* or stragglers, but perhaps missed PW picked up late on the 5th.

82 'Part played by Guards Armoured', pp.3–4; L.F. Ellis, *Welsh Guards at War* (Aldershot: Gale & Polden,

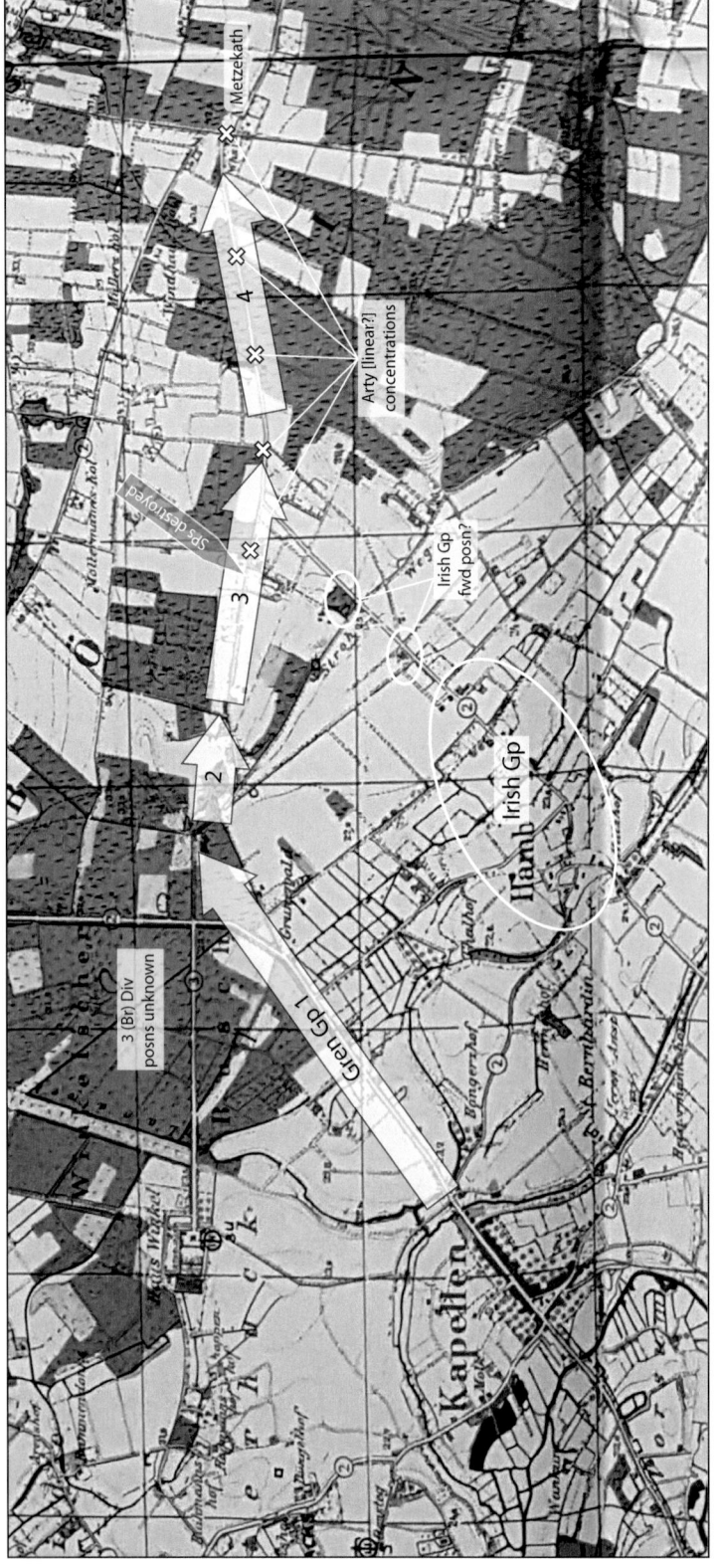

Map 38: Grenadier Group actions 5 March. (National Archives, author's photograph)

cost us some seventy casualties, life was pure peace. Even the rain and shells stopped [but] I'm afraid we wasted our time in Tilburg last February studying means of capturing the bridge intact by an armoured dash'.[83]

Conclusion

Charles Dick argues that Montgomery so doubted the abilities of his troops that he refused to form a corps de chasse. This may have been true for 1944, but over one week in 1945, 30 Corps attempted to breakout and pursue with 53 Division, 8 Armoured Brigade, then Guards Armoured Division. Each could be considered a corps de chasse and each could be considered a failure.[84] The first attempt was three days late, the second a day late, and the third was anything up to three weeks late. Then, once they were committed, each organisation was too slow to adapt to changing circumstances. These similarities might suggest an underpinning cultural characteristic, but a deeper examination shows that each attempt was afflicted by a different combination of deficiencies in planning, tactical logistics, command systems and inter-arm cooperation.

The 53 Division attempt lost tempo at both ends, with the focus on Operation Blockbuster transforming Operation Leek from a pursuit into a series of improvised break-in battles, essentially an attempt to repeat the success of Veritable's first days, but on the fly, with unfamiliar armoured support and infantry drained by weeks in the field. And it faced opposition stronger than on D-Day, particularly in artillery which was 'generally agreed to have been heavier than any we have encountered previously in the campaign.'[85] When the wide flanking movement by 1 East Lancs unhinged the defence, it was almost by accident, so what was 'probably our most hard fought and costly action of the campaign' ended in an anti-climax that caught 53 Division by surprise.[86]

It could be argued that 8 Armoured Brigade's breakout and pursuit failed because 53 Division lost contact with the enemy and had no reserve ready to exploit. This likely gave the Germans a 12-hour head start, but the rest of the delay came from the susceptibility of armour-heavy forces to tactical logistic problems. When 8 Armoured set out to chase four or five German SPs, it did so with over 100 tanks. Any number of tanks would have been susceptible to the culvert craters and mines the Germans left behind (while infantry could usually sneak around them) but 100 tanks took a long time to transition through stop-start cycles as they moved aside to let engineers through or get fuel trucks forward. Those 100 tanks needed a new road making for them though Weeze. Mass compounded tactical logistic problems so, even though it was virtually unopposed, the corps de chasse advanced at only 13 kilometres a day, about the same rate as 227 Brigade's largely dismounted and opposed advance on D-Day. Even then, the fastest segment of the advance was between Kevelaer and Geldern, when 158 Brigade's infantry took over and walked between objectives.

Yet the main drag on tempo for 8 Armoured Brigade was the need to handover a large section of its supply route to Guards Armoured Division, which was so hungry for road space it undermined the formations around it. Being so much larger, Guards Armoured moved even slower than 8 Armoured Brigade and its movement demanded administration via a command system so frail that 3 Division needed four hours' notice of any change to the Guards' movement plans. This

---

    1946), pp.269–271; Erskine, *Scots Guards*, pp.415–420; 2 Scots Guards and 2 Welsh Guards diaries.
83   Fitzgerald, *Irish Guards*, p.559.
84   2 Canadian Corps made other corps de chasse attempts that week.
85   ISUM 192.
86   Exham, 'Assault on the Reichswald', p12.

combination of size and complexity created a tailback all the way to Kevelaer.[87] The tailback was one reason 8 Armoured could not assault the Spandicker Ley: the logistic support needed for an armoured brigade to complete an opposed river crossing had great difficulty passing through an armoured division.

Another reason 8 Armoured could not assault was the poor combat performance of Sherman-equipped formations. Almost as soon as it left Weeze, the 8 Armoured group fell for a false front where one anti-tank gun forced a dismounted, armour-free clearance of Kevelaer. Then at the Spandicker Ley a few machine-guns, a suspicious tank track and impending darkness meant there was no attempt at assault. Guards Armoured had combat effectiveness problems too. The Irish Group's attack through Hamb used a mass of artillery then armour to hit an empty hamlet whereupon its 60 tanks and 500 infantry were stopped by a single tank casualty. The following day, the Grenadier Group launched with the same 1:1 structure, but when it met just four SPs (two of which were promptly disabled) it reverted to deliberate attacks dominated by artillery and infantry.[88] Perhaps these reversions to infantry assault reflect a deserved caution; although the accounts are vague, the Irish Group's loss of nine Shermans on the second move from Hamb suggest a problem with tanks, tactics, or both. The better documented losses to 13/18 Hussars supporting 2 Mons north of Weeze were similarly severe when they too were advancing towards concealed tank destroyers.

These losses and the extent to which caution was deserved bring this assessment uncomfortably close to the vigorous debate over the technological merits of Second World War armoured vehicles. That debate is outside the scope of the current assessment but needs some comment beyond the familiar comparisons of armour, firepower, and mobility.[89] Despite many fine qualities, Shermans were large targets, most had weak armour, and crews felt this qualitative disadvantage keenly.[90] Then, compared to the Churchill (and to the German turretless vehicles they usually faced in Veritable) the Sherman's height, narrow tracks, and high gearing made it far less capable off-road. The Sherman's approach to German defences was therefore much more predictable and ambush-able, even against hastily erected screens like that north of Hamb. Poor off-road performance also reduced the opportunities to collaborate with infantry and therefore curtailed the longer-term development of cooperation skills. Darkness, close terrain, command expectations, and ergonomics further reduced the opportunity for cooperation, widening the skills gap between Sherman and Churchill crews and, it must be assumed, between the crews of Shermans and German turretless vehicles.[91]

Looking across Veritable actions suggests a hierarchy of effectiveness, with familiar Churchills at the top and unfamiliar Shermans at the bottom, while familiar Shermans and unfamiliar Churchills competed for second place. The disjointed attacks around Weeze suggest 53 Division

---

87 Guards Armoured, 3 and 53 Division comms logs, 4–5 March.
88 The woodland task and losses from earlier battles do not fully explain the need for 5 Brigade to borrow 5 Coldstrem Guards. There was also briefly a scheme to borrow 8 Brigade from 3 Division (3 Division comms log).
89 Although these issues are covered by sources noted previously, this is one area where social media has helped uncover a wealth of previously unexamined material.
90 The Sherman was comfortable, reliable, easy to mass produce, transportable, maintainable, and repairable, but many units felt (like 4/7 DG in Ch 4) that they were backing a loser even in a fair fight. By advancing on roads the Sherman rarely had a fair fight.
91 On ergonomics, the Sherman commander sat a metre higher than the *Jagdpanzer IV* commander, who was near eye level with his supporting infantry and so had easier communication, a shared perspective and less need to dismount. This is the most extreme example; the approximate vehicle heights (from online sources) are: Sherman M4A2, 2.85m; *Jagdpanther*, 2.71m; Churchill IV, 2.45m; *Sturmgeschütz IV*, 2.20m *Jagdpanzer IV*, 1.85m.

suffered greatly in the switch from familiar Churchills to unfamiliar Shermans. But 8 Armoured suffered too, being swapped from 43 Division where they had begun to have a good effect, to the less familiar 53 Division without any familiarisation. The same problem influenced 8 Armoured's stint as corps de chasse. That attempt at breakout and pursuit failed to pressure the German retreat because the Sherman units were in an unfamiliar golf bag, their tanks were perceived to be ineffective, their heavy formation was susceptible to delay, and the Brigade had to give up its road space to Guards Armoured.

That the Guards had fewer golf bag problems is perhaps reflected in the successful troop-platoon attack out of Hamb; an attack in darkness being something many Sherman units would not countenance. Later the same day the Grenadiers destroyed two SPs by outflanking their ambush, something many Sherman units never had the chance to do. Yet this success prompted the Guards to switch to attacks where the two arms were apparently separated by lack of confidence in the Sherman's ability to face German armour or fight in woods. Ultimately however, Guards Armoured failed as a corps de chasse because it was simply too heavy to fight in Northwest Europe. Like a miniature version of 30 Corps, it had too much mass to reach the velocity it needed to achieve operational effect. By the time it solved one logistic or tactical problem, the enemy had created another.

The variation in Guards Armoured's combat effectiveness was hidden by the Division's post-operation report, which quickly clothed the naked truths of the breakout attempt, losing all the confusion, most of the delays, and presenting favourable outcomes wherever possible.[92] Likewise, 8 Armoured Brigade, after clamouring for a breakout role, omitted its lacklustre performance from its many memoirs and histories.[93] In contrast, the experience of 53 Division during its breakout attempt was swallowed up by the mythos of mines and mud that grew up to describe its relatively brief and relatively painless experience in the Reichswald. In this way the ponderous deployment of armoured formations, their vulnerability to a few well-placed tank destroyers and *Panzerfaust*, and the consequent caution, discoordination, and reversion to an infantry-artillery slog were forgotten. But so too was the full value of the German approach to delay battles (which has been critical to western allies ever since) and the vulnerability of that approach to a timely flanking attack. Instead, a historiographic omission has helped perpetuate the myths around manoeuvre warfare and British lethargy. And so, the tangible, repairable problems with force design in 53 Division, 8 Armoured Brigade, and Guards Armoured Division were allowed to persist and be transmitted to later generations of fighting formations.

---

92 'Part played by Guards Armoured' claimed, for example, that the Irish Group reached the high ground north of Hamb on the 4th.

93 For example, Christopherson and Holland's *Englishman at War* (pp.387, 489–491, 515) bemoans the repeated penny packeting of the Brigade but despite the concentration under 53 Division aligning with the Brigade's self-image, it is skimmed over and presented as a loose collection of engineering anecdotes. Anon, *8th Armoured*, (p.28) describes the whole advance in one paragraph.

8

Battle Morale

4 TO 7 MARCH BÖNNINGHARDT PLATEAU – MORALE INDICATORS – 4 RWF ON POINT AGAIN – ARMOUR UNAVAILABLE – A CHURCHILLIAN FOOTNOTE – 4 WELCH IN THE CAULDRON – THE SPEAR TIP BLUNTED – RICHARDSON AND BALCHIN – REVERSING COLOSSAL CRACKS?

Will Versus Skill

Neither side of the British Army effectiveness debate pays much attention to the potential for tactical events to enhance or degrade morale. The notable exception is Jonathan Fennell's work, which links will and skill, and even summarises Veritable to show how command interventions stabilised soldier morale in Northwest Europe. Fennell combines indicators of morale, including censorship-based morale surveys, battle exhaustion cases, sickness rates, self-inflicted wounds, absence without leave, and desertion, to generate monthly morale scores for Second British Army and First Canadian Army.[1] By combining these indicators Fennell shows how, following a near-crisis in Normandy, there was a period of morale recovery, then little measurable change until the end of the war.

Fennell defines morale as 'the willingness of an individual or group to engage in an action required by an authority or institution'. His assessment shows how improving soldier welfare bolstered morale then (following Buckley and Forrester) suggests morale was enhanced by adopting operational techniques that allowed British soldiers to believe they could beat the *Wehrmacht*.[2] This argument is persuasive, and there was no repeat of the Normandy morale scare, but Fennell's indicators refer to whole armies over the course of the campaign.[3] Likewise, his summary of Veritable follows the core narrative of an operation where 30 Corps was 'assigned the key role of advancing through the Reichswald Forest' but after a promising start reverted to a 'slogging match'.[4] Yet

---

[1] J. Fennell, 'Re-evaluating Combat Cohesion: The British Second Army in the Northwest Europe Campaign of the Second World War', A. King, *Frontline: Combat and Cohesion in the Twenty-First Century* (Oxford: University Press, 2015), pp.139–153; *People's War*, pp.513–519.

[2] Welfare measures included improving rest camps, entertainments and supplies of mail, beer, cigarettes, and fresh food.

[3] 'Combat Cohesion' (p.154) eschews tactics; *People's War* (pp.525–539) includes tactics and occasional reference to specific formations but is necessarily abstract in the presentation of tactical events due to its multi-theatre focus.

[4] *People's War*, pp.589–590.

despite the slog, centralised morale indicators remained high and so Fennell presents Veritable as evidence that 21st Army Group was 'fast becoming as professional, capable and ruthless as was required to decisively overcome their German counterparts.'[5]

As with other sources that have used Veritable to help assess aspects of British Army effectiveness, there is a danger that Fennell's top-down assessment masks the importance of tactical events on soldiers' will to fight and the resulting operational impact. There is no opportunity to interrogate centralised morale indicators directly, but Frank Richardson's *Fighting Spirit* previously applied part of that dataset at a much lower level, comparing battle exhaustion rates in divisions in Veritable to illustrate his characterisation of morale.[6] Richardson borrows Slim's definition: 'High morale means that every individual in a group will work – or fight – and, if needed, will give his last ounce of effort in its service.'[7] Although Richardson makes scant reference to tactical detail, by describing the assessment of battle exhaustion at divisional rather than army level, he exposes some of the limitations of centralised morale indicators.

To illustrate those limitations and to link morale with manoeuvre, this chapter returns to 53 Division on the Spandicker Ley and two battles that bookend the Division's advance across the Bönninghardt plateau: 4 RWF (De Horst, Chapter 2) attacking the plateau's western edge on 4 March, and 4 Welch (flamed in Chapter 7) attacking the eastern edge two nights later. Where the previous chapter showed how British force design almost precluded manoeuvre warfare, this chapter partly reverses the Colossal Cracks view to show how the lack of manoeuvre undermined morale.

Spandicker Ley

It was 17:00 on 4 March when 1 Oxford Bucks led 8 Armoured Brigade to the Spandicker Ley and made their report of Spandaus and *Tiger* tracks. Their report joined the list of mixed messages 53 Division had received since leaving Weeze. On one hand, Blockbuster had faltered in the face of German resistance and even the headlong advance of Ninth US Army had lost momentum against a stiffening defence. On the other hand, Guards Armoured was about to launch its attack on Hamb, and 53 Division's own progress had met only stragglers who reported German armour, artillery and headquarters withdrawing over the Rhine. Intelligence assessments reflected this ambivalence by speculating on a German collapse from the rear while remaining wary of a hard defence across the plateau.[8]

That ambivalence coloured 53 Division's response to the immediate tactical problem (Map 39). The first part of the problem was the blown bridge where the Weseler Strasse crossed the Spandicker Ley, then an unnamed hamlet just across the stream was followed by up to 400 metres of open ground that rose gently towards the forested ridge at the edge of the plateau. Although 53 Division did not know it, the hamlet and ridge were held by two weakened companies of *FJR 21*, amounting to just 100 men who had escaped the fall of Goch. Those defenders lacked armour and anti-tank guns, and had open flanks, making them an ideal target for a quick attack by a corps de chasse. A quick attack was feasible and was what the corps de chasse was designed to do: a Sherwood Rangers squadron had found a way through Issum just behind 1 Oxford Bucks and patrols had found intact crossings over the Spandicker Ley north of the Weseler Strasse. Somehow these opportunities for rapidity were mislaid among the radio chatter of traffic control. So, in

---

5 *People's War*, p.595.
6 F. M. Richardson, *Fighting Spirit: Psychological Factors in War* (London: Leo Cooper, 1978).
7 *Fighting Spirit*, p.4.
8 53 Division ISUM 199.

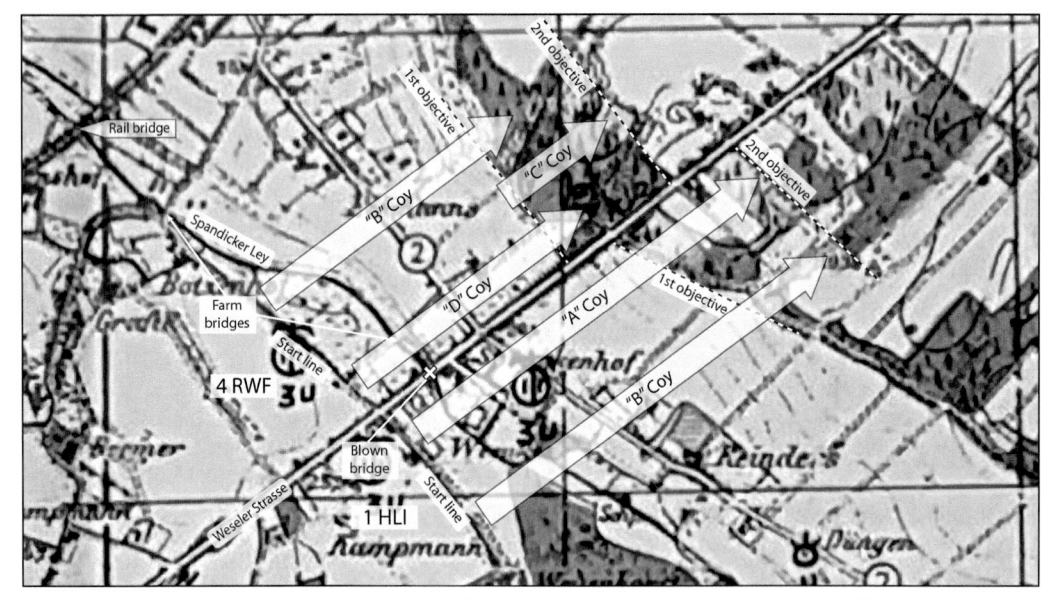

Map 39: The Spandicker Ley plan. (National Archives, author's photograph)

addition to the logistic and Sherman problems noted in Chapter 7, a third reason for 8 Armoured not attacking was confusion. The result was a reversion to type: 53 Division arranged an echelon change and an infantry assault while 8 Armoured Brigade curled up for the night. The brief swan was over, the slog was about to resume.[9]

The new plan called for 71 Brigade to take 1 Oxford Bucks back under command, then launch a brigade attack that would cross Bönninghardt plateau in a single bound and secure the small town of Alpen. From the far edge of the plateau, British artillery observers would dominate the low ground all the way to the Wesel bridges, raining fire on German defenders, and surely turn the withdrawal into a rout. It was assumed that Guards Armoured Division would be pulling ahead by that time and so 158 and 160 Brigade would exploit south and east (around Alpen at Map 36) while an armoured regiment would be kept on short notice for a dash to Wesel if the Guards were waylaid.

The first phase of the 71 Brigade attack (outlined at Map 39) would create a bridgehead over the Spandicker Ley and silence the German machine-guns to allow engineers to lay a new bridge. Once the bridge was in, armour would cross and support a rapid advance to contact across the plateau. This plan was issued while 4 RWF and 1 HLI, the infantry assigned to creating the bridgehead, were still at least five kilometres from the start line. Both battalions piled into lorries, then rushed forward through the traffic, leaving behind their heavier weapons and attached tank destroyers to avoid congestion.[10] Artillery units had similar movement problems, so 71 Brigade was to attack with only a few regiments of 25pdrs in support and had to share these guns with Guards Armoured Division. As noted previously, nearby Shermans that could have provided fire from the home bank, and maybe crossed to give close support, had been stood down for the night.[11]

Despite travelling light, 4 RWF and 1 HLI reached the start line two hours late. It was dark, they had no air photographs, and no information concerning their northern and southern boundaries, so their plans were based on a map reconnaissance and a sketchy handover from 1 Oxford Bucks.

---

9   53 Division comms log; Oxf Bucks diary.
10 160 Brigade and 53 Division comms logs 4–6 March.
11 53 Division diary; OO 34, 53 HQRA diary.

A series of 'weak' artillery concentrations were due to start at 22:30, the advance at 23:00, and bridging work just before midnight.[12] The attack would lack the mass of a set-piece action and, as it came six hours after the initial contact, also lacked the velocity of a quick assault by 8 Armoured. The intention was for a middle way, like the Oxford Bucks wood clearance into Kevelaer. Unlike the Kevelaer action, the defenders at the edge of the plateau were intent on holding their ground, at least for a while, and the attacking force was "tired". Like "disorganised" and "sticky", the British Army used "tired" to mean something far worse than its modern everyday usage. In this case it meant that 4 RWF were back leading the assault just three days after losing 30 percent of their fighting strength in Weeze; it meant they were grieving, fearful, sleep deprived, and so short of trained troops they had to assault with only three companies.

The opening artillery concentrations fell on the start line and although this caused casualties among 1 Oxford Bucks and 1 HLI, none were reported in 4 RWF. The RWF attack launched on time and soon crossed the Spandicker Ley, with "B" Company wading through the stream and "D" using one of the intact farm bridges. German outposts in the hamlet were quickly overcome and sent rearward as prisoners. At that point it is not clear whether the fire plan was too weak or had moved on too quickly, but defenders in the treeline were not suppressed and as 4 RWF began the gentle ascent, they were caught in the open by interlocking arcs of machinegun tracer. "D" Company was pinned down on the right, but on the left, "B" reached the cover of the woods, unknowingly turning the German flank. However, "B" Company was then exposed and isolated at the bottom of the ridge and hit by defensive mortar fire that continued until 02:00 (5 March). By that time, two platoons had been forced to withdraw, leaving only one platoon on the first objective line (Map 40).[13]

Fearing a rout, Major de Brett, 4 RWF's acting Commanding Officer, made a desperate request for armoured support. At one point he asked the Brigade Commander to personally order the tanks forward, but to no avail; the Sherwood Rangers could not be raised. There had been no further progress at 03:00, when "C" Company came up from reserve and joined "D" in the hamlet.[14] De Brett then repeated his plea for armour: 'If tks play my 'C' Coy will advance at about 0345 hrs to secure BUCKET [the top of the ridge]. Warn 1 HLI to take advantage of the adv. Crossing is scarcely an obstacle according to reports but understand br is in progress.'[15] On two points de Brett was mistaken: no bridging had been brought up and while a Churchill might have crossed the Spandicker Ley (as they had the comparable Leigraaf on D-Day), a two-metre-wide stream was considered an insurmountable obstacle for a Sherman. Ten minutes later, another request for tank support acknowledged that bridging had not started but suggested the Sherwood Rangers could use "D" Company's farm bridge or another that had been found further north. Once again, armour was not forthcoming, but "C" attacked anyway and managed to reach the treeline.[16]

South of Weseler Strasse, 1 HLI had also begun the battle 'very tired' and with only three companies, but their attack had been ruined by artillery fratricide on the start line.[17] Fifteen minutes into the fire plan, they requested its cancellation but were forced to endure because 71 Brigade could not contact the guns. Forty-five minutes after that, the fire plan had moved on but

---

12   4 RWF and 1 HLI diaries.
13   4 RWF, 1 HLI and 71 Brigade diaries.
14   71 Brigade comms log; 4 RWF diary; Kemp and Graves, *Red Dragon*, pp.261–262. Riley et al, *Regimental Records* (p.763) reports "A" Coy going forward but this contradicts the diary, and no other source mentions them, so it seems this was a misreading of 'a company'.
15   71 Brigade comms log 050340, possibly a delayed rebroadcast. Note de Brett could not speak directly to 1 HLI.
16   71 Brigade and Division comms logs.
17   1 HLI diary.

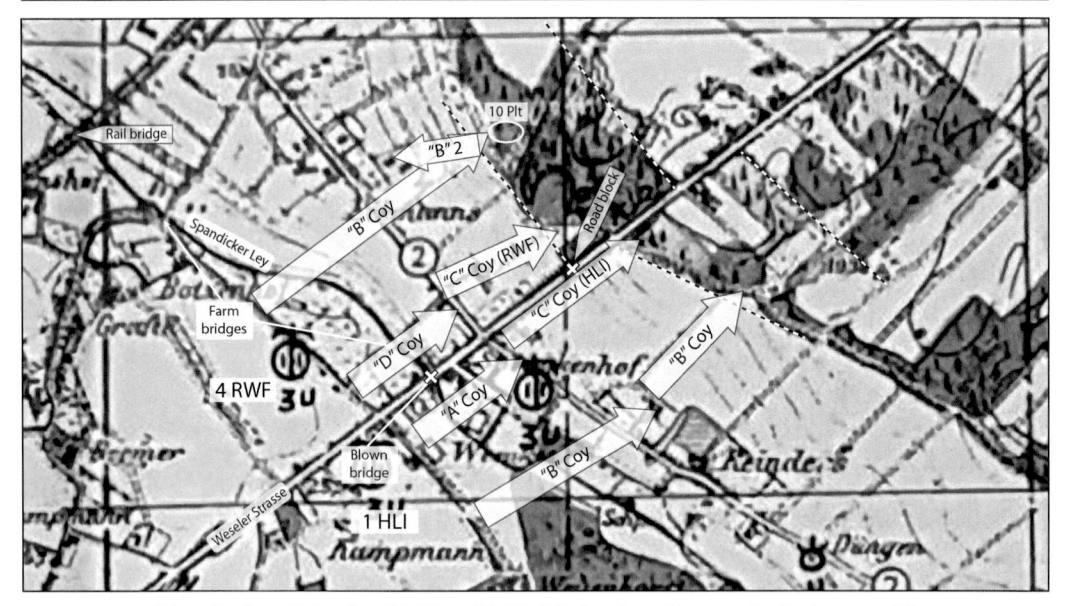

Map 40: Spandicker Ley 23:00 to 04:30. (National Archives, author's photograph)

the companies had not, euphemistically describing themselves as 'disorganised' by friendly fire.[18] Moving up from reserve, 1 HLI's "C" Company took over and crept up a roadside ditch into the treeline. Here they were stalled by a mined roadblock at the base of the ridge, but they disabled some of the machine-gun teams with flanking fire. This allowed the HLI "B" Company to get into the edge of the wood but no further.

Bridging began at 04:30 but by that time the battalions had committed all their deployable companies and secured fewer than half their objectives.[19] Drained by losses and fatigue, lacking armour and with limited artillery to balance the odds, they had been stymied by the firepower of German machine-guns. However, the Welsh battalions were unaware of their numerical superiority or the potential to outflank and infiltrate. If anything, FJR 21 had the more tenuous position. Weak to begin with, they had taken losses, been under constant pressure through the night and must have known that British armour would come forward once the crossing was completed.

That desperate balance was tipped by the arrival of a German counterattack force of 180 men from the machine-gun training battalion of *10. Fallschirmjäger-Division*.[20] The counter began by infiltrating along the RWF side of the road at 05:00 (Counter 1 at Map 41). Then a series of sharp contacts followed as the paratroopers probed the British left until they found the lone "B" Company platoon and attacked it, killing and capturing some fusiliers, and driving off the rest (Counter 2). Their success was then reinforced by a few SPs from *FJ-Stug-Bde 12*. At 05:30 this combined force attacked towards the HLI side of the road, forcing their "C" Company to withdraw in haste (Counter 3).[21]

---

18   1 HLI diary. 147 Field Regiment (8 Armoured's 25pdrs) appears to have been controlling the fireplan.
19   Division comms log. An additional friction at this time was Winston Churchill's visit to theatre, which involved road closures, a demonstration of bridge laying and a demand to meet 71 Brigade staff. (041745: 'Churchill himself caused 2 hrs delay.' 042155: 'Bull elephant [Churchill] to meet your SEAGUL [sic, likely Brigade Major] as soon as possible.') The reason for the meeting is unstated, but likely related to the replacement of the acting Brigade commander.
20   Not the same *Lehr* battalion reported near Weeze.
21   53 Division ISUM 200, & 201; 4 RWF and 1 HLI diaries. The composition of the defending and

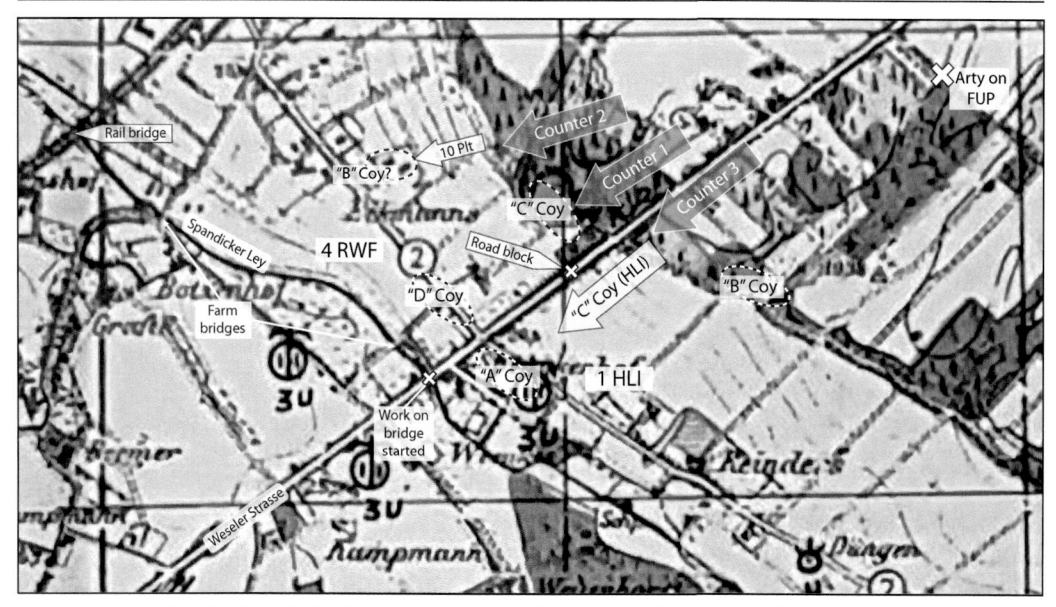

Map 41: Spandicker Ley counterattacks. (National Archives, author's photograph)

On 4 RWF's side of the road, "B" Company reported armour to their front, and the situation looked desperate, with a rumour of *Tiger II*s in the counterattack. At 05:10, 4 RWF was pleading for more sappers to help complete the bridging work, which Major de Brett thought would take just half an hour if personnel were made available. Additional engineers came forward from 8 Armoured Brigade, but under insistent mortar fire their work took longer than 30 minutes. Unknown to the British, the German counter (itself comprised of stressed, tired men) had culminated by 06:00, then at 07:00, with some daylight and a complete bridge, a Sherwood Rangers troop was finally sent into action.

These four tanks had little effect on their own, so another troop was sent across 20 minutes later and began blasting the roadblock.[22] Even this small force (four 75mm Shermans and four Fireflies) tipped the balance against the defenders, who withdrew into the sparse woods behind the ridge. Here they were spotted by a British airborne artillery observer, who believed they were regrouping for another counter. There is no record of the effect of this fire on the German forming-up place ("Arty on FUP" at northeast of Map 41) but 147 Regiment alone fired nearly 1,000 rounds.[23] This ended the Spandicker Ley battle but left neither side in control of the ridge. Parts of 4 RWF and 1 HLI had come close to rout after advancing just 600 metres of the expected 6,000, and 4 RWF had to be relieved as a matter of urgency.[24]

---

counterattack forces is the most tenuous presented in this book because diaries and ISUMs were written by especially tired men looking to being relieved, with little incentive to disseminate intelligence. The organisation presented is the best fit to sources, later unit movements in 52 Division ISUM 86 (7 Mar) and the *FJ* tendency for weak screens with strong counters. The groupings roughly match German online fora (e.g., lexikon-der-wehrmacht.de) which have *FJ-Stug-Brigade 12* with *StuG III* (75mm) and *StuH 42* (low velocity 105mm) in the area but the main body of *10. FJD* moving from Italy to Hungary. The SPs may be the two withdrawn from Metzekath.

22 The SRY diary suggests four troops deployed, but 53 Division sources and 8 Armoured Brigade diary have only two.
23 71 Brigade and Division comms logs; 8 Armoured Brigade diary.
24 The most complete German account found for the Spandicker Ley battles (Bosch, *Zweite Weltkrieg*, p.273) is

Plateau Slog

At 01:00, about an hour after 4 RWF and 1 HLI found themselves stuck at the bottom of the ridge, 53 Division issued an operation order that imagined 71 Brigade would soon be across the plateau and into Alpen. Staff then spent most of 5 March trying to rework that optimism into a sledgehammer blow but congestion, fatigue, competition for artillery, and a planning schism caused the renewed attack to mutate into a compromise where units successively bit and held 500- to 1,500-metre stretches of road or forest (Map 42).[25] The delay gave the Germans seven hours to form a hasty defence along the plateau. To the south of the Weseler Strasse, *Die Leucht* forest was held by *190. Division* units who had been hastily withdrawn from the Maas while Weeze was abandoned. The road and the area north of it were held by a composite force based around *FJR 21* and the SPs from the night before.[26]

British intelligence assessed that, 'It would be in keeping with Bosche policy to rescue his elite tps – in this case his paratps – as he has done with his SS in the past, leaving his lower class tps to stand and perish.'[27] This policy, and a twice-fired British barrage, may explain the lack of enthusiasm in *190. Division*, because the first plateau attack (1/5 Welch, southwest corner of Map 42) reported no casualties but collected 130 prisoners. The second attack (7 RWF) was more problematic, with communication difficulties contributing to the death of their Commanding Officer. The third attack (1/5 Welch, again) was another unopposed advance that took casualties only from indirect fire.[28] The fourth attack (1 East Lancs) had a fire plan that accidentally overlapped 7 RWF and 1/5 Welch positions, perhaps explaining some of the casualties to artillery in those units. The East Lancs broke into the hamlet of Pöttershof early on the 6th, but their night attack had no armoured support, and so suffered considerably when a pair of assault guns began firing down the road at first light.[29] By that time, it was evident that the greatest resistance was from the *Fallschirmjäger* and armour around buildings on the Weseler Strasse or firing onto the road from the north, so the fifth attack (2 Mons) sidestepped to the right and followed a weak narrow barrage along the edge of Die Leucht. With support from half a squadron of 13/18 Hussars, 2 Mons managed to exploit beyond their objective, but suffered heavy casualties, including three Shermans destroyed.[30]

---

three sentences where 71 Brigade quickly formed a bridgehead then attacked with tank support as darkness fell and the *Fallschirmjäger* defenders fought to the last.

25　53 Division and 30 Corps diaries; Division 00 34; Barclay, *53rd (Welsh)*, p.141. The schism is related to failed communication between Division Main and Tac HQs. Raw reports from Tac to Corps accurately echo battalion sources but the output from Main was disconnected and optimistic, suggesting a desire to present a positive image. Barclay, *53rd (Welsh)* follows Main's upbeat message and its maps are uncharacteristically inaccurate for these battles.

26　52 Division ISUM 86. Meindl (interview, pp.16–17) recalls giving *190. Division* the order to defend the southern edge of the plateau on the 5th but is vague on which units were deployed.

27　53 Division ISUM 200, supported by 52 Division ISUM 86.

28　53 Division, 8 Armoured Brigade, 1/5 Welch and 7 RWF diaries; Division ISUM 201; J. de Courcy, *The History of The Welch Regiment 1919–1951* (Cardiff: Western Mail & Echo, 1952), pp.282–283; Lindsay, *Sherwood Rangers*, pp.152–153; Barclay, *53rd (Welsh)*, p.142; CWGC.

29　There are no reports of artillery fratricide, but the first three attacks overlap in a way that often coincides with fratricide, like the Irish Group in Ch 7.

30　160 Brigade and 53 Division comms logs; 160 Brigade, 1 East Lancs, 2 Mons, 13/18 Hussars, and 81 Field Regiment diaries; Anon, *History of The East Lancashire Regiment in the War 1939–1945* (Manchester: Rawson, 1953), pp.178–181; CWGC. The Mons barrage was 1,000m wide, with 200m lifts and, it seems, only two field regiments involved. Echoing previous divergence of unfamiliar unit accounts, 2 Mons have a single assault gun lobbing indirect shots, 13/18 Hussars have their tanks destroyed by multiple SPs engaging from all sides, including a (probably) notional *Jagdpanther*.

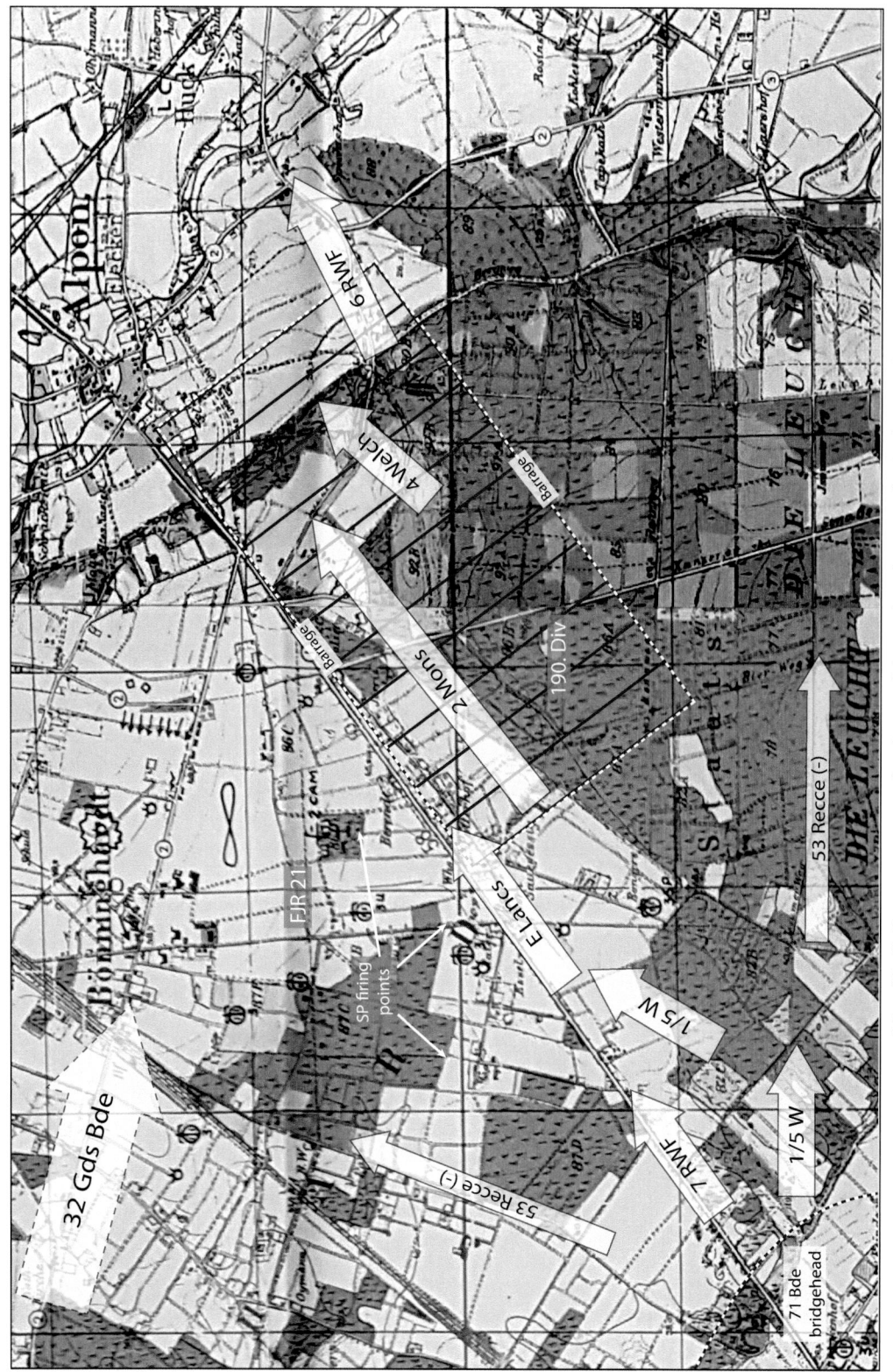

Map 42: 53 Division crossing the plateau. (National Archives, author's photograph)

Alpen Overlook

By noon on the 6th, 3,000 men and 60 armoured vehicles were crammed into the narrow strip of land along the Weseler Strasse, which was under German fire for most of its length. Marching into this congested space came 4 Welch. These were the same men who captured Starfish Wood on 24 February, then 'dug and dug; it seemed the only hope of survival', fell victim to the Crocodile fratricide, and then spent two nights under fire in the same waterlogged trenches.[31] After a few days recovering in Goch (and therefore playing only a minor role in the later Weeze attacks) 4 Welch were called forward on 5 March but 'owing to traffic jams', spent the whole day travelling to billets in Geldern.[32] Their Commanding Officer, Lieutenant Colonel Frisby, attended a 160 Brigade orders group at 01:30 on the 6th, gave his own orders at 03:00, then at 06:00, the Battalion began a 10-kilometre route march to the Spandicker Ley, walking being the quickest way to get forward.[33]

Early versions of the Brigade plan had 4 Welch marching along the Weseler Strasse, passing through 2 Mons, then following the Mons barrage to secure a strip of heather and woodland that overlooked Alpen from the eastern edge of the plateau. The overlook would be the ideal spot for artillery observers to dominate the low ground, but unfortunately for 4 Welch the Germans knew this too. Also, despite all its transport and communication problems, 53 Division was still nearly three kilometres ahead of Guards Armoured, which was due to attack Bönninghardt village at noon (northwest of Map 42). The Welsh barrage would end at noon too, when almost all 30 Corps artillery would switch to supporting the Guards. Realising a frontal assault would be foolhardy in these circumstances, Frisby span up a new plan at the side of the road. In another example of tactical manoeuvre and cleverness, he replaced the lost fire plan with tree cover and a less obvious attack axis, hooking around to the south for a "silent" attack with artillery on-call if communications allowed, and a half squadron of 13/18 Hussars if the ground allowed.[34] The later phases of the advance were poorly recorded and genuinely confusing to both soldier and historian, but a rough outline is shown at Map 43.

In addition to the usual radio problems, coordination was degraded by fatigue, with perhaps five hours sleep at best, a long, burdened route march, and then another four kilometres moving tactically. At 15:00, "A" and "D" Companies (centre and reserve) reported they were close to their objectives but under heavy fire from mortars and assault guns. By 16:25 these companies were on their objectives and digging in but there was no news from "C" Company (forward left), while "B" (forward right) had become disoriented and fallen behind the advance. An hour later "B" was on its objective, but there was still no contact with "C" Company.[35]

The other companies reported high casualties 'due mostly to shelling and mortar fire' and two recently promoted company commanders were wounded.[36] Despite their unfamiliarity with 4 Welch and their inexperience at fighting in woods, the Hussars provided good close support

---

31 Courcy, *Welch Regiment*, p.242.
32 4 Welch diary. 160 Brigade had 750 vehicles, but 30 Corps limited movement to 100 vehicles per hour.
33 4 Welch and 2 Mons diaries; Division comms log. 2 Mons attended a 160 Brigade orders group 2hrs before 4 Welch. There are often small discrepancies in recorded timings but here it seems Brigade tasked dispersed units in turn, with unavoidable loss of context and coordination, e.g., units unable to work through the detail of boundaries or "what if?" courses of action.
34 4 Welch diary; 160 Brigade comms log; Courcy, *Welch Regiment*, pp.243–244.
35 4 Welch diary; Courcy, *Welch Regiment*, pp.243–244. The end points of the arrows in Map 43 are from the diary's trace of positions at 070800 but the routes are a best guess because (like earlier Brigade orders) Colonel Frisby briefed companies 'verbally and individually'. 'News of ops from Coys extremely scanty due to screening of W/T [radio] by dense wood.'
36 Major Clement joined the Battalion in January and Major Jones was promoted to Company Command on 13 February. 4 Welch field return, 26 February.

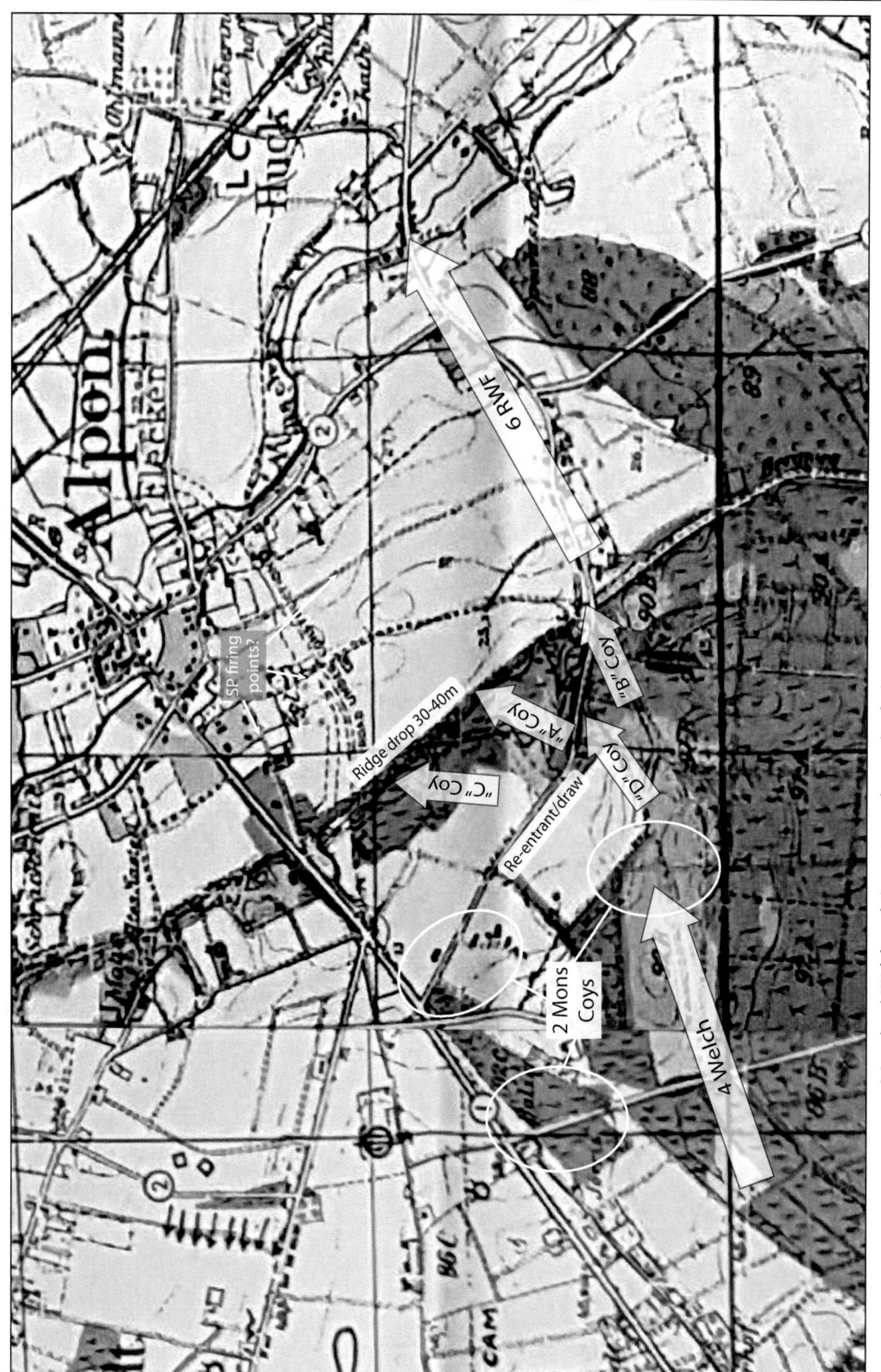

Map 43: 4 Welch and 6 RWF attacks south of Alpen. (National Archives, author's photograph)

wherever they could. One Sherman was destroyed by a German SP but only one bogged, and that was while traversing German trenches. Echoing 9 RTR's Broederbosch experience, two of the three tanks supporting "C" Company lost their turret traverse, but crews were pleasantly surprised to discover 'they could mow down trees of 12" diameter with ease.'[37]

At 18:30, when the overlook seemed almost secure, 53 Division launched its final Veritable attack using 6 RWF, who had suffered so terribly attacking Weeze ('not yet to be...' quote in Chapter 7). The ill effects of their Weeze experience were perhaps reflected in Colonel Exham's absence from their 05:00 orders group and his later evacuation to the UK, but 6 RWF had luck on their side for this battle. Attacking to the right of 4 Welch to capture a hamlet and a spur of woodland with support from a full squadron of Shermans, plus tank destroyers and Crocodiles, they had three times the armour support of 4 Welch. This support was effective despite frictions and darkness, and 6 RWF rolled over patchy opposition suffering few casualties.[38]

Yet the main reason for 6 RWF's lucky break was that German attention was sharply focused on pounding 4 Welch on the overlook. The 4 Welch "C" Company, closest to Alpen and with no reliable communications suffered the worst. In the early evening a 'very obscure' report came in from a runner, confirming that "C" Company had reached their objective in dense forest but were then forced to pull back 100 metres due to 'extremely hy and accurate fire at close range by SP Guns.'[39] The ability of 4 Welch to retaliate was severely limited due to the difficulty of getting armour or towed anti-tank guns forward. With both of their artillery observers wounded and infantry radios unworkable, 4 Welch called for fire by sending runners back to the Hussars who relayed target details through 8 Armoured Brigade and then to the guns, which made effective correction of fire almost impossible. The dismounted Carrier Platoon reinforced "C" at 21:30 but the position remained tenuous; the company commander, company sergeant major and all but one of the platoon officers and platoon sergeants had been killed or wounded. Many men were missing presumed dead and at one point "C" was down to just eight men commanded by the Hussars' squadron leader.[40]

Casualty evacuation became 4 Welch's main effort, with wounded soldiers manhandled in darkness through hundreds of metres of dense underbrush to the nearest forest ride then transferred to a vehicle. All the Battalion's tracked transport was set to this task and by 05:00 on 7 March (D+27) every casualty had been evacuated except for those 'killed during darkness' who could not be found.[41] Company positions were stable by 08:00 and mortar fire had become sporadic, but the Battalion HQ was often under indirect fire from the Alpen assault guns. At 09:00, 4 Welch learned they were to be relieved, having lost 27 killed, 65 wounded and 25 missing; over 20 percent of their fighting strength.[42] Relief came that afternoon when the plateau was taken over by soldiers from 52 Lowland Division, whose front had opened up when Weeze collapsed.

Later that day, part of 53 Division stopped off in Goch, where an embedded journalist wrote a summary of their Veritable experience:

---

37   13/18 Hussars diary. This revelation, weeks after 9 RTR developed their woodland fighting system, is another indicator of the limitation of lessons transfer and of Sherman units not considering close support.
38   6 RWF diary, OO 15, and 16; CWGC; 4 Welch diary. 160 Brigade diary has one killed, nine wounded. Surviving orders and Anon, *Caernarvon and Anglesey* (p.102) are vague and inaccurate for this attack.
39   4 Welch diary.
40   4 Welch, 13/18 Hussars and 160 Brigade diaries.
41   4 Welch diary; MM citation Lance Corporal Hanna (WO 373/54/436).
42   4 Welch diary; 160 Brigade Appendix A; Courcy *Welch Regiment*, pp.236–241; CWGC. Fourteen of the missing were later found alive. Courcy claims 'desperate resistance from paratroops hidden in the woods', and the Bn diary claimed 63 PW 'all from Parachute Regts' but PW identification is weak for this action and does not match later assessments, e.g., 52 Division ISUM 86.

They have foot-slogged 40 miles in a month, fighting for every yard. They have fired 1,000,000 rounds of machine-gun ammunition alone. They have had the longest, bitterest, sustained fighting of the war, and they are today, very, very tired.

And yet, as they sit here in the ruins, drinking interminable mugs of teas, they seem, apart from that weariness, entirely unaffected by their experiences.

Man, it seems, can get used to anything, and always endure a little more. If there is any maximum of endurance, however, then the men of the 53rd who fought in Normandy and in the Ardennes and before in Hertogenbosch have surely set it in the Rhineland.[43]

This romantic view (the journalist makes no mention of the near routs or battle exhaustion cases) resonated with the Division's staff, who proudly added copies of the article to their intelligence summaries.

Fighting Spirit

Frank Richardson's *Fighting Spirit* discusses esprit, leadership, and regimental pride but majors on the prevention and treatment of battle exhaustion because, as chief medic for 15 Division, that was one of his core roles.[44] Richardson's comparison of divisions (Table 2) conflates battle exhaustion and morale to imply that 15 Division had the highest morale in Veritable, and 53 Division the lowest.[45] A pro-British author might interpret the data as implying that 15 Division was an early adopter of Montgomery's functional doctrine, while an anti-British author might surmise that 53 Division suffered more from the British disease.[46] However, both those views are framed by top-down concepts like Montgomery's Colossal Cracks. From the nearly-bottom-up perspective, there was certainly an exhaustion problem in 53 Division, but its extent and causation are open to question, and the link to morale is not as straightforward as Richardson suggests.

Table 2: 30 Corps Battle Casualties and Battle Exhaustion Cases During Veritable

	Battle casualties	Battle exhaustion cases	Exhaustion as a percentage of total casualties
15 Division	1,084	98	8.3
Gds Armd Div	449	55	10.9
51 Division	1,211	173	12.5
43 Division	640	98	13.2
3 Division	706	113	13.5
52 Division	376	93	20
53 Division	1,695	456	21

---

43 V. Thompson, 'They Fought Non-Stop for a Month', *Daily Herald*, 12 March 1945, typed copy from 53 HQRA diary.
44 Richardson repeats themes from Moran, *Anatomy of Courage*, B.L. Montgomery, *Morale in Battle: Analysis*, (Hanover: BAOR, 1946), and J.C.M. Baynes, *Morale: A Study of Men and Courage. The Second Scottish Rifles at the Battle of Neuve Chapelle 1915* (London: Cassell, 1967).
45 *Fighting Spirit*, p.175. While suggesting cautious interpretation of statistics, Richardson (pp.120–122) claims his figures underplay the effectiveness of treatment and suggests the morale difference was greater than indicated by Table 2.
46 Forrester, *Monty's Functional* (Kindle 2368-2381, 3092-3140) pitches 53 Division as another of the slow learners. Note how the unfashionably pedestrian 52 Division scores nearly as poorly as 53 Division on Table 2.

One problem with Table 2 is that it presents the number of cases reported to 30 Corps, when the two central pillars of Richardson's method were to treat at battalion or company level, while stridently encouraging units to keep their case numbers low. He later upgraded this to an 'all-out attack' using a published health ladder to chastise units with too many reported cases.[47] This might be a minor confound were all divisions using the same approach, but 15 Division was at the forefront of this trend, while the less-fashionable 53 Division stuck with the official procedure of treating at division or corps and did not overtly encourage its units to minimise case numbers.[48] The centralised official procedure had helped to spark the Normandy morale scare when exhaustion rates influenced decisions about disbanding units and replacing commanders.[49] Under such pressures there can be little doubt that regimental officers (like today's middle management) were susceptible to playing the system and manipulating the indicator rather than addressing the underlying problem.[50] So, while Richardson's forward treatment idea is now considered best practice, the fixation on case numbers is strongly discouraged because it tends to hide problems.[51] It is not clear whether 15 Division even considered soldiers treated at battalion and company to be cases worthy of reporting to Corps but it would certainly have been far easier to overlook battle exhaustion cases spread among 36 company headquarters than in one divisional treatment centre.

Richardson's figures also overlook the varied experience of divisions during and prior to Veritable. After Blerick on 3 December, 15 Division had 'seven rather dreary weeks' defending on the Maas, then began preparing for Veritable, giving it two months where casualties were negligible, and the men were rotated out of line to all those morale-bolstering facilities instigated since Normandy.[52] By contrast, after fighting just south of Blerick, 53 Division spent three weeks on the Maas then a month in the Ardennes, experiencing some intense combat in harsh conditions. The Division's unluckiest unit during the Bulge fighting was 1 East Lancs, who suffered more casualties in a week than the whole of 15 Division did in the two months preceding Veritable.[53]

The tables were turned somewhat during the first fortnight of Veritable, when 15 Division suffered higher casualties on the main effort than 53 did in the Reichswald (Figure 22).[54] But even then, most of 15 Division was on the 30 Corps main supply route, and many men slept in civilian buildings with notably well-stocked cellars, while 53 Division suffered the strained logistics of "Chewing Gum Alley" and most of its men slept in the open.[55] The Reichswald experience needs to be contextualised, because it would be no great hardship for a competent infantry unit to spend

---

47　*Fighting Spirit*, pp.108–109, 119–120.
48　Unlike the decline reported in 15 Division (*Fighting Spirit*, p.176) Bolland's, *Team Spirit* (p.56) shows no drop in 53 Division's exhaustion rates as the campaign progresses.
49　*Fighting Spirit*, pp.117–118; G. Brown, 'Dig for Bloody Victory: The British Soldier's Experience of Trench Warfare, 1939–45' (Oxford University DPhil, 2012), pp.194–197. A. King, 'Why did 51st Highland Division Fail? A case-study in command and combat effectiveness', *British Journal of Military History*, 4:1, 2017.
50　Fixation on performance indicators notoriously encouraged call centre staff pick up the phone then put it straight back down and led hospital management to take the wheels off trolleys to classify them as beds. J. Seddon, *Freedom from Command and Control: a Better Way to Make Work Work* (Buckingham: Vanguard Education, 2003); S. Caulkin, 'The rule is simple: be careful what you measure', *Observer*, 10 Feb 2008.
51　NATO Standard AMedP-8.6, Forward Mental Health Care, 2019.
52　Martin *15th Scottish*, pp.220, 216–224.
53　Barclay, *53rd (Welsh)*, pp.94–111; CWGC.
54　To minimise reporting biases such as inconsistencies in unit casualty recording, Figure 22 combines CWGC data on deaths in infantry battalions. In the first fortnight 15 Division suffered 270 deaths compared to 53 Division's 176, but over the whole operation, 15 Division lost 276 to 53 Div's 417.
55　"Chewing Gum Alley" was a nickname given to 53 Division's main supply route through the Reichswald. The earliest public reference seems to be J. Illingworth 'Northern Bayonets Took the Reichswald', Yorkshire Post, 16 Feb 1945, 1 East Lancs diary, Mar 45.

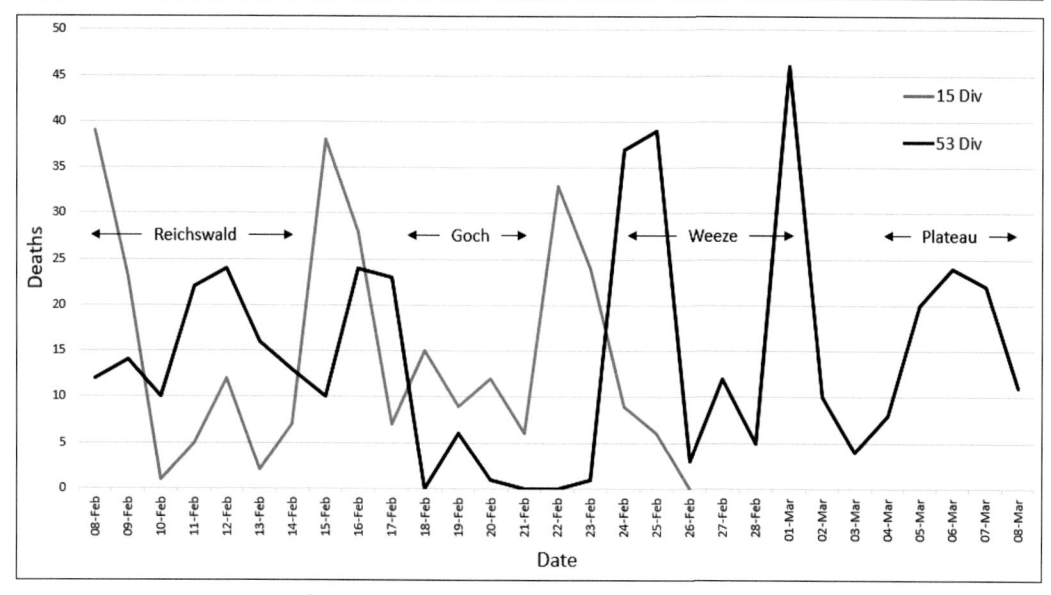

Figure 22: Infantry deaths per day for 15 and 53 Divisions during Veritable.

10 days under canvas on exercise today. In 1945 however, British equipment and training were designed around centralised feeding, rotation to billets, and access to good roads, all of which failed in the Reichswald. In the Reichswald, hot meals and even drinking water were in short supply, and the "canvas" that men slept under was often just a greatcoat and gas cape. So, men spent days soaked through, hungry and shivering in waterlogged slit trenches. Then of course, 15 Division was relieved after 17 days, while 53 Division endured another 10 days of intense combat.

Richardson also assumed a linear relationship between battle exhaustion and casualties, where exhaustion cases would stay around 15 percent of total casualties unless his treatment methods were applied. In contrast, most research describes a non-linear phenomenon, where soldiers and units gradually lose effectiveness until they break at a critical threshold.[56] Defence research simulations, for example, often use 25 percent casualties as the point beyond which subunits can no longer attack.[57] Alternatively, Swank and Marchand's pivotal study of combat neuroses has soldiers reaching 'maximum efficiency' after 10 days on operations, then from 30 days onward passing through worsening stages of battle exhaustion, sometimes reaching a vegetative state unless rested for a considerable period.[58]

The Swank and Marchand model might suggest little difference between 15 and 53 Division if both were fresh at the start of Veritable, but including the Ardennes experience would have 53's troops exhausted before they captured Weeze. By the time Weeze was captured most companies had also exceeded 25 percent casualties. Whether the tipping point was days in combat, privation,

---

56 S.A. Stouffer, et al, *The American Soldier, Vol. 2: Combat and Its Aftermath* (Princeton: University Press, 1949), pp.284–289. T. Copp, 'To the Last Canadian?: Casualties in the 21st Army Group' *Canadian Military History*, 18:1 (2009) pp.3–6.
57 R. L. Helmbold, 'Decision in Battle: Breakpoint Hypotheses and Engagement Termination Data' (Rand report, 1971).
58 R. L. Swank and W.E. Marchand, 'Combat neuroses: development of combat exhaustion', *Archives of Neurology and Psychiatry* 55 (1946), pp.236–247. Their graph still informs military research: B. Connable, et al, 'Will to Fight: Analyzing, Modeling, and Simulating the Will to Fight of Military Units' (Rand report, 2018), p.124.

casualties, failed attacks, or a combination of these, 53 Division's troops were much more likely to have crossed the Rubicon than any other Veritable division. The accessible casualty data (Figure 23) gives only the weakest indication of 53 Division reaching a tipping point during Veritable, with exhaustion seeming to increase faster than physical casualties.[59] But contrary to Richardson's assumptions, this dataset shows a relationship that is not linear, with battle exhaustion ranging from zero to 80 percent of total casualties in a formation that used a consistent treatment method. In other words, battle exhaustion was clearly subject to factors other than battle casualties and treatment methods.

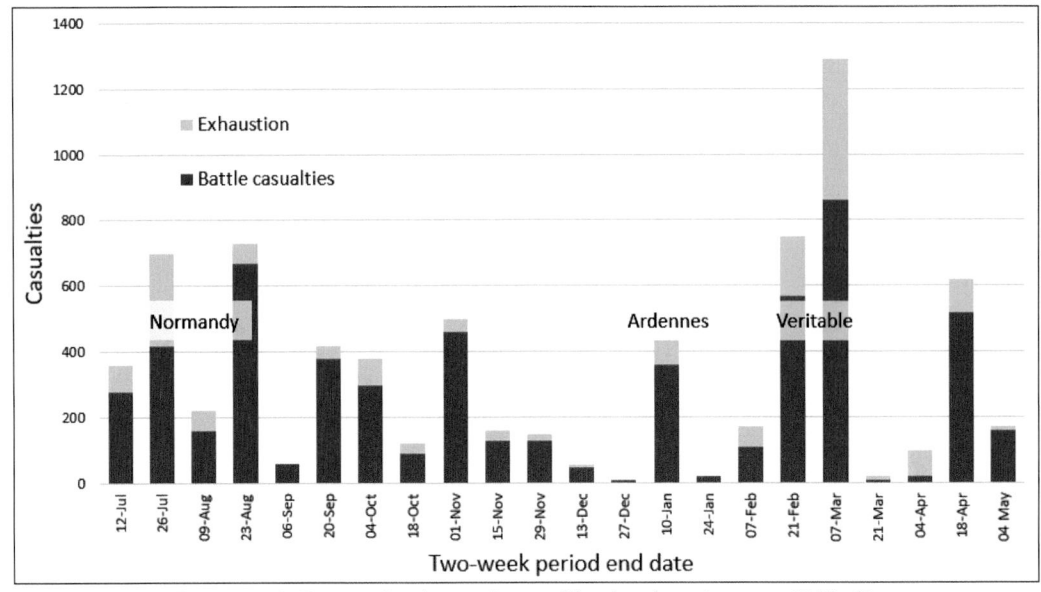

Figure 23: 53 Division battle casualties and battle exhaustion cases 1944–45.

Other centralised indicators of morale suffer similar limitations. Morale surveys, for example, hinged on censoring letters, which was performed inconsistently, or not at all when soldiers were too busy or too fatigued to write home.[60] On the few occasions when morale surveys have been used to examine divisions, the large proportion of rear area troops sampled has masked the state of morale in the combat arms.[61] Likewise, conviction rates for absence without leave and desertion were biased by the difficulty of absconding in contact and by units being more lenient after periods of intense combat, thereby artificially capping the number of incidents during periods where morale would be at its lowest.[62]

These limitations have led defence researchers to explore a concept outlined in 'Battle Morale', a 1945 paper by Brigadier Nigel Balchin, then Deputy Scientific Advisor to the Army Council.

---

59 Bolland, *Team Spirit*, p.56. No equivalent data was found for 15 Div. Although outside the scope of the current assessment it would be useful (but difficult) to examine the interaction in more detail using diary data on casualties and privation over the course of a campaign.
60 Fennell, 'Combat Cohesion' (p.141) notes that during Goodwood barely one percent of surveyed letters came from the divisions fighting the operation.
61 Fennell, *People's War*, pp.528–529.
62 These and other morale data biases are eloquently explored in C. A. Bielecki, 'British Infantry Morale during the Italian Campaign, 1943–1945' (UCL PhD thesis, 2006), passim.

Balchin was exasperated by the morale debate which, just like Richardson's *Fighting Spirit*, repeatedly switched from the 'stage of woolly abstractions in which people talk solemnly of "leadership" or "discipline" or "group spirit" without ever defining the meaning of these phrases in practice; and the all-too-concrete stage, in which the whole subject suddenly degenerates into discussions about supplies of beer'.[63] Balchin combined operational research, including the Swann Report, to look past high-level indicators to examine: 'the state of mind or spirit that determines the voluntary behaviour of troops in battle.'[64] Despite the awkward allusion to spirit, the core of battle morale is the observation that victory is usually achieved when 'the enemy <u>decides</u> not to fight on and retreats or surrenders.'[65] This decision depended on a soldier's 'estimate of his own chance of escaping death or injury, and on the chance of success of the enterprise in which he is engaged.' Later studies characterised this as the "is it worth it?" calculation.[66] Although this view was novel in Balchin's time, the same heuristics for assessing rewards and costs have since become fundamental to wide swathes of psychology, sociology, and economics.[67]

Balchin's battle morale concept surpasses fighting spirit because it accepts that combat behaviour is dependent on the tactical situation and recognises that soldiers are (at least partly) rational beings who can estimate the chances of success and injury. So, when "B" Company of 4 RWF recoiled from one side of the Bönninghardt plateau, or "C" Company of 4 Welch withdrew from the other side, it was not so much because their intrinsic will to fight had changed, but because the chance of success was low and the chance of injury high. Likewise, of the thousands of German soldiers who surrendered or withdrew during Veritable, most did so when they were outgunned, outflanked or in some other way outfought. So, unlike top-down indicators, the battle morale concept has potential to highlight the interaction of tactical events on casualty and surrender rates, and therefore to contribute to a richer picture of British Army effectiveness.

Unfortunately, although published studies broadly describe tactical failure lowering morale, primary sources are naturally reticent about recording events that could embarrass or incriminate their friends, and this is evident in the records of 4 Welch's experience. As Figure 24 suggests, 4 Welch suffered their worst casualties in the *47. Panzerkorps* counterattack, in the flame fratricide and artillery pounding in Starfish Wood, then when they were exposed on Alpen overlook.[68] The *47. Panzerkorps* counter was either not spotted by Allied intelligence, or not communicated to units in a meaningful way and, although defeated, that surprise cost British lives and caused days of operational dithering. Yet the cause and effect are barely mentioned in published sources.[69] The flame fratricide was part of a failed divisional operation, and neither fratricide nor failure are explicit in most accounts.[70] Finally, Alpen overlook was the result of 4 Welch being pushed

---

63 N. M. Balchin, 'Battle Morale', 1945. Reprinted in D. Rowland, 'Combat Degradation' (unpublished Defence Evaluation and Research Agency report, 1996), Appendix A. Part of this is reproduced in N. M. Balchin, 'Some Aspects of Psychological Warfare' War Office 1945 (WO 291/2316).
64 Balchin/Rowland, 'Battle Morale', p.A2.
65 Balchin/Rowland, p.A3, original emphasis.
66 Balchin/Rowland, p.A3; L. Murray, *Brains and Bullets: How Psychology Wins Wars* (London: Biteback, 2013).
67 "Is it worth it?" is fundamental to game theory, which Balchin was likely familiar with given his background as an industrial psychologist, and later to social exchange theory (K. S. Cook, *Social Exchange Theory* (London: Sage, 1987). Military applications coalesce around the aggressive altruism fundamental to S. L. A. Marshall, *Men Against Fire: The Problem of Battle Command* (New York: Infantry Journal, 1947) and Rowland, *Stress of Battle*.
68 Chart based on CWGC data. 4 Welch did not record casualties or PW. 160 Brigade casualty sheets for Feb could not be found and 8 Mar is illegible; a cautious reading suggests 99 casualties in 4 Welch on 7–8 Mar.
69 BAOR, *Tour* (p.57); Ellis, *Victory* (p.265).
70 Roberts, *Enshrined in Stone* (p.325), a memoir self-published 50 years after the event, is the only source with any detail on the fratricide.

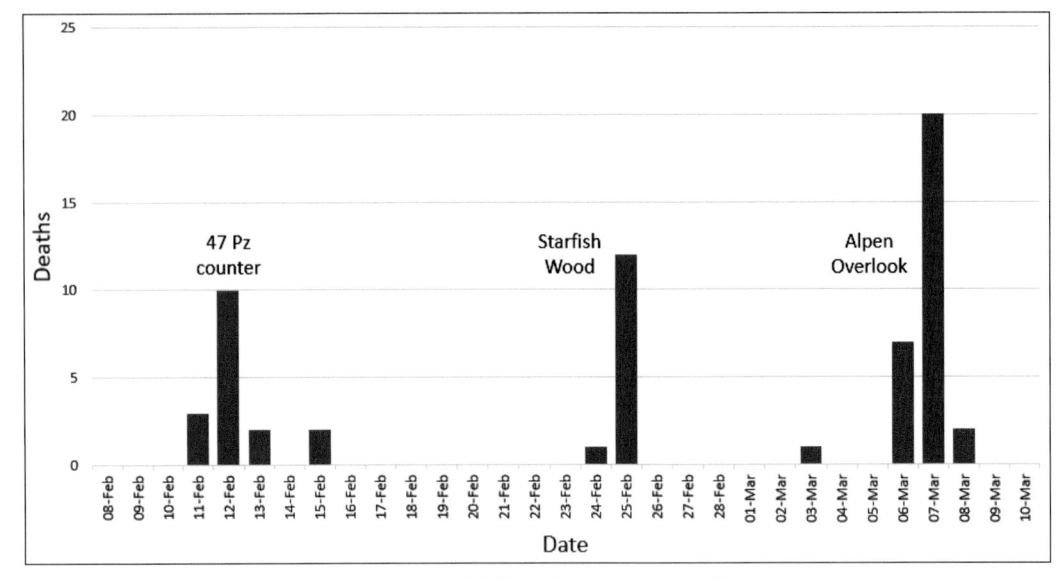

Figure 24: 4 Welch deaths during Veritable.

onto an exposed position then left hanging when 53 Division failed to assault Alpen as planned. Yet rather than examine causation, the Division blamed Guards Armoured and Ninth US Army for not capturing the town.[71] The tendency to shift the blame or to not record failures prevents a robust assessment of battle morale.

Despite similar obscuration, 4 RWF's experience suggests a relationship between casualties, battle exhaustion, and battle morale, as indicated by Figure 25.[72] With no major losses since Normandy, the Battalion had time to absorb replacements, learn, and train.[73] This was reflected in their success at De Horst, which was as near perfection as any battle could be. Difficulties and casualties began to mount that evening, as the Battalion entered the Reichswald through German defensive fire, then spent days repairing roads, digging out mired vehicles, and sleeping rough, largely because of the fumbled pass around Materborn. Although 4 RWF escaped the worst of the *47. Panzerkorps* counter, they suffered casualties in an attack on Asperden Bridge on the 13th, then during subsequent patrolling actions and artillery duels. Their attack into northern Goch on the 19th was another successful barrage-hug, but cost them 29 men, mostly to artillery and sniping after the attack.[74]

Given their light casualties up to that point, it could be argued that most of 4 RWF were not suffering from battle exhaustion, but plain old exhaustion from sleep loss, physical fatigue, and exposure. Whether following the official regime or Richardson's decentralised alternative, the treatment involved warmth, food, shelter, and sleep, with extreme cases given heavy doses of sleep medication.[75] It is therefore impossible to determine how much the treatments only repaired ordi-

---

71   160 Brigade diary: 'neither the Gds Armoured Division nor US tps on our right captured ALPON 1531 which meant that we received the undivided attentions of the enemy for far longer than was intended or anticipated.' Two days earlier, 53 Division had requested US forces be prevented from attacking Alpen (Corps diary 050230).
72   4 RWF summary sheet.
73   Riley et al, *Regimental Records*, pp.717–721; CWGC.
74   4 RWF and intelligence log, 8–19 Feb; CWGC; Riley et al, *Regimental Records*, pp.745–755.
75   4 RWF diary; Courcy, *Welch Regiment*, pp.236–239; Riley et al, *Regimental Records*, pp.754–756; *Fighting Spirit*, p.76. Swank and Marchand, 'Combat exhaustion'. Use of sleep medication, such as sodium amytal,

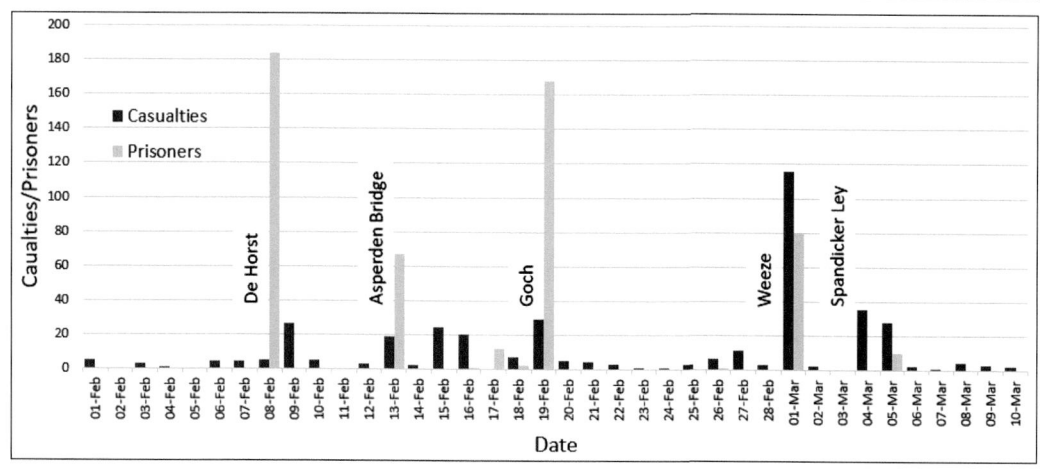

Figure 25: 4 Royal Welch Fusiliers casualties and prisoners during Veritable.

nary exhaustion, and how much they addressed the added grief and stress of battle exhaustion.[76] There are indications that the treatment between the Reichswald and Weeze did not address all the morale problems in 4 RWF, with staff fending off strident appeals for leave while sending deserving men on courses to give them a break. Meanwhile, the Battalion absorbed at least 48 replacements, half going to "A" Company who had been most 'heavily stonked and sniped' following the Goch attack.[77] This made the post-Goch "A" Company a particularly fragile mix of tired, traumatised veterans and replacements of unknown quality, which was why they stayed in reserve for the Weeze attack and were not deployed at all at Spandicker Ley.

As Figure 25 suggests, 4 RWF's losses consisted of those sustained in attacks (the five named points), attrition from indirect fire (larger unlabelled bars), and what could be called ambient casualties (the smaller bars before and during Veritable).[78] Indirect fire and ambient casualties must have sapped willpower and fed exhaustion, but the attacks mattered most because they required men to advance into danger. The average Veritable attack cost a battalion 10 percent of its fighting strength, and the cumulative effect of these losses is where the "is it worth it?" concept becomes useful.[79] When a soldier knows there is a one-in-ten chance he will be killed or wounded every time he attacks, his commitment will suffer; when he mourns the death or injury of one-in-ten of his friends after every attack, his resolve will loosen. Repeat this process enough times and it will change the "is it worth it?" calculation.

The calculation trickled up the layers of command, with several observers relating an "after you" spirit among formations during Veritable.[80] The consequences can also perhaps be glimpsed

---

gets only the briefest mention in historical sources: T. Copp, Review of *The Canadian Army and the Normandy Campaign*, by John English, *Canadian Historical Review*, 73 (4), 1992, pp.551–553.

76   This raises the concern that by hiding the supposed major symptom of weak morale, Richardson's faster return to duty may have forced poorly motivated men to find subtler ways to avoid combat.

77   4 RWF diary, 19 February. *Regimental Records* (p.755) suggests that on 21 February 4 RWF was 297 men short of establishment, 6 RWF 276, and 7 RWF 365. These figures do not tally with return sheets and are likely totals for the whole of Veritable.

78   Diary: summary sheets and part one orders.

79   In the 45 battles where reliable casualty figures could be determined, the average attacking battalion lost 9.84 percent of its fighting strength.

80   As when 43 Division handed Goch to 15 Div. 'G.I. Thomas was visibly pleased with his bargain, and I was sure his troops would be thankful to be spared the severe fighting.' Henniker, *Image*, p.236.

when the Sherwood Rangers were unobtainable at Spandicker Ley, when those Irish Guards tanks mysteriously went off air and bogged at Hamb, and in a dozen other actions where armour was seen to hang back from the fight. The infantry also seem to have become more cautious as Veritable progressed, with companies more likely to get pinned down in later actions, but infantry reticence is more difficult to spot than armour failing to arrive on time.[81] These are only glimpses, but it is reasonable to accept that repeated tactical failures eroded battle morale by making the chance of success appear too low and the blood price too high.

Conclusion

The British Army effectiveness debate could be characterised as an argument over the components of fighting power, with anti-British authors seeing weaknesses in the conceptual (how to fight) and morale (will to fight) components countered by reliance on the physical component (firepower and armoured mass). In contrast, pro-British authors see a conceptual and moral/morale improvement leading to less reliance on physical power. By examining the issue from a nearly-bottom-up perspective, previous chapters have exposed weaknesses in force design that prevented much of the conceptual improvement from being implemented, thereby making tactical failure more likely. Then, despite the inherent difficulties in measuring morale, this chapter has indicated how those failures compounded the effects of fatigue and stress, further reducing the chance of tactical success.

The relationship introduced in this chapter is therefore a partial reversal of the Colossal Cracks idea because the attempt to strike a heavy blow was so often counterproductive. Most battles in Veritable involved an intermediate combat intensity where set-piece attacks were too slow, but fluid advances-to-contact too weak. As we saw in Chapter 5, British doctrine was fixated on the extremes of deliberately slogging through a fixed defence or spontaneously swanning over country almost devoid of enemy. It was as if 21 Army Group's force design was built around having only two speed settings: a low grinder gear for breaking-in and high freewheeler for exploit and pursuit. But then British problems with command systems, tactical logistics and inter-arm cooperation made it difficult to engage a middle gear that would suit activity between these extremes.

From Materborn to Alpen, the transition cost of shifting gear from slog to swan was so great that German forces were able to form new fronts, making the swan inappropriate and forcing a reversion to slog. The result was a repeated failure to combine mass and velocity, and a series of disjointed partial successes that placed an unnecessarily high demand on troops, thereby upsetting the battle morale calculation. The psychological effect of failure is readily perceived but impossible to quantify, especially in retrospect. The reticence of primary sources and the complexity of collective stress, grief, fear, fatigue, guilt, and despair means accounts offer only hints of the "is it worth it?" calculation, but the logic seems undeniable.

As battle morale waned, casualties and privation changed units and helped to change the nature of the battles they fought. When 4 RWF launched their D-Day attack on De Horst, their battalion group was a cohesive, well-trained, combined arms team. They were attacking an objective all the officers had studied, and all the men had been briefed on. They were striking what was widely

---

81 Armoured regiments suffered horrific losses earlier in the war, the Sherwood Rangers saw more war than most, and their squadrons took 40 percent casualties during Veritable. SRY diary Feb-Mar; Lindsay, *Sherwood Rangers*, pp.149–153; CWGC. Infantry caution may be reflected in Figure 25 as attackers failed to close with defenders and therefore took more casualties (due to spending longer exposed to fire) and fewer prisoners, but attacker caution is currently inseparable from inter-arm cooperation and command system failures.

believed to be the final blow on the Reich, a blow expected to punch through the crust of the Siegfried Line then dash across the Rhine and into the heart of Germany. A very different 4 RWF crossed the Spandicker Ley 25 days later: their armour and much of their artillery was provided by strangers and since crossing the start line on 8 February they had suffered 295 infantry casualties, 59 percent of their fighting strength. Each company was a collection of half-trained strangers clustered round a nub of exhausted veterans and there was a danger that men would transition between these two extremes without experiencing Swank and Marchand's zone of 'maximum efficiency'. This unfortunate collective was attacking an ill-defined objective that none of their officers had seen in an ambiguous offensive that had dragged on for far too long.

We can assume that 4 Welch began Veritable as a cohesive unit too, but they never had chance to show it while stumbling around in the Reichswald or being battered at Starfish Wood and Alpen overlook. At the end of each action, all they had to show for their losses was another few hectares of splintered German forest.

It is no revelation that repeated costly attacks erode morale, but it is a phenomenon that is overlooked when histories rely on top-down sources, or when gross indicators of morale are too readily associated with the quality of individuals or organisations. The Welsh Division had a morale problem, but it was of a different nature to the problem Richardson suggested, and it was not the fault of the Division nor the men in it. The Division's force design meant it lacked a gear between slog and swan, and this prevented rapid manoeuvre, increased casualties and privation, reduced morale and created a corrosive feedback loop that required an extended period out of contact to remedy.

Centralised indicators of morale were useful to 21st Army Group because they alerted formations to potential problems. Commanders could then compare the alert to facts on the ground and decide whether the morale indicator reflected a failure to care for troops, a reasonable reaction to a hard fight, or a data processing blip, and then take corrective action. Historians can re-use these indicators as a handrail to explore morale and high-level policy, but interpretation below that level is problematic because command corrections are hidden from the historical record. The biggest problem with centralised indicators is that they encourage a top-down view of morale shaped on strategic and operational timescales. The unwarlike British soldier was certainly "browned off" by the campaign dragging on, but that was not the only story.[82] Centralised indicators say little about morale where it matters most, in combat.[83] The indicators therefore present a view of morale as something outside the remit of junior commanders, when in reality captains, colour sergeants and corporals fought the morale battle every day.

The battle morale concept is more applicable than top-down views which inevitably homogenise and become detached from the fighting arms. It is difficult to judge battle morale from a distance, but primary sources contain no evidence of British soldiers suffering from an intrinsic deficit of will, or even skill. Instead, the evidence points to their will being degraded and their skill diluted as they slogged through Veritable. Indeed, when their higher organisation provided the basic requirements of timely, accurate artillery and familiar armoured support, they beat the *Wehrmacht* every time. But as Veritable progressed, the problems with planning, tactical logistics, command systems and inter-arm cooperation created a succession of battles where the cost was high and the benefit low. As a result, when soldiers asked themselves "is it worth it?" the answer was much more likely to be "no".

---

82 Allport, *Browned off.*
83 Bielecki's central finding in 'British Infantry Morale during the Italian Campaign', passim.

Conclusion: Memory and Imagination

8 TO 10 MARCH – WESEL POCKET – MYTHS AND MINI MYTHS – HOW THEY FOUGHT – UNSEEN THINGS – BONEY AND BASIL – LESSONS FOR THE FUTURE

Historiography and Effectiveness

Veritable ended with a bang and a whimper. On the Allied side, 53 Division's relief coincided with a ponderous reorganisation as 2 Canadian Corps took on responsibility for the Wesel pocket. Thirty Corps was therefore denied the chance to reach Wesel, but Allied soldiers kept slogging forward to capture bridges that Allied aviators kept trying to destroy, eventually turning Wesel into a muddy pond.[1] On the morning of 10 March, having successfully evacuated all but a few hundred troops, *1. Fallschirm-Armee* blew the last bridge.[2] To add insult to injury, US troops simply walked to the broken bridges and claimed the symbolic victory while the Anglo-Canadian force was replanning its sweep of the emptied pocket.

In the end, Veritable's "forgotten victory" was closer to being an obscured failure because, although ultimately driven back across the Rhine, Schlemm's troops achieved their aim of delaying First Canadian Army. The delay lasted for far longer than Schlemm could have hoped and it stifled the true objective of 21st Army Group and 30 Corps, a rapid crossing at Wesel. That aim had always been partly obscured, but the longer the operation dragged on, the more Veritable's ambitions were retrospectively downgraded. It is tempting to speculate about the operational and strategic impact had Veritable been launched with a force design that was a better fit to 21st Army Group's enemy, ground, and technology. With less focus on mass and firepower and without a schism between British and Canadian plans, Veritable could have launched weeks earlier on harder ground and perhaps achieved surprise. Even without those advantages, a better application of artillery suppression, tactical logistics, command system design and armour-infantry cooperation would have reached Wesel more quickly, potentially seizing the bridges as hoped and putting the Allies over the Rhine six weeks earlier than the Plunder/Varsity crossings.

Ian Hamilton observed that 'On the actual day of battle naked truths may be picked up for the asking; by the following morning they have already begun to get into their uniforms.'[3] More

---

1   Bomber Command campaign diary, Mar 1945, nationalarchives.gov.uk.
2   52 Division ISUM 89. Meindl (NARA FMS B-093, p.20) has the bridges blown at 05:00; Stimpel, *Fallschirmtruppe* (pp.366, 375) has 04:00 and has the German defence close to collapse before the Allied reorganisation.
3   I. S. M. Hamilton, *A Staff Officers Scrap Book During the Russo-Japanese War* (London: Edward Arnold, 1907), v.

recently Steven Zaloga noted how, 'Famous battles become encrusted in myths and legends.'[4] There are many naked truths in Veritable's primary sources and picking them up then joining them together has shown how even this less-than-famous operation has become encrusted in myth. The strands of omission, obfuscation, and exaggeration in the Veritable core narrative include tanks sunk to their turret rings in the mud (actually one tank in a stream), 53 Division's 5,000 casualties in the Reichswald (actually under 1,000), and the operation ending on 26 February (10 March is the most appropriate date).[5] Then there are dozens of mundane mini myths, like the battery of 88s in Kranenburg (it was a lone gun), the troop of *Jagdpanther* captured on the 9th (none were encountered until the 10th), or Goch being captured on the 19th (it was the 21st).

Big or small, Veritable's myths gained traction because they aligned with the narrative of mines and mud, exaggerated the strength of the defence or the purity of the planning and thereby excused the lack of progress. Even the attrition and slow progress were partly illusion, with advance rates similar to those in Normandy and British units capturing defenders by the hundred when their force design allowed.[6] Progress only seemed more sluggish because commanders were constantly expecting mass and firepower to bring about a collapse from the rear and a return to the great swan of the previous August. But where the historiographic focus on Normandy's slow progress has created cycles of blame that eventually coalesced into an informed and quite balanced picture, Veritable's seeming drabness has allowed the mines and mud narrative to go unchallenged.

There is no hard evidence of a plot to hide the truth, more a congruence of convenient storylines. There were multiple instances of radio operators hearing only the armour and artillery officers who dominated the airwaves with their powerful radios and partial pictures of battle, then intelligence officers' best guesses and commanding officers' praise for their men, with this amalgamation topped off by Montgomery's nightly missives to Alanbrooke. That patchwork of parochial sources was compiled into the first wave of narrative by planners who only saw the ground after thousands of vehicles and artillery rounds had torn it to shreds. Later authors had little access to war diaries and communication logs, so cognitive "bias" drew them to the story sketched by the first wave of historiography.[7]

Historical research tends to be a top-down process because people usually take an interest in a whole war then drill down through campaign, operation, and battle. So, research usually begins with an unavoidably homogenised cultural-personal perspective (Montgomery embodying the

---

4   S. J. Zaloga, 'Debunking the Omaha Beach Legend: The Use of Armored "Funnies" on D-Day', *Journal of Military History*, 85, (Jan 2021), pp.134–162.

5   Casualty figure from J. Ellis, *The Sharp End of War: The Fighting Man in World War II* (London: David & Charles, 1980), p.169. Ellis adds that this was over nine days and claims it represents half the Division's casualties in Northwest Europe and half of 30 Corps' casualties in Veritable. The Division's figures in Bollard's *Team Spirit* gives 730 killed and wounded plus 450 sick and 180 exhaustion cases for a maximum of 1,360 for the 14 days from 7–21 February, which includes their time in the Reichswald and several forays outside it. As related in Chapter 8, 53 Division suffered more casualties in the following fortnight (920 + 410 + 430 = 1,760). More recently, the 5,000 in nine days was repeated in A. Beevor, *The Second World War* (London: Phoenix, 2012), Kindle 12781. The 5,000 seems to have its roots in Horrocks et al, *Corps Commander*, p.185.

6   R. L. Helmbold, 'A Compilation of Data on Advance in Land Combat Operations' (US Army Concepts Analysis Agency report, 1990), Annex A, pp.235–236. The advance rate also appears close to that in the 100 days of 1918. J. Boff, 'Combined Arms during the Hundred Days Campaign, August-November 1918', *War in History* 17(4), 2010, p.459.

7   This is no criticism of those authors. As noted previously, cognitive biases evolved as efficient ways to find meaning in data. The current author has suffered from the occasional ill effects of that efficiency, in the most extreme instance, spending weeks convinced there was a massive artillery fratricide near Afferden, only to find an illusion created by a diary typo and a fondness for revisionism. Most of this author's self-generated falsehoods were simpler confusions over casualties, timings or start lines.

British Way, for example) so even when authors identify tangible components of failure they are attributed to those cultural-personal characteristics rather than the prosaic interactions of force design. And then, whatever their specific interest, such histories tend to express what people at the top believed, or what they wanted others to believe. In this way, published histories usually hide the tactical detail that is of most value to soldiers and military analysts.

A top-down focus makes it difficult to apply the lessons of history because, even if they are valid, cultural-personal factors are extremely resistant to change. If the British Army expected to go to war next year, for example, it could not hope to change national and organisation culture or the personalities of its commanders and soldiers. However, the army could adapt its command systems to have a more appropriate balance of plan, direction, and influence, it could train to integrate artillery suppression with ground manoeuvre, it could incorporate tactical logistic constraints into mission planning and execution, and it could develop organisations that maximise the potential for close cooperation between infantry and armour. It would be difficult to implement these aspects of force design, but they are far more amenable to change than the intangibles that have dominated historical and topical debates on effectiveness.

Questions and Answers

This book opened with the question: 'How did British units and formations fight in Operation Veritable?' The answer has many facets, and these are reflected in the theme of each chapter. In Chapter 1, Veritable's vaunted planning was shown to be subject to weak intelligence and a curious bifurcation that suggests a schism between the Canadian and British headquarters. Later chapters showed how headquarters continued to generate untimely, almost outlandish schemes focused on distant objectives while seeming to ignore immediate tactical problems. Yet there was considerable variance. No plans completely survived contact with the enemy, but those that avoided detailed end states appear to have cost fewer British lives – and by capturing more defenders, cost fewer German lives too.[8] In Chapter 2, the (again vaunted) use of artillery firepower on D-Day was seen to be overkill that showed how much the army had forgotten how to achieve the 1918 "preventing" aspect of suppression. Later chapters showed how attacks could succeed with only 15 minutes' preparatory fire, but only if the assault came soon after. Attacks frequently failed because units did not, or could not, hug their fire plans.

In Chapter 3, the delayed breakthrough by 15 Division was shown to be more a function of tactical logistics than mines and mud, with the Division's problems exacerbated by artillery overkill and unnecessary armoured mass. Although later tactical logistic problems seemed less intense, this was largely because the accrued destruction of routes and the ungainly bulk of 30 Corps created operational scale problems that limited the forward accumulation of fire and mass.[9] In Chapter 4, the fumbled pass between 15 and 43 Division was shown to be due more to a dysfunctional command system than Horrocks's half-admitted mistake. This dysfunction persisted throughout the operation, with every division launching at least one attack that stumbled because it relied on centralised direction over radio nets that were known to be unworkable. Another aspect of inter-arm cooperation was examined in Chapter 5, which showed 52 Lowland Division's supposed flank protection task to be a bold attempt at regaining operational momentum. That attempt failed, in part, because of the golf bag conception of armoured support to infantry divisions, a problem

---

8   Quantification of this phenomenon was another of the side quests that could not fit in the current assessment.
9   Secondary sources (e.g., Whitakers' *Rhineland* and Copp's, *Brigade*) provide strong indications that Blockbuster, which had the time to accumulate mass and fire, suffered severe tactical logistics problems.

that was baked into 21st Army Group's organisational structure, leaving both arms dangerously exposed throughout Veritable.

The overlap of themes became explicit in Chapter 6, which challenged the narrative of armoured elan and urban attrition in Goch. Many of the problems in Goch came from airpower overkill and the northern operation's irrational planning process. Then tactical logistics unhinged the northern attack while the command system and the golf bag degraded coordination in both halves of the town. The interactive impact became clearer in Chapter 7, where force design factors combined to undermine performance in the fundamental roles that 21st Army Group was created to perform. From the edge of Weeze to the Bönninghardt plateau, an infantry division, an armoured brigade, and an armoured division were shown to be unsuited to breakthrough and breakout operations. This seems to have been repeated right across the area of operations. Chapter 8 capped all the previous chapters to show how this organisational inability to conduct manoeuvre warfare demanded an unnecessary reversion to a laborious slog that exhausted men, particularly the infantry, and upset the "is it worth it?" calculation of battle morale. It therefore showed how fundamental and correctable force design problems stacked up to undermine each component of fighting power.

The interaction of force design problems constantly created feedback loops during Veritable. Mass and firepower overkill drained tactical velocity, but then reduced operational tempo by demanding unnecessary quantities of munitions and machines. Reduced tempo exhausted men by leaving them exposed for longer than they were trained or equipped to endure, which further undermined team working and trust between armour and infantry, increasing the tendency for golf bag organisations to fight as separate arms, negating days of planning and making the carefully accrued mass yet more superfluous.[10] Concurrent with those loops, golf bag organisations strained the command system by attempting to combine untested radio nets and parochial doctrines, while demanding that supporting arms travel long distances across the operational area, unnecessarily eroding roads, men, and machines. (Recall 6 KOSB's armoured support doubling the road damage after dropping the Battalion on the Materborn Feature, or 8 Royal Scots armour doing the same in northern Goch, then multiply that effect across the operational area.) The resulting repetition of the break-in battle exhausted soldiers, and in so doing encouraged overworked commanders to double down on their fallback option: uncoordinated firepower and mass.

Meanwhile, fragile radio communications separated infantry and artillery, contributing to a high rate of fratricide. A Canadian study conducted during Veritable put the number of Allied casualties to friendly artillery at between seven and 21 percent of the total. The actions examined for the current assessment support splitting the difference at around 15 percent.[11] This figure is alarmingly close to the 19 percent attributed to German small arms, and considerably greater than the six percent benchmark for friendly fire casualties in a First World War barrage. Artillery fratricide was also a major factor in five of the failed attacks in the current assessment and, considering the tendency to underreport such events, was likely a factor in as many more. The high chance

---

10   The effect of fatigue on teamworking is under-researched (S. Banks, et al, 'Effects of fatigue on teams and their role in 24/7 operations', *Sleep Medicine Reviews*, 48, (2019)) but is familiar to trainers, who often see command teams unravel due to sleep loss. The loss of empathy (the basic ability to understand another's perspective) and the truncation of context are common and were likely part of the miscommunication that compounded Horrocks's "mistake" in Ch 4.

11   This is another of those tantalising glimpses mentioned earlier. The figures are the extremes presented in Brigadier E. C. Plow's study of munition fragments removed from casualties and could only be found in Appendix L of Copp's *Cinderella Army*. Copp and Buckley opt for 'as high as 19 percent'. Copp, *Cinderella Army*, pp.291, 338–340; Buckley, *Monty's Men*, p.272.

of fratricide very probably undermined the essential trust between infantryman and gunner, the coordination of fire and assault, and therefore the value of suppression.[12]

Late war written doctrine demanded local commanders chase opportunities to maintain momentum and espoused a form of command-by-influence, but the negative aspects of British force design conspired to prevent it, enforcing a mix of command using plan and direction.[13] So, when 227 Brigade secured Kranenburg, when 5 DCLI reached Nutterden, or when 1 Oxford Bucks reached the Spandicker Ley, combinations of the golf bag, tactical logistics, command system foibles, and exhaustion stifled the application of initiative. To exploit opportunities as doctrine espoused, local commanders needed to use engineers, armour, or infantry that they did not command and often could not speak to, or they needed to cancel a fire plan but lacked authority to do so. Complicated task organisation and fragile radio nets meant there were always unreachable components of the friendly force. So, in dozens of battles company commanders had to decide between following a fire plan that might fall on their own men or waiting for armour that might never arrive. This problem is more mundane but no less damaging than having the wrong command ethos.

Other loops are less visible to the historical record and can only be cautiously suggested here. The golf bag approach to an infantry division's organic assets seems to have been predicated on flawed assumptions about the mobility of tracked vehicles and the agility of radio-based command-by-direction. These flaws limited the effectiveness of the divisions' own mortars, tank destroyers, and engineers, but can be best illustrated through reference to machine-guns. The Bren was outmatched and often outnumbered by German weapons, but the Vickers was a division-controlled asset transported by carrier. The original concept of guns dashing to the point of need was undermined by congestion and communication difficulties, so the guns were rarely available when local counterattacks came. In most attacks, the Vickers was relegated to pre-planned indirect pepper pot fire. Perhaps the most telling limitation was that there was no capacity for a platoon or company to quickly arrange a fire support base for an assault, except by using the Bren, with its real and perceived inferiorities.[14]

Another less visible feedback loop began with formation reconnaissance units, which were so affected by poor deployability and perceived vulnerability that they were easily forced into bottlenecks that could be corked by a few men and a machine gun, as with 43 Recce on the Materborn Feature. During the whole month of Veritable, there appear to be only two examples of advances successfully led by formation reconnaissance and both were on bypassed flanks that the Germans had abandoned.[15] The reconnaissance troops in armoured regiments were similarly afflicted, but further degraded by golf bagging. Because armour usually supported an infantry brigade at short notice, there was little opportunity to use the regiment's reconnaissance troop. Meanwhile, infantry brigades and battalions made the detailed plans but had no officially designated reconnaissance

---

12 Contrary to the mines and mud narrative, the Canadian wounds study also found 4 percent of casualties were caused by the combination of mines and grenades, way behind German artillery, German small arms, and Allied artillery. J. B. Coates and J. C. Beyer (eds), *Wound Ballistics in World War II: Supplemented by Experiences in the Korean War* (Washington: Office of the Surgeon General, 1962) has mines accounting for 0 to 10 percent of total casualties depending on the sampling method. The battle descriptions for this assessment suggest the effect of mines on advance rates was marginal and appears no greater than in other operations.

13 For example, Montgomery, *Armoured Division in Battle*, passim.

14 The Bren issue was examined briefly in Chapter 5. For Vickers limitations see 'Machine Gun Platoon of WW2' at vickersmg.blog, and its roots in 1918 doctrine: War Office, *SS192 The Employment of Machine Guns, Part I, Tactical* (London: War Office, 1918), p.10.

15 52 Recce on the right flank after Weeze fell and 43 Recce on the left flank during Blockbuster.

element with which to explore routes and objectives. Early-war battalions used carrier platoons as fighting reconnaissance but long before Veritable their deployability and vulnerability usually relegated them to a resupply role.[16] At the same time, dismounted reconnaissance was a high-risk activity; as Major Brodie of 5 Black Watch noted, 'the very word patrol could send shivers down people's backs.'[17] Many units cultivated semi-elite patrol platoons, but tired soldiers found the task particularly daunting, so exhaustion helped to rob units of their most trusted source of information, creating another negative cycle.[18]

Reconnaissance problems also collided with German adaptation, notably the devaluing of signals intelligence as the *Wehrmacht* increased its use of civilian telephone networks. Then, while Allied air supremacy made aerial reconnaissance much easier, it was weather dependent and German forces got better at hiding. Even when German units were detected from above, it could be days between sighting and report, especially when waiting for aerial photography to be integrated into defence overprints. Hence, plans were frequently based on the mixture of assumption, rumour, and the "map recce" that caused so many of the problems around Afferden and Weeze. Units often attacked blind, effectively using their main force as reconnaissance, and having been mauled so often (forward companies usually suffered the worst casualties) this increased the suppressive power of a few well-placed machine-guns and anti-armour weapons.

These interacting problems exacerbated the slog or swan dilemma. With sufficient preparation time 21st Army Group's deliberate break-in battles were usually successful even against prepared defences in unfavourable terrain. Alternatively, with the right weather, clear roads, and disheartened stragglers as opposition, British forces could exploit and pursue at an impressive rate. But with no middle gears suitable for fluid fighting against formed enemy in close terrain, operations mutated into the multitude of hasty break-in battles that epitomised Veritable after D-Day. Then breakout and exploit/pursue operations, like that south of Weeze, fell short due to the need for centrally controlled reorganisation to shift gear from slog to swan and back again. That awkward gear change also made it more difficult for British units to win the civil engineering arms race so, while British sappers performed remarkable feats to cross obstacles, 21st Army Group's force design gave German pioneers more time to lay their traps.

Historians rarely have the time or sources to examine these interactions, and so the effectiveness debate has been unavoidably shallow. The anti-British author, with access only to top-down criticisms and some bottom-up grumbling, attributed poor British Army performance to a national malaise: bad commanders, bad soldiers, or both. Later pro-British authors, with access to official narratives and the correspondence of generals, found 21st Army Group countered poor tactical technique and questionable morale with superior mass, firepower and, by the time of Veritable, something akin to operational art.[19] The more detailed tactical analysis underpinning the current assessment suggests this argument has missed the fundamental problem because it has been based on data unsuited to assessing tactical matters. Rather than commanders or soldiers being ineffective, flaws in force design prevented them from achieving their collective potential.

---

16 The main exception is the Wasp, but primary sources barely mention them, as with 10 HLI in Kranenburg.
17 R. Grant, *51st Highland Division at War*, p.111.
18 The author was alerted to this phenomenon by John Cotterill, who developed the theory through his own soldiering experience and conversations with veterans. A similar feedback loop is central to T. Ashworth, *Trench Warfare 1914–1918: The Live and Let Live System* (London: Pan, 2000), passim. Patrolling for the sake of another formation must have been particularly unpopular and ineffective (e.g., the 51 Division reports before the 53 Division attack on Weeze).
19 Buckley, *Monty's*, pp.296–303 also includes engineering and medicine, both of which were difficult to assess here but appear to have been excellent given their logistic and command system constraints.

Memory and Imagination

The roots of the British Army's force design problems stretch back beyond the practical limits of root cause analysis, but there are repeated links to the last years of the First World War, and these all seem related to what Fuller described as 'a clash between two schools of thought, one relying on memory and the other on imagination.'[20] In 1916 tank tactics might have been hampered by a lack of imagination as Fuller claimed, but many of the force design problems in Veritable stemmed from a post-1918 glut of imagination untempered by memory of what worked and how it worked. Inter-war technophilia had the bomber, the tank and the radio message always getting through. The details of how artillery suppressed were forgotten and, one suspects, the details of infantry-armour cooperation, planning, tactical logistics and command systems were forgotten too. Artisan experience was pushed to the fringes by eloquent strategic theorising.

There were many extensions of Fuller's Plan 1919 concept (examined in Chapter 5) but one of the most illuminating is Liddell Hart's *The Future of Infantry*, which proposed one light tank for every four infantrymen, and a third of the infantry mounted in carriers.

> While these motorized units would naturally form a longer column than present units when in movement, they would in reality be shorter and so easier to move. It should always be remembered that military movement is a space-time problem. "Road-space" in the practical sense is not a question of the length of road that a unit occupies at any moment but of the <u>time during which</u> it is occupied.[21]

This instance of imagination unfettered by memory wished away anti-armour weapons, competent resistance, terrain bottlenecks, damage to highways, the logistic tail, rest, and maintenance. It imagined swanning with constant forward movement but had no slogging and nothing between the two extremes. Ironically, Liddell Hart's concept was aimed at reducing the burden on the infantry but, when taken to extremes, combined with artillery overkill, and applied in real terrain between Nijmegen and Wesel, it had the opposite effect, forcing the infantry to spend days digging out bogged vehicles or waiting in traffic jams.

The inter-war victory of imagination over memory skewed the evolution of armour and infantry organisations that put 21st Army Group into Northwest Europe with the golf bag problem baked into its force design. Judging by formations' efforts to develop semi-permanent associations this was a known problem, but its full impact was not appreciated. There were enough tanks available to give each infantry division at least one permanent armoured regiment but this seemingly obvious solution was not adopted before Veritable because it would have involved the unimaginably challenging task of a major restructuring in contact. In this light, Pamphlet 63's equivocation and Montgomery's rebranding of armoured brigades seem more like a sensible balance between aspirations and achievability. However, it remains a mystery why the New Model divisions lost their armour in 1943 rather than have a less radical restructure that allowed infantry and armour to retain familiar support from the other arm.[22]

---

20   Fuller, *Memoirs*, vii.
21   B. H. Liddell Hart, *The Future of Infantry* (London: Faber & Faber, 1933), p.47, original emphasis.
22   Dividing the independent Armoured Brigades would give one regiment per inf div. To get two regts per Division would require two Armoured divs be disbanded. This author could find no objective assessment of why the New Model divisions lost their tanks but did not really know where to look. The difficulty of a major change in command, structures, training, and logistics while in contact can be glimpsed in T. Farrell, F. Osinga and J. A. Russell (eds), *Military Adaptation in Afghanistan* (Stanford: University Press, 2013), passim.

The same unfettered enthusiasm was applied to command systems. Noting the limits of command-by-plan, the Kirke Report's recommendations on 'How to Convert a *"Break In"* into a *"Break Through"*' included wider adoption of decentralised command-by-influence. Yet this was only presented as an interim measure, as it was 'not a satisfactory substitute for the continuous control from above which constitutes the difference between generalship and a mere dog fight; between reinforcing success and hammering away at failure in the manner so adversely commentated upon in the Official Histories of the War.'[23] And so, despite identifying problems with radio frequency interference when only a handful of radios were deployed, the Kirke Report proposed widespread adoption of radio as the means of enabling command-by-direction. As with mechanising to increase mobility or the psychological effects of artillery bombardment, radio was a sound technological solution that was taken beyond the point of diminishing returns to a state where combat effectiveness was degraded by having too much of a good thing. The imagination of theorists and technology advocates was allowed to override practitioners' memory of field conditions and the knowable limitations of radio networks (or artillery fire or tracked vehicles). Fuller, Liddell Hart and the committees responsible for British force design often seem to have assumed the British Army would never fight a competent enemy in Northwest Europe, or in winter.

Outcomes

Although this book has been necessarily critical of the British Army, it is the impersonal criticism born of root cause analysis, it being easier to see flaws than perfection. The criticism is neither anti-British nor anti-Canadian and it is hoped the assessment shows the pro- and anti- arguments to be irrelevant constraints on objectivity. German and American armies experienced similar problems, and while they seem to have suffered less, a more detailed analysis would be needed to determine how much of this seeming was a reality, and how much can be attributed to superior post-war public relations.

This assessment has detected many tangible aspects of British Army force design because it benefitted from access to multiple primary sources that were practically unreachable for earlier generations of researchers. The assessment also benefitted from having the time for mistakes to be made and corrected, *though errors no doubt remain*. Although the assessment has dug deeper into tactical events than many previous studies, most of the Veritable battles could not be analysed, and many that were analysed could not fit the word count. Even so, the written product contains hundreds of frustrating contractions of tactical events, with almost every sentence leaving something unsaid. Likewise, the theme of each chapter could easily expand to fill a PhD project, without escaping the bounds of Veritable. Dozens of smaller questions remain unexplored because sources provide only glimpses of artisan experience, such as armoured flamethrower use, infiltration tactics, unit reinforcement, field craft training, or the arcane art of the signaller. Meanwhile, sources relating to higher headquarters, tactical air, medical services, combat engineering, 2 Canadian Corps, *1. Fallschirm-Armee* and the German civilian population have been detected but barely explored due to time constraints.

Yet, despite its restrictions, the approach used in *Slog or Swan* has exposed the limitations of Veritable's core narrative, suggested a more reliable alternative, and produced a richer picture of British Army effectiveness. By examining an operation from near the bottom and using the most complete and consistent primary source data available, this assessment has uncovered the mechanism that forced the British Army to slog through Operation Veritable. It is an approach to studying effectiveness that should be applied to other theatres, armies, and conflicts.

---

23 Kirke Report, pp.16–17. Note reference to the middle years of the war; later mobility seems to have been forgotten.

Bibliography

Primary Sources

National Archives War Diaries and Communication Logs
WO 171/346, 4076 & 4077, 30 Corps "G" Branch
WO 171/4103 & 4104, Guards Armoured Division
WO 171/4129 & 4130, 3 British Division
WO 171/4194, 15 Scottish Division
WO 171/4197, 15 Division HQRA
WO 171/4198, 15 Division HQRE
WO 171/4199, 15 Scottish Reconnaissance Regiment
WO 171/4200, 15 Division Signals
WO 171/4201, 15 Division Royal Army Service Corps
WO 171/4206, 4207 & 4208, 43 Wessex Division
WO 171/4215, 43 Reconnaissance Regiment
WO 171/4245, 51 Highland Division
WO 171/4260, 52 Lowland Division
WO 171/4264, 52 Division HQRA
WO 171/4276 & 4277, 53 Welsh Division
WO 171/4281, 53 Reconnaissance Regiment
WO 171/4282 & 4283, 53 Division HQRA
WO 171/4297, 79 Armoured Division
WO 171/4318, 5 Guards Armoured Brigade
WO 171/4321, 6 Guards Armoured [formerly Tank] Brigade
WO 171/4327, 8 Armoured Brigade
WO 171/4357, 32 Guards Brigade
WO 171/4363, 34 Armoured [formerly Tank] Brigade
WO 171/4366, 44 Lowland Brigade
WO 171/4368, 46 Highland Brigade
WO 171/4384, 71 Infantry Brigade
WO 171/4389, 129 Infantry Brigade
WO 171/4391, 130 Infantry Brigade
WO 171/4406, 152 Infantry Brigade
WO 171/4409, 153 Infantry Brigade
WO 171/4412, 154 Infantry Brigade
WO 171/4413, 155 Infantry Brigade
WO 171/4417, 156 Infantry Brigade
WO 171/4420, 157 Highland Light Infantry Brigade
WO 171/4423, 158 North Wales Brigade
WO 171/4428, 160 South Wales Brigade
WO 171/4437, 214 Infantry Brigade
WO 171/4440, 227 Highland Brigade

BIBLIOGRAPHY

WO 171/4685, 4th/7th Royal Dragoon Guards (4/7 DG)
WO 171/4687, 22nd Dragoons (22 Dgns)
WO 171/4691, 13th/18th Royal Hussars (Queen Mary's Own) (13/18 H)
WO 171/4696, 2nd Derbyshire Yeomanry
WO 171/4702, 1st Lothians and Border Yeomanry (1 Lothians)
WO 171/4704, Nottinghamshire (Sherwood Rangers) Yeomanry (SRY)
WO 171/4713, 9th Battalion, Royal Tank Regiment (9 RTR)
WO 171/4717, 107th Regiment, Royal Armoured Corps (King's Own) (107 RAC)
WO 171/4718, 141st Regiment, Royal Armoured Corps (The Buffs) (141 RAC)
WO 171/4721, 147th Regiment, Royal Armoured Corps (147 RAC)
WO 171/4722, 49th Armoured Personnel Carrier Regiment, (49 APC)
WO 171/4784, 198 (Anti-Tank) Battery (Self-Propelled) (198 SP AT Bty)
WO 171/4824, 79th Field Regiment RA
WO 171/4825, 80th Field Regiment RA
WO 171/4826, 81st Field Regiment RA
WO 171/4844, 133rd Field Regiment RA
WO 171/4952, 102nd Light Anti-Aircraft Regiment (102 LAA).
WO 171/5141, 1st (Armoured) Battalion, Coldstream Guards (1 CG).
WO 171/5142, 4th (Tank) Battalion, Coldstream Guards (4 CG).
WO 171/5143, 5th Battalion, Coldstream Guards (5 CG).
WO 171/5144, 1st (Motor) Battalion, Grenadier Guards (1 GG).
WO 171/5145, 2nd (Armoured) Battalion, Grenadier Guards (2 GG)
WO 171/5146, 4th (Tank) Battalion, Grenadier Guards (4 GG)
WO 171/5147, 2nd (Armoured) Battalion, Irish Guards (2 IG)
WO 171/5148, 3rd Battalion, Irish Guards (3 IG)
WO 171/5149, 2nd Battalion, Scots Guards (2 SG)
WO 171/5150, 3rd (Tank) Battalion, Scots Guards (3 SG)
WO 171/5152, 2nd (Armoured Reconnaissance) Battalion, Welsh Guards (2 WG)
WO 171/5153, 2nd Battalion, Argyll and Sutherland Highlanders (2 A&SH)
WO 171/5154, 7th Battalion, Argyll and Sutherland Highlanders (7 A&SH)
WO 171/5158, 1st Battalion, Black Watch (Royal Highland Regiment) (1 BW)
WO 171/5159, 5th Battalion, Black Watch (Royal Highland Regiment) (5 BW)
WO 171/5160, 7th Battalion, Black Watch (Royal Highland Regiment) (7 BW)
WO 171/5164, 5th Battalion, Queen's Own Cameron Highlanders (5 Cam H)
WO 171/5166, 6th Battalion, Cameronians (Scottish Rifles) (6 Cams)
WO 171/5168, 9th Battalion, Cameronians (Scottish Rifles) (9 Cams)
WO 171/5174, 4th Battalion, Dorsetshire Regiment (4 Dorset)
WO 171/5175, 5th Battalion, Dorsetshire Regiment (5 Dorset)
WO 171/5178 & 5179, 5th Battalion, Duke of Cornwall's Light Infantry (5 DCLI)
WO 171/5191, 1st Battalion, Glasgow Highlanders (Highland Light Infantry) (1 Glas H)
WO 171/5193, 2nd Battalion, Glasgow Highlanders (Highland Light Infantry) (2 Glas H)
WO 171/5196, 1st Battalion, Gordon Highlanders (1 Gordons)
WO 171/5197, 2nd Battalion, Gordon Highlanders (2 Gordons)
WO 171/5198, 5th/7th Battalion, Gordon Highlanders (5/7 Gordons)
WO 171/5200, 7th Battalion, Hampshire Regiment (7 Hamps)
WO 171/5202, 1st Battalion, Highland Light Infantry (1 HLI)
WO 171/5203, 5th Battalion, Highland Light Infantry (5 HLI)
WO 171/5204, 6th Battalion, Highland Light Infantry (6 HLI)
WO 171/5207, 10th Battalion, Highland Light Infantry (10 HLI)

WO 171/5213, 12th Battalion, King's Royal Rifle Corps (Queen's Westminsters) (12 KRRC)
WO 171/5215, 4th Battalion, King's Own Scottish Borderers (4 KOSB)
WO 171/5216, 5th Battalion, King's Own Scottish Borderers (5 KOSB)
WO 171/5217, 6th Battalion, King's Own Scottish Borderers (6 KOSB)
WO 171/5224, 1st Battalion, East Lancashire Regiment (1 East Lancs)
WO 171/5234, 1st (Machine Gun) Battalion, Manchester Regiment (1 Manch)
WO 171/5238, 7th (Machine Gun) Battalion, Manchester Regiment (7 Manch)
WO 171/5245, 2nd Battalion, Monmouthshire Regiment (2 Mons)
WO 171/5253, 1st Battalion, Oxfordshire and Buckinghamshire Light Infantry (1 Oxf Bucks)
WO 171/5258, 8th Battalion, Royal Scots (Royal Regiment) (8 RS)
WO 171/5259, 7th/9th (Highlanders) Battalion, Royal Scots (7/9 RS)
WO 171/5262, 4th/5th Battalion, Royal Scots Fusiliers (4/5 RSF)
WO 171/5263, 6th Battalion, Royal Scots Fusiliers (6 RSF)
WO 171/5267, 2nd Battalion, Seaforth Highlanders (2 Seaforth)
WO 171/5268, 5th Battalion, Seaforth Highlanders (5 Seaforth)
WO 171/5270, 7th Battalion, Seaforth Highlanders (7 Seaforth)
WO 171/5271, 4th Battalion, Somerset Light Infantry (4 SLI)
WO 171/5272, 7th Battalion, Somerset Light Infantry (7 SLI)
WO 171/5281, 4th Battalion, Royal Welch Fusiliers (4 RWF)
WO 171/5283, 6th Battalion, Royal Welch Fusiliers (6 RWF)
WO 171/5284, 7th Battalion, Royal Welch Fusiliers (7 RWF|)
WO 171/5286, 4th Battalion, Welch Regiment (4 Welch)
WO 171/5287, 1st/5th Battalion, Welch Regiment (1/5 Welch)
WO 171/5290, 4th Battalion, Wiltshire Regiment (4 Wilts)
WO 171/5291, 5th Battalion, Wiltshire Regiment (5 Wilts)
WO 171/5292, 1st Battalion, Worcestershire Regiment (1 Worc)
WO 171/5317 & 5318, 6th Assault Regiment, Royal Engineers
WO 171/5325, 81st Assault Squadron, Royal Engineers
WO 171/5329, 284th Squadron, Royal Engineers
WO 205/9, 21 Army Group, Concerning Operations 'VERITABLE' and 'GRENADE'
WO 205/247, 21 Army Group Future Operations Planning
WO 205/954, 30 Corps daily diary of events
WO 205/955, Operation Veritable: 15 Division wireless logs
WO 205/956, Operation Veritable: 43 Division wireless logs
WO 205/957, Operation Veritable: 51 Division operations logs
WO 205/958, Operation Veritable: 53 Division operations logs

Unpublished Post-Operation Reports and Operational Research
CAB 44/258 & CAB 44/257, Harris, G.W. 'Liberation Campaign North-West Europe: The Battle of the Rhineland' Parts I and Part II
CAB 44/312, Canadian Military Headquarters, 'Memorandum on Rhineland' 1956.
CAB 80/77/19, Anon, 'Fire Support of Seaborne Landings Against a Heavily Defended Coast. Summary of a Report by an Inter-Service Committee.' 1943
CAB 106/974, 21 Army Group, 'Report on Operation "Blackcock"'
CAB 106/991, Anon, 'Memorandum: Operation Veritable.' MORU, October 1946
WO 205/952a, 'Operations of 21 Army Group, 6 June 1944 – 5 May 1945'
WO 205/961, 34 Armd Bde, 'Seven days fighting through the Reichswald'
WO 205/972a, Notes on the Operations of 21 Army Group
WO 205/1164, Anon, 'The Morale Effects of Artillery' MORU Memorandum No. 7, 1946

WO 223/94, 53 Recce Regt, 'Operation "Veritable"'
WO 232/38, Department of Tactical Investigation, 'Employment of tanks with infantry: operational reports; radio communications reports and trials'
WO 291/1331, Johnson, P. 'Effect of counter-battery fire in Operation Veritable' ORS 2 Report No. 29, April 1945
WO 291/2316, Balchin, N.M. 'Some Aspects of Psychological Warfare', War Office, 1945

Award Citations
WO 373/53/398, DCM citation, Sargeant Telfor
WO 373/53/461, MC citation, Major Murray
WO 373/53/483, MM citation, Lance Corporal Whittaker
WO 373/52/698, MC citation, Lieutenant Hands
WO 373/53/738, MC citation, Major Brodie
WO 373/53/740, DSO citation, Lieutenant Colonel Bramwell
WO 373/53/761, MC citation, Major Fife
WO 373/53/764, MC citation, Major Tinniswood
WO 373/53/787, MM citation, Sargeant Campbell
WO 373/53/810, MM citation, Fusilier Henderson
WO 373/53/813, MM citation, Private Lindie
WO 373/54/436, MM citation Lance Corporal Hanna
WO 373/54/940, MM citation, Guardsman Veale

Books and Published Pamphlets

Addison, P. and Calder, D. (eds), *Time to Kill: The Soldier's Experience of War in the West 1939–1945* (London: Pimlico, 1997)
Advocate, *From Normandy to the Baltic: The Story of the 44th Lowland Infantry Brigade of the 15th Scottish Division from D Day to the End of the War in Europe* (Germany: Wasers, 2017 [1945])
Allport, A., *Browned off and Bloody-minded: The British Soldier goes to War* (London: Yale, 2015)
Anon, *A Short History of the 6th (Caernarvon and Anglesey) Battalion the Royal Welch Fusiliers, North West Europe, June 1944 to May 1945* (Caernarvon: Evans, 1946)
Anon, *An Account of the Operations of Second Army in Europe 1944–1945, Vol. 2* (Germany: HQ Second Army, 1945), WO 205/972c
Anon, *History of The East Lancashire Regiment in the War 1939–1945* (Manchester: Rawson, 1953)
Anon, *Report of Signal Division Supreme Headquarters Allied Expeditionary Force in Operation "Overlord"* (Germany: Publisher unknown, 1945)
Anon, *The 8th Armoured Brigade, 1939–1945* (Hanover: Publisher unknown, 1946)
Anon, *The History of Headquarters Royal Artillery, 52nd Lowland Division during the German War, 1939–1945* (Delbruck: Publisher unknown, 1945)
Anon, *The Wiltshire Regiment in the Second World War – 5th Battalion* (Salisbury: Rifles Museum, 2011)
Anon, *War History of the 4th Battalion, King's Own Scottish Borderers, 1939–1945* (Halle: KOSB, 1946)
Archer, L. and Haasler, T., *Sturmtiger: The Combat History of Sturmmörser Kompanies 1001–1002* (Old Heathfield: Panzerwrecks, 2021)
Ashworth, T., *Trench Warfare 1914–1918: The Live and Let Live System* (London: Pan, 2000).
Australian Army Research Centre, *Urban Warfare: A Practitioners Annotated Bibliography* (Canberra: AARC, 2021)

Babington Macaulay, T., *The History of England from the Accession of James II* (Philadelphia: Porter & Coates, 1855)

Baggaley, J. R. P., *The 6th (Border) Battalion The King's Own Scottish Borderers 1939–1945* (Germany: Publisher unknown, 1945)

Bailey, J. R. A., *Field Artillery and Firepower* (Oxford: Military Press, 1989)

Barclay, C. N., *The History of the 53rd (Welsh) Division in the Second World War* (London: Clowes, 1955)

Barclay, C. N., *The History of the Cameronians (Scottish Rifles), Vol. III. 1933–1946* (London: Sifton Praed, 1957)

Baynes, J. C. M., *Morale: A Study of Men and Courage. The Second Scottish Rifles at the Battle of Neuve Chapelle 1915* (London: Cassell, 1967)

Beale, P., *Tank Tracks: 9th Battalion Royal Tank Regiment at War 1940–45* (Stroud: Budding Books, 1995)

Beevor, A., *The Second World War* (London: Phoenix, 2012)

Beevor, A., *Arnhem: The Battle for the Bridges, 1944* (London: Viking, 2019)

Bercuson, D. J., *Battalion of Heroes: The Calgary Highlanders in World War II* (Calgary: Empire, 1994)

Biddle, S. D., *Military Power: Explaining Victory and Defeat in Modern Battle* (Princeton: University Press, 2004)

Bidwell, S. and Graham, D., *Fire-Power. The British Army Weapons and Theories of War 1904–1945* (Barnsley: Pen & Sword, 2004 [1982]).

Blake, G., *Mountain and Flood. The History of the 52nd (Lowland) Division, 1939–1946* (Glasgow: Jackson, 1950).

Bolland, A. D., *Team Spirit: The Administration of an Infantry Division during "Operation Overlord"* (Aldershot: Gale & Polden, 1948)

Borthwick, A., *Battalion: A British Infantry Unit's actions from El Alamein to the Elbe. 1942–1945* (London: Baton Wicks, 2001 [1946]).

Bosch, H., *Der Zweite Weltkrieg zwischen Rhein und Maas* (Geldern: District Historical Association, 1977)

Brander, A. M., *The Royal Scots (The Royal Regiment)* (London: Leo Cooper, 1975)

British Army of the Rhine, *Administrative History of 21 Army Group* (Hanover: Publisher unknown, 1945)

British Army of the Rhine, *Battlefield Tour, Operation Veritable. 30 Corps Operations Between the Rivers Maas and Rhine, 8–10 February 1945.* (Germany: BAOR, 1947), WO 106/5846

British Army of the Rhine, *Royal Engineers Battlefield Tour: The Seine to the Rhine* (Hanover: BAOR, 1947)

Buckley, J. D., *British Armour in the Normandy Campaign 1944* (London: Routledge, 2004)

Buckley, J. D., *Monty's Men: The British Army and the Liberation or Europe, 1944–45* (New Haven CT: Yale, 2014)

Caddick-Adams, P., *1945: Victory in the West* (London: Penguin, 2022)

Carver, M., *Out of Step: The Memoirs of Field Marshal Lord Carver* (London: Penguin, 1990)

Christopherson S. and Holland, J. (ed.), *An Englishman at War: The Wartime Diaries of Stanley Christopherson, DCO MC TD, 1939–45* (London, Corgi: 2020)

Clark, L., *Arnhem. Jumping the Rhine 1944 and 1945* (London: Headline, 2009)

Clark, L., *Orne Bridgehead* (Stroud: Sutton, 2004)

Coates, J.B. and Beyer J.C. (eds), *Wound Ballistics in World War II: Supplemented by Experiences in the Korean War* (Washington: Office of the Surgeon General, 1962)

Colvin, T., *The Noise of Battle: The British Army and the Last Breakthrough Battle West of the Rhine, February-March 1945* (Solihull: Helion, 2016)

Cook, K. S. (ed.) *Social Exchange Theory* (London: Sage, 1987)
Copp, T., *Cinderella Army: The Canadians in Northwest Europe, 1944–1945* (Toronto: University Press, 2006)
Copp, T., *Fields of Fire: The Canadians in Normandy* (Toronto: University Press, 2003)
Copp, T. (ed.), *Montgomery's Scientists. Operational Research in Northwest Europe. The Work of No.2 Operational Research Section with 21st Army Group June 1944 to July 1945* (Waterloo ON: Laurier Centre, 2000)
Copp, T., *The Brigade. The Fifth Canadian Infantry Brigade in World War II* (Mechanicsburg: Stackpole, 2007)
Copp T. and Vogel, R., *Maple Leaf Route: Victory.* (Alma OT: Maple Leaf Route, 1988)
Courcy, J. de, *The History of The Welch Regiment 1919–1951* (Cardiff: Western Mail & Echo, 1952)
Cowper, J. M., *The King's Own: The Story of a Royal Regiment, Vol. III. 1914–1950* (Aldershot: Regimental Association, 1957).
Creveld, M., *Supplying War: Logistics from Wallenstein to Patton* (Cambridge: University Press, 2004)
Creveld, M., Brower K. S. and Canby, S. L., *Air Power and Maneuver Warfare* (Montgomery AL: Air University, 1994)
Crow, D., *British and Commonwealth Armoured Formations (1919–46)* (Windsor: Profile, 1972)
Cuthbert, S.J., *We Shall Fight in the Streets* (Aldershot: Gale & Polden, 1942)
Czerwinski, T., *Coping with the Bounds: Speculations on Nonlinearity in Military Affairs* (Washington DC: Command & Control Research Program, 1998)
D'Este, C., *Decision in Normandy* (London: Harper Collins, 1983)
Darby, H. and Cunliffe, M., *A Short History of 21 Army Group* (Aldershot: Gale & Polden, 1949)
Delaney, D. E., *Corps Commanders: Five British and Canadian Generals at War, 1939–45* (Vancouver: UBC Press, 2011)
Department of the Army, *FM 100-2-1 The Soviet Army: Operations and Tactics* (Washington: Army, 1984)
Development, Concepts and Doctrine Centre, *Future of Command and Control*, (Swindon: DCDC, 2017)
Development, Concepts and Doctrine Centre, *Understanding and Intelligence* (Shrivenham: DCDC, 2011)
Dick, C. J., *From Victory to Stalemate: The Western Front, Summer 1944* (Lawrence KS: University Press, 2016)
Dickson, P. D., *A Thoroughly Canadian General: a biography of General H.D.G. Crerar* (Toronto: University Press, 2008)
DiMarco, L. A., *Concrete Hell: Urban Warfare from Stalingrad to Iraq* (New York: Osprey, 2012)
Directorate General of Development and Doctrine, *Operations* (Warminster: DGD&D, 1994).
Dupuy, T. N., *Future Wars: The World's Most Dangerous Flashpoints* (London: Sidgwick & Jackson, 1992)
Doubler, M.D., *Busting the Bocage: American Combined Armed Operations in France, 6 June – 31 July 1944* (Fort Leavenworth: Combat Studies Institute, 1988).
Dyson, S., *Tank Twins*, (Barnsley: Leo Cooper, 2004).
"EGYPTFORCE", *Street Fighting for Junior Officers*, (London: Publisher unknown, 1919)
Ellis, J., *Brute Force: Allied Strategy and Tactics in The Second World War* (London: Deutsch, 1990)
Ellis, J., *The Sharp End of War: The Fighting Man in World War II* (London: David & Charles, 1980)
Ellis, L. F., *Victory in the West. Vol. II* (London: HMSO, 1968)
Ellis, L. F., *Welsh Guards at War* (Aldershot: Gale & Polden, 1946)
Elstob, P., *Battle of the Reichswald* (London: Macdonald, 1971)

Erskine, D., *The Scots Guards 1919–1955* (London: Clowes, 1956)
Essame, H., *The 43rd Wessex Division at War 1944–1945* (London: Clowes, 1952)
Farrell, C., *Reflections 1939–1945: A Scots Guards Officer in Training and War* (Edinburgh: Pentland Press, 2000)
Farrell, T., Osinga F. and Russell, J.A. (eds), *Military Adaptation in Afghanistan* (Stanford: University Press, 2013)
Fennell, J., *Fighting the People's War: The British and Commonwealth Armies and the Second World War* (Cambridge: University Press, 2019)
Fitzgerald, D. J. L., *History of the Irish Guards in the Second World War* (Aldershot: Gale & Polden, 1949)
Fletcher, D., *Sherman Crab Flail Tank* (Oxford: Osprey, 2007)
Fletcher, D., *The Great Tank Scandal: British Armour in the Second World War: Part 1* (London: HMSO, 1989)
Ford, K., *A Luftwaffe General: General der Fallschirmtruppe Alfred Schlemm* (Southampton: Self-published, 2018)
Ford, K., *Assault on Germany: The Battle for Geilenkirchen* (Newton Abbot: David & Charles, 1989)
Ford, K., *The Rhineland 1945: The Last Killing Ground in the West* (Botley: Osprey, 2000)
Forbes, P., *The Grenadier Guards in the War of 1939–1945* (Aldershot: Gale & Polden, 1949)
Forester, C. S., *The Good Shepherd* (London: Four Square, 1955)
Forrester, C., *Monty's Functional Doctrine: Combined Arms Doctrine in British 21st Army Group in Northwest Europe, 1944–45* (Solihull: Helion, 2015)
Fraser, D., *And We Shall Shock Them: The British Army in the Second World War* (London: Hodder & Stoughton, 1983)
French, D., *Raising Churchill's Army. The British Army and the War Against Germany 1919–1945* (Oxford: University Press, 2000)
Fuller, J. F. C., *Memoirs of an Unconventional Soldier* (London: Nicholson & Watson, 1936).
Gee, J. W., *Wingspan: The Recollections of a Bomber Pilot* (Unknown: Self-published, 1988).
Gill, R. and Graves, J., *Club Route in Europe: The story of 30 Corps in the European Campaign* (Hanover: 30 Corps, 1946)
Glasgow Highlanders Benevolent Fund, *Concise Official History: 2nd Battalion the Glasgow Highlanders* (Lubeck: Glasgow Highlanders, 1946)
Grant, R., *The 51st Highland Division at War* (Shepperton: Ian Allan, 1977)
Greenwood, T., *D-Day to Victory* (London: Simon & Schuster, 2012)
Guderian, H. G., *From Normandy to the Ruhr: With the 116th Panzer Division in World War II* (Bedford PA: AUSA, 2001)
Gunning, H., *Borderers in Battle. The War Story of The King's Own Scottish Borderers 1939–1945* (Edinburgh: Martin, 1948)
Hamilton, I. S. M., *A Staff Officers Scrap Book During the Russo-Japanese War*, (London: Edward Arnold, 1907)
Hamilton, N., *Monty: The Battles of Field Marshal Bernard Montgomery* (London: Hodder & Stoughton, 1994)
Hamilton, N., *Monty: The Field Marshal, 1944–1976* (London: Hamish Hamilton, 1986)
Harclerode, P., *Arnhem: A Tragedy of Errors* (London: Arms & Armour, 1994)
Harris, J. P., *Men, ideas and tanks: British military thought and armoured forces, 1903–39* (Manchester: University Press, 1995)
Hart, S. A., *Montgomery and "Colossal Cracks": The 21st Army Group in Northwest Europe, 1944–45* (Westport CT: Stackpole, 2000)
Hastings, M., *Armageddon: The Battle for Germany 1944–45* (Basingstoke: Macmillan, 2011)

Hastings, M., *Overlord: D-Day and the Battle for Normandy 1944* (London: Pan, 1985)
Henniker, M., *An Image of War* (London: Leo Cooper, 1987)
Headquarters Doctrine and Training, *Generic Enemy (Mobile Forces) Part 1: Operational Art & Tactical Doctrine* (Upavon: HQDT, 1996)
Heuer, R. J., *Psychology of Intelligence Analysis* (Langley VA: CIA, 1999)
Holborn, A., *The 56th Infantry Brigade and D-Day: An Independent Infantry Brigade and the Campaign in North West Europe 1944–1945* (London: Continuum, 2010)
Holland, J., *Brothers in Arms: One Legendary Tank Regiment's Bloody War from D-Day to VE-Day* (London: Bantam, 2021)
Horrocks, B., *A Full Life* (London: Collins, 1960)
Horrocks, B., Belfield, E. and Essame, H., *Corps Commander* (Toronto: Griffin House, 1979).
Howard, M. and Sparrow, J., *The Coldstream Guards, 1920–1946* (Oxford: University Press, 1951)
Jary, S., *18 Platoon* (Winchester: Light Infantry, 2003)
Johnston, R. T., Steward D. N. and Dunlop, A. I., *The Story of the 10th Bn. The Highland Light Infantry 1944–1945* (Uckfield: Naval & Military, 2020 [1945])
Joint Chiefs of Staff (US), *Joint Logistics* (Washington: Joint Chiefs, 2019)
Keegan, J. D. P., *Face of Battle: A Study of Agincourt, Waterloo and the Somme* (London: Barrie & Jenkins, 1976)
Kemp, J. C., *The History of the Royal Scots Fusiliers 1919–1959* (Glasgow: Maclehose, 1963)
Kemp, P. K. and Graves, J., *The Red Dragon: The Story of the Royal Welch Fusiliers 1919–1945* (Aldershot: Gale & Polden, 1960)
King, A., *Frontline: Combat and Cohesion in the Twenty-First Century* (Oxford: University Press, 2015)
King, A., *Urban Warfare in the Twenty-First Century* (Cambridge: Polity, 2021)
Kirke W. M. St G., Armitage, C. C., Bartholomew, A. W., Fisher, B. D., Howard-Vyse, R. G. H., Kennedy, J., McCulloch, A. J., McNamara, A. E. and Selby, A. R., *Report of the Committee on the Lessons of the Great War (The Kirke Report)*, British Army Review reprint (Upavon: DGD&D, 2001 [1932])
Knight, D., *The Land Mattress in Canadian Service* (Ottawa: Service Publications, 2003)
Land Warfare Centre, *Formation Tactics* (Army Field Manual Vol. 1 Part 1) (Upavon: LWC, 2007)
Land Warfare Development Centre, *Urban Tactical Handbook* (Warminster: LWDC, 2016)
Latino, R.J., *Patient Safety: The PROACT® Root Cause Analysis Approach* (London: CRC Press, 2009)
Lawton, C.G., *Path of the Lion, 1944–1945*, (Ahrensburg: Publisher unknown, 1946)
Liddell Hart, B. H., *Future of Infantry* (London: Faber & Faber, 1933)
Liddell Hart, B. H., *History of the Second World War* (London: Cassel, 1970)
Liddell Hart, B. H., *Thoughts on War* (London: Faber & Faber, 1943)
Lindsay, M., *So Few Got Through: The Diary of an Infantry Officer* (London: Collins, 1946).
Lindsay, T. M., *Sherwood Rangers* (London: Burrup, Mathieson & Co, 1952)
MacDonald, C. B., *Siegfried Line Campaign* (Washington: Centre for Military History, 1993)
MacDonald, C. B., *A Time for Trumpets: The Untold Story of the Battle of the Bulge* (London: Harper Collins, 2018)
Marshall, S. L. A., *Men Against Fire: The Problem of Battle Command* (New York: Infantry Journal, 1947)
Marshall, S. L. A., *Soldier Load and the Mobility of a Nation* (Quantico: Marine Corps Association, 1950).
Martin, H. G., *History of the 15th Scottish Division 1939–1945* (Smalldale: MLRS, 2006 [1948])
McCann, C. (ed.), *The Human in Command: Exploring the Modern Military Experience*, (New York: Springer, 2000)

McBain, S. W. (ed.), *A Regiment at War: The Royal Scots 1939–45* (Edinburgh: Pentland, 1988)
McElwee, W. L., *History of the Argyll & Sutherland Highlanders 2nd Battalion (Reconstituted): European Campaign 1944–45* (London: Thomas Nelson & Sons, 1949)
McGregor, J., *The Spirit of Angus* (Chichester: Phillimore, 1988)
McKee, A., *The Race for the Rhine Bridges* (London: Pan, 1956)
Meredith, J. L. J., *From Normandy to Hanover: The Story of The Seventh Battalion, The Somerset Light Infantry (Prince Albert's)* (Hanover: Publisher unknown, 1945)
Middlebrook, M., *The First Day on the Somme* (London: Penguin, 2001)
Middlebrook, M. and Everitt, C., *The Bomber Command War Diaries: An Operational Reference Book, 1939–1945* (Barnsley: Pen & Sword, 2014)
Miles, W., *The Life of a Regiment: History of the Gordon Highlanders. Volume V 1919–1945* (Aberdeen: Publisher unknown, 1961)
Milligan, D. P. B., *View from a Forgotten Hedgerow* (Glebe NSW: Self-published, 1993)
Ministry of Defence, *Army Field Manual 2/6: Operations in Woods and Forests* (MOD, Undated)
Ministry of Defence, *Future Operating Environment 2035* (Shrivenham: MOD, 2015).
Montgomery, B. L., *21 Army Group: Normandy to the Baltic*, (London: Hutchinson & Co, 1946).
Montgomery, B. L., *High Command in War* (Germany: 21 Army Group, 1945)
Montgomery, B. L., *Morale in Battle: Analysis* (Hanover: BAOR, 1946)
Montgomery, B. L., *The Armoured Division in Battle* (Holland: 21 Army Group, 1944)
Moran, Lord (Wilson, C. McM.), *The Anatomy of Courage* (London: Constable, 1945)
Müller, R. D. (ed.), *Das Deutsche Reich und der Zweite Weltkrieg – Band 10/1: Der Zusammenbruch des Deutschen Reiches 1945* (München: Deutsche Verlags-Anstalt, 2008)
Murray, L., *Brains and Bullets: How Psychology Wins Wars* (London: Biteback, 2013)
Naveh, S., *In Pursuit of Military Excellence: The Evolution of Operational Theory* (London: Cass, 1997)
Neville, J. E. H., *The Oxfordshire & Buckinghamshire Light Infantry War Chronicle, Vol. IV* (Aldershot: Gale & Polden, 1954)
Oatts, L. B., *Proud Heritage: The Story of the Highland Light Infantry (vol.4)* (Glasgow: Grant, 1963)
Oatts, L. B., *The Highland Light Infantry* (London: Leo Cooper, 1969)
Parker, T. W. and Thompson, W. J., *Conquer: The Story of Ninth Army, 1944–1945* (Washington: Infantry Journal, 1947)
Pemberton, A.L., *The Development of Artillery Tactics and Equipment* (London: War Office, 1951)
Perrow, C., *Normal Accidents: Living with High-Risk Technologies* (New York: Basic, 1984).
Place, T. H., *Military Training in the British Army, 1940–1944* (London: Cass, 2000)
Prior, R. and Wilson, T., *Command on the Western Front: The Military Career of Sir Henry Rawlinson 1914–1918* (Barnsley, Pen & Sword, 2004)
Retter, L., Hernandez, Z., Caves, B., Hughes M. and Knack, A., *Global Mobility: Force Design 2040* (Cambridge MA: Rand, 2021)
Randel, P. B., *A Short History of 30 Corps in the European Campaign 1944–1945*, (Hanover: 30 Corps, 1945)
Richardson, F. M., *Fighting Spirit: Psychological Factors in War* (London: Leo Cooper, 1978).
Riley, J., Crocker, P. and Sinnett, R., *Regimental Records of the Royal Welch Fusiliers, Vol. V (2)*, (Warwick: Helion, 2018).
Roberts, J. H., *Enshrined in Stone: 1st Battalion (43rd) The Oxfordshire & Buckinghamshire Light Infantry in the Second World War* (Witney: Boldacre, 1994)
Roberts, J. H., *Welsh Bridges to the Elbe* (Witney: Boldacre, 2000)
Rosse, Earl of (Parsons, L. M. H.) and Hill, E. R., *The Story of The Guards Armoured Division* (London: Geoffrey Bles, 1956)

Rowland, D., *The Stress of Battle: Quantifying Human Performance in Combat* (London: HMSO, 2006)

Royal Artillery, *Programme Shoots (Barrages and Concentrations)* (Larkhill: Publisher unknown, 1942)

Russell, D. F. O., *War History of the 7th Bn. The Black Watch (R. H. R.)* (Markinch: Markinch, 1948)

Ryan, C., *A Bridge Too Far* (Bungay: Richard Clay, 1975)

Salmond, J. B., *The History of the 51st Highland Division* (Edinburgh: Blackwood & Son, 1953)

Samuels, M., *Command or Control? Command, Training and Tactics in the British and German Armies, 1888–1918* (London: Cass, 1995)

Scarfe, N., *Assault Division* (London: Collins, 1947)

Schein, E. H. and Schein, P., *Organizational Culture and Leadership* (London: Wiley & Son, 2016)

Schofield, V., *The Black Watch: Fighting in the Frontline 1899–2006*, (London: Head of Zeus, 2017)

Scott, A., Packer C. and Groves, J., *Record of a Reconnaissance Regiment: History of the 43rd Reconnaissance Regiment (The Gloucester Regiment) 1939 – 1945* (Bristol: White Swan, 1949)

Scull, L. V., *49th Unparalleled: The Story of the 49th Battalion Royal Tank Regiment Later Designated as an Armoured Personnel Carrier Regiment, 1939–1945* (Bovington: Tank Museum, 2002)

Seddon, J., *Freedom from Command and Control: a better way to make work work* (Buckingham: Vanguard Education, 2003)

Seventy-Ninth Armoured Division, *Final Report* (Germany: 21 Army Group, 1945)

Sheffield G. and Todman D. (eds), *Command and Control on the Western Front: The British Army's Experience 1914–1918* (Stroud: Spellmount, 2007)

Short, N., *Hitler's Siegfried Line* (Stroud: Sutton, 2002)

Snell, E.S., *The Scottish Volunteers* (Eastbourne: Menin House, 2009)

Stacey, C.P., *Official History of the Canadian Army in the Second World War. Volume III, The Victory Campaign* (Ottawa: Queen's Printer, 1960)

Steinhardt, F. P., *Panzer Lehr Division 1944–45* (Solihull: Helion, 2010)

Stimpel, H., *Die deutsche Fallschirmtruppe 1942–1945: Einsätze auf Kriegsschauplätzen im Osten und Westen* (Hamburg: Mittler & Sohn, 2001)

Stirling, J. D. P., *The First and The Last. The Story of the 4th/7th Royal Dragoon Guards 1939–1945* (London: Art & Education, 1946)

Stockings, C., *Bardia: Myth Reality and the Heirs of Anzac* (Sydney: UNSW, 2009)

Storr, J., *Something Rotten: Land Command in the 21st Century* (Havant: Howgate, 2022)

Stouffer, S.A., Lumsdaine, A. A., Lumsdaine, M. H., Williams, R. M., Smith, M. B., Janis, I. L., Star, S.A. and Cottrell, L. S., *The American Soldier. Vol. 2: Combat and Its Aftermath* (Princeton: University Press, 1949)

Sym J. (ed.), *Seaforth Highlanders* (Aldershot: Gale & Polden, 1962)

Taylor, A. J. P., *War By Time-Table: How the First World War Began* (London: Macdonald, 1974)

Taylor, G., *Infantry Colonel* (Upton: Self-published, 1990)

Thompson, R.W., *The Battle for the Rhineland*, (London: Westholme, 1958)

Twenty-First Army Group, *Operational Research in North West Europe* (Hanover: 21 Army Group, 1945), WO 205/1164

Twenty-First Army Group, *Operation Veritable. Clearing the Area Between the R Maas and the R Rhine, 8 Feb – 10 Mar 1945*, (Hanover: 21 Army Group, 1945), WO 205/953 & CAB 106/991

United States Marine Corps, *Force Design 2030* (Arlington VA: USMC, 2020)

United States Marine Corps, *Tactical-Level Logistics* (Twentynine Palms: USMC, 2016)

Urquhart, R. E., *Arnhem* (London: Pan, 1960)

War Department, *Field Artillery Field Manual: Firing, FM 6-40* (Washington: War Department, 1939)
War Office, *Field Service Regulations 1909* (London: War Office, 1912)
War Office, *Military Training Pamphlet No. 55: Fighting in Built-Up Areas* (London: War Office, 1943)
War Office, *Military Training Pamphlet No. 63: The Co-operation of Tanks with Infantry Divisions* (London: War Office, 1944)
War Office, *Infantry Training, Part VIII.- Fieldcraft, Battle Drill, Section and Platoon Tactics 1944* (London: War Office, 1944)
War Office, *SS98/4 Artillery in Offensive Operations* (London: War Office, 1916)
War Office, *SS139/4 Artillery in Offensive Operations* (London: War Office, 1917)
War Office, *SS192 The Employment of Machine Guns, Part I, Tactical* (London: War Office, 1918)
Warner, P., *D-Day Landings* (London: Random House, 1990)
Warner, P., *Horrocks: The General Who Led from the Front* (London: Sphere, 1984)
Warner, P., *Phantom* (Barnsley: Pen & Sword, 2005)
Whitaker, W. D. and Whitaker, S., *Rhineland. The Battle to End the War* (London: Leo Cooper, 1989)
Whitfield, T. D. W., *Time Spent, or The History of the 52nd Lowland Divisional Reconnaissance Regiment* (Hamilton: Publisher unknown, 1946)
White, P., *With the Jocks. A Soldier's Struggle for Europe 1944–45* (Stroud: Sutton, 2000)
Williams, J., *Long Left Flank: The Hard-Fought Way to the Reich 1944–1945* (London: Leo Cooper, 1988)
Winslow, P. D. and Brassey, B., *153rd Leicestershire Yeomanry Field Regiment R.A., T.A., 1939–1945*, (Uckfield: Naval & Military, 2015 [1945])
Woollcombe, R., *Lion Rampant, The Memoirs of an Infantry Officer from D-Day to the Rhineland* (London: Black & White, 2014 [1955])
Woolward, W. A., *A Short Account of the 1st Lothians and Border Yeomanry in the campaigns of 1940 and 1944–45*, (Edinburgh: Publisher unknown, 1946)
Xenophon, *Anabasis* (Gutenberg eBook, 2013 [c380BCE])
Yeide, H., *The Infantry's Armour: The US Army's Separate Tank Battalions in World War II* (Mechanicsburg: Stackpole, 2010)
Zuehlke, M., *Forgotten Victory. First Canadian Army and the Cruel Winter of 1944–45* (Madeira Park: Douglas & McIntyre, 2014)

Theses, Chapters, Articles, and Unpublished Reports

Anon, '134th Infantry Regiment report of action against the enemy, March 1 to March 31, 1945', transcript at coulthart.com
Anon, '35th Infantry Division report of action against the enemy – March 1945', transcript at coulthart.com
Anon, 'Command and Control (C2) Agility' (NATO, 2014)
Anon, 'Field Artillery, Volume 6, Ballistics and Ammunition' (Department of National Defence, Canada, 1992)
Anon, 'German Wehrmacht in the last days of the war' (NARA FMS C-020, undated)
Anon, 'History of 154 Infantry Brigade in North West Europe', transcript at 51hd.co.uk
Anon, 'NATO Standard AMedP-8.6, Forward Mental Health Care', (NATO, 2019)
Anon, 'Denkmalbereichssatzung Orstkern Kranenburg', (Unknown, 1991)

Balchin, N. M., 'Battle Morale'. In Rowland, D. 'Combat Degradation' (Defence Evaluation and Research Agency, 1996)

Banks, S., Landon, L. B., Dorrian, J., Waggoner, L. B., Centofanti, S., Roma, P. G. and Van Bongen, H. P. A., 'Effects of fatigue on teams and their role in 24/7 operations', *Sleep Medicine Reviews*, 48 (Sept 2019)

Becke, A. F., 'The Coming of the Creeping Barrage', *Journal of the Royal Artillery* 58:1 (1938)

Bielecki, C.A., 'British Infantry Morale during the Italian Campaign, 1943–1945' (UCL PhD thesis, 2006).

Blauensteiner, E., 'II Parachute Corps (19 Sep. 1944–10 Mar. 1945)' (NARA FMS B-262, 1950)

Boff, J., 'Combined Arms during the Hundred Days Campaign, August-November 1918', *War in History* 17(4) (2010), 459–478

Brown, G., 'Dig for Bloody Victory: The British Soldier's Experience of Trench Warfare, 1939–45', (Oxford University DPhil, 2012)

Buckholt, L. G. M., 'Signal Security in the Ardennes Offensive' (Command and General Staff College Masters' thesis, 1997)

Buckley, J., 'Montgomery: Command and Leadership in the 21st Army Group, 1944–45', presentation to Joint Command and Staff College, 2014

Caulkin, S., 'The rule is simple: be careful what you measure', *Observer*, 10 Feb 2008.

Clayton, J. D., 'The Battle of the Sambre, 4 November 1918', (Birmingham PhD thesis, 2015).

Conacher J. B. and Harrison, W. E. C., 'Operation "Veritable": The winter offensive between the Maas and the Rhine, 8–25 Feb 45 (preliminary report)' (Canadian Military Headquarters, report no.155, 1946)

Connable, B., McNerney, J., Marcellino, W., Frank, A., Hargrove, H., Posard, M. N., Zimmerman, S. R., Lander, N,, Castillo, J. J. and Sladden, J., 'Will to Fight: Analyzing, Modeling, and Simulating the Will to Fight of Military Units' (Rand, 2018)

Copp, T., 'Operational Research and 21st Army Group' *Canadian Military History*, 3(1) (1994), 71–84

Copp, T., Review of *The Canadian Army and the Normandy Campaign: A Study of Failure in High Command*, by John A. English. *Canadian Historical Review*, 73 (4) (1992), 551–553

Copp, T., 'To the Last Canadian?: Casualties in the 21st Army Group' *Canadian Military History*, 18:1 (2009) 3–6

Craggs, T., 'An "Unspectacular" War? Reconstructing the history of the 2nd Battalion East Yorkshire Regiment during the Second World War', (Sheffield University PhD thesis, 2007).

Daniels, K. F., 'The Distribution Dilemma: That Last Tactical Mile', *Army Logistician* 40(5) (2008)

Davis, M. A., 'Armor Attacks in Restrictive Terrain: is Current Doctrine Adequate?' (Fort Leavenworth Command and General Staff College monograph, 1995)

Devine, L. P., 'The British Way of War in North West Europe 1944–45: A Study of Two Infantry Divisions' (Plymouth University PhD thesis, 2013)

Directorate of Combat Developments, 'The Fort Sill Fire Suppression Symposium' (Fort Sill: DCD, 1980)

Dorward, J. C. and Strong, R. E., 'The effects of bombardment, the current state of knowledge.' (Military Operational Research Unit (MORU) Report No. 3, 1946)

Exham, K. G., 'The Assault on the Reichswald' and 'The Battle of Weeze', unpublished report chapters kindly provided by RWF Museum

Fiebig, H., 'The 84th Infantry Division during the battles from the Reichswald to Wesel' (NARA FMS B-843,1948)

French, C. F., 'The 51st (Highland) Division During the First World War' (Glasgow University PhD thesis, 2006)

French, D., '"Tommy is No Soldier": The Morale of the Second British Army in Normandy, June–August 1944', *Journal of Strategic Studies*, (1996) 19

Hanscomb, R. D., 'A Review of Urban Battles in Germany 1945', (Defence Operational Analysis Establishment Working Paper 662/5, 1983)

Harris, P. 'An Examination of the use of Tanks in the "Hundred Days Campaign" of 1918' (University of Wolverhampton PhD thesis, 2020)

Hart, R. A. 'Feeding Mars: The Role of Logistics in The German Defeat in Normandy, 1944', *War in History*, 3 (4), (1996) 418–435

Hart, S. A. 'Field Marshal Montgomery, 21st Army Group and North-West Europe, 1944–45' (KCL PhD thesis, 1995)

Helmbold, R. L. 'A Compilation of Data on Advance in Land Combat Operations' (US Army Concepts Analysis Agency, 1990)

Helmbold, R. L. 'Decision in Battle: Breakpoint Hypotheses and Engagement Termination Data' (Rand, 1971)

Henderson, C. W. P. 'Participation of 6th (Border) Battalion, The King's Own Scottish Borderers in the first phase of Operation "Veritable".' Undated file T1/34, KOSB Museum

Henderson, D. M. 'Operation Enterprise. The Allied Crossing of the River Elbe 1945 – The End and the Beginning', paper to British Commission for Military History, July 2007

Hooker, R.D. 'The Tyranny of Battle Drill 6' (Modern War Institute, mwi.usma.edu 2021)

Hughes, J. 'The Monstrous Anger of the Guns: The Development of British Artillery Tactics 1914–1918' (University of Adelaide PhD thesis, 1992)

King, A. 'Why did 51st Highland Division Fail? A case-study in command and combat effectiveness', *British Journal of Military History*, 4:1, (2017)

Macdonald, J.A. 'In search of Veritable: Training the Canadian Army staff officer, 1899 to 1945' (Royal Military College of Canada Master's thesis, 1992).

Marble, W. S. 'The infantry cannot do with a gun less: the place of artillery in the BEF, 1914–1918' (King's College London PhD thesis, 1998)

Margry, K. (ed.), *After the Battle*, (2013) No.159

Marsden, J. L., 'Span of Command and Control in the British Army: an Initial Study' (Defence Evaluation and Research Agency report, 1996)

Mayer, P.A. 'Operation "Blockbuster": the Canadian offensive west of the Rhine, 26 Feb – 23 Mar 45 (preliminary report)' (Canadian Military Headquarters, report no. 171, 1947)

McCann, C. A., Pigeau, R. and English, A. 'Analysing Command Challenges using the C2 framework', (Defence Research and Development Canada, 2003)

Meindl, E., 'II Parachute Corps: Part 3, Rhineland (15 Sep 1944 to 21 Mar 1945)' (NARA FMS B-093, 1947)

Montgomery, B. L. 'Personal message from the C-in-C (To be read out to all Troops)' February 1945

Neame, P. 'The Challenges of Leadership During the Falklands War by a Veteran', presentation at Royal Military Academy, Sandhurst, 19 Nov 2022

Redfern J. M. and Cornett A.M., 'The challenging world of command and support relationships', www.army.mil

Rooney, D. 'Opening the Second Draft of History: Liberation Campaign 1944–45', *Mars & Clio*, Autumn 2024, pp.12–25, in press

Rowland, D. 'Combat Degradation' (Defence Evaluation and Research Agency, 1996)

Rowland, D. 'Tracked Vehicle Ground Pressure and its Effect on Soft Ground Performance', (undated conference paper *c*. 1980)

Spencer, J. 'Why Militaries Must Destroy Cities to Save Them' (mwi.usma.edu, 2018)

Stone, T. R. 'He had the guts to say no: A Military Biography of General William Hood Simpson' (Rice University PhD thesis, 1974)
Swank, R. L. and Marchand, W.E. 'Combat neuroses: development of combat exhaustion', *Archives of Neurology and Psychiatry* 55 (1946), 236–247
Thomas, T. L. 'The Battle for Grozny: Deadly Classroom for Urban Combat' *Parameters* (Summer 1999), 87–101
Thornton R. C. and Watson, D. 'Historical Analysis of Infantry Defence in Woods' (Defence Operational Analysis Centre, 1993)
Vego, M. 'On Operational Art', *Strategos*, 1/2 (2017), 15–39
Wangen, G. B., Hellesen, N., Torres, H. and Brækken, E., 'An Empirical Study of Root-Cause Analysis in Information Security Management', Emerging Security Information Systems and Technologies, 2017
Wood, J., 'Captive Historians, Captivated Audience: The German Military History Program, 1945–1961', *Journal of Military History*, 69 (2005), 123–147
Zaloga, S. J., 'Debunking the Omaha Beach Legend: The Use of Armored "Funnies" on D-Day', *Journal of Military History*, 85, (2021), 134–162

Videos

British Army, *Fighting In Built Up Areas (FIBUA), Part 3: Goch* (c1984). Available as online stream
Dennis, J. (dir.), *Battle for the Rhineland* (Services Sound and Video Corporation, 1984). Three parts, widely available online

Online Sources

15thscottishdivisionwardiaries.co.uk. All the main diaries from 15 Division
51hd.co.uk, 51st Highland Division Museum. Many out of print sources
armyuniversity.edu/carl, Ike Skelton Combined Arms Research Library. History and doctrine
coulhart.com, US 35 Division and 134 Infantry Regiment after-action reports
cwgc.org, Commonwealth War Graves Commission. Searchable and downloadable database
chotiedarling.co.uk. Unpublished information on 52 Reconnaissance Regiment
dtic.mil, Defense Technical Information Centre. Downloadable research papers
feldgrau.net. Threads on German war experience
lexikon-der-wehrmacht.de. Exhaustive German organisation and operation summaries
mwi.usma.edu, Modern War Institute. Includes many articles on urban operations
nationalarchives.gov.uk. Access to diaries and reports including downloadable information
nigelef.tripod.com, British Artillery in World War 2. A trove of gunnery information
vickersmg.blog, The Vickers Machine gun. Articles on Vickers guns, their use, and organisations
wftw.nl, Wireless for the Warrior. Links to publications on British communications equipment
ww2talk.com. Many detailed Veritable threads include action outside the thesis scope

Index

People, places, operations and concepts

Afferden, xxiii, 122, 126-129, 130, 131, 133, 134, 135, 136, 137, 140, 142, 146, 147, 148, 155, 162, 217, 221

Alpen (Alpon), 186, 198, 202, 204, 205, 206, 211-212, 214, 215

Arnhem, xiii, xv, xvii, xviii, xx, 29, 31-34, 47, 127, 143, 170, 171

Asperden, xvii, xxiii, 39, 146, 155, 156, 157, 158, 212-213

Balchin, Nigel, x, 196, 210-211

Barber, Colin, 30, 59, 89, 103, 105-106, 113, 117-118, 120, 145, 147-148, 167

Barrage hugging, 50-51, 52, 54-55, 57, 60, 62, 66, 70, 74, 80-81, 212, 218

Blerick, 82, 89, 143, 144, 147, 166, 168, 172, 208

Bönninghardt, xxiii, 170, 186, 191, 196, 197, 198, 208, 211, 219

Buckley, John, xii, xix-xxi, 48, 102, 122, 170, 196, 221

Churchill, Winston, 196, 200

Colossal Cracks, xviii-xix, 123, 142, 196, 197, 207, 214

Command system(s), xxi, xxii, xxiv, 46, 101, 102-103, 105, 106, 113, 117-121, 136, 137, 171-172, 185, 193, 214, 215, 216, 218-219, 220, 221, 222-223

Crerar, Harry, xvi, 30, 34, 36, 41-42, 46, 47, 53, 56, 141

Cumming-Bruce, Henry, 59, 88, 89, 103, 106, 117, 118, 145, 147, 150-151, 154

De Horst, 55, 60-61, 62, 64, 160, 179, 197, 212, 213, 214

Emmerich, xiii, xxiii, 31, 34, 37, 39, 105, 123
Essame, Herbert, 96, 103, 108, 113, 114

Fiebig, Heinz, 42-43, 44-46, 72, 98, 108
Fighting power, xix, 141, 171, 214-215, 219
Fuller, J.F.C., 137, 222, 223

Geilenkirchen, 34, 35, 51, 78
Geldern, xiii, xvii, xxiii, 39, 41, 46, 173, 186, 187, 188, 189, 193, 204
Gennep, xviii, xxiii, 31, 39, 124, 127, 129, 131, 134, 144, 156, 168, 175
Goch, xiii, xvii, xxiii, 35, 37, 39, 41, 46, 52, 96, 101, 104, 105, 107, 109-110, 113, 117, 120, 121, 123, 124, 136, 143-170, 171, 172, 173-174, 175, 179, 180, 182, 185, 197, 204, 206, 209, 212, 213, 217, 219
Groesbeek, xxiii, 37, 44, 55, 59, 60, 72, 82, 84, 86, 94, 100, 102

Hamb, 189-193, 194, 195, 197, 214
Hastings, Max, xii, xix-xxi, 31, 48-49, 123, 170
Hochwald, xxiii, 39, 41, 46, 124, 186
Horrocks, Brian, xii-xiv, xx, xxi, 30, 34, 35, 41, 47, 52, 53, 56, 59, 64, 80, 92, 94, 101-103, 105, 107, 108, 114, 117, 118, 120, 124, 136, 141, 145, 147, 166, 167, 172, 185, 189, 217, 218, 219

Issum, xxiii, 186, 187, 188, 197

Kalkar (Calcar), xxiii, 39, 104, 105, 124, 146
Kapellen, xxiii, 186, 188, 189, 191
Kevelaer, xxiii, 41, 173, 186, 187, 188-189, 193, 194, 199
Kleve (Cleve), xii, xiii, xxiii, 31, 34, 35, 37, 39, 41, 42, 45, 46, 52-53, 90, 95, 96, 97, 101, 104, 105-108, 110, 111-114, 116, 119, 120-121, 123, 144, 146, 166
Kranenburg, xxiii, 48, 55, 64-71, 74, 78, 84, 87, 88, 92, 94, 97, 107, 117, 147, 217, 220, 221

INDEX

Liddell Hart, Basil, xviii, xix, 82, 137, 222, 223

Materborn, xxiii, 39, 41, 90, 95, 96-97, 98, 99, 100, 101, 103, 104, 105, 106, 107-121, 124, 137, 146, 180, 185, 189, 212, 214, 219, 220
Meindl, Eugen, 43, 46, 148, 159, 160, 162, 202, 216
Metzekath, 190, 191-192, 201
Montgomery, Bernard, xv, xvi, xix, xxi, 30-35, 36, 39, 41, 46, 97, 102-103, 107, 108, 114, 123, 124, 137-138, 140, 141, 171, 185, 193, 207, 217-218, 220, 222
Morale, xix, xxii, xxvi, 31, 51-52, 54, 59, 123, 129, 132, 140, 141, 142, 160, 170-172, 196-215, 219, 221
Moyland, xxiii, 123, 147

Nijmegen, xiii, xxiii, 31-32, 34, 37, 41, 42, 45, 83, 84, 88, 92, 93, 100, 105, 106, 108, 112, 117, 143, 170, 222
Normandy, xiv, xv-xvi, xvii-xviii, xx, xxii, xxv, 48, 85, 99, 103, 112, 122, 137, 141, 148, 171, 181, 185, 196, 207, 208, 209, 212, 217
Nutterden, xxiii, 92, 94-96, 97, 98, 104, 106-108, 120, 220

Operation Blackcock, 86, 99, 119,127
Operation Blockbuster, xvi, 172-173, 175, 180, 188, 193, 197, 218, 220
Operation Bluecoat, 171
Operation Clipper, 34, 51-53, 56, 57, 78, 80
Operation Daffodil, xix, 181-185
Operation Goodwood, 122, 138, 187, 210
Operation Grenade, xii-xiv, xviii, 36, 46, 101, 175
Operation Leek, xix, 172-181, 193
Operation Market Garden, xvi-xviii, xx, xxii, 29, 31-32, 60, 138, 188
Operation Overlord, xv
Operation Plunder/Varsity, 216
Operation Spider, xix, 147-155
Operation Sprat, xix, 136
Operation Ventilate, 36, 45, 46, 124, 125
Operation *Wacht am Rhein* (and Ardennes), 35, 36, 47, 207, 208, 209

Reichswald, xii, xiii, xvii, xviii, xxiii, 30, 32, 37-41, 43, 44, 55, 56, 59, 60, 63, 64, 72, 75-77, 78, 86, 96, 97, 109, 110, 116, 123, 124, 127, 129, 132, 133, 137, 155, 172, 185, 195, 196, 208-209, 212-213, 215, 217
Rennie, Tom, 30, 59, 124, 136, 145, 162
Richardson, Frank, 196, 197, 207-212, 213, 215
Ruhr, xiii, xv, 31-35, 46

Scheldt, 34, 86, 127
Schlemm, Alfred, 42-43, 45-46, 53, 96, 97, 108, 216
Simonds, Guy, xiv, 30, 42
Simpson, William, 36, 42
Stolpi, xi, 74, 117
Suppression / suppressive fire, xiv, xxii, xxiv, 48-59, 62, 64, 69, 72, 74, 77-81, 96, 99, 113, 122, 131, 150, 167, 171, 191, 199, 216, 218, 220, 221, 222
Swann, Michael, 48, 49, 51, 53, 54, 56-59, 77-80, 86, 87, 129, 211

Tactical logistics, xxii, xxiv, 82-84, 97-100, 105, 150, 160, 171-172, 193, 214, 215, 216, 218-219, 220, 222
Tactical psychology, x, xiv, xxii, 211
Thomas, Ivor, 30, 103, 113, 143, 145, 147, 148, 167, 213
Tiger Corner, 111, 113, 115-116

Venlo, xiii, 34, 36, 41, 44, 45, 46

Weeze, xvii, xx, xxvii, 39, 41, 110, 123-126, 130, 134, 136, 138, 146, 149, 158, 162, 165-166, 170-186, 188, 189, 193-194, 197, 199, 200, 202, 204, 206, 209, 213, 219, 220, 221
Wesel, xii, xiii, xxiii, 32, 34, 35-36, 37-41, 42, 45, 52, 56, 105, 117, 124, 143, 144, 170, 186, 188, 191, 198, 216, 222
Winnekendonk, xxiii, 175, 186, 189
Wyler, xxiii, 39, 74-75, 88, 92, 93

Xanten, xxiii, 39, 41, 46, 55, 105, 144, 175, 186

Yorkshire Bridge, 181-182, 183, 184

Allied formations

1 British Airborne Division, 31-32
2 Canadian Corps, xiv, xvi, 34-35, 36, 41, 42, 172-173, 175, 180, 186, 188, 193, 216, 223
2 Canadian Division, 30, 39-40, 42, 56, 62, 71, 74, 125
3 British Division, 172, 180, 181, 188-189, 193, 194, 207
3 Canadian Division, 30, 39-40, 42, 70, 88, 97, 119, 123
6 Guards Armoured (Tank) Brigade, xxvi, 139
8 Armoured Brigade, 141, 170, 171-173, 181, 185-188, 193-195, 197-198, 199, 200, 201, 206
15 Scottish Division, xi, xxv, xxvi, 39-41, 46, 48, 56, 59, 60, 61, 62, 64-73, 74, 84, 86-98, 101-108, 109, 110, 111, 113, 117, 119, 120, 123, 124, 138, 141, 142, 144-155, 160, 166-169, 172, 174, 175, 176, 177, 207-209, 210, 213, 218
34 Armoured (Tank) Brigade, xxvi, 45, 60, 127, 138
35 US Division, 172, 186, 187
43 Wessex Division, xxv, xxvi, 30, 34, 40, 41, 44, 46, 60, 96, 98, 99, 101-103, 105, 107-120, 123, 124, 138, 140, 141, 142, 146-148, 150, 151, 167, 172, 195, 207, 213, 218
44 Lowland Brigade, 82, 88-96, 105-106, 108, 144-155, 158, 159-162, 166-168, 170

51 Highland Division, xviii, xxvi, 39, 40, 41, 43, 46, 56, 60, 61, 75-77, 80, 86, 87, 88, 123, 124, 129, 130, 131, 134, 136, 141, 145-146, 148, 150, 155-160, 162-169, 172, 174, 175, 177, 207, 208, 221
52 Lowland Division, xi, xv, xvii, xxvi, 122-142, 147, 148, 155, 156, 186, 201, 202, 206, 207, 216, 218
53 Welsh Division, xviii, xxv, xxvi, 39, 40, 41, 45, 46, 52, 59-64, 71, 73, 74, 76, 82, 84, 88, 90, 95, 96, 97, 104, 110, 111, 114, 115, 116, 119, 123, 127, 133, 137, 141, 145, 146, 150, 156, 160, 161, 170-189, 191, 193-195, 196-215, 216, 217, 221
79 Armoured Division, xv, xxvi, 86, 89, 91
82 US Airborne Division, 31, 37, 62
153 Highland Brigade, 144-146, 155-169, 173, 175
First Canadian Army, xii-xviii, 31, 34-36, 39-42, 46, 47, 118, 125, 180, 188, 196, 216, 218
Guards Armoured Division, xxvi, 30, 40, 41, 96, 98, 105, 124, 138, 141, 170, 172, 187-195, 197, 198, 204, 212
Ninth US Army, xii, xiii, 36, 172, 186, 187, 197, 212, 216
Second British Army, 31-33, 36, 124, 125, 196

Allied units

13/18 Hussars, 74, 137, 175, 178, 179, 181, 194, 202, 204, 206-207
15 Scottish Reconnaissance Regiment, 105-106, 107, 108, 110, 120
22 Dragoons, 87, 93, 148, 150
43 Reconnaissance Regiment, 108, 109-112, 117, 220
49 Armoured Personnel Carrier Regiment, 154, 172, 175
52 Reconnaissance Regiment, 125, 126, 129, 134, 136, 220
53 Reconnaissance Regiment, xv, 173, 176, 177, 178, 181-182, 203

Argyll and Sutherland Highlanders, 44, 59, 64, 66, 68, 69, 70-71, 73, 74, 78, 84-85, 87, 88, 140, 165, 166

Black Watch (Royal Highland Regiment), 61, 75-77, 78, 143, 145, 157-169, 172, 173, 221

Calgary Highlanders, 56, 74-75, 78, 80, 88, 93, 137

Cameronians (Scottish Rifles), 56, 71, 72-73, 74, 78, 80, 88, 92
Coldstream Guards, x, 72, 187, 188, 191-192, 194

Derbyshire Yeomanry, 131
Dorsetshire Regiment, 51, 110
Duke of Cornwall's Light Infantry, 103, 108-118, 120, 137, 138, 189, 220

East Lancashire Regiment, 173, 184-185, 187, 193, 202, 203, 208
East Yorkshire Regiment, 181

Glasgow Highlanders (Highland Light Infantry) 36, 70, 71, 72, 73, 80, 87, 88, 125, 127, 129, 130, 134-135, 142
Gordon Highlanders, 75, 76-77, 78, 80, 90, 92, 94-97, 98, 104, 144, 158-159, 162-164, 165, 168, 175
Grenadier Guards, 89, 93-94, 139, 145, 146, 150-155, 160, 170, 187, 188, 189, 191-192, 194